the NAME QUEST

"No one has ever met God completely or exhaustively. But God invites you to know Him. Like a clear trail in a forest, the names of God lead you deeper into the heart of God. In his book, *The Name Quest,* John Avery leads us deeper into God's heart. Enjoy the journey!"

—**Floyd McClung**, International Director, All Nations, which seeks to make disciples and train leaders to ignite church planting movements among the neglected peoples of the earth.

"Encyclopedic in its scope, *The Name Quest* leaves no "stone" unturned in its author's search for names, titles and descriptions of the persons of the Trinity found in the Bible. The word in quotes is a pun intended: John Avery's fine volume includes 180 sidebars, two of which list every occurrence of "stone" ("chief cornerstone," "cornerstone," "living stone," "stone," "stone of Israel," "stone of stumbling") in the Old and New Testaments together with the Hebrew/Greek words they represent and the verses where they are found. The other 178 treat similarly every occurrence of each of the many hundreds of other divine names, titles and descriptions (Avery calls them a "kaleidoscope," a fitting term indeed) in the Bible. The bulk of Avery's book is given to lively expositions of God's acts in creation and redemption, his nature, his miracles, his incarnation, his wisdom, his blessing, his relationship to his people, his timelessness, his faithfulness, his love, his justice, his kingdom, his glory—and more. Avery's writing style is now lively, now challenging, always engrossing. The book leads us through Scripture sometimes chronologically, sometimes theologically. In short, *The Name Quest* is well worth reading through from cover to cover, and prayerfully at that."

—**Ronald Youngblood**, Professor emeritus of Old Testament and Hebrew at Bethel University, St. Paul, MN. The author/editor/co-editor of more than twenty volumes, he began his work as a translator/editor of the New International Version in 1970 and continues to serve on its Committee on Bible Translation.

"John Avery has done a masterful job explaining all the biblical names of God in his creative and informative book, *The Name Quest*. If you're looking for an exciting Bible study that will help transform you into the image of the heavenly Father, this book is for you. I strongly recommend *The Name Quest* both for young students of the word and for seasoned ministers."

—**Peter J. Iliyn**, North American Director, YWAM

"*The Name Quest*, is both light heartedly delightful and deeply thoughtful. It engages the theological mind with a fresh and lively tone. As a First Nations person, I particularly enjoyed the stories which carried the Quest of the book like a tugboat hauling weighty and worthy matters."

—**Cheryl Bear-Barnetson**, Native Musician
and Foursquare Pastoral Overseer, Canada.
Cheryl is from Nadleh Whut'en First Nation in British Columbia. She and her family plan to visit every First Nations community in Canada and the USA re-telling the story of Jesus in a Native way. www.cherylbear.com

"What's in a name? John Avery takes us on the ultimate exploration of the Ultimate Name. With both exhaustive research and engaging narrative, John's work and wit will be a blessing to any sojourner's quest. Layperson, teacher, and serious seeker alike will be challenged and edified."

—**Sam Skillern**, Salem Leadership Foundation, www.salemLF.org

"John Avery will take you into a rediscovery of your intimacy with God and into the depths of the Father as you read *The Name Quest*. As John points out, 'at every twist, a new perspective on God emerges.' This is timely and a must read!"

—**Carl Wills**, Core Team leader, Pioneer Network UK

"The theme and direction of *The Name Quest* captured me because the names of God have been significant in my life. Approaching God's names from the point of view of relationship with Him is more important than a simple academic study of the meanings and significance of God's names. *The*

Name Quest is a welcome addition to what is available now. The writing style is engaging, and the illustrations are well placed and helpful. The chapter that focuses on the raising of Lazarus is very good, and the four challenges to faith are well stated and touched me."

—**Gordon Bergman**, Pastor of Pastoral Care,
Salem Alliance Church, and Leader of SalemNet

"An amazing book! John Avery has managed to weave together a reasoned and scholarly book, which also utilises his gift for story-telling to bring familiar Biblical events to life and a brilliant use of analogy to explain concepts. From its opening pages *The Name Quest* demonstrates the depth and breadth of the author's insight into the Biblical narrative, encouraging the reader both to delve into its intricate detail and to step back and consider God's eternal purposes. It is a book that expands our view of the God who is far beyond the limits of our understanding, but its thought-provoking insights also have the capacity to deeply affect our personal lives in ways that are practical and down-to-earth. *The Name Quest* is the fruit of years of background study mixed with the author's own experience of growing in the knowledge of God and His character. It is an absolute treasure trove for all who long to know God more, understand His ways better and become more like Him."

—**Liz Woods**, MBE, Former member of staff at the Garden Tomb, Jerusalem

NAME QUEST

Explore the Names of God to
Grow in Faith and Get to Know Him Better

JOHN AVERY

NEW YORK

the NAME QUEST

Explore the Names of God to Grow in Faith and Get to Know Him Better

© 2015 John Avery.

Published in New York, New York, by Morgan James Publishing. Morgan James and The Entrepreneurial Publisher are trademarks of Morgan James, LLC.
www.MorganJamesPublishing.com

The Morgan James Speakers Group can bring authors to your live event. For more information or to book an event visit The Morgan James Speakers Group at www.TheMorganJamesSpeakersGroup.com.

A FREE eBook edition is available with the purchase of this print book

CLEARLY PRINT YOUR NAME IN THE BOX ABOVE

Instructions to claim your free eBook edition:
1. Download the BitLit app for Android or iOS
2. Write your name in UPPER CASE in the box
3. Use the BitLit app to submit a photo
4. Download your eBook to any device

ISBN 978-1-63047-159-0 paperback
ISBN 978-1-63047-160-6 eBook
ISBN 978-1-63047-161-3 hardcover
Library of Congress Control Number:
2014933879

Cover Design by:
Rachel Lopez
www.r2cdesign.com

Interior Design by:
Bonnie Bushman
bonnie@caboodlegraphics.com

In an effort to support local communities, raise awareness and funds, Morgan James Publishing donates a percentage of all book sales for the life of each book to Habitat for Humanity Peninsula and Greater Williamsburg.

Get involved today, visit
www.MorganJamesBuilds.com

Habitat for Humanity®
Peninsula and
Greater Williamsburg
Building Partner

ABBREVIATIONS

NASB   Unless otherwise noted, Scripture is taken from the NEW AMERICAN STANDARD BIBLE®, Copyright © 1960,1962, 1963,1968,1971,1972,1973,1975,1977,1995 by The Lockman Foundation. Used by permission.

NIV   THE HOLY BIBLE, NEW INTERNATIONAL VERSION®, NIV® Copyright © 1973, 1978, 1984, 2011 by Biblica, Inc.™ Used by permission. All rights reserved worldwide.

MSG   Scripture taken from *The Message*. Copyright © 1993, 1994, 1995, 1996, 2000, 2001, 2002. Used by permission of NavPress Publishing Group.

NKJV   Scripture taken from the New King James Version®. Copyright © 1982 by Thomas Nelson, Inc. Used by permission. All rights reserved.

AB   Amplified Bible (1987).

Darby   The Darby Translation (1890).

ESV   English Standard Version (2001).

Holman   Holman Christian Standard Bible (2009).

JB   Jerusalem Bible (1966).

KJV   The King James Version.

NEB   New English Bible (1961).

NKJV   New King James Version (1998).

RSV   Revised Standard Version (1971).

YLT   Young's Literal Translation of the Bible (1898).

TWOT   *Theological Wordbook of the Old Testament* Ed. R. Laird Harris (Moody Press, 1980).

DSS   Michael Wise, Martin Abegg Jr., and Edward Cook, *A New Translation, The Dead Sea Scrolls* (Harper One, 2005).

Ant.   Flavius Josephus, *Antiquities.*

War   Flavius Josephus, *The Jewish War.*

NTPG   N. T. Wright, *The New Testament and the People of God* (Fortress Press, Minneapolis, 1992).

JVG   N. T. Wright, *Jesus and the Victory of God* (Fortress Press, Minneapolis, 1996).

RSG   N. T. Wright, *The Resurrection of the Son of God* (Fortress Press, Minneapolis, 2003).

Eng.   English.

Heb.   Hebrew.

Gk.   Greek.

Aram.   Aramaic.

CONTENTS

THANKS TO:

Writing a book is like embarking on a major expedition; only the efforts of a team of people make it possible.

My thanks go to the members of St. Croix Christian Church who endured my first sermon forays into the subject of the names of God.

The friends who read early draft chapters and made helpful comments are too numerous to mention individually. Thanks for going the extra mile are due to Beth Hunter, Wendy Hall, Karen Hawkins, Jan Vickers, Janet Spingath, Marlin Brownell, Fred Lykins, Kathy Scriven, Les Yoder, and my wife, Janet.

Being part of a Writers' Group proved invaluable. My special thanks to Sam Hall, Lindy Swanson, and others who joined us for a season. They honed my early efforts and helped me to navigate away from tortuous and torturous rabbit trails.

Liz Woods spent hundreds of hours editing my rudimentary Hebrew, checking Bible references, and making many helpful comments. Special thanks to her.

Professional editing is essential. I am very grateful to Andy Butcher, and to Pamela Guerrieri and Scott Jones of Proofed to Perfection for their attention to detail. Also, thanks to George Guntermann for his final check of the manuscript, and to Matthew Lanser and Jason Hare for proofreading the Hebrew.

My thanks to David Hancock, Margo Toulouse, and the entire team at Morgan James Publishing who enabled the "expedition" to reach its goal.

And to you, the reader: if God blessed you through this book, I thank you in advance for telling others about it so that they can benefit from their own exploration of the names of God—to His glory.

—John Avery
www.NamesForGod.net

THE CAMEL BRAND

*The two most important days of your life are the day you were born and
the day you discover why.*

—Unknown[1]

Scooping up a handful of dried fruit, Abdullah flicked aside the flap of his
tent and emerged blinking into the bright desert sunrise. With no time
to stretch and yawn, he went straight to the fire pit, tossed yesterday's
newspaper and a leather pouch onto the ground, and took out his lighter.
One deft flick was enough to set some dry palm fronds crackling. Adding
a few sticks and pieces from a broken crate, he soon had a respectable fire.
Flaming wood slowly turned into glowing charcoal. Abdullah squatted in the
dust, savoring some dates and spitting the seeds into the embers.

It was a glorious start to his day. The rising sun was painting a colorful
masterpiece over a wispy canvas of clouds—carnelian fading through pink
to tangerine. Two palm trees leaned in, creating the perfect frame. But the
splendor extended past them and across most of the sky, making it impossible
to fully appreciate the sunrise from any single vantage point. Yesterday had
been glorious too, and Abdullah still basked in joy and relief. He had received

news from the municipal court that he had won his case. Justice had been served; a reckless driver would be compensating Abdullah for killing one of his camels.

Abdullah flicked through his newspaper, skipping most of the headlines. He was hunting for the sports pages, but one article arrested his eye. It compared present conditions in Iraq with life under Saddam Hussein.

Saddam's brazen attitude toward the rest of the world, along with the ensuing wars, had brought Iraq and Islam into the spotlight for many ordinary people. Questions arose about the nature of the Christian God versus Allah and other gods. Did it really matter which god a person believed in or what that god's name was? Visiting western journalists, who were embedded with troops headquartered in Saddam's Al Hillah palace, didn't seem to think so. They spoke of learning to be tolerant, emphasizing the role of individual choice in religion. This was not what Abdullah had been taught as a Shiite Muslim.

Christian foreigners had challenged much of Abdullah's education. Significant differences separated their beliefs from his. They claimed that God had sent to earth a son, who had died and been resurrected. How preposterous! Nonetheless, their Bible and his Qur'an contained some similar stories and shared a few of the same characters: Abraham, his son Ishmael, and Isa, whom English speakers called Jesus.

The Bible mentioned Babel, which was just down the road from Al Hillah, where Abdullah's black goat-hair tent stood. Nimrod the hunter had first put Abdullah's neighborhood on the world map by including Babel in his kingdom. In Nimrod's day, Babel (meaning "Gate to God") was as far as humans had gone on their journey from Eden to fill the earth. They had decided to settle on the plain and make a great name for themselves so that they would not be scattered. They erected a huge tower so high that some said it touched heaven. Their early construction project ended in a confusion of languages and the race scattered to form many nations. Babel and its offspring, Babylon, had long ago crumbled into the dust now piled in the mounds, which broke up Abdullah's horizon in the direction of Baghdad. The region seemed destined to be a crossroads. Nations had met here repeatedly, approaching each other like cars at an unmarked junction, unsure about how to negotiate it safely. Some of those meetings proved to be damaging collisions of world powers—battles that changed the course of history. Each empire was shunted aside by its successor.

The picture accompanying the newspaper article caught Abdullah's attention. It showed a huge poster of Saddam Hussein that was mounted on a Baghdad tower block. Years ago, angry crowds had ripped down the poster and burnt it. They were glad to be rid of him. Saddam's plans had included rebuilding the ruins of Babylon. Saddam had hung a portrait of himself and the biblical King Nebuchadnezzar at the entrance to Babylon's ruins, inscribing some bricks: "This was built by Saddam Hussein, son of Nebuchadnezzar, to glorify Iraq."[2] Abdullah wondered how Saddam had felt each time he drove past those images. Was he genuinely seeking greatness for Iraq? Or was he simply out to make a name for himself, as Nebuchadnezzar had been?

Abdullah chuckled as he thought about that intriguing king who had crushed so many neighboring nations, razing Jerusalem and its temple. Nebuchadnezzar had devised the legendary hanging gardens that supposedly lay beneath the mounds. He must have been very rich. The Bible said that he had commissioned a ninety-foot, gold image of himself. Then God humbled Nebuchadnezzar. What happened to that image? It too became part of the dust heaps.

Gathering more wood, Abdullah fed the glowing embers. No fire was necessary for warmth here. After all, by midday he would not be able to walk barefoot over the hot sand with its long story. Abdullah had built his fire for work. Abdullah opened the leather pouch and took out a crude tool, a wooden grip attached to a metal shaft ending in a piece of bent black steel. It was his branding iron. A few yards from his tent, a stout pen held a small herd of camels. They were females with calves. The time had come to brand the year's young—to mark them indelibly with his ownership. That mark, burned through a few millimeters of thick hide on their necks, secured their value, distinguishing them from unclaimed strays. In the lawsuit against his neighbor, who had argued that the animal he had run over was his own, the mark was indisputable evidence of Abdullah's ownership.

Abdullah felt a certain pleasure and significance in the power of the branding iron that he wielded in his hand. These were his animals. He had plans to breed a large, valuable herd to leave to his children. He wondered what mark he would make on history. Would his descendants remember him for as long as they had Nimrod or Nebuchadnezzar? Would his legacy be of value, or would people be glad to see his face no more? Worse, would God intervene to humble or crush him?

He pushed the end of the brand under the embers and left it there until it glowed like the clouds in the sunlight.

A KALEIDOSCOPE OF NAMES

What numbers are to a mathematician and what colors are to a landscape artist, names are to Christian language.
                    —**Eugene Peterson**, *The Jesus Way*

T his book is about God's names. More importantly, it's about God branding His character into our lives—the character to which His names point. As we spend time getting to know God, we grow more like Him. Understanding His names helps us understand His nature.

It takes about five hundred biblical names and titles to express every aspect of God's being. These names are like a kaleidoscope of complementary colors; they are difficult to organize but always beautiful. Strictly speaking, there are only two true names of God, the personal names: *Yahweh* and Jesus. Most of what we call "names" are really titles. God's titles tell us what He does or they aptly describe what He is like (though Jesus' enemies invented some names to deride Him). The Bible does not distinguish names from titles, so neither will I. Most of the time, it is simpler to call the titles of God "names." Surprisingly few of them are stated by the Bible to be actual names of God.[3]

My beloved
Heb.: *Dodi*
(Isa. 5:1)

My well beloved
Heb.: *Yedidi*
(Isa. 5:1)

The boundary between names and mere descriptions is hazy, which explains why one writer's list of God's names might be longer than another's. During one worship service, I reflected on that hazy distinction. The congregation was singing a song that referred to God as "my garden." The songwriter had invented his own metaphorical name for God. The prophet Isaiah did the same; he called God **My beloved** and **My well beloved**.[4] Terms of endearment are admirable. I have included many biblical ones because they flesh out our picture of God. Far from playing to the idea that God is what you make Him to be, such expressive names point to an important truth—God meets us on our level, using language that we can understand. As Eugene Peterson explains:

> When the writers of Scripture use metaphor, we get involved with God, whether we want to or not, sometimes whether we know it or not. . . . The quickest and most available access to the invisible by means of language is through metaphor, a word that names the visible (or audible, or touchable). A metaphor is a word that carries us across the abyss separating the invisible from the visible.[5]

I have omitted many names of God that crossed the hazy line. Names not found in the Bible are normally beyond the scope of this book, though I mention some because they are commonly mistaken as genuine names of God.[6] They are often the products of antiquated translation language or a hymn writer's expressive poetry. **Holy Ghost** is an example of a name that has become unfashionable.

Hold the Pigeonholes

One God
Heb.: *'El 'ekhad*
(Mal. 2:10)

In a sense, God's most fundamental name is *'El 'ekhad*, **One God**.[7] This name describes a basic aspect of His nature: He is the sole divine being in the universe.

Some people argue that if God had intended to convey absolute oneness, He would have chosen the word *yakhid*. *'Ekhad* can express compound unity (like one bunch of many grapes).[8] The doctrine of the Trinity—three persons in One God—expresses this complex unity. God is one Person, so Jesus commanded His disciples to baptize new believers "in the name [singular] of the Father and the Son and the Holy Spirit" (Matt. 28:19). Unfortunately, classifying God's names according to the Trinity would produce tedious repetitions.

The Old Testament refers to God using three primary names. *Yahweh* (translated as LORD)[9] and *'Elohim* (God) form the basis of many compound names, while a third, *'Adonai* (Lord or Master), does so less often. These terms make for a better classification system, but drawbacks remain. Sometimes two or more of the primary roots form a compound name.[10] In addition, similar descriptive suffixes combine with different primary names, as in *Yahweh tseva'ot* (LORD of hosts) and *'Elohim tseva'ot* (God of hosts). That system also leaves a residual miscellaneous section, which includes simple names like "Creator." Neat classifications of God's names don't work well and they're so dry! Praise is most natural when it flows from a relationship, not from a Rolodex.

That's why we don't find God's names neatly catalogued in the Bible. (www. NamesForGod.net provides a list.) God wants each of us to pursue relationship with Him, as He really is: a single personality with a multifaceted character. Personalities are too complex to compartmentalize; they are integrated and dynamic. We can't dissect His characteristics and expect Him to remain God.[11] This book clusters God's names in chapters, around common themes: who He is and what He does. Approaching Him in that way ensures that we will have meaningful relationships with Him. Every name of God helps us relate to Him as the dynamic being that He is.

One powerful exercise for growing closer to Him is to reflect on the character of God that underlies His names. There are other benefits too: Our meditations transform life's challenges into potent fuel for the fire of faith. Confidence in His practical care for us increases. We also gain greater authority to bless others. Our passion to bear and proclaim His name, and to magnify and praise Him, grows. We profane His name less and honor it more. Our walk through life aligns better with Him, bringing Him greater glory. The church that gathers and prays in His name becomes more aware of His presence and more effective in His work. Together we approach our high destiny of being called by His name.

Spinning the Kaleidoscope

Turning a kaleidoscope produces fascinating patterns as the tiny colored tiles tumble into novel arrangements. Read this book in the same way that you would look into a kaleidoscope. When you turn to a new chapter, you will find a fresh combination of names around a central theme—usually an attribute or activity of God. Some names will be mentioned in more than one chapter (without repeating all the background information) because they are components of several patterns. Remember, God is a personality and His attributes are intricately interrelated.

The chapters of human history and of our individual lives also unfold rather like a rotating kaleidoscope. At every twist, a new perspective on God emerges. Sometimes these perspectives are similar to what we've seen before, but sometimes they are quite fresh. The same colors are present, but each rotation produces another unique arrangement of tiles, with a new emphasis. Unlike a kaleidoscope, God's intentional self-disclosure is no random generation of patterns. Instead, in God's controlling hands, all of our circumstances work to deepen our relationships with Him.

Chapter 1

WHAT'S IN A NAME?

"Don't stand chattering to yourself like that," Humpty Dumpty said, looking at her for the first time, *"but tell me your name and your business."*

"My name is Alice, but . . ."

"It's a stupid name enough!" Humpty Dumpty interrupted impatiently. *"What does it mean?"*

"Must a name mean something?" Alice asked doubtfully.

"Of course it must," Humpty Dumpty said with a short laugh: *"my name means the shape I am—and a good handsome shape it is, too. With a name like yours, you might be any shape, almost."*

—**Lewis Carroll**, *Through the Looking Glass*

Names are verbal handles—handles for relationships. When my wife, Janet, calls my name, I know I've forgotten something. "John, get up! You didn't put the garbage bin out last night. Quick, the truck's coming down the road." Rudely awakened, I stumble out of bed, pull on a dressing gown, slip sockless into unlaced shoes, and stagger out to the street with the trash. I'm the breakfast show for a sleepy and bored garbage hauler.

Janet and I are British, so at three o'clock on a weekend afternoon, Janet usually makes a cup of tea. Often I'm at the bottom of our half-acre garden coaxing vegetables or pulling weeds. She shouts, "John, tea's made." Neighbors look up quizzically as I wipe my hands and walk self-consciously back to the house.

Names work well for getting a person's attention quickly, but as relationships grow closer, we call each other by name less often in everyday conversation. Unless we are upset, shouting from a distance, addressing each other in a crowd, or urgently needing attention, Janet and I tend not to use each other's names. With no children at home, we take it for granted that when one of us is talking, it must be to the other.

Much of the time, however, people do use names to identify each other. Having a name is part of being an individual.[12] Names often express an established identity, but they may also impart a new one. For instance, when a woman voluntarily takes her husband's last name in marriage, it marks her added identity as his wife.[13] In tender moments, Janet and I use pet names.

Parents do the most naming, but lovers, friends, and enemies give names to each other too. We like some names; others we dislike. Some fit; a few do not. Pet names express love and value; nicknames can be endearing or defaming. Whether we like them or not, we all have at least one name.

God named people in the Bible, and He changed names. But God doesn't just attach a new label, He transforms people from the inside out. Some biblical names have the future in mind, and these names speak of a desired quality or a reputation that God intends to form in the person.[14] When we surrender our lives to Jesus' lordship, we accept His ownership and we receive a new identity in Him. The change in our character follows more slowly, but His goal is for us to become like Him.

In the Bible, the Hebrew word *shem* means "name." *Hashem* represents everything about God. Notice how this works in the following examples:

- When the Bible says His name is lovely, it is because He is lovely (Ps. 135:1–3).
- His name is great, holy, and awesome, as He is great, holy, and awesome (Pss. 99:3; 111:9).
- It was said of Levi that he "stood in awe of My name" (Mal. 2:4–5), meaning that Levi revered God.

- We sing and praise all the glory wrapped up in His name (Ps. 66:1–2).
- To boast of His name is to put one's trust in His strength publicly (Ps. 20:7).
- Levitical blessings rested on the authority represented by His name (Num. 6:22–27; Deut. 10:8; 1 Chron. 23:13). Often, His names declare His superiority over the creation and other so-called gods.
- To praise and bless His name is to show gratitude for His works and speak highly of His character (Deut. 32:1–4; Pss. 7:17; 48:10; 89:12, 16; 92:1; 113:1–4; 145:1–2, 21; 148:5; Neh. 9:5).

But what do we mean by the character of God? Since God is a personality, the use of names in human cultures can teach us things about Him. Human names often have to do with roles. In God's case, His roles reflect His character.

Role Call

I hardly spoke a word on my first day of high school. A noisy bus, smelling of diesel, had swept me away from a long summer break and dropped me off at an unfamiliar school. I knew five boys; the other eight hundred students were much larger and louder than I liked. Somehow, I resisted the urge to run.

My clearest memory of that day is of our class teacher taking out his roll book and checking off our names. British grammar schools had a custom of addressing students by their last names. For seven years, I became simply "Avery" to teachers. My friends, to mock my curly hair, which I spent hours trying to smooth down, nicknamed me "Fuzzy." Other students received scarring labels that took years to heal from.

As the teacher went around the room, we had to call out our names. There was a Baker, my friend Thatcher, and a Brown, who was somewhat tanned when we looked closely. Another boy told us that he had acquired his surname when his parents had adopted him. The next boy had a rare name: Vazquez. He gained privileged first-name status and went by "Mario" for the rest of his time at school because no one dared humiliate himself trying to pronounce his last name.

The class comedians began to surface during this exercise. Smith pronounced his name so roughly that the teacher asked how many fs it contained. Clark emphasized that he spelled his name "without an *e*." So, everyone began calling him "Clark without an *e*."

Completing the roll book helped the teacher maintain class discipline because names are handles for authority too. The teachers who learned our names the fastest had the most orderly classes. These teachers had the power to single us out, get our attention, and write us up for detention after school.

Many surnames reflect a family's historical occupation. People used to know each other by their craft, their role in life. Some of my peers bore occupational names, presumably because their ancestors worked as village blacksmiths and bakers. Thatchers were roofers. The Clarks—with or without *e*'s—were administrators and the Vazquezes did goodness-knows-what in Spain. My own family name, Avery, derives from an older form, Aubry. Its history is not entirely clear, though the name might have Scottish or Norman roots, and it might have something to do with royalty. I am still hoping to inherit a castle.

After college, I moved away from my home culture to teach in a Kenyan village. There, families gave newborn babies several names. In addition to having an everyday personal name, each child would receive a name based on his or her birth event: the time of day, the season of the year, memorable incidents, and even notable weather. Later in life, children received additional names as they entered adulthood or experienced a life milestone. When a village elder died, his name often passed to a related child to continue his memory.

Of course, God's names far surpass the way human societies give and use names, but there are some parallels. God repeats many of His actions so that we recognize patterns and come to identify Him with role titles, like Creator and Savior. God's activity often produced recordable historical events, and some of His names remind us of those events. Bible heroes applied new names for God to physical monuments to mark times when God's attributes overflowed in special actions. Later on, we will consider the naming of three altars, a mountainside, and a city.[15] The names were given to these things to remind people of certain attributes and actions of God. Writers often use them as names of God. Other names point prophetically to future events that have already been fulfilled or are awaiting fulfillment upon Jesus' return.

When God acts, He does so to magnify His name.[16] His deeds in history continue to bring Him glory, as demonstrations of who He is. God arranged for Pharaoh to make decisions about Israel that ultimately displayed God's sovereignty and glory and "made a name" for Him.[17]

God's names are always more significant than mere labels used to address Him. All of God's names, even those that point to His actions or memorialize events, are condensed expressions of His character. They are packed with meaning, giving glimpses into the depths of His being. They express His many wonderful attributes and point to His true nature. The names are handles that facilitate our relationship with a personal God.

The Benefits of Knowing the God behind the Names

There are five broad ways in which understanding God's names benefits us:

- It helps us accomplish the human quest for a worthwhile legacy.
- Some of us need help escaping unpleasant labels and growing in character.
- We all need greater alignment with the character that underlies His names.
- We can get to know Him better through all of life's events.
- Our confidence to use His name in various ways grows.

Let's examine each of these benefits in turn:

The Human Name Quest

Biblical cultures paid attention to the meanings of names; names in the Bible usually mark characteristics, reputations, or events. Take one walk-on Bible character, Abigail. She said contemptuously of her husband Nabal (meaning "fool"), "As his name is, so is he" (1 Sam. 25:25).

The prayer of another minor player, Jabez, suggests a quest to shake off the stigma of his name. His mother called him Jabez because she bore him with pain (1 Chron. 4:9–10). Jabez hated to be pained or to cause pain ("Jabez" can mean either), so he prayed hard.

Because of their connection to character and reputation, names are important to us and to God. While the Hebrew word *shem* underlies most instances of the word "name," occasionally *zekher* is used instead.[18] Twice, the name *Yahweh* is called His *zekher* or memorial-name. In Exodus, God said, "This is My name forever, and this is My memorial-name to all generations."[19] Three times *zekher* parallels *shem*—evidence of the connection between names and a lasting memory or enduring reputation.

Isaiah said, "Your name [*shem*], even Your memory [*zekher*], is the desire of our souls."[20]

God cares about how we view Him and how we use His name. We must not take His name in vain,[21] swear falsely by it (stating an untruth while attaching God's name to make it seem sincere), or profane it.[22] We can identify with His concern because we know how much it hurts when people mock or misrepresent us. On the other hand, we love to blow our own horns and bolster our reputations.

We energetically enhance or defend our reputations knowing that they will outrun us. The Bible notes the human desire to be remembered; this desire manifested itself as a hope that descendants would perpetuate one's name.[23] It was sad, even shameful, when this did not happen or when the memory was a bad one. King David's son Absalom felt compelled to build a monument outside Jerusalem because he had no son to continue his name.[24] Cutting off descendants to end the family name was a punishment in the Bible. God's destruction of Nineveh buried the city's name in dust.[25] No one wants that kind of destiny.

The Bible is the epic two-part story of humans on a name quest. The first part includes our search for an enduring good reputation. The inhabitants of Babel thought their tower would establish their name. That idea crashed, but the struggle continued. The second part of the Bible describes God's plan to secure our destiny for us.

Isaiah outlined the end of our quest: the names of those who forsake the Lord will remain as a curse, while His servants will receive a new and better name.[26] *Our* names endure when we become servants of *His* name. God said, "In My name his horn will be exalted" (Ps. 89:24). The highest destiny of both individuals and nations is to "give thanks to [God's] name" (Pss. 106:47; 140:13). Our greatest purpose in life is to boost God's reputation—the reputation to which His names point.

Naming the Change

Some people, like Jabez, feel held back from their destiny by shame or pain. Much of their identity seems bound up with past mistakes or with pain caused by deep wounds. The truth is that we all have downsides that we would rather not have named. Most of us choose the quick fix—we keep those downsides as private as we can. God has a better solution. He changes characters, extends forgiveness, and heals the memories of painful events, just as He did for Abraham and his family.

Jacob (the son of Isaac and grandson of Abraham), whose name meant "heel grasper," or "supplanter," must have felt relieved when God renamed him Israel, which means "he who strives with God" (Gen. 32:28).

Rachel, Jacob's wife, died giving birth to his twelfth son. As she died, she named the boy *Ben-'oni*, "son of my sorrow" (Gen. 35:16–19). Jacob renamed him Benjamin, "son of the right hand," perhaps to remove any stigma of sorrow.

In the Bible, as people like Abraham and Jacob grew closer to God, they often received new names. The new name sealed and declared a character change wrought in the presence of God. But, don't think you must run out and register a new name to obtain new character traits. What matters most is a change of heart. God's solution for those who are desperate to escape shameful habits and burdensome backgrounds is to know Him better. God is gathering a huge family of changed people whose hearts are imprinted with His character.

God's Fingerprint

What does the often-used expression, "in His name," mean? Jeremiah gave us a principle concerning prophecy "in His name." He said that true prophecy originates in the "council" of the Lord—from being in His presence.[27] We read that the prophets spoke "in the name of the LORD." This phrase was no mere packing slip attached to the message; it was a seal of authenticity. True prophets, from Moses onward, received their messages straight from God.[28] If a prophecy came to pass, it was because God had revealed the matter, so the prophet carried His authority. Conversely, if the words did not originate with God, the prophecy would fail.[29] Jeremiah denounced the utterances of false prophets, who thought that they could simply label their words "in the name of the LORD" and get away with it. Such words were misleading. These words failed because people had conceived them, rather than the God of truth.[30] In God's presence, the true prophet heard God's intentions. His heart began to beat with the heart of God. The divine heartbeat resonated through the words he spoke, and those words eventually became part of history.

Actions that are truly done "in God's name" will correlate with His nature. When we read of Old Testament battles being fought "in God's name," this phrase was not a political tool to justify the fight or rubber-stamp the party cause (though history provides plenty of examples of its abuse).[31] Rather, the warriors were contending for God's will and ways.[32] When David fought Goliath, he was assured of victory because his alignment with God's purposes positioned him to receive God's backing.[33]

The principle of alignment extends to the rest of life. In Old Testament times, the Israelites were "God's people," a community called by His name and living in that name.[34] Religion was no secondary category for them. The entire social structure, from the family level to the national level, was under God's rule. God governed relationships, agriculture, land ownership, commerce, etc. God's blessing was proportional to Israel's obedience to His commands. The ideal Israel could rely on God to defend her. God had a reputation for faithfulness to His people.[35] Today, Christians are defined by faith in Jesus. So long as we remain "set apart"—dedicated to living God's way—the communal description, "God's people," is apt.[36] When we are aligned with God, all of His words seem sweet to us—yes, even His commands.[37]

Jesus emphasized that to minister "in the name of the Lord" means to be in harmony with His Father's will.[38] Jesus came in the Lord's name, so He was blessed.[39] Our words and actions indicate the source of our lives. They bring honor or shame to Him, depending on who we are in harmony with.[40] Those who align themselves with God's desires might very well see miracles, because His power is at hand when we live and act for Him.[41] Praying in His name means making requests that are consistent with His character and will. Jesus promised to grant such petitions for the Father's glory.[42] When we exhort people "by the name of the Lord," we are appealing to them to honor God by living according to His will.[43] That was Paul's prayer for the Thessalonians—to live up to their calling and to glorify the Lord's name.[44]

Being a people called by His name and doing everything "in His name" implies far more than displaying a brand mark on a few square inches of thick skin. It is more like the mark left in precious metals when they are refined. Each smelter leaves its own distinct atomic fingerprint, which is a unique combination of trace elements within the metal. When scientists need to determine the origin or authenticity of a metallic object, they conduct a high-tech assay to reveal the fingerprint. We're like the metal: as we repeatedly submit our lives to God's refining work, His character grows in us. Of course, refining is a process. In our lifetimes, we will never be completely refined. But people called by His name gradually shine with more of His characteristics.

Message in a Bottle

Any study of God's nature, including a study of the names that point to His nature, is limited. God's names express just a drop of the vast ocean of His being, so we can never comprehend Him completely.

For three years, Janet and I pastored a church on the island of St. Croix. Cotton-ball clouds sailed lazily overhead through a hazy blue sky, framed by crowded coconut palms. Strange as it may seem in the picture-perfect Caribbean, those clouds are a vital water distribution system. The spring water we bought at the store had a story. The tropical sun sucks up water from the Atlantic Ocean and the clouds deliver it to the hills. If those photogenic clouds were to pose for postcards for too long, the plants and animals would slowly expire. It is only when the clouds turn an ugly gray and drop their moisture that the *guts* (as the local creeks are called) start to run again. The water on my desk had been "bottled at source" and was a tiny representation of the ocean from which it had come.

Most of us know that water is colorless, but the skipper of a Caribbean charter yacht told me the following story. A passenger asked him to scoop up a sample of seawater so that she could show her mainland friends its beautiful azure color. She was surprised to discover that the color vanished as soon as it left the sea.

Each name of God is an imperfect compression of His attributes into human language and imagery. Words in a book only paddle on the shore of His oceanic nature. All writers run the risk of seeing the color drain out when their pens touch paper. Nonetheless, God wants us to know Him—so He reveals His names.

Becoming acquainted with someone usually involves exchanging names. Often, when God revealed Himself afresh, a new name accompanied His revelation. Frequently, God revealed more of Himself to biblical heroes during times of personal or national crisis. They sometimes framed the revelation into names, which memorialized the incidents. In joy and relief, Hagar, the maid of Abraham's wife, Sarah, honored God with the name *'El ro'i*, which means **God who sees**. He saw her desperation and He took care of her. Two other good examples are Abraham and Jacob, whose faith and relationship with God grew.

A similar relationship progression is discernible in Israel's national history. The first part of our Bible[45] (the Jewish Scriptures that Jesus and New Testament writers used) tells of God's covenant-based relationship with Israel. The second part tells of the new covenant that Jesus secured. This covenant offers the entire human race far greater intimacy with God than Israel ever experienced.

Until Jesus came, people groped after relationships with God, like children before Christmas. We sometimes catch children sneaking quick investigations of the presents—a little poke here, a rattle there. They lift one to gauge its weight. Some try squeezing the gift to determine what shape hides beneath the wrapping paper. The upturned corners of the gift-wrapping show where they have peeked in. Each tiny view gives an accurate glimpse of the gift inside, but children rarely get enough clues to guess exactly what the gift is. The combined evidence builds a vague picture of the concealed present. Nevertheless, final confirmation and full enjoyment of the gift must wait until Christmas, when they can tear the wrapping away.

Well, Christmas has come and God has lifted the wrappings of spiritual blindness that once separated us from Him. His ultimate revelation went beyond written or spoken names to a flesh-and-blood expression of the Personality behind the names. Yes, a measure of mystery about His name will remain until the end,[46] but in Jesus—the Word of God—our eyes have been opened. We can relate to God and live as people called by His name.

So, if you consider your present understanding and experience of God to be like a pale, pint-sized portion of a billion gallons, be encouraged. The One who is the source of life loves to meet us in the thick of life and deepen His relationship with us. We only have to ask Him to meet us as we are.

Calling with Confidence

Our confidence to ask God for things grows as we get to know Him through His names. In addition, "calling on His name" comes with many promises.[47]

In the beginning, no names appear in the recorded conversations between Adam and God. The birth of Adam's first grandson, Enosh, marks the turning point when people "began to call upon the name of the LORD" (Gen. 4:26; 5:3–6). Why did humans wait for 235 years? No one noted the reason for the delay, so we can only speculate. Perhaps Adam and his family knew God so intimately that spoken names were unnecessary or too limiting. Maybe there was no crowd of rival gods to distinguish Him from. Or were there no problems or frustrations to elicit a cry for help? Perhaps our race had already fallen into the do-it-yourself mantrap of coping without calling for help.

The name Enosh may provide a clue as to why things changed, if his name hints at human weakness.[48] Perhaps people had begun to recognize their need for God. In any case, relating to God requires communication.

Calling on God does not imply that we must shout to be heard. God is certainly listening. However, calling requires a mixture of humility and faith. The Bible states a profound truth when it says that our help is in His name: dependence on God is healthy.[49]

God's people don't just petition Him for things, they seek Him for Himself and they worship Him sacrificially.[50] Belief in His name is fundamental to our relationship as adopted children,[51] and it produces great joy and abundant life.[52] When we gather "in His name," His presence is ensured.[53] An inheritance awaits everyone who fears His name.[54] "Those who love His name will dwell in [Zion]." (Ps. 69:35–36)

We may call on His name and experience His response in numerous situations. When we repent, we receive forgiveness.[55] The power to heal and do miraculous works is in His name.[56] In His name, the disciples drove demons out.[57] It might seem strange, but the prophet Elisha even used God's name to curse two lads who mocked his baldness. (Don't try that at home!)[58] We call on Him for deliverance and thank Him for salvation.[59] In fact, there is no other name by which we can be saved.[60]

God also promises security and deliverance: "I will set Him securely on high, because he has known My name" (Ps. 91:14; see also Ps. 20:1). "The name of the LORD is a strong tower; the righteous runs into it and is safe." (Prov. 18:10) The humble find refuge in His name.[61] Jesus asked the Father to keep His followers in His name.[62]

As we experience God's faithful answers to our cries, our confidence to petition Him increases. Learning His names well enough to reel them off as Bible trivia might help us remember His character, attributes, and activities, but such intellectual knowledge is relatively inconsequential. Experiential knowledge of a responsive God is a more substantial buttress of faith.[63] Acquiring such knowledge is a journey of adventure—so let's begin.

Chapter 2

A FAITH JOURNEY

Every day you may make progress. Every step may be fruitful. Yet there will stretch out before you an ever-lengthening, ever-ascending, ever-improving path. You know you will never get to the end of the journey. But this, so far from discouraging, only adds to the joy and glory of the climb.
—Sir Winston Churchill

My heart almost stopped when I saw the raging river. "Oh, no. I didn't expect any of this," I said to myself. I had hoped to refill my canteen but the river was brown with mud and undrinkable. Twenty minutes of searching confirmed my predicament. There was no clean water source nearby, and I had miles to go.

I was camped with bow-hunting friends in northeastern Oregon on the plateau overlooking Hell's Canyon. I had tagged along not to shoot elk, but to shoot photographs of the dramatic scenery. When I planned my hike, the route looked straightforward. The tiny wisps of smoke a mile down across the river assured me that the brush fire was no threat. I packed plenty of food and carried three pints of water. At first, the trail, with its multiple switchbacks, was easy. The final descent was cross-country over loose scree. I descended at a fast pace. It took just three hours to reach the Snake River. My knees trembled from the constant jarring of 5,600 downward steps and the final controlled slide. I was exhausted and my adventure had turned into a potentially life-threatening endurance test.

The valley was a suntrap that was far hotter than the breezy rim. The brush fire had consumed acres of vegetation on both sides of the river, leaving smoldering stumps. The charred landscape absorbed the sun's rays, and the canyon had become a broiling oven. Each step kicked up a plume of soot and ash—thank goodness for hiking boots. Now I faced a grueling 5,600-foot struggle up the valley side through a torturous, dehydrating furnace. I would be hiking upward at a very slow pace. That day, I learned the importance of proper preparation. I had not carried enough water.

The Faith Canteen

Our journey through the names of God begins at a dry period in the life of Moses and Israel. It might seem like an odd place to start—farther down the path of Bible history than expected. Why not begin with Adam or Abraham? After all, it was during Adam's life that people began calling on the Lord's name.[64] We start in Exodus because in that book, Israel encountered a historic challenge, and Moses was ill prepared, just as I was for my hike. God revealed Himself to a new degree to prepare Moses and His people. He expanded their knowledge of one of the three primary names we will consider in this chapter. That revelation launched them on their journey.

We also start with Moses because our own lives are full of new challenges. Each challenge is an opportunity for us to discover more of who He is. Each fresh insight spurs us on.

The exodus from Egypt and the subsequent journey to the promised land of Canaan were momentous. They marked the beginning of Israel's life as a nation.[65] Crossing Sinai was like traversing a birth canal, and Moses was the spiritual midwife. When a midwife hands a mother her baby, a deep bonding begins. The Israelites met God in a new, more personal way in Sinai, and their relationship with God was initiated and defined there. The laws that God revealed at Mount Sinai were actually the details of a covenant—the provisions governing the relationship.

God chose Moses to lead the crucial mission. Moses was to take the Hebrew people out of Egyptian isolation, through the baking Sinai Desert, to a promised land of intimacy with God. A challenge like that required spiritual preparation. Moses would have to draw on His relationship with God as if he were drinking from a hiker's canteen. He would be living a life of faith.

We often talk about our Christian lives in terms of faith.[66] Faith rests on two foundations:

- Truths stated about God, which we can choose to believe or not believe.
- Experiences of Him that reinforce those truths but can never replace them.

Typically, our challenge is to believe God's truth before we receive the reinforcing experience.

Did Moses' water bottle contain enough faith? God ensured that it did by increasing Moses' knowledge of Himself. He will do the same for us.

Thirsty Leader, Thirsty People

As a young man, Moses had witnessed an Egyptian taskmaster abusing a Hebrew slave. Most Hebrews had learned to hide their horror, shut up, and look busy; they had lost faith and hope for deliverance. Moses, on the other hand, reacted impulsively and killed the Egyptian.

The murder failed to catapult him into the role of revolutionary leader. Israel shunned him and Pharaoh issued a death warrant. Moses' early longing to see justice for his people went unsatisfied, draining his confidence in God's commitment to Israel.[67] Moses' long exile in Sinai prevented him from worshiping God with them. Spiritually and geographically, he entered a desert. The spiritual water bottle of his life—his faith in God—needed refilling. Yet God chose him as leader of the exodus. So, how did God replenish Moses' faith?

Three Primary Names for God

In Exodus 3, God called to Moses from a burning bush and identified Himself as "'the **God of your father**, the **God of Abraham**, the **God of Isaac**, and the **God of Jacob**.' Then Moses hid his face, for he was afraid to look at God" (v. 6). God assured him that He had seen the affliction of His people and He had heard their cries. "Come now, and I will send you to Pharaoh, so that you may bring My people, the sons of Israel, out of Egypt" (v. 10).

Moses responded to God as if someone had asked him to cross a stormy ocean right after learning to swim. Moses disguised his objections in a series of questions. He hoped that God would let him off with a nice campfire story about a blazing bush—which wasn't really burning—to tell his grandchildren. Moses' second point anticipated Israel's inquiry. He said to God, "Behold, I am going to the sons of Israel, and I will say to them, 'The **God of your fathers** has sent me to you.' Now they may say to me, 'What is His name?' What shall I say to them?" (v. 13)

> **God of your father**
> Heb.: *'Elohei 'avikha*
> (Gen. 31:29)
> **God of Abraham**
> Heb.: *'Elohei 'Avraham*
> (Gen. 31:42)
> **God of Isaac**
> Heb.: *'Elohei Yitskhaq*
> (Gen. 28:13)
> **God of Jacob**
> Heb.: *'Elohei Ya'aqov*
> (Ex. 3:6)

Evidently, a message from a God accredited by the patriarchs (or fathers of the nation), Abraham, Isaac, and Jacob, wasn't enough. The family relationship didn't motivate Moses to go, and it didn't persuade him that the people would follow. Moses reckoned that the knowledge of God that he and Israel shared was insufficient. Moses wanted the God of their fathers to identify Himself in a new way. He needed proof that God had more than an exciting escape plan. Moses wanted God to assure him that He could competently provide follow-up care for His people.

In Hebrew, the question, "What is His name?" (v. 13) is a way of inquiring about His character, rather than just His identity.[68] The Israelites already knew God by several names, including three primary ones: *'Adonai*, *'Elohim*, and *Yahweh*.[69] The last two in particular are like rootstocks onto which various descriptive words are grafted to form most of God's compound names. Let's consider the primary names.

Adonai

First is *'Adonai*. Its shorter form is *'Adon* and both of these forms mean **Lord**.[70] The root expresses ownership or mastery over others. In the Bible, *'Adon* usually refers to men. For instance, Sarah and the household servants used it of Abraham.[71] Elijah the prophet and Joab, King David's chief of staff, were also addressed that way.[72]

> **Lord or Master**
> Aram.: *Mare'*
> (Dan. 2:47; 5:23)
> Heb.: *'Adonai, 'Adon*

The standard plural form *'adonim* often refers to false "lords."[73] When Moses called the Israelites to recommit themselves to God, he used two names: **God of gods** and **Lord of lords**. Both of these names express God's extensive mastery. *'Adonai* is a special plural of *'adon* that intensifies the word's meaning, perhaps emphasizing the Lord's majesty.

God gives us freedom to choose Him as our owner, Lord, and Master. Just as any reasonable human master provides his servants with all of the resources needed to perform his will, so our heavenly Master supplies everything for us.[74] He is a master who deserves respect.[75]

Elohim

God
Heb.: *'Elohim, 'El, 'Eloah*
Aram.: *'Elah*
Gk.: *Theos*

'Elohim is generally translated "**God**," though occasionally it refers to angels or judges. A common convention is to use the lowercase, g-o-d, when referring to deities other than the Christian God. We honor only Him with a capitalized proper name.

T. E. Lawrence (of Arabia) once commented on our little word "god": "We lost much eloquence when making him the shortest and ugliest of our monosyllables."[76] The word "god" probably derives from an Indo-European word, *ghut*, "That which is invoked."[77] Entering old Germanic languages, it became *guth*. That word branched into *gott* (German), *gut* (Scandinavian), and "god." Ulfilas, a fourth-century missionary, was the first to adopt the word for his translation of Scripture into Gothic. To the Goths of Eastern Europe, the word denoted a supreme, uncreated Creator. The missionary gladly accepted their three-letter linguistic peg, but he hung on it the biblical details of God's character.

The Good Spirit
Heb.: *Haruakh hattovah*
(Neh. 9:20; Ps. 143:10)

Great and awesome God
Heb.: *Ha'El haggadol wehannora'*
(Deut. 7:21; Dan. 9:4)

Our English word suggests an emphasis on a specific aspect of His nature: goodness. However, the word "god" is etymologically unconnected to "good." The roots of *'Elohim* lie elsewhere.

'Elohim is related to two other words that are also translated "God": *'El* and *'Eloah*. The root meaning of both is might or strength. *El* is sometimes associated with fear. The descriptions "greatly feared" and "**great and awesome God**" are examples.[78] The name **fear of Isaac** may derive from that understanding of God's

nature. However, while God is the object of fear, He is also a refuge from fear. There is room for both senses.

Hebrew belongs to the family of Semitic languages that are spoken by people who descended from Noah's son, Shem. Hebrew, Arabic, and Aramaic are like cousins; they share a family likeness. During their exile in Babylon, the Jews adopted Aramaic as their everyday language, and they returned to Judah with it. They relegated Hebrew to Scripture and ceremony. Old Testament books written after the exile often use the Aramaic name *'Elah* (notice how similar it is to *Allah*). Jesus probably spoke Aramaic and Hebrew—and perhaps Greek too. Matthew recorded in Hebrew what Jesus cried to God from the cross; Mark preserved the Aramaic: "'*Eloi, Eloi, lama sabachthani?*' which is translated, 'My God, My God, why have you forsaken Me?'" (Mark 15:34[79]) While the other languages also used *'El* and *'Eloah* for their gods, only Hebrew used *'Elohim*. (See www.NamesForGod.net/bible-pronunciation for information about the languages of the Bible.)

'Elohim is unusual. Although it is the plural of *'Eloah*, it speaks of the One God.[80] In the Old Testament, it mostly accompanies singular verbs, adjectives, and pronouns. Like *'Adonai*, it has been called a "plural of majesty" indicating the elevated rank of God, who surpasses all created things. As such, *'Elohim* highlights the majestic transcendence of God and His supernatural nature.

Some scholars deny that Hebrew has a plural of majesty. So, it is reasonable to take the plural *'Elohim* (and *'Adonai*) as evidence of the Trinity. Also, the fact that God refers to Himself using the plural pronouns "us" and "our" is "marvelously consistent with" the doctrine of the Trinity.[81] "In the beginning *'Elohim* created . . ." says Genesis 1:1.[82] Later, " *'Elohim* said, 'Let *Us* make man in *Our* image, according to *Our* likeness'" (Gen. 1:26, my italics).[83]

Now, Elohim is no impersonal energy or good force. C. S. Lewis comments on this belief of pantheism:

> Pantheists usually believe that God, so to speak, animates the universe as you animate your body: that the universe almost *is* God, so that if it did not exist He would not exist either, and anything you find in the universe is a part of god. The Christian idea is quite different. They think God invented and made the universe—like a man making a picture or composing a tune. A painter is not a picture, and he does not die if his picture is destroyed.[84]

God, whose nature finds partial expression in the word *'Elohim*, transcends the cosmos. He created it. He is independent of it, yet He has a sustaining relationship with it and with us. The names *'El, 'Eloah,* and *'Elohim* all point to His majestic supremacy.

Yahweh

The Old Testament uses a third word even more often than *'Adonai* or *'Elohim*. Rather mysteriously, we can't be sure of the pronunciation because we only know the four consonants. They are equivalent to the English *YHWH* and scholars call them the Tetragrammaton.

Written Hebrew differs from most languages in that it has few vowel letters; Modern Hebrew represents vowels using tiny dots and dashes. These are called vowel points, and for most words they indicate pronunciation. We don't know how Moses and his people pronounced *YHWH* because the vowel points were added much later, long after people had forgotten the pronunciation.[85]

LORD (Yahweh, Jehovah)
Heb.: *YHWH*
(Ex. 6:3)
Heb.: *Yah*
(Ex. 15:2; 17:15–16; Ps. 118:14)
Gk.: *Kyrios*

Some think it sounded like **Jehovah**, a pronunciation that was first mentioned in the thirteenth century.[86] Others prefer **Yahweh** because ancient writers implied that pronunciation.[87] We will use the word *Yahweh*.

Yah is a short form of *Yahweh*. Many Jews had personal names that were compounds with *Yah*; the earliest example is *Yehoshua'* (Joshua in English). In this word, the first syllable derives from *Yah*. Until Moses renamed him, he was Hoshea (salvation). By renaming him, Moses ensured that Joshua's name emphasized Yah as the source of salvation.[88] Over the years, the spelling of *Yehoshua'* shortened to *Yeshua'* ("Jesus" in English), but the meaning, "Yah is salvation," remains the same.

We are familiar with *Yah* at the end of the word *hallelujah*, which means, "Praise Yah" or "Praise the LORD."[89] We should practice this jubilant shout because it's the chorus to heaven's songs.

Psalm 68:4 tells us that God's name is *Yah*. Most English Bibles translate both *Yah* and *Yahweh* as "**LORD**" in all capitals. This is done to distinguish these two words from *'Adonai*, which is translated as "Lord." The Jerusalem Bible helpfully retains *Yahweh*.

The three names can appear in combination with each other. Here are some examples, including the typical English translations:

- *Yahweh 'Elohim*—LORD God (Gen. 2:4; 3:23).
- *Yahweh 'elohekha*—LORD your God (Ex. 20:1–7).
- *'Adonai Yahweh*[90]—Lord GOD, or Sovereign LORD (NIV) (Gen. 15:2, 8; Ps. 71:5; Ezek. 2:4; Amos 7:1).
- *Ha'adon Yahweh*—The Lord GOD (Ex. 23:17; 34:23).
- *Yahweh 'adonenu*—GOD our Lord (Ps. 8:1).
- *Yahweh 'adonai*—GOD the Lord, or Sovereign LORD (NIV) (Ps. 68:20).
- *'Elohai wa'donai*—my God and my Lord (Ps. 35:23).
- *'Adonai 'elohai*—O Lord my God (Ps. 38:15).
- *'El 'Elohim Yahweh*—The Mighty One, God, the LORD (Josh. 22:22; Ps. 50:1).
- *Yah Yahweh*—LORD GOD, or GOD the LORD (Isa. 12:2; 26:4, KJV has LORD JEHOVAH).
- *Yahweh 'elohei Yisra'el*—LORD, God of Israel (Josh. 14:14; Judg. 5:3; Ps. 59:5).
- *Ha'el Yahweh*—God the LORD (Ps. 85:8).

'El, 'Eloah, and *'Elohim* are generic names. *Yahweh* (and *Yah* in Ps. 68:4) is the personal name of the God of Israel.[91] *Yahweh* never occurs in the form "my Yahweh" or "the Yahweh."

Think of it this way: in an audience with royalty or a president, people would say, "Your Majesty," "Your Royal Highness," or "Mr. President." These are titles of rank. Their families address them with more familiar terms like "Mother," "Father," or their personal names. *Yahweh* is God's personal name. He revealed it to us because He wants us to be part of His royal family.

Tiptoeing around God's Name

Why does so much obscurity surround the divine name? The Jews were anxious not to inadvertently deface it.[92] They avoided permanent records of its full form by inscribing just the consonants. Today, some people prefer to write "G—d" out of similar reverence.

With the exception of priests, it became customary to refrain from vocalizing *Yahweh*.[93] Ordinary Jews still use substitutes; many occur in the Bible. The name *'Adonai* predominated, so the vowel points inserted above *YHWH* in later texts were those of *'Adonai*. They indicated: "For '*Yahweh*'

read '*'Adonai*.'"[94] Other substitutes are used: "the Blessed One,"[95] "Heaven,"
"Power," and "Power of God."[96] When Peter wrote of the "Majestic glory," he
might have been using another substitute.[97] Similarly, the writer of Hebrews
called God the "Majesty on high."[98] *'Avir* (Mighty One) and *pakhad* ("fear,"
as in the **fear of Isaac**) are Old Testament examples.[99] In the Aramaic
translations (Targums), *memra'* (the Word), was another roundabout
reference to God.[100] One Dead Sea Scroll used the first Hebrew letters of the
titles: "A man must not swear either by Aleph and Lamedh (*'Elohim*) or by
Aleph and Daleth (*'Adonai*)."[101]

Another method is to insert "*hashem*" (the name) in the text. This phrase
is shorthand for the sum total of His Being—His character or nature. That
includes His will, the expression of His will, and all of the authority and power
that accomplish His purposes. Even the apostles spoke of being worthy to
suffer for the sake of "the name."[102] If these subsitutions seem like an odd
custom, consider our own oblique phrase "for goodness' sake."

Hebrew priests were trained which name to use as they recited the liturgy.
However, in the third century BC they stopped vocalizing the name *Yahweh*.[103]
The Jews eventually forgot the original pronunciation.

According to one Jewish tradition, the coming Messiah would be able to
pronounce the divine name. Over the centuries, certain Jewish mystics claimed
to have deciphered the secret name. They received the title "*Ba'al hashem*,"
which means "masters (or possessors) of the name."

The Angel of the LORD

The angel of Yahweh who appeared to Moses in a blazing bush needs to be
identified.[104] Who was this mysterious messenger who occasionally visited
biblical heroes? He was no ordinary angelic envoy, as we can tell from
later incidents.

Judges 13 uses two different phrases to describe the angel who encountered
Samson's parents. He came to announce that Manoah's barren wife would have
a child, Samson. Manoah's wife said, "A *man of 'Elohim* came to me and his
appearance was like the appearance of the *angel of 'Elohim*, very awesome. And
I did not ask him where he came from, nor did he tell me his name" (vv. 6, 10).

When Manoah inquired about the angel's name, he responded, "Why do
you ask my name, seeing it is wonderful?" (v. 18).[105] The angel lived up to that
claim; he "performed wonders" with the sacrifice and "ascended in the flame

of the altar" (vv. 19–20). Manoah, who initially did not even know that the visitor was an angel, concluded, "We will surely die, for we have seen '*Elohim*'" (vv. 16, 22).

The Old Testament refers to the angel of Yahweh in terms ranging from "man of Elohim," to "angel of Yahweh/Elohim," to being Elohim Himself. When the Israelites set out on their wilderness journey, the escorting angel was to be obeyed as God's representative, "since My name is in him" (Ex. 23:20–23). Elsewhere, he is equated with the Savior who delivered Israel from Egypt and he is described as the very presence of God.[106] The connection is so strong that we can conclude that the angel of Yahweh is a manifestation of God Himself.[107] J. A. Motyer asks rhetorically, "Where else in Scripture is there One who is identical with Yahweh and yet distinct?"[108]

Moses' encounter fits the pattern. Just two verses after the angel spoke, Elohim Himself addressed Moses from the bush.[109]

Please Call Me John

When God spoke to Moses, He introduced Himself using names that were familiar to Israel. Yahweh told Moses that He was the **God of your fathers**. Then He emphasized His personal name, *Yahweh*. "Thus you shall say to the sons of Israel, '*Yahweh*, the '*Elohim* of your fathers, the '*Elohim* of Abraham, the '*Elohim* of Isaac, and the '*Elohim* of Jacob, has sent me to you.'" (Ex. 3:15) Moses was to lead the nation into a deeper relationship with God based on His personal name.

I have lived in three African cultures—once as a pastor and twice as a missionary. I admired the respect that people in African cultures give their leaders, but I wanted to establish an informal relationship. When people called me "Pastor Avery," I would say, "Please, call me John." A few younger people shuffled their feet and mumbled my first name. Others managed a slightly less formal, "Pastor John." Even when I left the pastoral position, they still preferred to use the title.

Some people balk at the idea that our relationships with God can be reverent yet informal and intimate. No doubt, this skepticism is another effect of sin separating us from God. Nonetheless, God values authenticity over formality in our relationships with Him.

The name *Yahweh* was not new to Israel. Like the other two primary names, *Yahweh* occurs throughout the book of Genesis; it was part of Hebrew heritage.

However, intellectual knowledge of God's name didn't amount to sufficient faith in Yahweh for their journey. Their "faith canteen" had too little in it. This fact is hinted at in a confusing and almost contradictory later statement: "*'Elohim* spoke further to Moses and said to him, 'I am *Yahweh* and I appeared to Abraham, Isaac, and Jacob, as *'El shaddai*, but by My name, *Yahweh*, I did not make myself known to them'" (Ex. 6:3).

God Almighty
Heb.: *'El shaddai*
(Gen. 17:1; Ex. 6:3)

At face value, the verse suggests that the patriarchs didn't know the name *Yahweh*. Nevertheless, they had used it.[110] So, what did God mean? The circumstances in which the patriarchs spoke the name *Yahweh* in Genesis shed light on their relationships.

Family Reunions

Abram (who later became Abraham) had visions of Yahweh and heard His voice.[111] Abraham spoke the name *Yahweh* (seventy-three times). So did Abraham's servant. Rebekah's brother, Laban, and Abraham's nephew Lot also used it. Abraham's wife, Sarah, called on it. His son Isaac used it fourteen times. His grandson Jacob invoked it fifteen times, and Jacob's wives, Rachel and Leah, spoke it.[112] Abraham's family certainly knew God's personal name, but how did they learn it?

It was only when Adam's grandson Enosh was born that people began calling on Yahweh.[113] Did the patriarchs' knowledge come from their very-great-grandfather Enosh? Let's have some fun speculating: Although there were many intervening generations between Enosh and Abraham, those generations overlapped a lot. While there is no evidence that anyone took nutritional supplements back then, people had huge life spans. So, if Abraham had attended family gatherings in Ur as a young man, his very-great-grandfather Noah would still have been alive, and he could have attended the reunions. Enosh (who lived until Noah was eighty-four) might have taught the name to Noah. Theoretically, it took just two links in a chain spanning generations to teach the family to call on Yahweh.

Of course, all this is speculative, but think of the impact it would have on our families if we went beyond naming God to recounting everything that He does for us.

The pattern in Genesis demonstrates that although people knew God's name *Yahweh* (however they pronounced it), typically they expressed His characteristics using other names. In Genesis, we find *Yahweh* alongside descriptive names compounded with *'El*:

- When Melchizedek blessed Abram in the name of *'El 'elyon* (God Most High), Abram graciously received the blessing. Later, though, he stated that his allegiance was to *'El Yahweh, 'El 'elyon*.[114] *'El 'elyon* might have originated as the name of a Canaanite god. If so, this meeting marked a clarification by Abram that Yahweh was the true God Most High.
- Hagar, Sarah's runaway maid, recognized Yahweh as *'El ro'i*, a God who sees.[115]
- To make a lasting covenant with Abimelech at Beersheba, Abraham invoked Yahweh using the name *'El 'olam*, the Everlasting God.[116]
- Not wanting Isaac to marry a Canaanite woman, Abraham had his servant swear by "*Yahweh*, the God of heaven and the God of earth" (Gen. 24:3) that he would find Isaac a wife from their own clan.
- Jacob knew Yahweh as the God of Bethel, and he later erected an altar to "God, the God of Israel" in acceptance of Yahweh as his God and of Jacob's own new name, Israel.[117]
- Only once in Genesis is the personal name *Yahweh* part of a descriptive compound name. When Abraham recognized God's provision of a ram to sacrifice instead of Isaac, he called the place *Yahweh yir'eh*, the LORD will provide.[118]

We will explore these great names of God in more detail later. For now, it is enough to recognize the sense of Exodus 6:3. Although the patriarchs called God *Yahweh*, they focused on characteristics encapsulated in the name *'El shaddai*, the Almighty God. It was as El shaddai that God met all three patriarchs, making and renewing covenant promises with them.[119] Using that name, they passed blessings on to the next generations.[120] The name *'El shaddai* expresses that He is completely able to accomplish His plans against all odds. That was how the patriarchs understood God; He had not made *fully known* the character underlying His name, *Yahweh*.[121] With Moses, the descendants of the patriarchs were about to progress. Yahweh was ready to pour a fresh revelation about His identity into Israel's water bottle. My, oh my, did they need it.

All Dried Up

The patriarch Jacob had arrived in Egypt with his faith intact. The embryonic nation had seen God do amazing things. Yet Jacob's son Joseph, who had been sold into slavery in Egypt by his brothers, did not use the name *Yahweh* at all. By Moses' time, the use of *Yahweh* was in decline.

We can imagine how the Israelites felt. Four centuries of servitude in Egypt had taken their toll. The recent years under Hebrew-hating pharaohs had been particularly harsh. Their faith evaporated quickly under the scorching Egyptian sun. Perhaps Moses anticipated the questions and the doubts, which must have multiplied like the population:

"Come on Moses. After four hundred years, does Yahweh still care what happens to us?"

"Is He able to do anything for us?"

"Why didn't He intervene years ago?"

"What about His promise to give us a land of our own? That fell flat!"

The Israelites were drained and weary. A life of faith seemed irrelevant in a society that scorned it. Alternative gods surrounded them. Huge pyramids, crammed with priceless treasures, honored the dead. The Israelites were trapped in a world that was opposed to the idea of there being one true living God. They still knew God, but their water bottle of faith-filled relationship with Him was almost dry. No wonder Moses expected objections. They might even ask, "What is His name?"

God had an answer for them all. Moses and Israel did not need to attain a certain standard of faith or spirituality before God would reveal Himself to them.

The Source

God's new revelation of His nature began with a play on words: " *'Elohim* said to Moses, 'I AM WHO I AM'; and He said, 'Thus you shall say to the sons of Israel, "I AM has sent me to you."'" (Ex. 3:14)

In Hebrew, the first capitalized phrase reads, " *'ehyeh 'asher 'ehyeh.*" The exact meaning remains obscure, but it uses a continuous form of the verb "to be." The phrase could be translated, "I was who I was," or even "I will be who I will be." The Greek translation[122] is *"ego eimi ho on"* (I am the Being). Yahweh, who calls Himself "I AM," is the One who simply *is*. He spans past, present, and future. Donald Miller puts it well: "Climbing inside letters, God explains, *I encompass, I am beyond existence, I am nothing you will understand, I have no beginning and no end, I am not like you, and yet I AM.*[123] God's nature, expressed in His name, is "dynamic and energetic, not static and frozen."[124] I gladly kept my boots on in the soot of Hell's Canyon; the fire of Yahweh's presence demanded that Moses remove his sandals and stand back.[125]

Any revelation of Yahweh is inevitably mysterious and difficult to grasp. He transcends ordinary existence, which makes Him almost unnameable. So, one commentator warns us: "As to the meaning of the name, we are safer if we find the character of God from His works and from the descriptions of Him in the Scripture, rather than to depend on a questionable etymology of His name."[126]

God compensated for His cryptic statement by providing a series of object lessons, which are easier to understand and remember than foreign word roots. He miraculously metamorphosed a stick into a writhing snake and then turned the snake back into a lifeless stick. He plagued Moses' hand with leprosy, and then healed it. The One with power to breathe life into dust turned water into blood as it hit the hot Egyptian sand.[127] Notice His comments to a stammering Moses: "Who has made man's mouth? Or who makes him mute or deaf, or seeing or blind? Is it not I, *Yahweh*?" (Ex. 4:11) Yahweh dramatically demonstrated that He, the sourceless One, is the origin, the sustainer, and the terminator of all life, intervening as and when He chooses.

Just as stage lights come on to illuminate a scene and prepare an audience for the players, so the bush provided a primer for the verbal revelation of Yahweh. The bush was God's first illustration of His rather shadowy name, *Yahweh*. Burning bushes normally become charred stumps like those I saw in Hell's Canyon. The Sinai bush transcended the laws of nature and gave Moses a glimpse into the supernatural realm, which was Yahweh's abode. The bush sprouted flames because the Sovereign who established nature's laws said so. Yahweh defines and initiates all existence.

The flaming delivery paints a picture of the One who simply *is*. Just as the fire required no natural fuel but was self-sustaining, so the I AM is "invincible, self-sufficient sovereignty."[128] He needs no energy supply. If I don't get cornflakes and caffeine in the morning, I fade; by lunchtime, I'm grouchy and lacking in energy. He, however, is inexhaustible; He does not expire. He does not depend on anyone else for His existence; He is utterly autonomous. J. I. Packer describes Yahweh as the "source and goal of all things that exist," the One who has "limitless life and power."[129] Yahweh vividly demonstrated that His power was available and sufficient to answer Israel's need. He was preparing to deal with His people's plight.

The angelic voice from the unconsumed bush was a message in itself. It stopped Moses in his tracks, but it also reflected God's heart. The "angel of Yahweh," who is at times God's undercover agent and at other times the embodiment of Yahweh, hand-delivered to Moses His message of committed love for Israel. Ablaze with Yahweh's presence, the bush reinforced His words: "I am indeed concerned about you and what has been done to you in Egypt" (Ex. 3:16).

Yahweh's revelation topped up Moses' water bottle of faith, but Moses thought that there was still a problem.

Strapping the Sandals Back On

Moses continued to argue with Elohim, making excuses.[130] "What if they will not believe me?" "Please, *'Adonai*, I have never been eloquent." Then, more honestly, but still calling Him *'Adonai*, he asked God to use someone else. Moses had taken off his sandals, but he wasn't ready to slip them back on and lead God's people.

How like Moses we can be. God warms us with His love when we worship Him. He illuminates our hearts with penetrating truth, and His power touches our lives. We should be able to trust Him, but when He calls for a step of faith, we hesitate. Are those experiences not enough to propel us forward, or do we have other problems?

Most of us want God to provide everything we need in advance of the journey—a trailer to tow around, loaded with supplies for every future difficulty. However, that's not God's way. There can be no camping next to burning bushes to preserve the experience, either. Encounters with God are refreshing and edifying. They make us feel good for a while, but they don't turn into stories—let alone history.

Like all journeys, faith journeys begin with a step. God wanted the newly refreshed Moses to start walking. So, having argued God into recruiting his brother, Aaron, as His spokesman, Moses slipped his sandals on and began striding—back to Egypt and forward into God's plan.

Drinking Little and Often

For forty years, Moses had been a desert exile who was afraid to face his own past. As he stepped out and witnessed God at work, he began to walk free from unbelief. He accepted his assignment to "speak in Your name" (Ex. 5:23) and he grew as a leader. The key to Moses' success lay in a process like the one I learned in Hell's Canyon.

How did I ever hike out of there after running out of water? Well, as I trudged up a side valley toward the rim, I noticed a line of scrubby bushes. The fire had scorched them, but they were otherwise green and healthy. A quick detour revealed a welcome sight: a tiny creek trickling between sleepy pools. The creek ran parallel to the first section of my path. It was little more than a ditch that was contaminated with branches and debris. Among the tangled bushes along its banks, I found black bear spoor and I caught occasional glimpses of small snakes darting for cover. It was counterintuitive to drink from it, but that creek held life-sustaining water. Belly ache was a better option than dehydration. Never mind the bugs and the bears, spluttering and splashing water all over my shirt, I quenched my thirst. Then I refilled my canteen and continued on my way. Until the trail veered away from the stream, I returned to the brook whenever I felt thirsty.

Moses had to learn to turn to God. Promised lands are rarely a single step away; the journey is often long and difficult. Pharaoh, and even Israel, opposed Moses immediately. Pharaoh objected, "Who is the LORD that I should obey His voice to let Israel go? I do not know the LORD, and besides, I will not let Israel go" (Ex. 5:2–4). Moses simplified things for him by referring to the more generic name, **God of the Hebrews**.[131] But Pharaoh had already made up his mind on the question of the ages: "Who is God and how will I respond to Him?" Pharaoh's heart was resistant. He pointed a long, bony finger to the doorway and roared, "Back to work!"

Nonetheless, Moses continued on his path of obedience. He turned to God at each hurdle and found Yahweh to be a reliable source of guidance and wisdom. At each step, God proved faithful and Moses' faith grew stronger; God repeatedly replenished His supply.

Shuttling between Yahweh and Pharaoh, Moses performed God's miraculous signs and delivered His ultimatums. "I will count slowly to ten and then . . . ." Ten plagues became ten plaques of victory over Egyptian gods. As the Hebrews witnessed the finger of God subduing Egypt, they stopped objecting. God was using Pharaoh's defiance for His own glory. By the time God reached the end of His countdown, Israel was ready to participate in the final plague—the death of firstborn sons. The people had to be ready because no family was safe from that midnight plague, unless they sacrificed a lamb.

So, each Israelite household killed a lamb and daubed the blood around the doorframe. The blood signaled Yahweh to pass over the home without striking their firstborn dead. Pharaoh had no such protection. Distraught at the loss of his own firstborn and the nightmare that was engulfing Egypt, he begged Moses and every last Hebrew to leave.

God had a final lesson for Egypt. Enveloped in a pillar of cloud and fire, Yahweh guided Israel to the Egyptian border. In his cycle of grief, Pharaoh quickly moved on to anger, and he sent a revengeful chariot regiment thundering after Israel. The cornered people panicked, but Moses turned to God again. God parted the sea for Israel. Then he triggered His trap and trounced Egypt.

God's Name: Made in Egypt

The exodus from Egypt was such a historic event that we're told He "divided the waters before them to make for Himself an everlasting name" (Isa. 63:11–12).[132] Repeatedly, the Old Testament singles it out as the classic demonstration of God's love for His people, His sovereignty over other gods, and His nature as a **Redeemer** and a **Deliverer**. Everyone learned more about Yahweh, including Egypt.[133] Three of God's four promises to Moses could be checked off (Ex. 6:2–8):

"I will bring you out from under the burdens of the Egyptians." Done.

"I will deliver you from their bondage." Done.

"I will also redeem you with an outstretched arm and with great judgments." Done.

Israel reached the far side of the Red Sea and burst into a triumphant song, celebrating Yahweh's salvation.[134] Her faith had grown. Yahweh would keep His fourth promise to take Israel for His people, and be their God. They would know Him as "*Yahweh* your *'Elohim*, who brought you out from under the burdens of the Egyptians" (Ex. 6:7). God's intervention in Egypt formed the basis for centuries of covenant relationship with Israel. The Sinai commandments defined the relationship.[135]

It sounds so promising, doesn't it? With such a momentous birth, Israel was poised for a glorious history. Sadly, Israel's faith in God was unsteady. The people continued to question His faithfulness. They turned to things that had the appearance of firmer promises that would be fulfilled more quickly, but those things were deceptions. Israel, like all humankind, fell short of the glory that God intended for them.

Chapter 3

A RAINBOW SPECTRUM OF GLORY

God appears, and God is light
to those poor souls who dwell in night;
but does a human form display
to those who dwell in realms of day.
—William Blake

The book of Daniel is full of dramatic stories. One tells about King Nebuchadnezzar setting up his golden image on a plain and then ordering his subjects to bow their knees and swear allegiance to it. The towering image provided a focal point for people to glorify their king. Their obeisance demonstrated submission to the king's rule over all of their affairs, even though they did it under great duress. Daniel's three tongue-twisting friends, Shadrach, Meshach, and Abednego, refused to bow down, so Nebuchadnezzar's warriors threw them into a raging furnace. The only things that burned were their ropes and the guards who had pushed them in. Mysteriously, a fourth man appeared in the flames looking "like a son of the gods" (Dan. 3:1–25).

At Belshazzar's feast, a ghostly hand inscribed a cryptic sentence on the wall and ruined a riotous party. Daniel interpreted the words as a warning— Belshazzar should humble himself and learn a lesson from his grandfather Nebuchadnezzar. Because of Nebuchadnezzar's pride, the glory of his kingdom had been removed from him for a while "until he recognized that the **Most High God** is ruler over the realm of mankind and that He sets over it whomever He wishes" (Dan. 2:37; 5:18–21). Belshazzar failed to give glory to God. He died that night.[136]

Glory belongs to God alone. Scripture calls Him **God of glory** and **Father of glory**. As **King of glory**, He loans us a little glory under a sort of copyright agreement, but He wants full credit for all the glory of human lives and activities. God said in Isaiah 42:8, "I am the LORD, that is My name; I will not give My glory to another, nor My praise to graven images." As His names imply, glory derives from Him and belongs to Him, the all-glorious One. Glory is connected to His names and to the image that He designed to focus and reflect His own glory. The story of glory began long before Daniel's kings.

King of glory
Heb.: *Melekh hakkavod*
(Ps. 24:7–10)

God of glory
Heb.: *'El hakkavod*
(Ps. 29:3)
Gk.: *Ho Theos tēs doxēs*
(Acts 7:2)

Father of glory
Gk.: *Ho patēr tēs doxēs*
(Eph. 1:17)

Glory: A Weighty Subject

What is glory? We all remember glorious days. Perhaps they were days of victory, accomplishment, vindication, or heroics. Perhaps they were days when we soaked up the magnificent beauty of a sunrise or a sunset silhouetting a splendid mountain. The adjective "glorious" could refer to a storm's fury or to the tranquility of a tropical beach. The Bible's concept of glory goes further. So, what exactly is glory and how does it affect us?

The most common Hebrew word for glory is *kavod*.[137] Its use in the contexts of the wealth of Jacob, and the strength of Assyria's army points to its root meaning.[138] *Kavod* derives from the same root as *kaved* (heavy). Abraham was "loaded,"[139] Jacob had purchasing power, and Assyria flexed her military muscles.

When *kavod* is used of God, it connotes weightiness in the sense of His power and authority. We use "weight" in a similarly figurative way to talk about influence. Influential people have "a lot of clout." We would say that their ideas carry "weight." In that sense, God is the heavyweight champion of the universe. The King of glory is weighty in power, might,[140] majesty, beauty, holiness, and righteousness.

The Greek translators of the Hebrew Scriptures used *doxa* for *kavod* to talk about glory. *Doxa* is appropriate because it connotes the fame, honor, reputation, and praise that *kavod* implies.[141]

God's Phenomenal Glory

Make no mistake, *kavod* leaves no room for subjective opinions about God; it speaks of substance. God's glory is so real that it sometimes becomes tangible.

Commentators say that glory is "the visible and supernatural manifestation of the supreme and incomparable majesty of God."[142] Glory is also "that which expresses His inherent majesty, which may or may not have some visible token."[143]

People paddling on a beach will experience the wake of a passing speedboat as the water surges around their feet. We experience glory like that wake. It is a consequence of God's presence; it touches us and occasionally overwhelms someone.

Throughout history, a pattern of physical phenomena accompanied revelations of God's glory. The phenomena were common at key times, such as the births of the universe, Israel, and God's Son, Jesus. God used such phenomena to deepen His relationship with people. It is as though God deliberately came close enough to attract attention by splashing them with His presence. But He intends for us to have more than just wet feet. He wants to excite us so that we run into the water to Him.

The Israelites observed the pattern of phenomena. They witnessed God's glorious presence in the pillar of fire and cloud, which led them through the wilderness.[144] They also noted His presence in the cloud covering Mount Sinai.[145] Moses visited with God in the cloud while the people perceived God's glory as a consuming fire and felt the ground shake.[146] Other notable phenomena were thunder, lightning, fire, smoke, earthquakes, shaking, darkness, and tempests. Often, people heard God's voice, perhaps accompanied by a trumpet sound. Some people were knocked down.[147] Centuries later, the prophet Isaiah saw smoke and angels when he encountered God in the temple.[148] The foundations shook and the prophet felt woefully wretched. Isaiah didn't just hear the angels proclaim God's glory; he witnessed it.[149]

The temple and tabernacle, and the ark of the covenant that they contained, were all so central to the manifestation of God's glory that we will return to them in the next chapter. For now, note that God dwelt between two angelic beings called cherubim, who covered the ark with their wings.[150] Every year, when the High Priest approached the ark, he saw the brightness of God's glory above it.

The Brightest Light

In biblical times, God's glory often produced fire or a bright light.[151] Wayne Grudem calls glory "the created brightness that surrounds God's revelation of Himself."[152]

Light is a significant biblical theme that is often linked with glory, so we must examine it in greater detail. Old Testament writers said, "The LORD is my light" (Ps. 27:1; Isa. 60:19–20). But He is more than a source of illumination for our path.

During Israel's exile in Babylon, Jewish Scripture commentators began using a special word for God's glorious presence: *shekhinah*. To a Jew, *shekhinah* suggests all of the phenomena associated with God's manifest presence, especially the light. Though the word is not in the Bible, it was in use by Jesus' time.

Some of God's names concern light. God is the **Light of Israel**, and Jesus, the **true light**, said, "I am the **light of the world**." He came as a **light to the nations**. When James spoke of the **Father of lights**, he meant the creator of the celestial bodies, but he also implied the source of moral, intellectual, and spiritual light. Jesus was heralded at birth as "a **light of revelation** to the Gentiles and the **glory of Your people Israel**" (Luke 2:32). After Jesus' resurrection, Paul equated Jesus with God, as the **Lord of glory**.

My light
Heb.: *'Ori*
(Ps. 27:1)

Light of Israel
Heb.: *'Or-Yisra'el*
(Isa. 10:17)

Light to the nations
Heb.: *'Or goyim*
(Isa. 42:6)

Light of revelation
Gk.: *Phōs eis apokalypsin*
(Luke 2:32)

Light of the world
Gk.: *To phōs tou kosmou*
(John 8:12)

True light
Gk.: *To phōs to alēthinon*
(John 1:9)

Father of lights
Gk.: *Ho patēr tōn phōtōn*
(Jas. 1:17)

Lord of glory
Gk.: *Ho kyrios tēs doxēs*
(1 Cor. 2:8)

Malachi coined a prophetic name: "For you who fear My name, the **sun of righteousness** will rise with healing in its wings" (Mal. 4:2). Some people expected the Messiah to come as a healer. Perhaps the woman with the disabling and humiliating hemorrhage was among them. Did she touch Jesus' fringe because she knew that the Hebrew word for the corner of a garment also means "wings"?[153] Either way, her bold faith bore fruit. She went home healed.

Sun of righteousness
Heb.: *Shemesh tsedaqah*
(Mal. 4:2)

Bright morning star
Gk.: *Ho astēr ho lampros ho prōinos*
(Rev. 22:16)

Morning star
Gk.: *Ho phōsphoros*
(2 Peter 1:19)

The glorified Jesus, who appeared to John, called Himself the **bright morning star**. This name evokes images of a star (or the planet Venus) shining bright and early, heralding daylight. Peter referred to Jesus as the **morning star** (literally "light bearer") who will arise in our hearts.[154] God promised the morning star to those who overcome.[155]

All this talk of fire, light, and earthquakes can be a little off-putting, so remember, glory implies beauty. True beauty includes every desirable attribute at once; God epitomizes it because He lacks no good thing.[156] Compared with the darkness of the godless, the brightness of God's presence is so attractive that it will draw nations to Him.[157] Glory is certainly powerful, but make no mistake—it is also beautiful.

A Rainbow of Glory

To Ezekiel, the radiant glory surrounding the enthroned Lord looked like a beautiful rainbow.[158] The rainbow brightens up a dramatic storm that rages through the first chapter of his prophecies. It resembled lapis lazuli, a semi-precious, cobalt-blue stone that represents riches. A rainbow conveniently illustrates God's glory.

Sunbeams form a rainbow when the rays pass through raindrops, which split the light into a continuous spectrum of colors. It's a law of physics that when light is shone through any prism—raindrops will do—it divides into its component wavelengths. Conversely, combining the primary colors will produce white light.

Just as a rainbow's beauty depends on all of its colors, so too everything God is and does contributes to His glory. God's glory is not simply another one of His attributes; it is the full spectrum of His nature. Yet, in another sense, each of God's attributes and actions carries its own weight and is itself glorious. The "name of God," like His glory, signifies the complete spectrum. Yet in each facet of His being, God is remarkable and many of His attributes are represented by specific names. There is a substantial correlation between God's glory and His names.

Let's observe several colorful rays of God's glory as they radiate from the prism of Scripture.

Creation

Creation is the first ray—a green one, no doubt. Psalm 19:1 says, "The heavens are telling of the glory of God; and their expanse is declaring the work of His hands." The animals He created and provides for declare His glory.[159] Isaiah saw angels called seraphim, who associated God's holiness with His glory filling the world: "Holy, Holy, Holy is the LORD of hosts, the whole earth is full of His glory" (Isa. 6:3). Creation points to the Creator.[160]

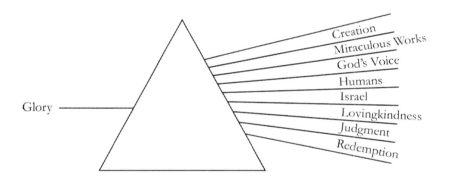

The Wonder Worker

Psalm 66:2–3 relates God's glory to a second ray—His miraculous works. "Sing the glory of His name; make His praise glorious. Say to God, 'How awesome are Your works! Because of the greatness of Your power Your enemies will give feigned obedience to You.'"[161]

God's very name is wonderful.[162] The Bible only uses the Hebrew word *pele'* to describe God's superhuman abilities. He is the **God who works wonders**, especially when caring for His people or bringing retribution. **Wonderful Counselor** describes the promised Child. David determined that, "on the glorious splendor of

God who works wonders
Heb.: *Ha'El 'oseh pele'*
(Ps. 77:14)

Wonderful Counselor
Heb.: *Pele' yo'ets*
(Isa. 9:6)

Your majesty, and on Your wonderful works, I will meditate" (Ps. 145:1–5; see also Isa. 28:29).

Although God can't be seen, He leaves signs. Pharaoh's courtiers dreaded the "finger of God."[163] Isaiah saw the "arm of the LORD" in miracles.[164] God's every act is like a tiny spectral line sparkling with more of His glory.

Weighty Words

Psalm 29 highlights a third ray, which is audible this time. The voice of God evokes the cry "Glory!"[165]

> The **God of glory** thunders, the LORD is over many waters. The voice of the LORD is powerful, the voice of the LORD is majestic. The voice of the LORD breaks the cedars.
>
> . . . The voice of the LORD hews out flames of fire. The voice of the LORD shakes the wilderness . . . The voice of the LORD makes the deer to calve and strips the forests bare; and in His temple everything says, "Glory!" (Ps. 29:3–9)

His voice is more than sound waves rippling through air, which are often resisted, distorted, deflected, or simply ignored. Every word from God carries weight. "'Is not My word like fire?' declares the LORD, 'and like a hammer which shatters a rock?'" (Jer. 23:29) His word is an irresistible instrument of action like a hammer or a sword.[166] His voice was the life-imparting trigger of creation: "By the word of the LORD the heavens were made, and by the breath of His mouth all their host. . . . He spoke, and it was done; He commanded, and it stood fast" (Ps. 33:6, 9). Genesis 1 states repeatedly that God only had to speak a word and creation happened.[167] If God wants to heal, He commands it.[168] God's words express His personality.

Words have their own life and power. When Isaac discovered that he had been tricked into blessing his son Jacob instead of Esau (Isaac's firstborn), Isaac said, "Yes, and he shall be blessed." He could do nothing, except give a residual blessing to Esau.[169] If this is true of human words then certainly God's word is irrevocable and irresistible—it doesn't return without getting the job done.[170]

Made in His Image

When the King of glory created humans in His image, His goal was to reflect His own glory. The first humans had intimate, harmonious relationships. Unconditional and selfless love motivated every thought, word, and action. People were another tangible manifestation of God's spectral beauty, a fuller manifestation than any ray that has been mentioned so far. Humans demonstrated the splendor of the King's reign over His creation. God designed us to act like billions of tiny prisms glinting with His glory—a miniature rainbow in human form.

However, the fall began a pattern of human independence from God and from one another; the prisms became tarnished and the harmony was destroyed. "All have sinned and fall short of the glory of God," pointed out Paul (Rom. 3:23). The whole race "exchanged the glory of the **incorruptible God**[171] for an image in the form of corruptible man and of birds and four-footed animals and crawling creatures" (Rom. 1:23 See also Ps. 106:20). Everyone, including the nation of Israel, traded "their glory for that which does not profit" (Jer. 2:11)—poor choice!

National Treasure

When God launched the nation of Israel by giving the Law at Sinai, He had a purpose: "Out of all nations you will be my treasured possession" (Ex. 19:5 NIV; Deut. 7:6; 26:18). The words "treasured possession" (*segullah*) cast Israel as a precious jewel that was on display for neighboring nations.[172] He crafted Israel as another ray of glory to sparkle like a diamond, reflecting and radiating His glory. The word "Jew" derives from "Judah," meaning "praise"—the nation was designed to praise God.[173] The national destiny is evident in the way that God referred to Israel before her exile as "everyone who is called by My name, and whom I have created for My glory" (Isa. 43:1–7).[174] Israel was passively glorious because the God of glory dwelt in the tabernacle right in her midst; but God designed her to glorify Him actively in her national character and relationships, and by cooperating with Him.

God always intended that "all the earth will be filled with the glory of the LORD" (Num. 14:21; Hab. 2:14). In God's plan, the Jews were to advertise the blessing of having a relationship with Him. This would attract foreigners who would in turn glorify Him.[175] But Israel failed to reveal His glory to the nations;[176] her sin dulled and marred the reflected glory. The Old Testament plot deals with that failure, and it emphasizes God's glorious lovingkindness and forbearance, but it also heralds His solution. Isaiah pointed beyond the blemished nation to a servant who would successfully glorify God.

An early example of Israel's shortfall and its consequences occurred in Samuel's day.

Sin abounded and even the priesthood was lax. God allowed the Philistines to capture the ark, where *shekhinah* glory was concentrated. Israel's defeat was both a response to and a symptom of her fall. The cry "Ichabod," which indicated, "the glory has departed from Israel," summarized Israel's condition (1 Sam. 4:21–22; Ps. 78:61).

That particular incident turned out to be only a temporary loss of God's presence. A few years later, under King David, the nation regained its passion for God, and David was able to restore the ark to the tabernacle. Isaiah said of God, "You have increased the nation, You are glorified" (Isa. 26:15). Those words could aptly describe God's blessing on David's kingdom too. But David's son Solomon planted seeds of national division and decline.

The Bright Side of Judgment

The next four hundred years were full of distrust and disloyalty toward God. As a result, Nebuchadnezzar dragged many Jews to exile in Babylon and destroyed two national symbols—he burned the temple and the ark disappeared from history. The exiled prophet Ezekiel envisioned the glory departing from the temple.[177] He also recognized a rather unexpected ray in God's rainbow of glory: judgment highlighted the glory of God's holiness.[178] However, Israel had lost what she most valued: the primary symbols of God dwelling with her in His glory.

Redemptive Glory

We might be justified in thinking that, in judging Israel, God had deleted glory from the national script. However, His judgment provided a backdrop for the beauty of redemption.[179] There's a growing prophetic drum roll in the period following the deportation to Babylon. The King of glory was about to astound Israel with His most spectacular ray: redemptive glory.

In fact, the drums began to beat out the theme of a coming deliverer much earlier. Certainly, those drums were beating at the nation's founding, but even when God created Adam and Eve, He told of a **seed** that would bruise the serpent's head. Before the exile to Babylon, Isaiah had prophesied that the **Redeemer** would deal with sins. He declared, "The LORD has redeemed Jacob and in Israel He shows forth His glory" (Isa. 44:23). He had hinted at the hero of redemption: "In that day the **Branch** of the LORD will be beautiful [*tsevi*] and glorious [*kavod*]" (Isa. 4:2). Few people had understood the significance of the prophecies, though many verses spoke of a restored and deepened relationship with Him, in which He would embrace all people.

> **Her Seed**
> Heb.: *Zar'ah*
> (Gen. 3:15)

Later in the exile, Ezekiel envisioned God's glory returning after years of absence because of Israel's sin.[180] It was a welcome forecast, but another four centuries would pass before the prophecy would find complete fulfillment in Jesus. Meanwhile, God planned to return a remnant of the Jews from Babylon to Israel to glorify His name, as the earlier exodus had done.[181] During national reconstruction, God spoke again of the temple, "I will fill this house with glory," and "the latter glory of this house will be greater than the former" (Hag. 2:5–9). The drumbeat grew louder, lifting national hopes and expectations.

A Phenomenal Birth

God's supreme spectacle began at Jesus' nativity with a dramatic build-up, a series of phenomena not seen together since the days of Moses or the temple dedication. Angels appeared. A priest became dumbstruck. Men and women were filled with the Holy Spirit, and an unborn baby bounced with joy—all signs that God was at work.[182]

Out in the fields were some shepherds. "An angel of the Lord suddenly stood before them, and the glory of the Lord shone around them; and they were terribly frightened." An angelic choir assembled, "praising God and saying, 'Glory to God in the highest, and on earth peace among men with whom He is pleased'" (Luke 2:8–14).

Mingling in the temple crowds was a man who was particularly alert to the signs. Simeon cradled the newborn Jesus, and with the soft but strong triumph of an elderly man reaching his goal, he declared, "My eyes have seen Your salvation . . . the glory of Your people Israel" (Luke 2:30–32).

Down by the River Jordan, after John had reluctantly baptized Jesus, "the Holy Spirit descended upon Him in bodily form like a dove, and a voice came out of heaven, 'You are My beloved Son, in You I am well-pleased'" (Luke 3:22). Isaiah 40:4–5 had indicated a particular sign to watch for. A voice would order obstructions to be cleared because, "the glory of the LORD will be revealed, and all flesh will see it together." Luke 3:1–6 describes John the Baptist's work in those terms. However, Luke introduced a subtle change. Whereas Isaiah wrote "glory," Luke used the term "salvation." God had given Israel a rich heritage in the area of salvation. His rout of Pharaoh's army at the Red Sea was the most celebrated deliverance. Global salvation was about to become the highlight of God's rainbow of glory.

On the Mount of Transfiguration, Peter, James, and John "were eyewitnesses of His majesty" (2 Peter 1:16). For a few moments, the light of glory resting on Jesus made His face shine and His clothes glow whiter than clothes in a laundry detergent advertisement. They saw His glory and they observed Moses and Elijah talking with Him. A cloud enveloped them, terrifying them so much that they fell on their faces. Then they heard the voice of God say, "This is My Son, My **Chosen One**; listen to Him" (Luke 9:28–36).[183] Peter later recounted, "When He received honor and glory from God the Father, such an utterance as this was made to Him by the **Majestic Glory**, 'This is My beloved Son with whom I am well-pleased'" (2 Peter 1:17–18). Peter had no need to pitch a tabernacle. John explained that God had become flesh, and He dwelt among us and we beheld His glory (John 1:14).

Majestic glory
Gk.: *Hē*
megaloprepēs doxa
(2 Peter 1:17)

A Word about The Word

John's words form the summit of a mountain of profound insight into Jesus' nature.

> *In the beginning was the Word, and the Word was with God, and the Word was God. He was in the beginning with God. All things came into being through Him, and apart from Him nothing came into being that has come into being.* (John 1:1–3)

Why did John immediately zoom in on the **Word** and use it to introduce us to Jesus? John understood the importance of the "word" in Jewish thinking, especially about creation. The Jews knew God's word was irresistible, irrevocable, and never returned void. They recognized it as another manifestation of His glory.

John added that the Word existed before anything else. This concept also applied to **Wisdom**, which Proverbs personifies as God's assistant at creation.[184] Later, Paul called God the **only wise God**.[185] Wisdom is associated with Jesus, who surpassed Solomon in wisdom.[186] Jesus had the **Spirit of the LORD** resting on Him, "the **spirit of wisdom and understanding**, the **spirit of counsel and strength**, and the **spirit of knowledge and the fear of the LORD**" (Isa. 11:2).

Colossians 2:2–3 says that Christ is **God's mystery**, "in whom are hidden all the treasures of wisdom and knowledge." Now, biblical mysteries are not dark, cryptic secrets with a hint of the spooky that are reserved for special initiates. Rather, they are open for all to discover. God reveals them to us by faith. Therefore, Jesus shines like an uncovered lamp, a radiant source of wisdom and knowledge.[187]

Word
Gk.: *Logos*
(John 1:1, 14)

Wisdom
Heb.: *Khokhmah*
(Prov. 8:12, 22–31)

Only wise God
Gk.: *Monos sophos Theos*
(Rom. 16:27)

Spirit of God
Heb.: *Ruakh 'Elohim*
(Gen. 1:2)

Spirit of the LORD
Heb.: *Ruakh Yahweh*
(Isa. 11:2; 61:1)
Gk.: *Pneuma Kyriou*
(Luke 4:18)

God's mystery
Gk.: *To mystērion tou Theou*
(Col. 2:2)

In his introduction, John emphasized that the Word (and by implication, Wisdom) was one with the creating word: "all things came into being through Him." He existed with God. In fact, "the Word was God."

Now, John understood the Greek perspective on the word (*logos*) too. *Logos* can also mean "mind" or "reason." Heraclitus, a Greek philosopher who lived in Ephesus in 560 BC, understood *logos* as a fundamental principle that orders everything. John appealed to that idea but pointed beyond a dull principle of logic to a rational Being: Jesus, who is God incarnate.

In Jesus, John recognized an astounding truth: Jesus embodied and completed those two ancient and pervasive philosophical insights. He had universal—not just Jewish—significance. The pre-existing, life-giving Word of God was also the spine of order behind the universe, superior to the material world that He had initiated. The Word was "in the beginning," and "the **Word of God**" was, in the end, the secret name that John saw written on our Lord. The Word of God brought irresistible judgment on His enemies.[188]

Word of God
Gk.: *Ho logos tou Theou*
(Rev. 19:13)

Word of Life
Gk.: *Ho logos tēs zōēs*
(1 John 1:1)

The Jews never expected the Word to become flesh, so John emphasized Jesus' closeness and vitality. John and some of his readers had physically touched Jesus. He described Jesus as, "What was from the beginning, what we have heard, what we have seen with our eyes, what we have looked at and touched with our hands, concerning the **Word of Life**." (1 John 1:1)

Jesus referred to Himself as a life-imparting Word. He said, "I am the **Resurrection** and the **Life**" (John 11:25; 14:6). He was instrumental in creation and He restored life to the dead.

Jesus claimed to be not only life, but also the light associated with glory. "In Him was life, and the life was the light of men" (John 1:4, 9). He was the **true light**. The word that spoke life and light into being is the best light. It is better than any secondary or artificial illumination.

During the Jewish Feast of Tabernacles (Booths or *Sukkot*), priests lit four lampstands in the temple court of women, which adjoined the treasury. The lamps served as a reminder of the pillar of fiery light that had guided Israel through the wilderness. They also brought to mind God's other *shekhinah* visitations.[189] At that feast, in the treasury, Jesus proclaimed, "I am the **Light of the world**" (John 8:12; 9:5; 12:46).

The Laser Light

Why does Scripture burst with so many names for Jesus? Because Jesus is more than a single splendid ray of God's glory, He radiates the full spectrum and is the very substance of glory. Each aspect of the life of "our **glorious Lord Jesus Christ**" (James 2:1) shines brilliantly. Each of Jesus' names points to an aspect of God's nature. Through the prism of Jesus, every color of the rainbow of God's glory refocuses into the brightest and purest glory possible. In Jesus, all of the fullness of the glory of God is concentrated to the intensity of a laser beam. It took an explosion of names to express His glory.

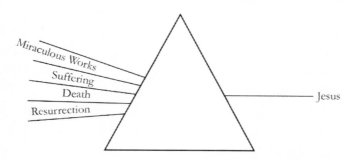

Jesus the Miracle Maker

John said that Jesus' first miracle, changing water into wine, manifested His glory.[190] Just as the deeds of God comprised one part of His spectrum of glory,[191] so Jesus' miracles resulted in recipients and observers giving glory to God. The multitudes "marveled as they saw the mute speaking, the crippled restored, and the lame walking, and the blind seeing; and they glorified the God of Israel" (Matt. 15:31).[192]

After Jesus raised a widow's son from the dead, "fear gripped them all, and they began glorifying God, saying, 'A **great prophet** has arisen among us!' and, 'God has visited His people!'" (Luke 7:16)

When Peter declared, "The **God of our fathers** has glorified His servant Jesus," (Acts 3:13) he might have been speaking of the vivid scene of a lame man leaping up and jumping around after he had been healed. Or perhaps he had the supremely glorious resurrection of Jesus in mind.

Dark Bands of Glory

Jesus' miracles were a popular attraction; not all of God's works are so appealing. Sometimes glory hides behind pain. For instance, Jesus told Martha that her faith would result in God's glory when He raised her brother, Lazarus, from the dead.[193] God takes even the dark strands of sickness and death, weaves them into His purposes, and uses them for His glory by demonstrating His power over them. Martha learned that God beckons people to swim in deeper glory. The lesson prepared Jesus' followers to witness His own agony turned to glory.

"Was it not necessary for the Christ to suffer these things and to enter into His glory?" Jesus asked two travelers who were going to Emmaus, and who were still mourning His death (Luke 24:26). The question presented a twist, not just to their thinking but also to the whole human mindset. Several verses describe Jesus' death and resurrection as the hour of His glory.[194] Jesus' path to ultimate glory meandered through humility, service, and suffering. Notice the progression: He was "made for a little while lower than the angels" and "because of the suffering of death crowned with glory and honor" (Heb. 2:9). The **Author of their salvation** was perfected through suffering in order to bring many sons to glory.[195]

The route that Jesus took—to glory via suffering—is sometimes the same route that we take.[196] Playing on the basic meaning of *kavod* ("weight" and "glory"), Paul quipped that our momentary light afflictions are an investment for a greater weight of future glory.[197] Knowing that his own death would somehow glorify God,[198] Peter encouraged us: "If you are reviled for the name of Christ, you are blessed, because the **Spirit of glory and of God** rests on you.

Spirit of glory and of God
Gk.: *To tēs doxēs kai to tou Theou pneuma*
(1 Pet 4:14)

God of all grace
Gk.: *Ho Theos pasēs charitos*
(1 Peter 5:10)

. . . If anyone suffers as a Christian, he is not to be ashamed, but is to glorify God in this name" (1 Peter 4:12–19). A deep desire to glorify God will help us endure suffering. Peter inspired us: "After you have suffered for a little while, the **God of all grace**, who called you to His eternal glory in Christ, will Himself perfect, confirm, strengthen and establish you" (1 Peter 5:10).

Resurrection Glory

Paul made it clear that Jesus "was raised from the dead through the glory of the Father" (Rom. 6:4). The story of Jesus' glory progresses all the way to heaven. Paul referred to Jesus' ascension as His being "taken up in glory" (1 Tim. 3:16). Incidentally, another cloud and "men in white" attended His ascension too.[199]

If the phenomena surrounding the birth, baptism, transfiguration, resurrection, and ascension of Christ were spectacular, it is no wonder the phenomena anticipated at His second coming are at least as glorious.[200] After Jesus returns, God's glory will light the New Jerusalem; its lamp will be the **Lamb**.[201] God's people will share in His glory.[202] Finally, God will spread His tabernacle again and dwell with us forever—something He has been planning for a very long time.[203]

Chapter 4

APPROACHING GLORY

For good ye are and bad, and like to coins,
some true, some light, but every one of you
stamp'd with the image of the King.
—Alfred, Lord Tennyson

G lory and space travel have two things in common; they are both difficult to explain and we can approach neither of them without proper preparation. Most of us struggle to imagine the sensation of a rocket propelling us beyond earth's gravity into orbit at 17,000 mph. Weightlessness sounds fun but a little weird. The math involved in rocket science requires more than ten fingers. When it comes to explanations of space travel, NASA does a great job.

Exhibiting Glory

NASA's exhibition at the Kennedy Space Center impressed Janet and me. It engaged each of our five senses, just as the "rays" of God's glory engaged His people. We saw photographs and read printed explanations. Audio recordings played at the touch of a button. One of our favorite presentations was the

Cinemax. Accompanied by surround sound, the 180-degree screen displayed earth from the perspective of a space shuttle orbiting two hundred miles above a dreary, east coast day.

Elsewhere, a man wearing a welding mask put heat-resistant tiles through their paces with a 2000 °F blowtorch. People could finger moon rock, buy inflatable rubber rockets for their nephews, and sample space-age ice cream.

The best exhibits were the ones we could enter. We peered inside a landing module in which Apollo astronauts had once returned to earth, and we puzzled how the crew had squeezed into it without getting painful cramps and cricked necks. The Saturn V rocket was impressive, but the walk-through space shuttle won the day.

Like the NASA exhibition, God's exhibition of glory featured one central exhibit: the ark of the covenant. It was housed first in the tabernacle and later in the temple. Those structures were like God's walk-through display of glory. God dwelt in them, and His people could experience His presence there.[204]

The ark was the centerpiece of the tabernacle and the temple. It was "called by the Name, the very name of the LORD of hosts who is enthroned above the Cherubim" (2 Sam. 6:2). Throughout Scripture, God's presence is associated with both His glory and His name. His glorious presence was notable at times of sacrifice, when Moses and Aaron blessed the people, and when they approached God with humility.[205]

Glory's Shadow

God designed the visible world to point to the invisible.[206] This is especially true for the tabernacle; every part modeled ("shadowed" is the New Testament word) what His eternal dwelling (heaven) is like.[207] Two of the items relate to God's glory:

Behind the veil, the "mercy seat" that covered the ark was a shadow of God's throne. Now, we know that God is enthroned on high, in heaven, and "upon the praises of Israel,"[208] but the Bible also says that He is enthroned above the cherubim.[209] Certainly, the foundations of His throne are righteousness and justice, and the earth is His footstool.[210] Yet David indicated that God's footstool was in the temple.[211] Israel focused her worship there.[212] On the annual Day of Atonement, the High Priest carried the sacrificial blood through the veil. When he sprinkled the blood on the mercy seat, it was as though all of Israel had stepped up to bow before the throne of the King of glory to be reconciled to Him. This earthly ritual shadowed the reality of the worship of the King in heaven.

Outside the veil stood a seven-branched lampstand called the *menorah* that was visible to everyone. During the tabernacle and temple periods, its oil-soaked wicks burned perpetually to light the sanctuary. Just a few feet behind the veil, the *menorah* symbolized God's greater glory. The King of glory included it to remind Israel that He dwelt with them.

However, the relationship between people and God was formalized. It had to be because it was damaged and difficult.

God in a Tent

Paul identified the central problem in our relationship with God. We fell short of the glory that God had intended for us.[213] The initial act and the ongoing pattern of rebellion made our relationships with God awkward to say the least. God is perfect and He tolerates no evil, so blemished people could no longer approach Him directly. God responded to sin with patience. He avoided destroying Adam by dismissing him from the garden, while He prepared for reconciliation. God stationed a guard at Eden,[214] but He maintained a degree of relationship through sacrifices, which were later centered in the tabernacle.

The precursor to the tabernacle was called the "tent of meeting." God's goal was to meet with people.[215] The tabernacle was a large tent, erected in the center of Israel's encampment for the glorious presence of God to reside. Without the tent, His glory would have overwhelmed people if they had approached in their sin. The God of glory wants to relate to people with all of His heart.[216] In Old Testament times, the tabernacle made that relationship possible.

God dwelt in a modular tent with His people on the move. Once Israel had completed the tabernacle, God's glory, which had earlier appeared on Sinai, consecrated and filled it.[217] God relocated to the temple to dwell with His people in the promised land. That permanent structure was built for His name. It nested in a city planned for His name, in a nation set apart for His name.[218] In response to praise, God filled the temple too.[219]

Interestingly, the word for tabernacle (*mishkan*) is related to the word *shekhinah*. *Shakhen* (neighbor) and the verb *shakhen* (to dwell) are part of the same word group. *Shekhinah*, a manifestation of God's

Mishkan	Tabernacle
Shakhen	Neighbor
Shakhen	To dwell
Shekhinah	

blazing glory, proved that the tent pitched in the middle of the camp was more than a showpiece. God dwelt in the neighborhood. He had planted His feet on earth among His people.[220] However, a heavy veil in front of the ark reminded everyone of the awkwardness of the relationship. Even so, wise people in Israel treasured God's glorious presence above everything else. David expressed his love for "the habitation of Your house and the place where Your glory dwells" (Ps. 26:8).

Too Hot to Handle

In one sense, the temple itself, as an architectural splendor, glorified God; however, that is secondary.[221] The glory of both the tabernacle and the temple depended on the presence of God above an ark that was about the size of a TV stand or a chest freezer. In a way that we can't fully understand, God's glory was concentrated in the space above and between two cherubim on the "mercy seat" (the lid covering the ark). Hebrews 9:5 even calls them the "cherubim of glory." That was where the Lord of hosts "sat."[222]

That focal point of glory is like what physicists struggle to create in order to stimulate the controlled fusion of hydrogen nuclei—a magnetic force field powerful enough to contain a glowing, ultra-hot reaction. This mirrors the dilemma faced by people of every era who seek a relationship with the God of glory. God is so glorious that an encounter with Him would overwhelm us mortals. God's presence is simply "too hot to handle."

The veil, which screened the ark, acted as a safety barrier. The thick curtain reminded the High Priest, who probably trembled as he went behind it to the ark once a year, to be scrupulously clean (in spiritual terms) before approaching—or he would die. Everywhere we look in the Old Testament, God, who desires intimacy, must nonetheless protect His people from full contact with His glory.

NASA deals with a problem rather like the one we have been considering. They have to balance participation with safety. Janet and I climbed some metal stairs onto a steel walkway. Then we entered a space shuttle. Although we could peer into the shuttle's cockpit, we could touch nothing. Mounted smack in front of our noses was a thick Plexiglas screen. It was there to protect delicate instruments from sticky fingers and to shield tourists, who were grounded by the walkway, from electrical hazards. Only astronauts could go closer.

Signposts to Blessing

High-voltage equipment usually has protective shields, and it comes with warnings and safety instructions. God provided his people with instructions too, teaching them how to relate to Him appropriately.

One summer vacation while I was in college, I volunteered at a Christian conference center. I took a sightseeing trip on a shoestring budget. I hitchhiked, slept in cheap hostels with rationed showers, and carried just a few extra clothes. When I returned, the director met me and announced, "The archbishop is visiting. Bathe, shave, and change your clothes. Then you can meet him." It is common for people to wear decent clothes and use deodorant out of respect for distinguished people. God is like that too; He has house rules—a dress code, if you like. But He actually provides the cleansing and the clothing.

God's Law contained instructions for a safe working relationship with Him.[223] The details were not the sadistic requirements of a killjoy; rather, they were signposts showing where the blessing of His presence faded and where the shadows of pain and danger began. The Law marked the boundary between good and evil, just like the rumble strips that edge some roads. When a driver veers over one, it sends a jarring warning of impending disaster. In the Law, God said, "I desire a relationship with you. Given that we are such vastly different beings, here's how it can happen." The Law was not meant to repel people but to draw them to God.

It was theoretically possible to obey the Law and be close to God. In practice, the Law provided a lesson about how needy we are. We need help to follow His ways and to change our hearts so that we can recognize God's goodness and get good and evil the right way round in our minds. One verse gives a fascinating insight into the Law's purpose: "This is the thing which the LORD has commanded you to do, that the glory of the LORD may appear to you."[224]

The Face of Glory

A chance to glimpse the glory of God—what a tantalizing yet confusing offer. The Bible says that no one can see God's face; yet a few people did see it. Jacob was surprised that he survived. Moses initially hid his face from God in the bush. Elijah wrapped a cloak around his head when God spoke. Samson's parents and Gideon all saw the face of the angel of God and remained unscathed.[225] Ordinary Israelites were afraid of even hearing God's voice; yet they saw Him "eye to eye" in the pillar of cloud and fire, and observed His glory on Sinai and after the first offerings.[226] Israel's elders ventured closer.[227] Although Moses survived his encounter with God, the people didn't want to push their luck—they begged Moses to represent them.[228] Moses obliged, and so began a thread of national expectation for a prophetic leader, ultimately fulfilled in Jesus.[229] Moses had a privileged position. "The LORD used to speak to Moses face to face, just as a man speaks to his friend" (Ex. 33:11)[230] But confusingly, when he asked to see God's glory, God denied him a view of His face.[231] A closer look at Exodus 33 and 34 will help us understand the problem that glory presents. It will also explain why the temple had a veil and why Eden is guarded.

God told Israel that He would appoint an angel to lead them from Mount Sinai to Canaan. His reason: "I will not go up in your midst, because you are an obstinate people, and I might destroy you on the way" (Ex. 33:1–5). Note the dilemma again: His presence is desirable, but the relationship is tricky for fallen humans.

When it came to the tabernacle, the people played it safe. The tabernacle was available for "everyone who sought the LORD," but the fearful people chose to watch and worship at a distance while Moses visited with God.[232] They paddled on the edge of glory, instead of swimming deeper. But Moses knew that God's presence indicates His favor, so he sought a guarantee that God would accompany Israel on their journey.[233]

Trying to cash in on the guarantee, Moses said, "I pray You, show me Your glory!" God replied, "I Myself will make all My goodness pass before you, and will proclaim the name of the LORD before you . . . you cannot see My face, for no man can see Me and live!" God arranged to place Moses in a crevasse at the summit of Mount Sinai and to shield him with His hand while His glory passed by. Then, as He removed His hand, He said, "You shall see My back ['*akhor*], but My face shall not be seen" (Ex. 33:18–23). However, some better translations than "back" are "afterglow" and "wake."[234] Moses experienced the ripples of God's glory.

In Scripture, God's glory and His face (*panim*) are connected. In light of all that we have said about glory so far, this is not surprising. The face best expresses character, attitude, sentiment, and beauty. In Hebrew, *panim* "can be a substitute for the self or the feelings of the self."[235] The reluctant prophet, Jonah, fled from the LORD's presence (*panim*).[236] The priestly blessing included a request: "The LORD make His face shine on you" (Num. 6:24–26;

see also Dan. 9:17). Isn't our biggest reward the sense that our heavenly Father is smiling at us in pleasure?

But what about the apparent contradiction? God told Moses that he couldn't see His face, but then He revealed His name and "wake." What does this mean? Let's clarify God's communication to Moses: "You cannot see my full glory, which includes my face, but you can see ripples of my glory—my goodness and my name." What Moses eventually saw was the "friendly" aspect of God's glory. From the standpoint of an unredeemed human, God's full-faced glory was too fierce. It would have killed him.

The tolerable ripples of God's glory came in the form of a proclamation emphasizing His goodness[237] and expanding on the familiar names *Yahweh* and *'El*. His goodness appears in eight qualities—six positive qualities and two seemingly negative qualities. The fact that God referred to the collection as His "name" demonstrates that names express character. One commentary calls them God's comeliness or beauty: "old truths but with a new splendour."[238]

When Moses reached the summit, "he called on the name of the LORD," who passed by in front of him and proclaimed:

> *Yahweh, Yahweh 'El,*
> compassionate [*rakhum*] and
> gracious [*khannun*],
> slow to anger, and
> abounding in lovingkindness [*khesed*]
> and truth [*'emet*];
> who keeps lovingkindness for thousands,
> who forgives [*nose*] iniquity, transgression, and sin;
> yet He will by no means leave the guilty unpunished,
> visiting the iniquity of fathers on the children and on the grandchildren
> to the third and fourth generations. (Ex. 34:5–7)[239]

While they are not true names (though elsewhere God's names incorporate many of these characteristics), all of them describe how God relates to His people. This is important, given the backstory. The passage records the events that occurred after Israel had offended God by making the golden calf and Moses had smashed the first copy of the Ten Commandments. Nonetheless, God proceeded to communicate His patience, mercy, and forgiveness. Unfortunately, human relationships are more easily broken than mended; with God, the pattern is reversed. God is so eager for relationship that His whole being, including the two "negatives" listed above, focuses on reconciliation. Let's break down what God showed Moses. Remember, this collection of attributes comprises the part of His glory that fallen humans can endure.

The adjective *rakhum* (compassionate) relates to *rekhem* (womb). God's compassion is stronger than a mother's love for her child.[240] He is a **compassionate God**. Elsewhere, *rakham* is translated to indicate God's mercy.[241] In the New Testament, He is the **Father of mercies**.[242]

"Gracious" (*khannun*) means "undeserved favor." It sometimes equates with mercy.[243] When God declared to Moses His sovereign choice over the exercise of graciousness and compassion, He was not expressing tight-fistedness, but His desire to bless some unexpected people.[244]

Compassionate God
Heb.: *'El rakhum*
(Deut. 4:31)

Gracious and compassionate God
Heb.: *'El-khannun werakhum*
(Neh. 9:31; Ps. 86:15; Jon. 4:2)

God who shows me loving kindness
Heb.: *'Elohei khasdi*
(Ps. 59:17)

My lovingkindness
Heb.: *Khasdi*
(Ps. 144:2)

The phrase, "slow to anger," literally means, "long-nosed." Now, what's that about? One function of the nose is to dissipate heat. It's a relief to know that a cooling mechanism exists to disperse the burning anger (literally, "the heat of the nostrils") of the Lord.[245] God tolerates a surprising amount of sin and is always ready to welcome back His people when they humble themselves and turn to Him for help. In Isaiah 48:9, God says of His forbearance with Israel: "For the sake of My name I delay My wrath."

God's lovingkindness (*khesed*) is an unbreakable loyal commitment to the people with whom He is in covenant. It is synonymous with His everlasting love.[246] He abounds with it and extends it to thousands of people. He is the **God who shows me lovingkindness**. He is also **my lovingkindness**.

'Aman	(To confirm, support, be certain)
'Emet	(Truth, something certain)
'Amen	(Truth, certainty)
'Emunah	(Faithfulness, steadiness, reliability).

Lovingkindness often parallels truth (*'emet*)[247] because *'emet* is part of a family of words that express certainty and reliability. He is true to His people. **God of truth** is a name in its own right. Another version is **true God**, a name that the New Testament gives to Jesus. One of Jesus' tasks was to bear witness to the truth;[248] another task was to send us the **Spirit of truth**. *'Emet* is not just truth in contrast to falsehood or fantasy; it is a loving loyalty that "stays true" through thick and thin. God's truth is so expansive that it fills the skies and the heavens.[249] Psalm 115:1 declares, "To Your name give glory because of Your lovingkindness, because of Your truth."

Deuteronomy 7:9 uses a word (*'aman*) related to truth, in a similar context. "The LORD your God, He is God, the **faithful God**, who keeps His covenant and His lovingkindness to a thousandth generation with those who love Him and keep His commandments." He is a **God of faithfulness**, certain and dependable. Faithfulness (dependability) is an often-celebrated attribute of God.[250] God's faithfulness in the face of our fickleness highlights His glory.[251]

Isaiah spoke about the **God of truth** using *'aman*'s little cousin *'amen*. It could also be translated "God of certainty." The Hebrew word *'amen* passed unmodified into many languages. It forms the bottom line of our prayers: our agreement with the petition and a statement of faith that God will grant it.[252] Jesus Himself guarantees God's faithfulness to His promises to us.[253] *'Amen* can also be translated as "truly," which often acts as an emphatic introduction to Jesus' statements. In Jesus, the names reunite. He is "**The Amen, the faithful and true Witness**," (Rev. 1:5; 3:14), and He is also called "**Faithful and True**" (Rev. 19:11).

Lastly, on the positive side, God forgives (lifts or bears away[254]) the weight of guilt that results from violating His laws. Psalm 99:8 calls Him a **forgiving**

God of truth
Heb.: *'El 'emet*
(Ps. 31:5)
Heb.: *'Elohei 'amen*
(Isa. 65:16)

True God
Heb.: *'Elohim 'emet*
(Jer. 10:10)
Gk.: *Ho alēthinos Theos*
(1 John 5:20)

The Faithful God
Heb.: *Ha'El hanne'eman*
(Deut. 7:9)

God of faithfulness
Heb.: *'El 'emunah*
(Deut. 32:4)

Spirit of truth
Gk.: *To pneuma tēs alētheias*
(John 14:17; 15:26; 16:13)

The Amen
Gk.: *Ho amēn*
(Rev. 3:14)

Faithful and true witness
Gk.: *Ho martys ho pistos kai alēthinos*
(Rev. 1:5; 3:14; 19:11)

Forgiving God
Heb.: *'El nose'*
(Ps. 99:8)

God of forgivenesses
Aram.: *'Eloah selikhot*
(Neh. 9:17)

God. Nehemiah 9:17 reiterates the words spoken to Moses.[255] "You are a **God of forgiveness**, gracious and compassionate; slow to anger and abounding in lovingkindness."

We must take God seriously, though, because He won't acquit or ignore (*naqqeh*) covenant violations, but He will visit (*poqed*) sanctions on four generations. At times, God appears in glory to punish unbelief and rebellion;

> **God who hides Himself**
> Heb.: *'El mistatter*
> (Isa. 45:15)

He is ready to avenge evil.[256] One form of punishment is for God to hide His smiling face.[257] His name, the **God who hides Himself**, was spoken during Israel's exile.[258]

Quite naturally, our tendency is to see God's glory in what is appealing. But even His punishments contain beauty; they are not so fierce or negative

> **Father of spirits**
> Gk.: *Ho patēr tōn pneumatōn*
> (Heb. 12:9)

as they might first appear. Rather, providing correction is an attribute of the **Father of spirits**, who lovingly disciplines His children so that they will mature. What at first might seem hard to us comes from God's loving heart.

What about the contradiction between Exodus 33:11, which tells us that Moses spoke with God face to face, and verse 20, which says that to do so spells death? Evidently, God reveals Himself by degrees. People in biblical times anticipated death when they witnessed a manifestation of God's glory. Some of them received privileged glimpses, not realizing that the brilliance that they observed was only a tiny, friendly fraction of the whole. On Mount Sinai, Moses encountered eight aspects of His goodness. Jesus alone could see His Father's full-faced glory because He shared it.[259]

In concluding the summit meeting, Moses bowed, asked forgiveness for Israel, and requested that God's presence remain with His people. God warned that He was a **Jealous God** who did not tolerate the worshipping of foreign gods.[260] Then He reissued the covenant commandments. Moses returned to the people with God's terms for their relationship with Him engraved on stone tablets, which he placed in the ark. Moses' face shone so brightly it frightened people. Imagine his radiance if he had been able to see the fullness of God's glory. When Moses finished speaking with the people, he wrapped a veil round his face.[261] Relationships with God were awkward, but God planned to fix them. The drums rolled as Jesus approached the stage.

Center Stage

Janet and I ended our visit to the Kennedy Space Center watching a presentation called The Astronaut Encounter. A crowd waddled like penguins squeezing through a gate that led into an arena. People spread out to sit on benches around a platform. The host did an excellent job of building excitement. She asked the audience, "Who would like to be an astronaut?" A dozen children (and a few adults) raised their hands. She interviewed a boy called Sam. Sam said that for all of his life he had watched shuttle launches, and he had pasted pictures into space albums. He longed to meet an astronaut, so this was his big day. Even some adults were on the edges of their seats. Finally, with the amplified words reverberating around the buildings, the emcee introduced the star: "And nowww, let's give a big handdd for Commander Rick Searfoss."

Rick, the commander of three shuttle missions, took the stage.[262] At last, we were seeing a real-life astronaut! He had handled controls that we had only glimpsed behind Plexiglas. He told of his trips into space, his years of preparation, the thrill of the launch, and his exhilarating view of earth. Rick answered our questions about rocket propulsion. He explained space travel and described what weightlessness does to a human body and mind. Rick Searfoss fascinated us more than the best displays.

The dramatic manifestations surrounding Jesus' birth and early ministry were God's build-up. They prepared alert people to encounter glory—glory wearing skin. The Jesus encounter surpassed any astronaut encounter. The Son of God stood in the center stage of human history, as a man to whom we can readily relate. John said, "The Word became flesh, and dwelt [eskēnōsen] among us, and we saw His glory, glory as of the only begotten from the Father, full of grace and truth" (John 1:14). In Jesus, God pitched a tent of human flesh so that all of the earth could see what glory looked like. Even when limited by a human body in a fallen world, glory is magnificent.

Mishkan	Tabernacle
Shakhen	Neighbor
Shakhen	To dwell
Shekhinah	
Eskēnōsen (Gk.)	Dwelt

Paul summarized Jesus' significance: "God . . . shone in our hearts to give the light of the knowledge of the glory of God in the face of Christ" (2 Cor. 4:6).

There are two kinds of movies about the life of Christ. One portrays Jesus as a straight-faced religious master who is detached, if not stern. Most of us prefer the second kind of movie, in which Jesus grins winsomely. Isn't this the Jesus of the Gospels? God's glory shines from a face with an inviting smile.

What a Character!

The book of Hebrews introduces Jesus as the ultimate upgrade to God's prophetic messengers: "He is the radiance [*apaugasma*] of [God's] glory and the exact representation [*charaktēr*] of His nature [*hypostaseōs*]" (Heb. 1:1–3).

The word *apaugasma* implies reflection, but it emphasizes radiance from within. Either way, God is the source of Jesus' glory. Jesus did exactly what God intended all humans, especially His chosen nation, to do: display His glory. *Charaktēr* is the word for an engraved die used to stamp a duplicate impression on an object, such as a coin. But Jesus is more than an impression of God; the word *hypostaseōs* indicates that all of God is invested in Christ. Hence, He is the "perfect imprint and very image of [God's] nature" (Heb. 1:1–3 AB).

Image of God
Gk.: *Eikōn tou Theou*
(2 Cor. 4:4)

Image of the invisible God
Gk.: *Eikōn tou Theou tou aoratou*
(Col. 1:15)

One early church leader used the word *charaktēr* to express that God made man in His image (1 Clement 33:4). Using a different word, Paul said that Jesus is the **image of God** and the **image** of the **invisible God**. "In Him all the fullness of **Deity** dwells in bodily form." (Col. 2:9)[263] Anyone who sees Jesus sees the Father (John 14:9). Jesus points to Him!

Jesus spoke of glory in terms of God's name: "The glory which You have given Me I have given to them . . . I have manifested Your name to the men whom You gave me" (John 17:1–6, 11–12, 22–26). Jesus could manifest the Father's name because, as the unmarred image of God, He embodied all of God's attributes.[264] Read His words again, replacing the phrase "Your name" with "the fullness of Your character":

> I have manifested the fullness of Your character to the men whom You gave me.

The Fierce and the Friendly

Jesus solved Moses' frustrating dilemma. Moses wanted to see God but he had to settle for seeing His "wake." "No one has seen God at any time; the only begotten God,[265] who is in the bosom of the Father, He has explained Him" (John 1:18). His most profound explanation came on the cross.

Jesus' humiliating death blended deep love and strong justice. The two sides of glory, the friendly and the fierce, from which God shielded Moses, are visible together in the crucifixion. God so loved us that He gave His only begotten Son to stand in the raging fire of judgment to receive our penalty for sin. Now we need not perish in the presence of His glory. Instead, we can fully relate to Him forever.[266] The rules for having a working relationship with God had finally progressed beyond unattainable legal requirements. Jesus faced God's judgment seat and took the heat for us. Now, through faith in Jesus and His death on the cross, we have access to the Father. That's "the gospel [good news] of the glory of Christ, who is the image of God."[267] The dilemma of the ages was resolved once and for all. Jesus restored our relationships with God.

The Family Business

God always longed to adopt more sons and daughters and bring them to glory.[268] In simple terms, the Trinity is "a well-adjusted family that wanted to get bigger."[269] God expanded His covenant with Israel to allow people from every tribe, tongue, and nation to praise His glory.[270] God patiently endured the vessels of wrath "to make known the riches of His glory upon vessels of mercy [Jews and Gentiles of faith in Jesus], which He prepared beforehand for glory" (Rom. 9:22–23). Israel largely failed to pass God's blessing on, but God drew the nations to Himself as Jesus was lifted up.

The arrival of Greek pilgrims asking to see Jesus marked the hour for the Son of Man to be glorified.[271] The prophecy of Isaiah had begun to pan out: "They cry out from the west concerning the majesty of the LORD. Therefore glorify the LORD in the east, the name of the LORD, the God of Israel, in the coastlands of the sea. From the ends of the earth we hear songs, 'Glory [*tsevi*] to the Righteous One'" (Isa. 24:14–16). Christ functioned as a **servant to the circumcision** to fulfill God's promises and so that Gentiles could "glorify God for His mercy" (Rom. 15:8–9). However, the church, which was born in a Jewish milieu, found Gentile inclusion difficult to swallow. That inclusion is one of the mysteries revealed by God and understood through faith.[272] Currently, history is marching toward the day when every knee will bow and every tongue will declare that Jesus is Lord to the glory of God.[273]

Salvation does more than restore the status quo; it transforms sin-afflicted, captive, and grieving people into new creatures. Isaiah predicted the transformation: "They will be called oaks of righteousness, the planting of the LORD, that He may be glorified" (Isa. 60:21; 61:1–3). Jesus changes the most derelict lives. Some renewal is almost immediate; the rest takes a lifetime of work on the part of the Holy Spirit.

Unveiling the Veil

How significant is the Holy Spirit? Let's return to the puzzling veil that Moses wore after receiving the Law. Paul provides an insightful perspective:

> *If the ministry of death, in letters engraved on stones, came with glory, so that the sons of Israel could not look intently at the face of Moses because of the glory of his face, fading as it was, how will the ministry of the Spirit fail to be even more with glory? For if the ministry of condemnation has glory, much more does the ministry of righteousness abound in glory. For indeed what had glory, in this case has no glory because of the glory that surpasses it. For if that which fades away was with glory, much more that which remains is in glory.* (2 Cor. 3:7–11)

Paul reasoned that if the impartation of the Law was a glorious event, then the "ministry of the Spirit" is even more glorious. The Israelites needed Moses' veil to protect them from the glory that was being reflected toward them, and to hide its fading.[274] We need no veil; we have nothing to fear and the Spirit's presence does not fade. Instead, "we all, with unveiled face, beholding[275] as in a mirror the glory of the Lord, are being transformed[276] into the same image from glory to glory" (2 Cor. 3:18). These words indicate a Spirit-mediated progression. For sure, the process awaits completion in heaven, but we already have the privilege of seeing more of God's glory than Moses did. It should show on our faces too.

In fact, God's presence is internal. Paul listed it as another mystery that the Bible reveals: "Christ in you, the hope of glory."[277] As believers, we receive God's indwelling Holy Spirit as though we were miniature tabernacles or temples.[278] When God camps in our hearts, our destiny to glorify Him is back on track. The experience of Christ living in us motivates us with the hope of greater glory to come. Paul described our present and future situations. We have obtained an "introduction by faith into this grace in which we stand; and we exalt in hope of the glory of God" (Rom. 5:2). We eagerly await "a Savior, the Lord Jesus Christ; who will transform the body of our humble state into conformity with the body of His glory" (Phil. 3:20–21). Jesus' work in us continues the fulfillment of Haggai's prophecy of a more glorious house.[279] Until Jesus returns, the church is the brightest token of God's glory, shining outside of heaven's veil for the world to see.[280]

John's revelation of heavenly reality began with a voice like a trumpet. John turned and saw seven golden lampstands. What arrested his eye, though, was Jesus, who stood among His churches and outshone them. Ultimately, Jesus replaces the temple *menorah*, the symbol of God's glory behind the shielding veil. John saw unscreened glory and he fell at God's feet.[281]

Astronaut Encounter

While Rick Searfoss stood at the podium sharing space anecdotes, he invited Sam to stand next to him, and he offered to answer a question. Startled by hearing his own voice in the speakers, Sam blurted out, "How do I become an astronaut?"

Human nature tries to emulate heroes. As images of God, we find our greatest fulfillment in becoming more like our heavenly hero. The horizon proscribed for our human potential is conformity to the image of Jesus.[282]

Jesus set an example for us in many ways. Even His attitude toward glory was different from our instinctive attitude. Rather than coveting glory from people, He valued only His Father's pleasure in His obedience. He did not seek glory for Himself. Unlike the Nebuchadnezzars and Belshazzars of the world, Jesus directed it all to God.[283] Consider His words and actions: "If I glorify Myself, My glory is nothing; it is My Father who glorifies Me" (John 8:54). When Satan offered Him the world's glory in exchange for worship, Jesus immediately refused.[284] Neither did Jesus glorify Himself by taking the role of High Priest upon Himself; God appointed Him.[285]

Jesus handled glory like a spotlight. He used His glory to highlight the outstanding features of His Father. The Father likewise pointed to Jesus, glorifying Him. This approach to glory was a major theme in Jesus' prayer in John 17. Having glorified His Father by accomplishing His assigned work, Jesus asked the Father to glorify Him in a way that would in turn glorify the Father. Jesus also sought to have the glory that He had once shared with the Father restored.[286] Jesus said that the Holy Spirit "will glorify Me; for He will take of Mine, and will disclose it to you" (John 16:14). The picture is one of mutual glorification, in which each member of the triune Godhead shines the spotlight of glory on the others.

What about the King of glory's plans to form His image in us? It comes as no surprise that the principle of mutual glorification extends to us. Our natural tendency is to build towers of self-aggrandizement, but our highest calling is to accept the King's rule over all of our affairs and live "to the praise of His glory" (Eph. 1:6, 12). (www.NamesForGod.net/glorifying-god gives a number of ways in which the Bible says we can bring glory to God.)

> *Now to Him who is able to keep you from stumbling, and to make you stand in the presence of His glory blameless with great joy, to the only God our Savior, through Jesus Christ our Lord, be glory, majesty, dominion and authority, before all time and now and forever. Amen.* (Jude 24–25)

Chapter 5

SCORCHED GROUND

Apart from Jesus, the presence of God is an object of terror, from which devils hide themselves in hell, and sinners weave aprons or hide among the trees. But in Him all barriers are broken down, all veils rent, all clouds dispersed, and the weakest believer may live, where Moses sojourned, in the midst of the fire, before whose consuming flames no impurity can stand.
—**F. B. Meyer**, *The Secret of Guidance*

"There's another one! On the left."

I saw what Janet was pointing at. Within minutes, flames engulfed the crown of the small tree. For an hour, we watched a wall of smoky fire consume a hillside.

"If only the wind would change direction."

Few people realize that wildfires are a danger on tropical islands. During the dry season on St. Croix in the US Virgin Islands, tall grass and wild tan-tan bushes desiccate under the blazing sun. A spark can ignite them. With continuous trade winds fanning the flames, fires occasionally threaten to destroy homes. A front of fire can race across acres of island. Hot flames reduce anything combustible to soot and cinders. Fire obeys a simple chemical formula: fuel plus air equals flames, smoke, and ashes.

Fires burn, hurt, and destroy. Those who have had close encounters with life-threatening infernos—not just hot barbeque coals or the cozy log fire in the hearth—know how terrifying they can be.

For part of our stay on St. Croix, Janet and I lived in a wooden cabin in a valley that was full of tan-tan and grass. During fire season, I jumped whenever my office phone rang. Was Janet calling me to rush home to hose down our house because of an advancing fire?

Many people are as apprehensive about God's holiness as I was about brush fires. We are instinctively aware of our vulnerability to raging wildfires. We know that the consuming flames are incompatible with our fragile selves. We understand that God's holiness and our fallen-ness don't mix. Even the thought of holiness can make us uncomfortable if it triggers feelings of guilt, shame, or unworthiness. Perhaps holiness seems like the Old Testament's dominant and dismal theme, and we don't want to be reminded of it. Maybe we would prefer to skip to the New Testament, which indicates how God provided us with a place of complete security.

Good news has the most impact when it follows on the heels of bad news. So, if a chapter on names that express God's holiness and judgment makes you jumpy, hang around for the good news. When we understand God's reaction to sin and how Jesus bore His wrath to shield us, then we can grasp the magnitude of God's redemptive love. A relationship with the Holy God is possible. Holiness doesn't have to burn us.

So, first let's consider what seems like bad news.

What a Difference!

The subject of the previous two chapters, God's glory, also evoked discomfort in those who witnessed it. So, is there a connection between glory and holiness? In a sense, there is. Glory and holiness both have to do with how different God is from His creation.

God's glory is a manifestation of His superiority; with His might, knowledge, timelessness, beauty, love, and righteousness, He outweighs us in every way. We most readily associate glory with brightness and beauty.

The main Hebrew word for "holy" (*qadosh*) means, "set apart." Numerous passages state that God's name is holy.[287] When we pray, "Hallowed be Your name," we are asking that people treat every aspect of God with honor and respect.[288] Nothing about Him should be profaned or treated as common or ordinary.[289] Isaiah and John glimpsed the throne room of the King of glory. Impressive attendant angels, called seraphim, declared to one another, "Holy, Holy, Holy, is the LORD of hosts, the whole earth is full of His glory" (Isa. 6:3). "The rare threefold repetition designates the superlative and calls attention to the infinite holiness of God."[290]

Holiness is not a commodity that we can measure, package, and deliver; holiness is a quality. We tend to associate holiness with perfection and righteousness. To be holy includes being "utterly pure in thought and attitude."[291] God is pure. He lacks no good attribute and He contains no trace of evil.[292] One New Testament word, *hagios*, which is often translated as **Holy One**, zooms in on God's moral perfection. The Bible frequently calls Him **Holy God**, **Holy One**, or the **Holy One of Israel**. His Spirit is the **Holy Spirit** or **Spirit of holiness**.[293]

Joshua warned that Israel would be unable to serve God in her own strength because His holiness is unattainable for humans.[294] "Who is able to stand before the LORD this Holy God?" asked the men of Beth Shemesh (1 Sam. 6:20). Everyone who heard the commandment to "be holy, for I the LORD your God am holy" (Lev. 19:2; 20:26; Eph. 1:4; 1 Peter 1:15) felt the awkward human dilemma: How on earth can we live with the holy God?

The inevitable reaction between perfection and imperfection shows up in the relationship between two Hebrew words, *qodesh* (holiness) and *tame'* (impure/unclean). They often butt heads in Scripture. Impurity infects the holy, hence the many laws concerning ritual cleanliness. One Bible teacher says, "*Kodesh* and *tamei* are contagious states which explode when mixed."[295] God's glory far surpasses the rest of creation, and it would overwhelm anyone. Similarly, His holiness and our unholiness, His perfection and our impurity, don't mix.

The Deity
Gk.: *Hē theotēs*
(Col. 2:9)

Holy One
Gk.: *Hagios*
(1 John 2:20)

Holy God
Heb.: *'Elohim qedoshim*
(Josh. 24:19)
'Elohim haqqadosh
(1 Sam. 6:20)
'El haqqadosh
(Isa. 5:16)

Holy One
Heb.: *Qadosh*
(Job 6:10; Hos. 11:9, 12; Hab. 1:12; 3:3)

Holy Spirit
Heb.: *Ruakh qodesh*
(Ps. 51:11; Isa. 63:10–11)
Gk.: *To pneuma to hagios*
(Matt. 1:18)

Spirit of holiness
Gk.: *Pneuma hagiōsynēs*
(Rom. 1:4)

The Old Testament seems to be full of examples of the reaction. When Yahweh's glory appeared to Israel outside their camp at Sinai, the people trembled and expected to die if they approached.[296] While wandering through the Sinai wilderness, they had several brushes with God; thousands of rebellious people died. The wicked Philistines, who briefly held Israel's ark captive, witnessed God's reaction to their idols.[297]

Another word, *khasid*, is also translated as "Holy One." It usually means "kind" or "pious."[298] New Testament writers wrap holiness, righteousness, and piety into one word, *hosios*, which is also translated "**Holy One**." Jesus connected these very attributes, appealing to His **Holy Father** and **Righteous Father**, in the belief that God would vindicate Him in resurrection.[299] In Acts, Luke interpreted Psalm 16:10 as a prophecy: Jesus, the Holy One, would not decay but would rise again.[300]

Holy One
Heb.: *Khasid*
(Ps. 16:10)
Gk.: *Hosios*
(Acts 2:27; 13:35;
Rev. 16:5)

Righteous God
Heb.: *'El-tsaddiq*
(Isa. 45:21)
Heb.: *'Elohei tsidqi*
(Ps. 4:1 NIV)
Heb.: *'Elohim tsaddiq*
(Ps. 7:9)

Righteousness means being and doing right. God sets that standard because He is utterly right. He is definitive. He draws the line. God is unique in the rightness of His judgments: "The LORD of hosts will be exalted in judgment, and the Holy God will show Himself holy in righteousness" (Isa. 5:16). He is called the **Righteous God** and the **Upright One**. Righteousness implies right-standing before God. If anyone had achieved God's standards, they could have approached God knowing they would be, well, all right.

Righteousness includes purity. God is so pure that He cannot even look at evil;[301] He eventually judges it. When God overlooked sins committed previously,[302] it was not a travesty of justice but a suspension of sentencing. He knew that Jesus would take the punishment on Himself later. Only briefly will God allow those who share His name through covenant relationships to profane his name.[303]

J. I. Packer's words summarize what we have been saying so far.

"Holy" is the word which the Bible uses to express all that is distinctive and transcendent in the revealed nature and character of the Creator, all that brings home to us the infinite distance and difference that there is between Him and ourselves. Holiness in this sense means, quite comprehensively, the "God-ness" of God, everything about Him which sets Him apart from man.

Later, he expands upon his definition:

The word points to God as standing above and apart from men, a different kind of being on a higher plane of existence. It focuses attention on everything in God that makes Him a proper object of awe and worship and reverent fear and that serves to remind His human creatures how ungodlike they really are. Thus it denotes, first, God's infinite greatness and power, contrasted with the smallness and weakness of us men and women; second, it denotes His perfect purity and uprightness which stand in glaring contrast with the unrighteousness and uncleanness of sinful humanity, and which call forth from Him that inflexible retributive reaction to sin which the Bible calls His "wrath" and "judgment."[304]

Unholy humans have tremendous intrinsic value because He made us in His image, but in no attribute do we match God. Human "holiness" always falls short of perfection. Its highest peaks are dedication, patience, gentleness, etc., but even our favorite holy men have flaws. In this world, sharing God's fullness, as Paul prayed,[305] amounts to demonstrating the complete range of His qualities, but in a reduced measure. In quantitative terms, we will never possess God's attributes to the extent that He does.

The Consuming Fire

God is so utterly different from us that Scripture describes Him as "a **consuming fire**," and it describes our lives as "tinder-dry grass."[306] Other passages describe war and God's tongue like sin-purging fires.[307]

Consuming fire
Heb.: *'Esh 'okhlah*
(Deut. 4:24)
Gk.: *Pyr katanaliskon*
(Heb. 12:29)

God's promise to consume the wicked Anakim ahead of Israel's invasion, was typical of the conquest of Canaan.[308] The Canaanites came under a ban or curse (*kherem*), not because their eviction was necessary to provide Israel with real estate, but as a judgment of their evil deeds. It was not primitive racism either; this treatment of sin applied universally and Israel herself received a warning to obey the consuming fire.[309]

The Old Testament's concluding verse deals with Israel and the problem of the curse (Mal. 4:6).

The curse (*kherem*) was the lowest, most shameful level in God's universe. Placing people under the curse was like discarding dry vegetation to a burn pile for incineration. In the end, gross and persistent sins were cut off, quarantined, and eradicated. For the Canaanites, that time came when Israel entered the land.

In Israel during the monarchy, the valley of Hinnom, which was just south of Jerusalem, served as the municipal dump. Sooty plumes and pungent odors regularly wafted through the streets. When garbage collection services are not provided, homeowners must dispose of their own trash. I spent one summer at a Christian conference center on Mount Carmel in Israel. No garbage truck stopped there. Instead, we had a large open pit behind the buildings. It was ten feet deep, strewn with rocks, and overgrown with thorns at the edges. We tossed our waste over a low wall into the pit. The heap grew until a volunteer climbed down, wary of snakes basking among the rocks, and put a match to it. One biblical word for hell, *Gehenna*, derives from *ge Hinnom*, the valley of Hinnom. It is an apt picture of hell. Hell is a cosmic burn pit for the devil and his angels; God never intended it for humans.[310] However, if we trash our relationship with God on earth, we get consigned to an eternity without Him.

"There's no cell service down here, but there's a pay phone near the furnace room."

"Cell Hell," by Fred Allen. Used with permission. www.OurDailyFred.com

People tend to trivialize heaven and hell. Heaven becomes the place of our dreams; hell is our worst nightmare. Heaven is 75 °F, and it rains only at night; cat-lovers keep clawless cats that play with indestructible mice. Hell might be an abysmal golf course, an endless traffic jam, or a shopping trip with no money. You fill in the blanks. In fact, heaven and hell are about dwelling eternally with God, in relationship with Him—or not.

Isaiah framed a vital question that pinpointed the crux of Old Testament religion: "Who among us can live with the consuming fire?" (Isa. 33:14–16[311]) It summarized the awkward human dilemma about unholy humans living with the Holy God. Isaiah answered it by describing the practical righteousness of a people who avoid evil and are scrupulously honest. The Law described that kind of lifestyle in detail. However, no one could reach the ideal. When people inevitably failed, the Jewish sacrificial system dealt with the uncleanness of sin. God, in His patience and mercy, provided sacrifices as a temporary measure to preserve His people. Fire consumed sacrifices instead of sinners.

Judging by God

God defines what is right, so only He can originate and administer true law. The Holy and Righteous God combines all three aspects of our justice systems—legislature, judiciary, and corrections. Isaiah calls Him the **Lawgiver**. The Hebrew word for lawgiver comes from the word for inscribing, which is exactly how God wrote the Law tablets for Moses on Sinai. James called God our **Lawgiver and Judge**. When it comes to consequences, He is the **God of recompense**.[312] That name emphasizes balanced justice. He rewards both good and bad accordingly. He imposes punitive or corrective sentences.

We might prefer it if God would omit the judgment part, but for God to be just He must judge anything that is opposed to holiness and righteousness. The Old Testament calls Him the *shofet* (judge).[313] He administers justice to the world.

Scripture shows that His is no rough justice. His punishment is carefully calculated and surgical, rather than being an uncontrolled fiery anger.[314] Abraham appealed to the **Judge of all the earth**, rhetorically asking, "Won't You deal justly?"[315]

In Hebrew, justice is closely related to righteousness. They reside in the Ruler, not in a statute book. God is perfect and His eyes penetrate human hearts,[316] so He knows exactly how and when to administer true justice. In the psalms, we read: "Righteous are You, O LORD, and upright are Your judgments" and "Righteousness and justice are

Lawgiver
Heb.: *Mekhoqeq*
(Isa. 33:22)
Gk.: *Nomothetēs*
(James 4:12)

Judge
Heb.: *Shofet*
(Ps. 50:6)
Gk.: *Kritēs*
(James 4:12; 5:9)

Judge of all the earth
Heb.: *Shofet kol-ha'arets*
(Gen. 18:25)

God of recompenses
Heb.: *'El gemulot*
(Jer. 51:56)

Righteous Judge
Heb.: *Shofet tsaddiq*
(Ps. 7:11)
Gk.: *Ho dikaios kritēs*
(2 Tim. 4:8)

God of justice
Heb.: *'Elohei mishpat*
(Isa. 30:18; Mal. 2:17)

**Judge of the living
and the dead**
Gk.: *Kritēs zōntōn kai
nekrōn*
(Acts 10:42)

God of vengeances
Heb.: *'El-neqamot*
(Ps. 94:1)

**Jealous and
avenging God**
Heb.: *'El qanno'
wenoqem*
(Nah. 1:2)

**God who executes
vengeance for me**
Heb.: *'El hannoten
neqamot li*
(2 Sam. 22:48;
Ps. 18:47)

the foundation of His throne."[317] God is aptly called the **Righteous Judge**, and the **God of justice**. Peter called Jesus the **Judge of the living and the dead**.[318] Peter also described the Holy One as an impartial judge. He said that Jesus, while suffering, "kept entrusting Himself to Him who judges righteously."[319] Jesus told a parable in which God's granting of justice was without question, but the challenge to us is to petition Him persistently.[320] In another parable, however, all judgments from the Son of Man, who is also the King, are suspended until He returns.[321]

God is also the **God of vengeance** and the **jealous and avenging God**[322] Just vengeance targets evil. Because God is vengeful on behalf of His people, He is called the **God who executes vengeance for me**. Even an unappealing attribute like vengeance is part of God's perfect nature. Another commentator said that "God cannot be true to His character of holiness and justice if He allows sin and rebellion to go unpunished . . . [He] must be the God of wrath in order for His mercy to have meaning."[323] Victims can take comfort in this, but for sinners it evokes fear.

Reverent Fear

The Old Testament's legal and sacrificial systems depended on a certain kind of fear. Fear first appears in the Bible when Adam, following his sinful disobedience, admits, "I was afraid."[324] The fall placed Adam and Eve in a position where God could have legitimately exercised His power to crush them to dust. God could have responded to their sin with wrath, and there would have been nothing capricious or malicious about His action. All of the ingredients were present for a reaction of judgment. Adam became aware of his problem and he was afraid.

While Israel camped at Mount Sinai, Moses offered a more comforting perspective on the fiery God who had set them trembling. "Do not be afraid; for God has come in order to test you, and in order that the fear of Him may remain with you, so that you may not sin." (Ex. 20:20)[325] How could Moses say, "Don't be afraid" and in the same breath talk about a lasting fear? It seems that God wanted to instill in the people a special sort of fear. The verse points to a difference between terror and reverent fear; the former paralyzes one's relationship with God, while the latter strengthens and secures it. This fear of the Lord leads to wisdom because it motivates people to obey God.[326] So what exactly is reverent fear? The changing coastline of St. Croix provides a good illustration:

Over the course of three years, I walked completely around the shores and cliffs of St. Croix—all eighty-three miles of them. The variety of the scenery impressed me. Many bays cooperate with the images in the tourist brochures, but the sea at the eastern headland is invariably rough and intimidating. On days when storms pass by, even tranquil waves in sheltered coves become destructive, and the friendly becomes frightening. After storms, the beaches looked as if a fleet of bulldozers had scoured them. Uprooted trees floundered in the waves; broken coral littered the shoreline.

Janet and I had the dubious privilege of experiencing hurricane Lenny battering St. Croix. It hit the island at Category 4. We sheltered in a safe concrete house with friends. Winds topped 130 mph. Ten inches of rain fell. The shutters vibrated like jackhammers as the wind and rain screamed by. The Weather Channel topped our TV ratings until the cables blew down. Then we tuned into local radio.

One host did a special show during hurricanes (for those who still had electricity). Live callers (whose phones still worked) spiced up his blow-by-blow account of the storm with reports from their neighborhoods (those who still had neighborhoods). At the height of the storm, a call came in about two surfers who had decided to hone their skills on the mammoth waves that were pounding the north shore. A nail-biting commentary ensued. The host described their struggle to avoid being pulverized on the rocks and their eventual success in safely reaching shore.

Storms are frightening, but sensible Caribbean islanders have learned that they can live with storms if they take precautions. This illustrates the reverent fear that the Bible speaks about. The fear of God is not a quivering, evasive terror but a humble respect for the Holy One and His standards. Surfing in a hurricane is generally agreed to be a crazy stunt, but careful fishermen can negotiate rocky headlands. They take the line dividing safety and danger seriously.

One writer sums up the difference between terror and reverent fear like this:

> There can be no religion at all without the awe of the creature in the presence of the Creator. The feeling of reverence, the awareness of God, is at once the prophylactic against sin, the dynamic of the Christian life, and the mainspring of Christian effort. But when reverence turns to fear in the lower sense of the term, then religion becomes a stunted and inadequate thing, which, because it has lost its grace, has lost its glory.[327]

Translations often interchange the words "revere" and "fear," so bear in mind what we have been considering—fear is a good thing. Isaiah 11:2 attributes the Spirit of the fear of the LORD to the Messiah. Moses' warning to Israel before they entered the promised land begins, "If you are not careful to observe all the words of this law which are written in this book, to fear this honored and awesome name, the LORD your God," you will be cursed (Deut. 28:58[328]). The Law acted like a highway rumble strip, warning where the edge of the road lies. Wise drivers respond to the judders. God's servants can "delight to revere Your name," and trust as they fear,[329] because reverent fear steers us away from the curse and toward blessing.

An appropriate fear of God's name will be evident in our behavior.[330] Fear means honoring and respecting Him, rather than despising Him. Fear results in confessing Him and not denying Him.[331] Fearing His name implies that we won't profane it or break His commands, although God's enemies revile and spurn His name.[332] Leviticus tells of one whose own name is forgotten, who was stoned for blaspheming God's name.[333] Such behavior invites the curse of God's judgment on our lives, just as standing in the way of a crashing wave or a raging fire invites disaster.[334]

❧

The Old Testament system we have been reviewing appears rather unattractive. This set of names tends to make us uncomfortable. Something inside us recollects a rumor of what J. I. Packer called God's "inflexible retributive reaction to sin," and we cower. Let's face it, at a glance, the Old Testament rumbles with declarations of holiness and demonstrations of judgment, especially on His enemies. For sinners like me, it's troubling. The subject sparks debates between objectors (Christian or otherwise) and defenders of the faith. Many people would prefer God to be an easygoing grandfather figure who pats us on the head and says "never mind" whenever we blow it. Instead, although we are assured of receiving a "fair trial," the equation remains the same: unholiness plus holiness equals judgment.

Fire burns, so we avoid fire.

Three Fire Drills

We typically exhibit at least one of three responses to the disquieting truth of the holy fire equation—three "fire drills."

Run

Our first response to a racing fire might well be to run like crazy. There are many ways to avoid any serious consideration of the difference between God's standards and our own lifestyle. We can dim the lights on reality or turn up the volume on our preferred set of distractions to drown out our conscience. Homemade anesthetics are everywhere.

Perhaps we attempt to tilt the equation in our favor by minimizing God's holiness in our minds, denying our failings, or puffing up our sense of worth. Just as we casually warm ourselves at a safe distance from our homely fires, so holiness is comfortably theoretical, as long as we avoid any close encounters with God.

Tremble

Some people live in anxiety, knowing that all of their attempts to satisfy God's high standards will fail. They shoot nervous glances over their shoulders. Aware that they could never outrun the flames, they tremble in terror.

Gideon's reaction to one particular divine encounter exemplifies this group. Gideon lived during the period of the judges. They played more than a judicial role; they were God's leaders and deliverers. Israel was stuck in a cycle at that time. When a neighboring nation oppressed her, she cried to God for help and He raised up a judge. The judge courageously repelled the enemy, but Israel became complacent and slipped back into her old sinful ways. A new oppressor was one of the consequences for her new sin.

We meet Gideon in Judges 6, when God's angelic recruiter called Gideon to resist the Midianites and their junior plundering partners, the Amalekites. Gideon wasn't sure who his visitor was, so he asked for ID. Then Gideon showed typical Middle Eastern hospitality by preparing a meal for his guest. Instead of eating it, the stranger had him place it on a boulder. Suddenly, with a touch of his staff, the meal was consumed (*'akhal*) by a burst of flame, and the angel vanished from sight. "When Gideon saw that he was the angel of the LORD, he said, 'Alas, O Lord GOD! For now I have seen the angel of the LORD face to face.'" (vv. 22–23)

Gideon knew that God sometimes manifested Himself as the angel of the Lord. He remembered God's response to Moses' request to see God's glory: "No man can see Me and live" (Ex. 33:20). Like us, Gideon had a background understanding of God's nature. He knew that his weak and doubting human condition was like tinder-dry grass before God's raging fire. So, having shaken God's hand only to have his home-cooking incinerated, the hospitable chef expected to be flambéed and consumed. In the instant following his realization that the strange stranger who had disappeared like a spirit was a manifestation of God Himself, Gideon's life flashed before him. We can imagine him glancing backward in anticipation of a thunderbolt, grasping the nearest tree to prevent himself from tumbling into a vast crack splitting the ground open, or tentatively feeling his limbs and expecting them to melt away. Gideon's concept of God was clear, so his cry was instinctive: "Alas, for I have seen the angel of the LORD." Fire burns.

Trembling, Gideon had no time to consider the difference between fear and reverence. He was scared to death and he needed God to intervene. And this is where the good news comes in.

Advance

God injected words of hope straight into Gideon's terror: "Peace to you, do not fear; you shall not die" (v. 23). The words are full of meaning. God's peace is more than tranquility or absence of hostility; it is a deep, wholesome sense of wellbeing that comes from being reconciled with God in a harmonious relationship.[335]

When Gideon embraced the prophetic good news, he began to exemplify a third group, which steps forward in faith. He built and named an altar, "the **LORD is peace**." It might seem strange to name a large pile of stones, but altars lasted many centuries in that semi-desert climate.[336] For years, Gideon's altar celebrated God's reassurance, and it served as a prophetic pointer to the ultimate peace-giver, Jesus. Just then, God had established a firebreak to stop the inevitable reaction between holiness and impurity. Gideon stepped into the firebreak, and we can too.

The Lord is peace
Jehovah shalom
(KJV)
Heb.: *Yahweh shalom*
(Judg. 6:24)

A History of Firebreaks

Crews fighting forest fires keep a careful eye on their escape route. If a wall of fire suddenly flares up, driven by a gusting wind and devouring fresh fuel, the firefighter must know exactly where to retreat.

Human minds will always struggle to comprehend the divine. Since God is holy, righteous, and committed to justice, how can His friendly qualities coexist with the fierce? When we do more than glance at the Old Testament, we see a broader, more accurate description of a God who displays both qualities. We must embrace that broad, biblical picture. God loves His created people so much that He does not want to consume us in the flames of judgment that leap from His holiness. Part of the first firebreak is God's choice to exercise mercy or suspend judgment.

Adam experienced God's restraint because God wanted reconciliation. God set a distance between both Adam and Eve and His holiness. He insulated the fallen first couple from certain destruction while preparing a way for the entire race to return to Him.

God revealed part of Himself to Moses while shielding him from flaming glory. In addition, God proclaimed a breadth of "fire-suppressing" qualities—grace, compassion, patience, and forgiveness.[337] Perhaps Gideon derived some peace from remembering what God had shown Moses. Later, Isaiah observed that God smiles on humble, contrite hearts because of His mercy.[338] Paul contrasted God's kindness toward people of faith with His severity toward transgressors.[339]

Old Testament Law also functioned as a firebreak. It delineated ideal human relationships with God. If people respected God's Law and stayed on the right

The LORD who sanctifies you
Yahweh meqaddishkhem
(Lev. 22:32)

side of the line, they could enjoy peace with God. When anyone failed, animal sacrifices secured justice; sacrifices took the heat of God's wrath in place of the offerer. Flames engulfed sacrifices to deal with impurity and to restore peace.[340]

Leviticus gives us another perspective on the Law:

> *You shall keep My commandments, and do them; I am the LORD. You shall not profane My holy name, but I will be sanctified among the sons of Israel; I am the LORD who sanctifies you, who brought you out from the land of Egypt, to be your God. I am the LORD.* (Lev. 22:31–33)

The Hebrew words for "sanctify" and "holiness" are related. Holiness indicates an object or person that is set apart; sanctification is the process of setting the object apart. Sanctification is the movement from being common to being set apart.

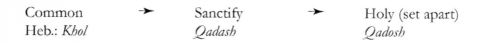

| Common | → | Sanctify | → | Holy (set apart) |
| Heb.: *Khol* | | *Qadash* | | *Qadosh* |

The names that describe God as a sanctifier usually accompany a call to obey His commandments. The commandments are His first plan to sanctify individuals, society, and Himself![341] In the above verses, God declared that Israel's obedience would sanctify *Him*; national submission to the law would set *Him* apart. Nathan Stone said, "All the institutions of ancient Israel's economy . . . were designed to insulate [Israel] for a while from the rest of mankind, and to make them the best possible instrument for God's purpose."[342] Of course, God never changes, but the way we live influences how others perceive Him. A godly lifestyle doesn't come naturally, so when Christians live it, other people conclude that the God we follow is different from their own "gods."

God did more than proscribe standards of behavior; the **LORD who sanctifies** also provided His people with a path into the set-apart lifestyle. The Law signposted blessings; it defined how to have a satisfying relationship with God. God's Law marked the boundary of the blessed life, but it was nonetheless His welcoming invitation to that life. God did not say "be holy, for I the LORD your God am holy" (Lev. 19:2) to ruin lives and spoil people's fun. The Law spelled out how to succeed at life. Outside the blessed place lay a lawless existence that was subject to God's judgment. The Law defined the edge of the firebreak.

Laws, sacrifices, and God's "friendly" face were all available to Gideon as reassuring firebreaks, but Gideon's altar anticipated a more robust solution. The Law was inadequate because human nature continually fails, wanders, and blatantly rebels. Ultimately, justice requires a more substantial penalty for my own sins, as well as those of the evil Canaanites, the hostile Philistines, and the straying Israelites. God promised to dwell with His people in a covenant of peace.[343] The good news was that God had a way to satisfy justice and make peace at the same time. He provided the best firebreak—something that had already been burned.

Scorched Earth

Fire crews sometimes use a drip torch to back-burn dry fuel hazards. The desiccated brush flares up, but it quickly burns out, leaving a scorched area. Firefighters retreat into the scorched area if the main front of fire threatens. The fire will halt before it reaches the crew because no fuel remains around them.

The holy God has provided spiritual scorched ground for His people to stand in. Instead of abandoning us to judgment, God sent Jesus to take the heat for our sins. He is the answer to Isaiah's question, "Who can live with the consuming fire?" Jesus imparts His holiness to us, and His Spirit empowers us to triumph over sin. The new formula goes like this:

> A perfect sacrifice satisfies God's holiness and justice, resulting in people having a restored relationship with God.

Each name of God speaks of just one facet of His nature. Reading the Bible selectively gives one an unbalanced view of Him. The cross provides the broadest, most balanced and appealing perspective on God. The friendly and the fierce met at Calvary. Jesus bore God's just judgment in His act of supreme substitutional love for us. The crucifixion combined God's burning wrath against sin with His deep love for us. Only Jesus could bear the combination.

This combination of justice and love is central to God's heart. Six times in the Bible the **Holy One of Israel** is called **Redeemer**.[344] On the cross, God lifted up both justice and love to demonstrate that He is both "a **Righteous God** and a **Savior**" (Isa. 45:21).

Oswald Chambers warned, "Never build your preaching of forgiveness on the fact that God is our Father and He will forgive us because He loves us. It is untrue to Jesus Christ's revelation of God; it makes the Cross unnecessary and the Redemption 'much ado about nothing.' If God does forgive sin, it is because of the Death of Christ."[345]

Holy One of God
Gk.: *Ho hagios tou Theou*
(Mark 1:24)

Holy and righteous One
Gk.: *Ho hagios kai dikaios*
(Acts 3:14)

Righteous One
Heb.: *Tsaddiq*
(Isa. 24:16)
Gk.: *Dikaios*
(Acts 7:52; 22:14)

LORD our righteousness
Heb.: *Yahweh tsidqenu*
(Jer. 23:6; 33:16)

Prince of Peace
Heb.: *Sar-shalom*
(Isa. 9:6)

God of peace
Gk.: *Ho Theos tēs eirēnēs*
(Rom. 15:33)

Lord of peace
Gk.: *Ho Kyrios tēs eirēnēs*
(2 Thess. 3:16)

Our Peace
Gk.: *Hē eirēnē hēmōn*
(Eph. 2:14)

Angels heralded Jesus' birth with the words, "peace among men." When Jesus, in Gethsemane, contemplated the heat of God's wrath, He was reluctant to drink the cup.[346] Jesus was widely recognized as an example of righteousness. Even demons testified that He was the **Holy One of God**.[347] New Testament preachers proclaimed the crucifixion of God's **Holy and righteous One**, which Isaiah had first announced.[348] Picture the divine Judge passing sentence on sinners and then leaving His bench to say, "I will pay the penalty Myself. Take the life of My precious, sinless Son." "By His knowledge, the **Righteous One**, My Servant, will justify the many, as He will bear their iniquities" (Isa. 53:11). Jeremiah prophesied about Jesus, the **righteous Branch** who combines righteousness and justice. Of all the names for God that were actually specified in the Old Testament as God's names, Jesus fulfills the last two: the **LORD our righteousness** and **Redeemer**. As Jesus hung on the cross, the full force of the shameful curse fell on Him.[349] He was the sacrifice and His life was consumed to provide our escape from fiery wrath. We can step into Jesus, our "scorched ground," and enjoy marvelous peace. Only the cross could simultaneously express God's love, mercy, and forgiveness, and yet still satisfy justice. Righteousness and peace kissed at Calvary.[350]

Peace is a New Testament theme[351] but it has Old Testament precursors apart from Gideon's example. Isaiah foretold the coming of a **Prince of Peace**.[352] In the New Testament, the eternal purpose of the **God** of peace[353] or **Lord of peace** finally became clear and Paul affectionately called Jesus, **Our Peace**.

Peace through the Blood

The New Testament presents four perspectives on how Jesus "made peace through the blood of His cross," (Col. 1:20) and it includes names that relate to three of them. The first perspective involves the words "righteousness" and "justification." Righteousness describes God's standard—a straight line, if you like. Justification is the process of alignment with that standard. My word processor is programmed to "left justify" the words I type. Each new line jumps to the left margin. God is our **Justifier** because He made correct alignment possible. Animal sacrifices are no longer the key to

Justifier
Gk.: *Ho dikaiōn*
(Rom. 3:26; 4:5; 8:33)

right standing with God. Now, faith in Jesus realigns us. We must exercise one tiny but vital choice: accepting Jesus by faith. Conversely, judgment remains for those who reject Him and His words.[354]

John announced the second perspective using a technical term: "We have an advocate with the Father, **Jesus Christ the Righteous**; and He Himself is the propitiation [*hilasmos*] for our sins" (1 John 2:1–2; 4:10; see also Rom. 3:25; Heb. 2:17). *Hilasmos* signifies an offering made to placate or appease an offended party. Jesus did something more fundamental than appeasement; He atoned for our sins.[355] If

Jesus Christ the righteous
Gk.: *Iēsous Christos dikaios*
(1 John 2:1)

someone dumped hazardous waste on your property, only a thorough cleanup would satisfy you. Jesus dealt fully with sin's defilement (an act called expiation), thus removing the object of God's anger. Technically speaking, His sacrifice had "the double effect of expiating the sin and thereby propitiating God."[356]

Hilasmos relates to the Greek word *hilasterion*. This was the word for the mercy seat covering the ark, the place of God's glorious presence. The High Priest sprinkled it with sacrificial blood on the Day of Atonement.[357] Using the legal metaphor again, Jesus approached the Judge's seat as both the sacrificial penalty and as our defense attorney. He paid our fine, so God blotted out our unrighteousness and credited us with Jesus' righteousness.

Thirdly, in Hebrews 12:18–24 the arrangement at Sinai is contrasted with our situation. We are not camped at a place where the raw, manifest glory of God induces terror. Rather, we stand before **God, the Judge of all**,

Judge of all
Gk.: *Kritēs pantōn*
(Heb. 12:23)

Mediator of a new covenant
Gk.: *Diathēkēs neas mesitēs*
(Heb. 12:24)

alongside "Jesus, the **mediator of a new covenant**." Jesus' sprinkled blood changes our response to the consuming fire; instead of fear, we can live at peace.[358] He is our immunity from judgment's flames.

Two words that we saw earlier, "sanctification" and "holiness," provide the fourth perspective. Sanctification is a cleansing process that results in holiness. Sometimes, holiness is represented as whiteness. Even one drop of "red" sin taints our life robes, making them "off-white" and unacceptable to God. The blood of Jesus laundered us clean again.[359] Jesus' sacrificial love for the church cleansed her and presented her in glorious, unblemished beauty.[360] Paul catalogued the behavior that once excluded us from God's kingdom, but he concluded, "You were washed . . . sanctified . . . justified in the name of the Lord Jesus Christ and in the Spirit of our God" (1 Cor. 6:9–11).

Jesus solved the dilemma about how to be holy. He altered the Law's operation in His followers' lives. Our holiness no longer depends on straining to comply with the Law and making bloody sacrifices when we fail. As the final sacrifice, Jesus ended that flawed system and imparted His holiness to us.[361] Unfortunately, we tend to revert to Old Testament religious thinking, and perhaps that's why we still feel uncomfortable discussing holiness. We must learn to resist relying on our own efforts and rituals. Instead, we must trust Jesus.

Burned is Beautiful

Pictures are often inadequate. Burnt earth sounds inhospitable, lifeless, black, and boring. J. I. Packer encapsulates many people's initial thoughts about holiness:

> The word "holiness" suggests to modern man something pale, anaemic, withdrawn, negative and passive. That shows how little modern man knows about it! Scriptural holiness is in fact the most positive, potent and often passionate quality of life that is ever seen.[362]

The haven of scorched ground, the place of holiness and righteousness that God puts us into (and puts into us), is filled with incredible satisfaction, joy, and freedom. In that haven, we enjoy a new degree of relationship with God. The most personalized forms of the names covered in this chapter found fulfillment in the crucifixion. Jesus became the **LORD our righteousness**[363] and **God of my righteousness**. In Jesus, God counts us righteous; there is no condemnation.[364] Consequently, the Bible refers to His people as "Jeshurun," the "righteous one(s)" or the "upright in heart." The **Upright One** relates to us as **God of Jeshurun**. Although the New Testament often translates *hagios* as "**Holy One**," in many contexts it means "saint."

God of my righteousness
Heb.: *'Elohei tsidqi*
(Ps. 4:1)

Upright One
Heb.: *Yashar*
(Isa. 26:7)

God of Jeshurun
Heb.: *'El Yeshurun*
(Deut. 33:26)

Gideon tasted peace but never completely understood it; our experience is fuller. Paul summarized it by saying, "Therefore, having been justified by faith, we have peace with God through our Lord Jesus Christ, through whom also we have obtained our introduction by faith into this grace in which we stand; and we exult in hope of the glory of God" (Rom. 5:1–2). Jesus introduced us to the life of grace, but Paul knew that holy living is an ongoing process, so he asked the **God of peace** to sanctify believers.[365] Grace is our resource package for the holy life. The indwelling Holy Spirit guides and empowers us to serve God in a way that Joshua had deemed impossible.[366]

A healthy relationship with the Lord grows in two directions. On the one hand, we develop a deepening knowledge of and reverence for the Holy and Righteous One. On the other hand, we develop a stronger grasp of the peace that Jesus obtained for us. Knowing the good news in light of the bad deepens our relationships with the Lord God.[367]

Chapter 6

PLEDGING ALLEGIANCE

I delight to come to my bearings—not walk in procession with pomp and parade, in a conspicuous place, but to walk even with the Builder of the universe, if I may.
—Henry David Thoreau, *Walden*

D on't you love it when your team is winning? In Psalm 24, David cheered God, the King of glory, who was victorious in war against His enemies. David asked rhetorically, "Who is this King of glory?" and his answer introduces another name. "The **LORD of hosts**, He is the King of glory" (Ps. 24:10).

We find kingship linked with the same name elsewhere. He is the "LORD of hosts, my **King** and my God" (Ps. 84:3). Isaiah looked into the throne room of "the King, the LORD of hosts" (Isa. 6:3, 5). The name is important because LORD of hosts is stated to be the name of God almost as often as *Yahweh* is.[368] The name is associated with His position as King, God of Israel, Redeemer, and Creator.[369] So, who is this LORD of hosts?

My King (King)
Heb.: *Malki (Melekh)*
(Ps. 84:3; Jer. 46:18; 48:15; 51:57)

LORD God of hosts
Heb.: *Yahweh 'Elohei tseva'ot*
(Amos 3:13; 4:13)

"**Lord Almighty**" is the usual New Testament equivalent of "Lord of hosts." English versions selected "Almighty" because of the way our Bible came to us. By about 200 BC, the Jews had produced a Greek Old Testament called the Septuagint.[370] In it, they often translated *Yahweh tseva'ot* with the words *Kyrios pantokratōr.* [371] *Pantokratōr* occurs in the Greek of Revelation 4:8 because that verse quotes Isaiah 6:3, along with Amos 3:13 and 4:13. In those verses, the Septuagint uses *pantokratōr. Pantokratōr* means "all power" and it correlates with the meaning of the Hebrew name. By choosing "Almighty," English translations emphasize that God is the supreme ruler. For the same reason, 2 Corinthians 6:18[372] and all nine occurrences in Revelation[373] substitute either "Lord Almighty" or "Lord God the Almighty" for the underlying *Yahweh tseva'ot* whom John saw enthroned (once, the KJV has "the **Lord God omnipotent** reigneth"[374]).

LORD God of hosts
Heb.: *Yahweh 'Elohei tseva'ot*
(Amos 3:13; 4:13)
Gk. OT: *Kyrios ho Theos ho pantokratōr*

Lord God the Almighty
Gk. NT: *Kyrios ho Theos ho pantokratōr*
(Rev 4:8)

Lord God omnipotent (KJV)
Latin NT: *Dei omnipotentis*
(Rev. 19:6)

I used to drive past a church called the Lord God of Sabaoth Lutheran Church. The name derives from another variation of **LORD of hosts**. In the New Testament, the similar name, **Lord of Sabaoth**, occurs twice.[375] Sabaoth is the anglicized form of the Hebrew word *tseva'ot* (hosts), which is usually translated as "Almighty."

"Almighty-ness . . . is not the power of doing anything or everything. Almighty-ness is the power to carry out the will of a Divine nature."[376] There are things God cannot do because they would be inconsistent with His nature: He will not lie. He cannot deny Himself. God cannot be tempted by

LORD of hosts
Heb.: *Yahweh tseva'ot*
(Isa. 1:9)
Gk. OT: *Kyrios Sabaōth*

Lord Almighty
(2 Cor. 6:18)
Heb.: *Yahweh tseva'ot*
Gk. OT and NT: *Kyrios pantokratōr*

Lord of Sabaoth
Gk. NT: *Kyrios Sabaōth*
(Rom. 9:29; James 5:4)

evil, and He tempts no one. He does not look at evil. He cannot cease existing or resign from being God. And He does not change.[377] But He is utterly capable of accomplishing His will.

Many names reflect God's supremacy. One verse calls Him the **Glory of Israel**; the Hebrew implies enduring pre-eminence and strength. God is the

Glory of Israel
Heb.: *Netsakh Yisra'el*
(1 Sam. 15:29)

mightiest warrior, the all-powerful King. When He fights his enemies, He wins; so it's good to be on His side.[378] Israel heard a three-fold description of God: "The LORD your God is the God of gods and the Lord of lords, the **great**, the **mighty**, and the **awesome God**" (Deut. 10:17–18). Those three adjectives occur often, in various combinations with God's names.[379]

The first adjective, *gadol* (great), refers to size and importance. It relates to *gadal* (to become great, or magnify), which urges us to increase God's honor. That is the essence of worship.[380]

God is the **great God**. The same name is another possible translation of *rav*, which elsewhere means "captain" or "chief." He is "the **LORD Most High** . . . a **great King over all the earth**." "The LORD is a **great God** and a **great King**." His name itself deserves to be described as great.[381]

The name **mighty God** is one name of the promised Child. That name and **Mighty One**, liken His strength to a warrior's strength. The Hebrew word *'addir*, which connotes superiority and majesty, also celebrates His might. So, He is called the **majestic One** and Psalm 8 exclaims, "O LORD, our Lord, how majestic is Your name in all the earth!"[382]

Another Hebrew word, *'avir*, features in the names **Mighty One of Jacob** and **Mighty One of Israel**. Even the primary name *'El* is rendered "Mighty One" in the composite name *'El 'Elohim Yahweh*, "the Mighty One, God, the LORD."[383] Two verses connect names that speak of might and majesty with *Yahweh tseva'ot*: Psalm 89:8 asks, "O **LORD God of hosts**, who is like You, O **mighty LORD**?" Jeremiah 32:18 says of the "**great and mighty God** . . . the **LORD of hosts** is His name."

New Testament writers echoed the same understanding of God's greatness, simply calling Him the **Power** or **Majestic Glory**.[384] Jesus, our High Priest, sits at the right hand of the **Majesty on high**, who is also called the **Majesty in the heavens**. Both

---

Great God
Heb.: *'El gadol*
(Ps. 95:3)
Heb.: *Ha'Elohim haggadol*
(Neh. 8:6)
Aram.: *'Elaha' rabba'*
(Ezra 5:8; Dan. 2:45)
Gk.: *Ho megas Theos*
(Titus 2:13)

Great King
Heb.: *Melekh gadol*
(Pss. 47:2; 95:3;
Mal. 1:14)

Mighty God
Heb.: *'El gibbor*
(Isa. 9:6; 10:21)

Great and mighty God
Heb.: *Ha'El haggadol haggibbor*
(Jer. 32:18)

Mighty One
Heb.: *Gibbor*
(Ps. 45:3)
Heb.: *'Addir*
(Isa. 10:34)
Gk.: *Ho dynatos*
(Luke 1:49)

Majestic One
Heb.: *'Addir*
(Isa. 33:21)

Mighty LORD
Heb.: *Khasin Yah*
(Ps. 89:8)

names might derive from another Hebrew expression for God, which is similar to *'El gadol*: "the Greatness in the heights."[385]

Paul called Christ the **power of God** and **wisdom of God**.[386] Coming full circle, **great God** describes Jesus.[387]

A Host of Hosts

The name *Yahweh tseva'ot* points beyond His inherent might to the hosts that He commands. So, who are the Lord's hosts? The Old Testament uses words like *tseva'ot* in contexts involving regimentation and dedication, such as temple service and war.[388] The term "hosts" can refer to all created things or to particular celestial bodies.[389] Telling of God's creative work, the prophets emphasized, "The **LORD God of hosts** is His name."[390] The term "hosts" can also refer to angels, like those who stunned the Bethlehem shepherds and who were on standby to rescue Jesus.[391] The Message Bible substitutes the wonderful title, "God of angel armies." All of God's hosts surround Him.[392] "Hosts of the LORD" sometimes denotes Israel.[393] As the **Commander of the host**, the Lord rules the armies of Israel, the world, and His own heavenly forces. All of these are potential "instruments of indignation" that are available to secure His victory.[394]

Power
Gk.: *Dynamis*
(Matt. 26:64)

Majesty on high
Gk.: *Megalōsynē en hypsēlois*
(Heb. 1:3)

Majesty in the heavens
Gk.: *Megalōsynē en tois ouranois*
(Heb. 8:1)

Commander of the host
Aram.: *Sar-hatsava'*
(Dan. 8:11)

What manifests as human, earthly warfare is often rooted in spiritual warfare. Our worst enemies are not flesh and blood; the key battles rage in heavenly places.[395] The LORD of hosts is sovereign over the idols, demons, and false gods of the world.[396] Consider what the LORD of hosts said to Zechariah: "Not by might nor by power, but by My spirit" (Zech. 4:6). Isaiah warned Israel not to trust horses or chariots but to look beyond the earthly to her true source of deliverance—the LORD of hosts.[397] Kay Arthur points out that *Yahweh tseva'ot* is "God's name for man's extremity." It occurs most frequently during periods of national distress.[398] Israel could rejoice that "the LORD of hosts is with us; the God of Jacob is our stronghold," because He ended wars aimed at destroying her.[399]

God isn't automatically on anyone's side, as Joshua's encounter with the mysterious "captain of the LORD's host" teaches us.[400]

Now it came about when Joshua was by Jericho, that he lifted up his eyes and looked, and behold, a man was standing opposite him with his sword drawn in his hand, and Joshua went to him and said to him, "Are you for us or for our adversaries?"

He said, "No; rather I indeed come now as captain of the host of the LORD."

And Joshua fell on his face to the earth, and bowed down, and said to him, "What has my lord to say to his servant?"

The captain of the LORD's host said to Joshua, "Remove your sandals from your feet, for the place where you are standing is holy." And Joshua did so. (Josh. 5:13–15)

The captain would not take sides. When it comes to allegiances, we are the ones who have to move—not God.

Game, Set, and Match

All of God's battles end in victory. He subdues His enemies and expands the number of His subjects. One day, even nations that previously warred against Jerusalem "will go up from year to year to worship the King, the LORD of hosts" (Zech. 14:16–17). Three biblical battles exemplify God's decisive victories.

The first battle happened shortly after Israel left Egypt. Hostile Amalekites attacked her from the rear:[401]

Moses said to Joshua, "Choose men for us and go out, fight against Amalek. Tomorrow I will station myself on the top of the hill with the staff of God in my hand."

Joshua did as Moses told him, and fought against Amalek; And Moses, Aaron, and Hur went up to the top of the hill. So it came about when Moses held his hand up, that Israel prevailed, and when he let his hand down, Amalek prevailed. But Moses' hands were heavy. Then they took a stone and put it under him, and he sat on it; and Aaron and Hur supported his hands, one on one side and one on the other. Thus his hands were steady until the sun set. So Joshua overwhelmed Amalek and his people with the edge of the sword. (Ex. 17:9–13)

The passage doesn't mention the LORD of hosts, but the principle is there—victory came as Israel looked to God for help. The lifting of Moses' staff of leadership was critical. When Moses raised his arms, the Israelites advanced; when he lowered them, Amalek prevailed. As Moses grew tired, Aaron and Hur propped up his arms and the staff. The staff symbolized God's power; the uplifted staff appealed to that power. Everyone was up in arms—Joshua with swords, Moses on the hill, and Amalek in surrender. The battle provides an example of teamwork producing victory. More importantly, it illustrates intercession—focused on God's resources to deliver His people. Israel's cheers and victory songs were boisterous after they won that battle.

To express his gratefulness, Moses built an altar and named it the LORD is my **banner**. Moses connected the altar with God's determination to eradicate the Amalekites.[402] Gideon's altar memorialized the peace of God; Moses' altar reminded Israel to pursue God's enemies. However, the book of Joshua, which records

The LORD is my banner
Jehovah nissi (KJV)
Heb.: *Yahweh nissi*
(Ex. 17:15)

Israel's conquest of the promised land of Canaan, doesn't mention any battles with Amalekites. They reappear later to harass Saul and David. Apparently, Joshua forgot the message of the altar; he left survivors. Anyhow, the name of the altar likened God to a banner, standard, rod, or flag, all of which are possible translations of the word *nes*. The Israelite warriors could rally behind God as if He were a modern flag leading their armored column to victory.

Today, the rallying point of our Christian lives is not our church, youth group, favorite band, or missionary work. Jesus alone deserves the highest place and all the cheers. We follow Him.

LORD of hosts—1   Amalek—0

Much later, David challenged Goliath "in the name of The LORD of hosts, the **God of the armies of Israel**." His battle was fought and won over the character and will of God. God came through for David and Israel; He vindicated His name.

God of the armies of Israel
Heb.: *'Elohei ma'arkhot Yisra'el*
(1 Sam. 17:45)

LORD of hosts—1   Goliath—0

Isaiah 37 tells how the Assyrian king Sennacherib besieged King Hezekiah and all of Jerusalem. Sennacherib mocked them, saying that they should not trust Egypt or God. He likened Israel's God to the other gods he had destroyed as he conquered large swaths of the Middle East. Hezekiah immediately enlisted Isaiah, hoping that the **living God** would rebuke Sennacherib (vv. 4, 17). In his prayer to the LORD of hosts, Isaiah presented this paraphrased challenge: "The gods of other nations failed them because they were not gods. Here's an opportunity to prove Yourself so that all of earth's kingdoms may know that You alone, LORD, are really God" (vv. 16–20). Then Isaiah delivered God's response. Sennacherib was arrogant and had blasphemed the **Holy One of Israel** (vv. 23, 29). Isaiah promised Hezekiah that "the zeal of the LORD of hosts" would deliver Israel and save a remnant (v. 32).

And He did. One angel and a family coup later, Sennacherib lost an army of 185,000, as well as his life and his empire (vv. 36–38).

LORD of hosts—1   Sennacherib—0

Crushing victories like the three examples excite us. It's great to be on the winning side of the LORD of hosts and moving up in the league, isn't it?

We can all think of areas in our lives in which we need God to break through so that His will is done. The more decisive the victory is, the better. When an Amalek harasses us, a Sennacherib besieges our families, or a Goliath torments us and taunts our relationship with God, let's lift our hands and cry out to our Banner, the LORD of hosts.

No Talent Spotting

We must not make the mistake of trying to buy God for our side. It seems that after every Super Bowl or Cup Final, a bidding war begins for the star players. God is not available for hire, and prayer is not a way to recruit God to our cause. Rather, prayer is conversation with God. Listening for His will is more important than asking Him to bless our agendas.

Israel made the mistake once, and they took a tumble in the league. Reflecting on a recent defeat at the hands of the Philistines, the army decided that having the LORD of hosts with them would guarantee future victory. In those days, the LORD of hosts was associated with the ark of the covenant, which was then kept in the town of Shiloh.[403] Ever since Moses had followed

God's blueprints and constructed the ark, God in all of His glory had dwelt between two cherubim over the ark. The ark stood in the tabernacle, among the people. After Israel was defeated, she wanted God to be even closer, right at the battlefront—her secret weapon to ensure victory. "Let us take to ourselves from Shiloh the ark of the covenant of the LORD, that it may come among us and deliver us from the power of our enemies." (1 Sam. 4:3)

Off marched Israel with a confident shout. The Philistines heard the noise, checked their intelligence reports, and realized that Israel was deploying the ark of the LORD. Unsure of the exact nature and number of the Israelite deity, they made a brave stand. Unexpectedly, they beat Israel severely and captured the ark. The glory of the God of Israel had departed.[404]

Good Question

After their earlier defeat, Israel asked an important question (1 Sam. 4:3): "Why has the LORD defeated us today before the Philistines?" It was a good question and the answer was worth waiting for. However, Israel didn't wait. Sadly, we often skip the question too. But, if we face repeated setbacks, defeats, or unfruitfulness, we should ask God whether something is affecting our relationship with Him.

The behavior of Israel's spiritual leaders explains her defeat. At the time, the elderly Eli served as High Priest. He had two sons, Hophni and Phinehas. They were the priests who were in charge of the day-to-day tabernacle services. Strangely, "they did not know the LORD" (1 Sam. 2:12). What a tragedy that those responsible for facilitating the relationship between the people and God did not know God. What a travesty that when they boiled the sacrifices they grabbed their biggest forks and fished the meaty chunks out of the cauldron for themselves. Also, "before they burned the fat, the priest's servant would come and say to the man who was sacrificing, 'Give the priest meat for roasting, as he will not take boiled meat from you, only raw'" (1 Sam. 2:15). This violated God's commands regarding sacrifices. They abused their position through manipulation and intimidation. To top it all, they slept with the serving women.[405] While Eli's sons "brought a curse on themselves," we're told that Eli "did not rebuke them" (1 Sam. 3:13). Eli allowed their behavior to continue; he acquiesced in the sins of his family.

Not surprisingly, God didn't have a lot to say to His people; "word from the LORD was rare in those days, visions were infrequent" (1 Sam. 3:1). Ark or no ark, God withheld the blessing of His presence because Israel knowingly fell short of the glory that He had intended for them.

We can also deduce the answer to the question from events subsequent to the Philistines capturing the ark. The Philistines took the ark to the temple of their idol, Dagon, in Ashdod. Dagon fell down in pieces and the people became diseased. Too hot to handle, they passed it on to Gath. Those folk also became sick. When Gath tried to pass the parcel to Ekron, that city rejected it and returned it to Israel on a cart pulled by two cows.[406]

Why was Israel defeated by Philistia? The answer is that the LORD of hosts will not associate with sin and idolatry. Israel had stepped out of His blessing. This is yet another application of the principle that we dealt with in the previous three chapters on His glory and His holiness. The blessings, protection, and victory of the LORD of hosts require more than superficial association with Him; we must establish a fundamental alignment between our lives and His.

Isaiah's glimpse into the throne room of "the King, the LORD of hosts" left him with a striking impression of God's holiness: "Holy, Holy, Holy, is the LORD of hosts."[407] Later, Isaiah linked several descriptive names of God while specifying that the LORD of hosts was His name. Evidently, holiness stood out. "Our **Redeemer**, the **LORD of hosts** is His name, the **Holy One of Israel**." (Isa. 47:4) "For your **husband** is your **Maker**, Whose name is the **LORD of hosts**; And your **Redeemer** is the **Holy One of Israel**, Who is called the **God of all the earth**." (Isa. 54:5)

Holiness is central to the character of the LORD of hosts; He does not mix with sin. When un-holiness approaches Him, it must be dealt with or a cry like Isaiah's will go up: "Woe is me, for I am ruined!" (Isa. 6:5).

When sin affects our relationships with God, He always has a solution. In Isaiah's case, an angel seared away his sin by touching his lips with a burning coal from the altar.[408] In our case, the sacrifice of Jesus, accepted by faith, cleanses all sin. Jesus took the heat of God's wrath.

John equated Jesus with the LORD of hosts when he stated that Isaiah saw Jesus' "glory, and he spoke of Him" (John 12:37–41). Jesus applied to Himself some of the words that the LORD of hosts had spoken to Isaiah.[409]

Wrapped up in more of Isaiah's words is an awesome choice: "It is the LORD of hosts whom you should regard as holy. And He shall be your fear, and He shall be your dread. Then He shall become a sanctuary; But to both the houses of Israel, a stone to strike and a rock to stumble over" (Isa. 8:13–14). Peter applied those words to Jesus—"a **living stone** . . . a **stone of stumbling** and a **rock of offense**" (1 Peter 2:4–8). We can take our pick. Through faith, we can choose Jesus as our sole source of holiness and receive sanctuary, or we can take offense, trip over Him, and lose everything.

Living stone
Gk.: *Lithos zaō*
(1 Pet. 2:4–5)

Stone of stumbling
Gk.: *Lithos proskommatos*
(Rom. 9:33;
1 Pet. 2:8)

Rock of offense
Gk.: *Petra skandalou*
(Rom. 9:33;
1 Pet. 2:8)

His Banner over Me is Love

Victory in spiritual warfare and in everyday life depends on God's presence; He cannot bless us if we live in sin. Our lives must come into alignment with His holy will and ways. He doesn't need to change; we do. Now, I am not suggesting that every struggle is a sign of sin. Nor am I saying that once we are in the Lord's will, everything gets easy. Life doesn't work that way. But, in general, good fruit grows when we align ourselves with Him and march under His banner.

So, how do we come under the Lord's banner? We hand the Holy Spirit the keys to our life and welcome His continuous scrutiny. We ask Him to convict us of sin so that we can repent and enjoy the "shower" of Jesus' cleansing blood. Sometimes we feel uncomfortable with the topic of conviction. But think about the last shower you took. Were you trembling at the knees and whimpering, "I am so dirty! When I turn on the water, I will dissolve and gurgle down the drain"? I doubt that anyone has that phobia.

So, why fear conviction? Perhaps we muddle it with condemnation. Satan loves to condemn. Condemnation is often broad and sweeping, directed toward no words or actions in particular, and it offers no remedy. It blankets us with negative thoughts about ourselves.

Conviction is much easier to deal with. The Holy Spirit puts His finger right on our sinful behavior or words, exposes the issue, and points us toward solutions. Conviction is a loving nudge into the presence of God.

King David experienced conviction after he committed adultery with Bathsheba. One evening, he looked down on his neighbor's property and spied her bathing.[410] He chose to entertain temptation. Being the king, no one questioned his orders when he arranged for her to visit him. Later, when he heard that she was pregnant, he scrambled to cover his tracks. Uriah, her husband, refused to dishonor his battlefront buddies by enjoying the pleasures of a night off with his wife. So David made one last desperate move. He ordered Uriah to the front lines, where he would meet with certain death. Then David married Bathsheba.

In David's case, conviction came via Nathan the prophet, but the Holy Spirit does the real work. Nathan cleverly told a sad tale of exploitation and injustice. A rich man stole a poor man's lamb because he was too stingy to cook his own lamb for a guest. The tale hooked David and he became indignant. At that point, Nathan delivered the convicting words, "You are the man" (2 Sam. 12:1–7). Right away, David admitted his sin and experienced God's forgiveness.

One part of aligning our lives with God is to have our sin dealt with; another aspect is changed behavior. Jesus is not just our Savior; He is our Lord. The word "lord" occurs in military, legal, and regal contexts, and it is associated with respect, headship, ownership, and mastery. It is no accident that "lord" forms part of so many of God's names. If we properly accept His Lordship, we submit to His standards, His will, and His ways. We give Him ownership and veto power over our decisions.

If I Be Lifted Up

Before we close this chapter, the name that Moses coined after Israel defeated Amalek, *Yahweh nissi*, the **LORD my banner**, needs to be examined. So, let's trace the use of the root word *nes*.

In Numbers 21, as a punishment for Israel's grumbling, fiery serpents from God bit and killed many people. God told Moses to attach a bronze serpent to a standard (*nes*) so that anyone who looked at it would be saved from the venom.[411] "*Nes*" indicates a conspicuous signal pole.

Isaiah prophesied of a day when a **shoot** and **branch** from the family of Jesse (King David's father) would arise. The **root of Jesse** would be filled with the Spirit of Yahweh and provide a signal (*nes*) and a lifted standard (*nes*) for the nations.[412]

The name *Yahweh nissi* finds fulfillment in Jesus, who spoke of His own body hanging on the cross in the same terms that Moses had used.[413] Lifted up from the earth, with nails puncturing His outstretched hands, He won a resounding victory over every force in the universe.[414] Our belief in Him detoxifies us from sin's venom and it frees us to live eternal lives. He is our shining banner against the enemy, sin, and sickness.

Retrieving the Ark of God's Presence

But what happened to the ark? We left it after it had "burnt" the iniquitous Philistines prompting them to dispatch it to the border of Israel. Israel experienced a troubled forty-year period after they chose Saul as king and he let them down. Then God selected David, a man after His own heart, to replace Saul.[415] "David became greater and greater, for the **LORD God of hosts** was with him." (2 Sam. 5:10) Meanwhile, the ark remained where the Philistine cows had taken it.

When David became king, he tried to retrieve "the ark of God which is called by the Name, the very name of the LORD of hosts who is enthroned above the cherubim" (2 Sam. 6:2). He made the first attempt with scant consideration of God's shipping instructions. The priests tried to move it on a cart. It wobbled and almost fell, but a well-meaning priest's son, called Uzzah, reached out to steady it. God struck him dead. David's paralyzing despair is evident: "How can the ark of the LORD come to me?" (2 Sam. 6:9–12) In fear, David stored the ark at the home of Obed-edom. But, when David saw how God had blessed Obed-edom, his longing for God's presence in His capital revived. David overcame his fear and studied the correct way for the ark to travel. "How can the ark return?" became a practical question.

It's another good question for us all. The question implies, "How can I know God's presence?" But it also implies, "How does God want me to live so that I am in harmony with His ways?" David learned from his failure, and willingly accepted God's lordship. When David aligned himself with God's method, he succeeded. The dancing began. Banners waved and the people rejoiced, as if to say, "God, we're glad to have You back." Then David "blessed the people in the name of the LORD of hosts" (2 Sam. 6:18). Israel began a seventy-year winning streak, growing greater than she ever would. The nation had turned from sin and aligned with God's ways, so the presence of the LORD of hosts returned to them.

Israel loved being on God's side, and she loved having David as her king. David's reign became the standard by which she would assess her future kings. Good kings promoted the temple, ruled justly over the people, and defeated Israel's enemies, just as David had felled Goliath and subdued other enemies. Unfortunately, many kings were evil. During their reigns, prophets pointed to David as a great king and promised an even greater ruler who would win a more decisive victory over a more sinister enemy.

Chapter 7

INTERSECTING WITH
THE EVERLASTING GOD

Those who are in Christ share with Him all the riches of limitless time and endless years. God never hurries. There are no deadlines against which He must work. Only to know this, is to quiet our spirits and relax our nerves. For those out of Christ, time is a devouring beast; before the sons of the new creation time crouches and purrs and licks their hands.
　　　　—**A.W. Tozer**, *The Knowledge of the Holy*[416]

"John! You remember how to read this, right?"

"Yes, Dad."

On previous trips, I had been able to follow our position on the map, so I felt confident. Besides, as a young teenager, I liked any excuse to sit in the front seat of the car.

"I know the way to within three miles of the freeway, John, but you must navigate after that."

That summer, long before GPS, our family traveled two hundred miles to the Brecon Beacons of South Wales. As we drove along an unfamiliar secondary road, I learned a valuable lesson.

"Where's our turning for the freeway, John?" asked my father impatiently.

"Hang on. I'm just finding where we are on the map," I replied, hiding my surprise.

Then three things happened simultaneously. Just as I found our location and my father recognized a landmark, we roared past the on-ramp. There was the freeway, only a few hundred yards away from us. It was running almost parallel to us, but we were not on it. Turnarounds were uncommon on narrow country roads, so a family tiff ensued, centered on my lack of navigational skills. I resolved that in future I would study the route before we set out and keep a close eye on the map during the journey.

Most of us have overshot an intended junction, so we know what this frustration feels like. Imagine what missing one of the major "intersections" of life would be like. Moses' reflections in Psalm 90 teach us about navigating through life.[417] He concluded with a cry for a meaningful life. It's a cry we can all relate to—a desire to accomplish something permanent. "Let the favor of the Lord our God be upon us; and confirm for us the work of our hands." (v. 17)

The key to the pathway of permanence lie in Moses' prayer for wisdom: "So teach us to number our days, that we may present to You a heart of wisdom."[418] The wise navigator checks the chart before departing. Along the way, he stays attentive to the route. Understanding the brevity of our lives in the span of eternity helps us take life seriously enough to produce an enduring legacy. So, let's view life from the perspective of eternity and learn more about the eternal God.

Beyond Space and Time

The vastness of space boggles our minds and gives us a little taste of eternity. Consider a few facts: Our own galaxy, the Milky Way, is one hundred thousand light years across; a ray of light from a peripheral star takes one hundred thousand years to reach a star on the opposite side of it. The universe contains billions of galaxies, and it is many orders of magnitude larger than our galaxy. It would take ninety-three billion years for light to cross the observable universe. We can convert that into speeds that humans have experienced. The space shuttle, cruising at 17,300 mph, would take about 3.9 million years to cross the Milky Way and 3,600,000 billion years to traverse the universe. In terms of eternity, it would merely be a blink of a beginning, yet it dwarfs our life spans. Compared with God, even those astounding lengths of time shrink. Moses said, "from everlasting ['*ad*] to everlasting ['*olam*], You are God" (Ps. 90:2).

As humans, we shudder as we struggle to comprehend eternity. In contrast with the eternal God, we seem insignificant and futile. Life is fragile too. Isaiah 40:6–8 likens humankind to dry vegetation.

All flesh is grass, and all its loveliness is like the flower of the field. The grass withers, the flower fades, when the breath of the LORD blows upon it; surely the people are grass. The grass withers, the flower fades, but the word of our God stands forever ['olam].

Scripture reminds anyone with an over-inflated ego,

He it is who reduces rulers to nothing, who makes the judges of the earth meaningless. Scarcely have they been planted, scarcely have they been sown, scarcely has their stock taken root in the earth, but He merely blows on them, and they wither, and the storm carries them away like stubble. (Isa. 40:23–24)

And

Man is like a mere breath; His days are like a passing shadow. (Ps. 144:4)[419]

Isaiah 40 contains hope too. God leads out the stars, calls them by name, and never misplaces them.[420] Despite our apparent smallness, God cares about us too. He goes on to ask:

*Why do you say, O Jacob, and assert, O Israel, 'My way is hidden from the LORD, and the justice due me escapes the notice of my God'? Do you not know? Have you not heard? The **Everlasting God**, the LORD, the Creator of the ends of the earth does not become weary or tired. His understanding is inscrutable. He gives strength to the weary, and to him who lacks might He increases power.* (Isa. 40:27–29)

The **God of my life** cares about our brief life spans. He is our **Redeemer from of old**.

Abraham called on *'El 'olam*, the **Everlasting God**, after covenanting with Abimelech at Beersheba (Gen. 21:32–33). He wanted the agreement to last. *'Olam* (and *'ad*, which is almost synonymous) indicates perpetuity looking either backward or forward. It can simply mean the farthest boundary of our understanding or experience. In the days of Abraham and Isaiah, the frontier lay no farther than where nomads with their portable tents and flocks could travel or where imaginations wandered when stirred by traders' tales from distant lands. Today, we can probe the edges of the universe, but God is bigger than the reach of travelogues and telescopes.

Everlasting God
Heb.: *'El 'olam*
(Gen. 21:33)
Heb.: *'Elohei 'olam*
(Isa. 40:28)

God of my life
Heb.: *'El khayyai*
(Ps. 42:8)

Living God
Heb.: *'Elohim khayyim*
(Jer. 10:10)
Aram.: *'Elaha' khayya'*
(Dan. 6:20, 26)

Our Redeemer from of old
Heb.: *Go'alenu me'olam*
(Isa. 63:16)

Naming the Eternal One

Psalm 135:13 notes, "Your name, O LORD, is everlasting." How appropriate that He "who is and who was and who is to come" (Rev. 1:4, 8; see also Rev. 4:8; 11:17; 16:5) is called the **beginning and end**, the **Alpha and Omega**, the **first and the last**.

Perhaps the Jewish equivalent of "alpha and omega" was also used to describe Him. Rabbis found it significant that the two alphabetical bookends (*alef* and *taw*), along with the middle letter of the Hebrew alphabet, spell the word *'emet* (*alef, mem, taw*)—"truth." They said, "The seal of the Holy One, blessed be He, is *'emet*."[421] God is the beginning, middle, and end of all things.

Beginning and end
Gk.: *Hē archē kai to telos*
(Rev. 21:6; 22:13)

Alpha and Omega
Gk.: *To alpha kai to ōmega*
(Rev. 1:8; 21:6; 22:13)

The First and the last
Heb.: *Hari'shon weha'akharon*
(Isa. 41:4; 44:6; 48:12)
Gk.: *Ho prōtos kai ho eschatos*
(Rev. 1:17; 2:8; 22:13)

In a world accustomed to a diluted and relative, nine-carat truth, it is reassuring that God's twenty-four-carat truth has eternal substance. God and genuine truth outlast time itself.[422] *'Emet* denotes reliability and faithfulness, and the **God of truth** is another of His names.[423] Jeremiah 10:10 connects *'Elohim 'emet* with *'olam*: "The LORD is the **true God**; He is the **living God** and the **everlasting King**."

Eternal Spirit
Gk.: *Pneuma aiōnios*
(Heb. 9:14)

Everlasting Rock
Rock eternal (NIV)
Rock of ages (Darby)
Heb.: *Tsur 'olamim*
(Isa. 26:4)

Everlasting King
Heb.: *Melekh 'olam*
(Jer. 10:10)

King of the nations
King of the ages (NIV, 1984)
King of saints (KJV)
Gk.: *Ho basileus tōn ethnōn*
(Rev. 15:3)

Him who lives forever
Heb.: *Khei ha'olam*
(Dan. 12:7)
Aram.: *Khai 'alma'*
(Dan. 4:34)
Gk.: *Zaō eis tous aiōnas tōn aiōnōn*
(Rev. 4:9–10; 10:6; 15:7)

High and exalted one
Heb.: *Ram wenissa*
(Isa. 57:15)

King eternal
Gk.: *Basileus tōn aiōnōn*
(1 Tim. 1:17)

Incorruptible God
Gk.: *Ho aphthartos Theos*
(Rom. 1:23)

Invisible God
Gk.: *Ho Theos ho aoratos*
(Col. 1:15)

Eternal God
Ancient God (MSG)
Heb.: *'Elohei qedem*
(Deut. 33:27)
Gk.: *Ho aiōnios Theos*
(Rom. 16:26)

Several other names express His everlasting nature: He is the **eternal Spirit**, an **everlasting Rock**.[424] He rules as **King of the ages** (NIV, 1984). Isaiah says that He is the "**high and exalted One** who lives forever [*shokhen 'ad*]." Daniel refers to "**Him who lives forever**."

All of those descriptions tie in with 1 Timothy 1:17, which tells of the **King eternal** (literally "King of ages") who is immortal and invisible (*aoratos*). The word "immortal" (*aphthartos*) stresses His incorruptible or undecaying nature. Paul called Him both the **incorruptible God** and the **invisible God**, and he mentioned His invisible nature and eternal power.[425]

A similar name is *'Elohei qedem*, the **Eternal God**. He "is a dwelling place, and underneath are the everlasting [*'olam*] arms." *Qedem* means "former" or "east," and it can also refer to idyllic situations like Eden, the exodus, or David's reign. "**Eternal God**" reappears in Romans 16:26, but the Greek word that is used there indicates an order of existence beyond time.

Daniel recounted his vision of the **Ancient of Days**. In Revelation, John described the Son of Man like Him.[426] So once again, the names culminate in Jesus. He is one with the Everlasting God, the Creator of time, matter, and life. He claimed to be the way, the truth, and the life.[427] In John 1:1–2, we read, "In the beginning was **the Word** and the Word was with God and the Word was God. He was in the beginning with God."[428] Jesus is life's source, the **Beginning of the creation of God**, **Him who has been from the beginning**, who has "neither beginning of days nor end of life" (Heb. 7:3). **The root and the descendant of David** infinitely preceded and outlasts King David and every created thing. Jesus is "the same yesterday and today and forever" (Heb. 13:8) because He is God and shares God's eternal nature.

As we survey the Bible, we discover that everything about God is everlasting: His truth, covenants, and lovingkindness (which boils down to faithfulness to His covenants).[429] His wisdom, righteousness, and salvation last forever.[430] Of His kingdom, His reign, and His throne Psalm 93:1–2 says, "The LORD reigns, He is clothed with majesty; The LORD has clothed and girded Himself with strength; Indeed, the world is firmly established, it will not be moved. Your throne is established from of old; You are from everlasting."[431] Another psalm on His greatness and lovingkindness concludes, "For such is God, Our God forever and ever ['olam wa'ed]; He will guide us until death" (Ps. 48:14).[432] Many of God's promises and laws are everlasting.[433] "The word of our God stands forever." (Isa. 40:8) Not surprisingly, we find that His purpose is eternal too.[434] In Isaiah 43:13, God states, "Even from eternity I am He . . . I act and who can reverse it?"

Ancient of Days
Aram.: *'Attiq yomin*
(Dan. 7:9, 13, 22)

Root and descendant of David
Gk.: *Hē rhiza kai to genos Dauid*
(Rev. 22:16)

Beginning of the creation of God
Gk.: *Hē archē tēs ktiseōs tou Theou*
(Rev. 3:14)

Him who has been from the beginning
Gk.: *Ho ēn ap' archēs*
(1 John 2:13–14)

Just a Moment

Let's compare God's eternal purposes to an infinite freeway. One British motorway, the M6, crosses the Midlands and continues north to Scotland. It is about two hundred miles long. In British traffic, it seems to take forever to travel along this road. Now, imagine a freeway with no beginning and no end, infinitely longer than the breadth of the universe. Such are God's purposes and nothing can ever interrupt His will. Nothing can divert or delay His purposes, or prevent them from being accomplished.

Isaiah 46:9–10 confirms this fact:

I am God, and there is no other; I am God, and there is no one like Me, declaring the end from the beginning and from ancient times things which have not been done, saying, "My purpose will be established and I will accomplish all My good pleasure."[435]

Again, the One who extends beyond conceptions and conclusions says, *"I am He, I am the **first**, I am also the **last"*** (Isa. 48:12). And Moses said, *"Before the mountains were born or You gave birth to the earth and the world, even from everlasting to everlasting, You are God"* (Ps. 90:2).

Another psalmist declared that God began history and one day will sum it up:

> *Of old You founded the earth, and the heavens are the work of Your hands. Even they will perish, but You endure; and all of them will wear out like a garment; like clothing You will change them and they will be changed. But You are the same, and Your years will not come to an end* (Ps. 102:25–27).

When God placed the sliver of human history into His eternal purposes, it was as though He drew a line across the endless freeway using an artist's ultra-fine pen. The thin line represents the period that He allotted for humans to inhabit the earth.

The Everlasting God created humans with numerous abilities, including the ability to make clocks. Humans have a highly developed sense of time. For some, this sense borders on being an obsession. Living inside the line, history seems long and slow. From the perspective of eternity, though, history is as long as a fine line is wide. "A thousand years in Your sight are like yesterday when it passes by, or as a watch in the night." (Ps. 90:4)

Time travels slowly enough for us to enjoy it and be tempted to waste it, but fast enough for us to notice it slipping away. Stop for a while to reflect on that thought and on Moses' other words. "As for the days of our life, they contain seventy years, or if due to strength, eighty years, yet their pride is but labor and sorrow; for soon it is gone and we fly away." (Ps. 90:10) It is sobering to realize that from God's perspective our lives last just a brief moment. Again, the cry rises: "Let the favor of the Lord our God be upon us; and confirm for us the work of our hands" (Ps. 90:17).

Time Travelers

The cry originates because God has "set eternity [*'olam*] in their heart" (Eccl. 3:11). A. W. Tozer comments on that verse,

I think He here sets forth both the glory and misery of man. To be made for eternity and forced to dwell in time is for mankind a tragedy of huge proportions. All within us cries for life and permanence and everything around us reminds us of mortality and change. Yet, that God has made us of the stuff of eternity is both a glory and a prophecy. A glory yet to be realized and a prophecy yet to be fulfilled.[436]

The everlasting God had a reason for placing each of us into eternity for our brief slice of time.

Where does the misery of mortality originate? The fact is, God created people from the stuff of eternity. He made us in His image, and He gave us the desire and potential to live forever. Bodies, thoughts, and feelings tend to preoccupy us. We forget the enduring part—the soul.[437]

Think of it in the following way. In space, there is no natural oxygen, and temperatures are three digits below freezing.[438] Astronauts must wear a space suit to survive in that inhospitable environment. God supplied the human soul with a body as its earth-suit. By breathing life into Adam's fleshy earth-suit, God introduced Adam to time and time to Adam. He wired the suit with a nervous system and set his soul in motion for eternity. Some earth-suits have added substance around the waist. Others have hair that grows thin or joints that stiffen and ache with age, but bodies are standard issue for life in the physical world. When the body dies, the soul immediately enters its eternal state. Either it meets God there and finds eternal satisfaction in Him or it is lost forever. Our destiny depends on whether we find the right path in this world.

When Adam fell, he started humans down a dead-end road, away from the freeway of God's purposes. The lost soul longs to return to God. The world around us urges our outer selves to derive identity and labels from it, but an inner voice whispers that our eternal destiny lies in allowing God to transform us.

So, how can the glory that Tozer points to be realized? As the eternal God scanned the pathways of time, He foresaw Adam's tragic choice. So, His plans included a way to reestablish a purposeful relationship with Him. The everlasting God sent His Son into human history on a mission. Increasing the magnification on the ultra-fine line of history reveals a microscopic focal point. God's endless freeway focuses on one moment.

The Focal Point

Along the M6 near Birmingham, there is a complex intersection called Spaghetti Junction. The name caught on because, seen from above, the intersection looks like a mishap in an Italian restaurant. Several roads join the M6 at this junction.

The focal point of God's purposes functions like a freeway intersection; it enables people to return to Him. The prophecies concerning Jesus were advanced road signs that were floodlit in the light of eternity: "One will go forth for Me to be **ruler** in Israel. His goings forth are from long ago, from the days of eternity" (Mic. 5:2). The **child** who fulfilled those words has as part of His name, **Eternal Father**, a name used to describe the perpetual head of a family or a clan. Jesus physically dwelt with us for three decades, but He is one with the Eternal Father, who outlives history.

Eternal Father
Everlasting Father
(KJV, NIV)
Heb.: *'Avi'ad*
(Isa. 9:6)

When God promised eternal life long ages ago, He had Jesus in mind.[439] Even before time began, Jesus' life was aimed at one event. Historically, His death took just a few hours and it happened in a land miles away from most of us. Nevertheless, Jesus' death at Calvary is the focal point of time that provides all of us with an on-ramp to eternity.

U Turns Permitted

Our lives may feel like the high street in rush hour, but that doesn't mean we are in a good place. Without God, every road is a spiritual side road.[440] Before life sweeps us along too far, we must realize that in God's eyes our lives are as brief as the sprouting and withering of grass. The wisdom that Moses requested includes the same perspective. It helps us take our span of "three score years and ten" seriously. From the perspective of eternity, our lives come and go in the blink of an eye, but we have enough time to turn from our errant ways to God's way.

God's on-ramp includes a tollgate. When we intersect with God's way by putting our faith in Christ, we arrive at the toll and we are waved through. Jesus has already paid the fee. If anyone misses the junction, then when their physical eyes close in death, their spiritual eyes will suddenly register where they are. The soul will gaze with sadness as it sails past its last opportunity to rejoin its Maker.

The day when God says, "Return, O children of men" (Ps. 90:3) will come for everyone. Our bodies wither and fade like a sunburned meadow; our genesis reverses, and our flesh turns to dust.[441] We revert to our most basic form: a soul that exists forever after.[442] Daniel 12:2 presents two options: everlasting life or everlasting contempt. Unless a person puts faith in Jesus during his or her life, the soul will make its passage through the eons, painfully aware of its missed destiny and always separated from God. The Bible presents hell's separation in strong language, describing it as eternal fire, punishment, judgment, and destruction.[443]

Jesus gave us the good news: "He who hears my word, and believes Him who sent Me, has eternal life, and does not come into judgment, but has passed out of death into life" (John 5:24). Later on, He said, "This is eternal life, that they may know You, the only true God, and Jesus Christ whom You have sent" (John 17:3). When we merge with the freeway of eternity, we gain new purpose and destiny. Isaiah says that includes an everlasting name better than sons and daughters.[444] So, check your map. Make sure that you are traveling on God's "everlasting way"[445] and that you have accepted your prepaid toll ticket.

Directing Traffic

Even believers sometimes amplify the inner whispers of eternity into cries of frustration at life's futility. Christian hearts long for significance. "Confirm for us the work of our hands," (v. 17) pleaded Moses, and so cries your heart and mine. Our eternal life is ensured, but we want to receive God's favor in our earthly lives. We want our handiwork to be of lasting value. Can we do anything to ensure that we bear enduring fruit?

Spaghetti Junction is synonymous with complexity. On one journey that I took with my parents as a teenager, we made a detour to avoid the junction. For many people, life is one big Spaghetti Junction; the confusion obscures God's on-ramp. Thankfully, road signs exist in His creation, in Scripture, and in the examples of other believers' lives. All the signs point to God. What could be more significant than for us to help people navigate the map of eternity and read God's signs? God will favor and confirm that kind of work.

Chapter 8

THE GODS
MUST BE CRAZY

The gods become gods by being believed in, and faith in the one God and the one Lord creates freedom no longer to recognize these powers.
—Hans Conzelmann

King Nebuchadnezzar was one of the greatest kings of Babylonia. He dominated vast swaths of the Middle East, subduing many kingdoms including Tyre, Egypt, and Judah. He subjected perhaps a million people to his brutal reign. His successes earned him the title "King of kings," which signifies supremacy.[446]

The title **King of kings** best fits God, as do the similar titles **Lord of lords**, **God of gods**, and **Prince of princes**. God reigns supreme over all other rulers, human and spiritual. Eventually, even Nebuchadnezzar acknowledged Him as "God of gods and a **Lord of kings**." Nebuchadnezzar built a temporary empire; the **God of heaven** rules an eternal kingdom that crushes all other kingdoms, including Babylon and its successors.[447]

All those titles reflect an eternal truth about God's dominion. However, His dominion is still unfolding in the everyday world. We await the fullness of God's kingdom. Ours is an age of two opposing kingdoms that are engaged in conflict on earth and in the heavens. Jesus proclaimed that the kingdom was at hand, and he commissioned His followers to spread the good news of the kingdom.[448] Satan is hell-bent on retaining his territory for as long as he can. He has agents in his service to help him.

Daniel 8 foretells a king who will oppose the **Prince of princes**. Daniel 11 describes a "despicable person" (he is also called a king) who struggles against God's people.[449] "Then . . . he will exalt and magnify himself above every god and will speak monstrous things against the God of gods" (Dan. 11:36).

The book of Revelation describes the endgame. A beast and ten kings will wage war against the **Lamb**, but "the Lamb will overcome them, because He is **Lord of lords** and **King of kings**" (Rev. 17:12–14). Then Jesus, the **Heir of all things**, will receive His appointed possessions, and the kingdom of this world will become the kingdom of our Lord and of His Christ.[450]

For believers, who are caught in the present struggle, a verse in Daniel provides another excellent reason to explore the names of God.

God of gods
Heb.: *'Elohei ha'elohim*
(Deut. 10:17;
Ps. 136:2)
Aram.: *'El 'elim*
(Dan. 11:36)
'Elah 'elahin
(Dan. 2:47)

King of kings
Heb.: *Melekh melakhim*
(Not used of God)
Gk.: *Basileus basileōn*
(1 Tim. 6:15;
Rev. 17:14; 19:16)

Lord of lords
Heb.: *'Adonei ha'adonim*
(Deut. 10:17;
Ps. 136:3)
Gk.: *Kyrios kyriōn*
(1 Tim. 6:15;
Rev. 17:14; 19:16)

Prince of princes
Aram.: *Sar-sarim*
(Dan. 8:25)

Lord of kings
Aram.: *Mare malkhin*
(Dan. 2:47)

Heir of all things
Gk.: *Klēronomos pantōn*
(Heb. 1:2)

The people who know their God will display strength and take action. (Dan. 11:32)

Let's begin by contrasting God's character and kingdom with Satan's. God is supreme, so what power do other spiritual beings have? In what sense is He the God of gods? And who or what are these gods anyway?

Gangbusters

I once attended a PowerPoint presentation by a police gang-response officer. He described the activities of local street gangs. Gangs have characteristic dress customs. Some gang members wear oversized pants as an identifying mark; others cut their hair in distinctive patterns. They even develop their own dialects. They fund their activities by dealing drugs and committing robberies. Rather confusingly, some gangs adopt more than one name. Gangs are territorial like dogs. They tag their hoods (neighborhoods) with property-defiling graffiti and they fight like dogs when lines are crossed. Occasionally, bullets fly and members die. Developing a behavior profile is the first step to ending their lawless reign of terror.

The Bible lists various evil beings, including gods, idols, and demons. Collectively, they function rather like a street gang. All of them unite around the common purpose of opposing God and His people. Some members appear harmless or eccentric; others are obviously malicious. In fact, all of them are evil. Their terrorizing activities span the inhabited globe. What's their aim? To consolidate a form of government that opposes the kingdom of God, and to draw people away from worshiping the true God.

Daniel 11 gives one snapshot into the activity of this gang and its agents. A little detective work into their activities and backgrounds, which are described throughout the Bible, produces a dossier on the gang of the gods. Let's review the entries:

Entry 1: The Gang of Three—Demons, Idols, and Gods

One dictionary defines a god as: "A being, regarded as possessing superhuman or supernatural qualities or powers, and made an object of worship or propitiation."[451]

In Chapter 5, we noted that propitiation involves offering a sacrifice to appease an offended party. In the Sinai wilderness, Israel chose the wrong party. She sinned by making sacrifices to three connected entities: demons, idols, and gods.

> *They made Him jealous with strange [gods];[452] with abominations they provoked Him to anger. They sacrificed to demons who were not God, to gods whom they have not known, new [gods] who came lately, whom your fathers did not dread. You neglected the **Rock** who begot you, and forgot the **God who gave you birth**. . . . They have made Me jealous with what is not God; they have provoked Me to anger with their idols.* (Deut. 32:16–18, 21)

God's jealous reaction is one subject discussed in the next chapter. For now, notice that the gang of three "is not God."[453] The gang members are clearly different in nature.

The biblical files imply that the word "god" is nothing more than a palatable name that people have been duped into giving to a demonic being. Paul stated that idolatry is empty in relation to God. He also exposed the underlying demonic forces that wait to pounce on those who dabble in idolatry.[454] Canaanite idols were referred to as demons.[455] So, the gang that we call gods and associate with idols is really a gang of demonic spirits that is under Satan's leadership. There is only one true God with supreme power.

The three are as deceptive and dangerous as spiritual icebergs. The idol is the most visible. It lies somewhere between an unusual souvenir from a tropical trip and a weird bust in a temple niche. Idols may appear harmless, but behind them are false gods who are demons ruled by the devil.

Entry 2: Idols

Idols themselves exist on four levels:

1. The least sinister idols are merely alluring objects. They attract attention but there is no spiritual entity behind them. Nebuchadnezzar's colossal image fits this category, as do most religious statues and vacation souvenirs. The worshipping of creatures rather than the Creator fits here too.[456]

2. Paul said that even greed amounts to idolatry.[457] Greed boils down to an intense desire to acquire something to satisfy the idol of self. These are the gods Donald Miller calls "our tiny invisible friends."[458] Paul wrote of certain "enemies of the cross," whose "god is their appetite."[459] Food or anything of which we say, "I must have more," can be an idol. Now, a craving for chocolate seems harmless enough, and in normal proportions it is, but urges that control us have strayed beyond healthy boundaries. Crossing those boundaries is what it means to succumb to temptation.[460] Such desires can open doors to demonic forces. Excessive desires behave like the worst idols, they hinder our relationships with God. They distract us or slime us with guilt and shame. After saying that the Old Testament warns Christians not to slip into evil cravings, immorality, and grumbling, Paul told us to flee from idolatry.[461]

Jesus pointed out, "No one can serve two masters [*kyrioi* also means "lords"] . . . You cannot serve God and mammon." To make His point, Jesus personified riches as Mammon. No one can serve God and riches. Under Satan's influence, wealth craves power and fights to be lord and master of our hearts.[462]

But isn't it our hearts that crave the idols? Donald Miller, with his typical honesty, exposes us all when he recounts his realization that, "I desired false gods because Jesus wouldn't jump through my hoops."[463] If it offers a fast track to selfish goals, it is probably a smooth-talking usurper.

3. Paul said that even "elemental things . . . which by nature are no gods" can enslave us.[464] He was referring to legalism and to false religions.

4. There are several Hebrew words for idols, some of which are rooted in the idea of fashioning an image, hence the term "graven images."[465] Idols of this type, like temple busts, are deliberately made to represent sinister spiritual beings. People who want to appease a god need something visible to sacrifice to. Scripture exposes the lie, pointing out that God "is to be feared above all gods. For all the gods of the peoples are idols."[466] Moses urged Israel to avoid "the graven images of their gods" (Deut. 7:25–26).

The Assyrian, Rabshakeh,[467] sent messengers with propaganda to the besieged king, Hezekiah, claiming that Assyria had destroyed other nations because their gods had failed to protect them. Hezekiah pointed to the biblical truth: "They were not gods but the work of men's hands, wood and stone" (Isa. 37:8–20).

Unaware of how different Yahweh is, Israel's enemies treated Him like their own gods. "They spoke of the **God of Jerusalem** as of the gods of the peoples of the earth, the work of men's hands" (2 Chron. 32:19).[468]

The most important god of the Canaanites, among whom Israel lived, was the storm god, Hadad. Usually he went by "*Ba'al*," which can mean "lord," "master," or even "husband." The term signifies ownership, slavery, and bondage. The Canaanites believed the seasons mirrored Ba'al's life, death, and resurrection cycle. In their worldview, he was responsible for rain, fertility, and harvest. After King Ahab married the Canaanite princess, Jezebel of Sidon, Ba'al worshipers infested Israel. Canaanite cult worship included gross sexual and sacrificial rites.[469] One mild example is the masochistic bloodletting that Ba'al's prophets performed during their showdown with Elijah.[470]

Various cities and regions had localized versions of Ba'al.[471] The Bible mentions Ba'al zebub, the god of Ekron.[472] That name literally means, "fly-lord," but it might be a slur on the Canaanite title Ba'al zebul (lord prince). When Pharisees accused Jesus of casting out demons "by <u>Beelzebul</u> the <u>ruler of the demons</u>," Ba'al zebub was probably in mind.[473] In His answer, Jesus equated Beelzebul with Satan. There may also be a disparaging word association with *zevel* (manure). Academic considerations aside, I vote for the flies. With their appetites for decay and death, they represent Satan's character best.

Less than two centuries before Jesus, Antiochus IV Epiphanes[474] introduced the worship of Greek gods to Israel, thus precipitating the Maccabean rebellion. The chief god, Zeus, had the Hebrew title *Ba'al shamayim* (Ba'al of heaven); privately, Jews dubbed Zeus, *shiqquts shomem*, the "abomination of desolation."[475] Jesus foresaw at least one abominable situation in the temple,[476] a day when Rome would cast off restraint and her legions would parade their ensigns inside Jerusalem.[477] The Bible associates desecration by pagans or by the Jews with judgment and desolation.

Isaiah mocks idols when he paints a picture of a man taking wood from a specially grown tree and using the pieces for different things. He burns half of the wood in the fire to roast meat, get warm, and be satisfied. With the other half, he makes a graven image and worships it. He prays to the idol: "Deliver me, for you are my god" (Isa. 44:14–20).[478]

Wouldn't it be nice if God forgave our sins and spared us the consequences? Isaiah's next words are surprising. God lets our idolatry affect us; He smears blindness over the eyes and hearts of those who worship idols in any form. In their deception, they think their wellbeing depends on such futile things. So, we should ask God to show us anything that we think we can't live without or anything that we desire more of. He can penetrate the deepest deception. Be warned, no kind of idolater has an inheritance in the Kingdom of God;[479] idolaters run with the wrong gang.

Entry 3: The Godfather and His Godchildren

The Satan of horror stories is scary enough to frighten us in the dark yet entertaining enough to laugh at with friends the next day. Movies give him a deep, gravelly voice and a syrupy deceptiveness. One passage in the book of Revelation exposes the real Satan using four names: "The great dragon was thrown down, the serpent of old [ancient serpent, NIV] who is called the devil and Satan, who deceives the whole world; he was thrown down to the earth, and his angels were thrown down with him" (Rev. 12:9).

Genesis 3:15 says the serpent has "seed," or offspring. They are presumably those angels and anyone else who chooses to follow him. Jesus also mentioned the devil's angels.[480] The fact that Satan is called the ruler of this world and the prince of the power of the air[481] confirms that he has subordinates, such as the princes of Persia and Greece.[482] Paul catalogued various entities: principalities, rulers, powers, authorities, world forces of this darkness, and spiritual forces of wickedness.[483] Evidently, the gang is a hierarchy that Satan rules.

Satan's angels are fallen angels that have their own identities. The angel of the abyss, or underworld, is named *Abaddōn* (from the Hebrew for "destruction") and *Apollyōn* (Greek for "destroyer").[484] It is unclear whether demons are angels, or beings that are subordinate to fallen angels.[485] Satan's hierarchy extends beyond the realm of spiritual beings. False christs and false prophets also serve Satan.[486] Daniel exposed the "despicable person" who was possessed by a demon and intent on promoting himself to the status of God. The hierarchy can infiltrate human organizations and individuals whenever they align themselves with Satan's purposes and make him their puppet-master, just as the kingdoms that opposed God and His people in the book of Daniel did.[487]

Revelation mentions two sinister beasts. Neither one is Satan, but both are his evil delegates. The dragon (Satan) gives to the first beast "his power and his throne and great authority." The beast's seven heads bear blasphemous names.[488] A second beast, which is subordinate to the first one, appears. It entices people to worship the first beast and its image, and to receive the mark of the beast's name or the mysterious "number of his name."[489]

The numerical value of the beast's name is an intriguing puzzle. The number given in early manuscripts is either 666 or 616. This could well be a simple code for a Roman emperor who had a reputation for persecuting Christians.[490] The number is connected with worshiping the beast and his image. One day, bearing either his name or number will be a prerequisite for conducting business. The number is that of a man, so receiving it as a mark is quite a comedown. Our true destiny includes the "seal of the living God" and a new name from Him.[491]

The phrase "was, and *is not*, and is about to come up" mocks the beast. It contrasts with the sweeping, timeless sovereignty of the eternal God, who "was and who *is* and who is to come."[492] The beast returns to destruction (*apoleia*); God comes to reign.

Another delegate in Satan's evil scheme is the Antichrist, who opposes Christ and is a dark alternative to Him. The Antichrist denies the Father and the Son, and Jesus' incarnation. John called him a deceiver and a liar. He mentioned many human antichrists who were once part of the church.[493] One overarching agent, the spirit of Antichrist, controls them all.

In his letter to the Thessalonians, Paul says that Jesus will not return until a falling away occurs. Then, "the man of lawlessness [sin, KJV] is revealed, the son of destruction,[494] who opposes and exalts himself above every so-called god or object of worship, so that he takes his seat in the temple of God, displaying himself as being God" (2 Thess. 2:3–4). The "lawless one" aligns with Satan.[495] The description fits a human agent under Satan's influence.

The beast, Antichrist, and son of destruction[496] all appear as different manifestations of the same subordinate of Satan.

Entry 4: Origins of a Tyrant

Two biblical passages tell of defeated kings of Babylon and Tyre.[497] On one level, the passages speak of historical human leaders; on another level, they personify evil. Because some verses suggest a fallen heavenly being, many interpreters think these passages provide glimpses into Satan's origin.

At first acquaintance, Satan seems like a nice fellow. In Eden, he was an anointed cherub (a kind of angel), but we soon realize his niceness is a front for the worst form of self-seeking. This "star of the morning, son of the dawn" (Isa. 14:12) took pride in his own beauty.[498] He became ambitious. He wanted to shoot for the top and become like the **Most High**.[499] So began his principal activity: redirecting worship from God to himself.

The phrase "star of the morning," or "day star," is a translation of a Hebrew word that means, "shining one," and it probably began as a reference to the planet Venus. The name Lucifer is one Latin word for the devil.[500] Jesus, the true **bright morning star**, outshines him by far.

Satan the archangel became God's archenemy. God evicted him from heaven and threw him down to the world's streets, where he and his gang now operate. Their objective is to keep people from worshiping the true God, and they will use any effective strategy. It doesn't have to be as blatant as Satanism or idol worship. They might tempt our runaway appetites and lure unsuspecting hearts deeper into bondage, but simple distractions using otherwise harmless trivia will do. Whatever the sales pitch is, lives that venture too close to icebergs risk becoming shipwrecked.

Entry 5: Character Profile

"Satan" is Hebrew for "adversary."[501] Greek translators used the word *diabolos*, which relates to the word "devil" and means "slanderer" or "accuser." Satan accused Joshua the High Priest and he continues to be the accuser of our brethren.[502]

Peter described the adversary as a roaring, devouring lion.[503] The book of Job presents the more typical legal picture of Satan approaching God to accuse Job of sin.[504] What a contrast with our **Advocate**. He was the atoning sacrifice for our sins and He justifies us before God.[505]

Temptation is another one of Satan's businesses. He successfully tempted David to count Israel. As the tempter, Satan confronted Jesus in the wilderness.[506] In Eden, he deceptively tempted Eve to "be like God, knowing good and evil" (Gen. 3:5, 13). Instead of receiving 20/20 vision, humans grew spiritual cataracts, our moral insight became smeared, and we fell from God's intended glory. The god of this world continues to blind eyes to the "light of the gospel of the glory of Christ, who is the image of God" (2 Cor. 4:3–4).

Satan works through delegated evil spirits in two main areas: physical and mental. Unclean spirits, spirits of infirmity, and dumb spirits can afflict the health of people. Spirits of divination, error, and false prophecy attack the truth.[507] Paul indicated that demonic false doctrines could capture people.[508] Strongholds of the mind are still pivotal in spiritual warfare.[509]

Shortly before New Testament times, various names were given to Satan. Paul used one of them: Belial.[510] The Dead Sea Scrolls portray Belial as an angel of darkness who opposes light.[511] The name means "worthless."[512]

The three accounts of the parable of the sower show that Satan, the devil, and the evil one are equivalent names.[513] Evil manifests itself in many ways, especially through stealing, killing, and destroying.[514] Satan is the enemy of the kingdom, and his subordinates include "sons" who share his characteristics.[515] He is "a liar and the father of lies." The devil sinned and was a murderer from the beginning.[516] The fear of death made us slaves, but Jesus delivered us and destroyed the devil's work. Jesus rendered "powerless him who had the power of death, that is, the devil" (Heb. 2:14–15). Although the devil has not yet been annihilated, like a wasted wasp, his stinger—the sting of death—is gone.

The evil one uses various wiles, scheming tricks, and snares.[517] He "disguises himself as an angel of light" (2 Cor. 11:14). For his first ploy, the tempter took the form of a <u>serpent</u>; it will also be one of his final manifestations.[518] Another form is the red <u>dragon</u> mentioned earlier.[519] The Greek word *drakōn* derives from *derkomai*, which means "to look at in a bewitching way." He loves to hold our attention like a coiled cobra preparing to strike.

All this talk about idols and demons might seem spooky or weird, but Satan uses fear and skepticism to make us reluctant to fight; those emotions are part of his deceptive strategy. Either he tempts us to shrug him off as an outdated superstition, or he convinces us that his power is greater than it actually is. In fact, God has charged the gang's ringleader and found him guilty. God allows Satan to remain on earth, where he awaits his final extradition and punishment. Remember what the Bible says about the gang's weapons: they have little real power. Jesus confiscated Satan's bullets when He conquered death. Now, deception and lies are the frightening, noisy blanks he fires to intimidate us. They are ineffective unless we listen to them. When we know God through Jesus, it is easier to recognize Satan's lies for what they are.

Entry 6: Satan's Hood

If Satan's power is broken, why do bad things happen to good people? Why does evil still pervade the world?

Evil exists wherever God's kingly rule is unwelcome. Sin is the choice to live outside of God's will. Habitual sin traps people in Satan's domain.[520] During the time of Israel's judges, God punished years of national disobedience by allowing foreign gods to ensnare Israel. Slavery to Satan was a form of punishment.[521]

Whenever we favor one of the enemy's values, we reject the opposite value in God's kingdom. For instance, hoarding is contrary to generosity, and bitterness blocks forgiveness. By the choices that they make, whole communities—not just individuals—remain under the dominion of darkness. When evil individuals or nations club together, it is hard to believe that Satan has "*little* real power." The darkness is palpable.

Paul contrasted life in the two kingdoms. Prior to knowing God, the Galatians were "slaves to those which by nature are no gods" (Gal. 4:8). When we welcome His reign, our liberty includes adoption into His family.[522] Later, Paul pointed to one of many challenges that believers face. Religious legalism tries to displace enthusiastic obedience that is based on a loving relationship with the King.[523] It's true that "the devil does some of his best work behind stained glass."[524]

The Bible's instructions for dealing with the enemy sound almost too simple: "Submit therefore to God. Resist the devil and he will flee from you" (James 4:7). In short, welcome the King's rule and turn from evil. Jesus' commission to extend the kingdom worldwide included His authority over Satan's gang.[525] In Jesus' name, believers cast out demons. Humble lives and prayers are effective against the gang. The word of God is our sword. God provides us with armor and weapons for the fight, but the list in Ephesians 6:10–17 begins, "in the strength of His might." The Lord deals with the enemy.[526]

Knowing God

Like it or not, all followers of Christ are involved in the battle as either imprisoned victims or active combatants. We are supposed to drive back Satan's defeated gang and free his captives. Having familiarized ourselves with the enemy's profile in the gang's dossier, we are ready to be briefed about our present task: a mopping up operation.

Daniel sounded the rallying cry: "The people who know their God will display strength and take action" (Dan. 11:32). The confidence to resist comes from knowing clearly that God surpasses Satan in every way. So, let's contrast their respective characteristics in four broad areas: creativity, power, love, and life.

God Gives Life

God's ability to create from nothing is unique.[527] He breathed life into all creation, including the invisible power structures that Satan loves to infiltrate: thrones, dominions, rulers, and authorities.[528] God gives life, freedom, and fulfillment; Satan destroys lives.[529]

God Laughs at His Enemies

Paul spoke of the **Blessed God**, which could literally mean "the happy God." He has every reason to be happy. Nothing intimidates Him: "He who sits in the heavens laughs" at his enemies.[530] Relative to God, Satan's power is tiny and temporary. "What god is there in heaven or on earth who can do such works and mighty acts as Yours?" (Deut. 3:24) Numerous names reflect God's superiority. He is "the blessed and only **Sovereign**, the **King of kings** and **Lord of lords**."

God holds Satan on a leash. Satan does only what God allows him to do. In contrast to idols, "our God is in the heavens; He does whatever He pleases" (Pss. 115:3–4; 135:5–6).

When Jesus encountered demons, they recognized Him as the Holy One. When He asked what their names were, they clammed up. We can imagine them smirking and chuckling when they said, "We know

Blessed God
Gk.: *Ho makarios Theos*
(1 Tim. 1:11)

Sovereign
Gk.: *Dynastēs*
(1 Tim. 6:15)

Head over all
Heb.: *Lekhol lero'sh*
(1 Chron. 29:11)

Head over all things
Gk.: *Hē kephalē hyper panta*
(Eph. 1:21–22)

Head over all rule and authority
Gk.: *Hē kephalē pasēs archēs kai exousias*
(Col. 2:10)

Most High
Heb.: *'Elyon*
(Num. 24:16;
Deut. 32:8)
Gk. NT: *Hypsistos*
(Luke 1:35, 76)

**God Most High/
Most High God**
Heb.: *'El 'elyon*
(Gen. 14:18–22;
Ps. 78:35)
Heb.: *'Elohim 'elyon*
(Pss. 57:2; 78: 56)
Aram.: *'Elaha' 'illaya'*
(Dan. 3:26; 4:2;
5:18, 21)
Gk. NT: *Ho Theos
tou hypsistou*
(Acts 16:17; Heb. 7:1)

LORD Most High
Heb.: *Yahweh 'elyon*
(Pss. 7:17; 47:2; 97:9)

Highest One
Aram.: *'Elyonin*
(Dan. 7:18, 22,
25, 27)
Gk. OT: *Hypsistos*

your name, you don't have ours. So we're in control."
But Jesus did not need their names. He easily expelled
them.[531] Jesus is "far above all rule and authority and
power and dominion, and every name that is named,
not only in this age but also in the one to come" (Eph.
1:21). He is the **Head over all rule and authority**.

Oaths often invoke an authority figure. To swear
by someone is to appeal to them as a witness of the
truth of a statement; the highest available authority
is usually chosen. David and Jonathan swore loyalty
to each other in God's name.[532] When God made
His promise to Abraham, "since He could swear by
no one greater, He swore by Himself" (Heb. 6:13).
He used expressions like, "as I live" (Num. 14:21). No
authority is higher than God.

Many of God's names are rooted in His authority
and power. Psalm 97:9 says: "For You are the **LORD
Most High** over all the earth; You are exalted far
above all gods." The main word in these names, *'elyon*,
sometimes indicates the highest or uppermost of pairs
or collections.[533] *'Elyon*, the name and status that Satan
coveted, is translated "**Most High**."[534]

'El 'elyon, **God Most High**, expresses the "exaltedness and overwhelming
majesty of God . . . the supremacy of the deity."[535] This name first occurs
when Abram meets Melchizedek, priest of God Most High. Melchizedek
blessed Abram in the name of "God Most High, **Possessor of heaven and
earth**." A few verses later, Abram clearly ascribed

God above
Heb.: *'El mimma'al*
(Job 31:28)

God on high
Heb.: *'Elohei marom*
(Mic. 6:6)

**Possessor of heaven
and earth**
Heb.: *Qoneh shamayim
wa'arets*
(Gen. 14:19)

that   name
to Yahweh.[536]

Appropriately, God is called the **Highest One**.
The New Testament uses the equivalent Greek word
(likewise, the Septuagint uses *hypsistos*) of the **Most
High**.[537] Uniquely, Job spoke of **God above**. Another
name, **God on high**, tells of His exaltation.

The Old Testament is replete with examples in
which *'elyon* is used alongside other important names

for God, such as *Yahweh*, *'El*, and *Shaddai*.[538] The psalmists cried for Israel's enemies to know that Yahweh was Most High over all the earth.[539]

Deuteronomy 10:17 says, "For the LORD your God is the **God of gods** and the **Lord of lords**." The passage proceeds to summarize His nature: "the great [*gadol*], the mighty [*gibbor*] and the awesome God who does not show partiality, nor take a bribe."[540] "The LORD is a **great God** and a **great King** [*melekh gadol*] above all gods" (Ps. 95:3). Moses sang of God's name: "I proclaim the name of the LORD; Ascribe greatness [*godel*] to our God" (Deut. 32:3).

Notice that the despicable person of Daniel 11 perpetuates Satan's struggle to be the greatest and "magnify himself above every god" (Dan. 11:36). Yet the Bible reminds us repeatedly (as in 2 Sam. 7:22), "For this reason You are great, O Lord GOD; for there is none like You, and there is no God besides You."

God's name is itself great.[541] The psalmist exclaimed, "How majestic is Your name in all the earth" (Ps. 8:1, 9). He used another word (*'addir*), which speaks of His superiority and elsewhere is rendered "**Mighty One**"[542] and "**Majestic One**."[543] His name is so great that nations will seek Him.[544]

Similarly, God is *'El gibbor*, **Mighty God**. Used of men, *gibbor* indicates heroism.[545] Then, of course, He is the **Almighty**.[546] "Who is like You among the gods, O LORD?" asked Moses.[547] "What god is great like our God?" demanded the author of Psalm 77:13. "He is to be feared above all gods," makes an apt reply to both of these questions.[548] Relative to Him, the gods are powerless, so Paul labeled them, "those which by nature are no gods" (Gal. 4:8; 1 Cor. 8:4). Instead, Paul called Jesus the **Great God**.[549] The gods, and Satan their ringleader, must be crazy to oppose Him.

The Bible records their craziness—the repeated collisions of demonic gods with the true God. Each time, God exposed their impotence. Consider the following selection:

God performed signs through Moses: plague upon plague, ten times. The Egyptian gods, at the bidding of magicians and priests, could not repeat Moses' miracles. God defeated them—with His finger.[550]

In Judges 6, Gideon smashed the altar of Ba'al, and the townsfolk wanted to lynch him. His father, Joash, spoke a truth that had the potential to demolish the strongholds in their minds. He said, "If he [Ba'al] is a god, let him contend for himself." He implied, "If he were real he could fight for himself. I won't defend a weak, upstart Canaanite god that we shouldn't be worshiping anyway!"[551]

When the Philistines stole the ark of God and put it in the temple of Dagon, their idol kept toppling over. The Philistines decided, "We don't want this God or His ark here; He disrupts our practices." They couldn't endure God.[552]

Elijah contested against the prophets of Ba'al on Mount Carmel. He drenched the altar, the firewood, and the offering with water. While Ba'al's prophets failed to ignite dry sticks, the true and living God sent fire from Heaven to consume Elijah's soggy sacrifice.[553]

Often Israel's enemies would mock her, saying, "The gods of the nations fell before our armies; your God will too." They considered the God of Israel to be just another species of national god.[554] Once, the Aramaeans mistook Him for a limited mountain god who had no authority in the valleys.[555]

Repeatedly, the **God of Israel** triumphed and laughed. He proved He was more than just another god with a small *g*. He is the God of the "small *g* gods."

God Loves

The fact that God has Satan on a leash does not make Him the source of evil. Evil comes from Satan, often as a consequence of human choices. Of course, God could instantly eradicate all evil, but that would override our free will and turn us into robots. Free will is the only context for a true love relationship.

The book of Job indicates that God allowed Satan a limited scope to afflict Job, but God did not initiate Job's suffering.[556] He cares so much about pain that He even collects our tears.[557] God used Job's suffering to do the most loving thing: deepen his relationship with Him. He will do that for us too.

Paul called Him, "the **God of love and peace**." God desires relationships with His covenant people.[558] "God, being rich in mercy, because of His great love" for us, exercised His might and delivered us from the prince of the power of the air. His act of mercy and grace freed us from Satan's bondage and from "the lusts of our flesh." As a result, we have privileged relationships with God. We are seated with Him in the heavenly places in Christ Jesus (Eph. 2:1–10).

God of love and peace
Gk.: *Ho Theos tēs agapēs kai eirēnēs*
(2 Cor. 13:11)

God Lives

Satan is not a rival "god of evil," He is a created being. God declares, "I am the **first** and I am the **last**, and there is no god besides me" (Isa. 44:6). On their own, idols are lifeless objects of worship.[559] The threats that the Assyrian captain, Rabshakeh, delivered were empty.[560] Assyria and other nations worshiped inanimate idols with just one spiritual entity behind them: Satan.

"The LORD is the **true God**; He is the **living God** [*Elohim khayyim*] and the **everlasting King**. At His wrath the earth quakes, and the nations cannot endure His indignation" (Jer. 10:10; see also Ps. 42:2; 1 Thess. 1:9). He is the **Only God**; by contrast, Satan was made.

Only God
Gk.: *Monos Theos*
(1 Tim 1:17)
The only true God
Gk.: *Ho monos alēthinos Theos*
(John 17:3)

Crossroads

The four areas in which the God of gods surpasses other gods converge in Jesus. Jesus came as a child, "in the strength of the LORD, in the majesty of the name of the LORD His God . . . At that time He will be great to the ends of the earth" (Mic. 5:4). The child **Immanuel** (God with us) bears the name of the **Mighty God**.[561] Jesus dwelt in flesh as the **Living and true God**. He gave us life and defined it relationally: "This is eternal life, that they may know You, the **only true God** and Jesus Christ" (John 17:3; see also John 17:6; 1 Thess. 1:9; 1 John 5:20). As one with the loving God, Jesus died to deliver His people from their bondage to sin.

Living and True God
Gk.: *Ho Theos zōntos kai alēthinos*
(1 Thess. 1:9)

Peter's confession of Jesus as "the Christ, the **Son of the living God**," (Matt. 16:13–17) happened close to a significant town: Caesarea-Philippi. Historically, the town was strategic because it guarded a major highway. A tributary of the River Jordan flows from a cavern at the base of a 130-foot cliff. Locals call the town Banias, which is derived from its Greek name, Paneas. The ruined temple to the Greek god Pan still attracts tourists. There is also evidence of much earlier Ba'al worship at this site. In Jesus' day, Banias had temples to Pan, and a white marble temple that King Herod the Great had dedicated to Caesar Augustus. Herod's narcissistic son Philip celebrated himself by renaming the town Caesarea-Philippi.

What a religious center![562] It was as if Jesus had arranged for the world's gods to witness Peter's proclamation of truth in their own backyard. He also declared, "The gates of Hades shall not prevail against" the church (Matt. 16:18, NKJV).

During His life, Jesus fought a running street battle with Satan and his gang. An early salvo came on the Mount of Temptation. Satan appealed to

Jesus' normal desires, trying to debase them. Jesus, of course, stood firmly. Later, praying in Gethsemane, Jesus resisted Satan, choosing instead to submit to God's reign. Finally, on the cross and in the grave, He seemed to laugh in the face of His archenemy. He served His arrest warrant, and rendered him powerless by conquering death.[563] His resurrection proved the supremacy of the God of gods. One day, God will receive universal reverence. "The LORD will be king over all the earth; in that day the LORD will be the only one and His name the only one" (Zech. 14:9). The gods were crazy to target Jesus; the crucifixion hastened their end. Through His crucifixion, Jesus became our Champion.

The Making of a Champion

In fairytales, the most intimidating character is the giant. Once upon a time, the reward for slaying one was half a kingdom and a princess' hand in marriage. In Israel's real-life history, the bounty on Goliath's head was less.[564] The prize fell short of half of Saul's small kingdom, and there was no mention of life, health, and disability insurance—important benefits for anyone tackling a giant. No one volunteered—that is, until David, the songwriting shepherd, arrived at the battlefront.

Goliath was no fairytale character; he stood nine feet and nine inches tall. Reflect on his body mass index, or BMI (the weight at which a person of a certain height feels his best—his optimum build). Goliath was off the charts; he felt his best at almost five hundred pounds. Larger than life, Goliath was the Philistines' champion (*gibbor*) mighty man.[565] *Gibbor* is the first of three Hebrew terms for a champion, two of which occur in the story of David and Goliath.

Champion (only the first is used of God) Heb.: *Rav* (*normally "chief" or "captain"*) (Isa. 19:19–20) *Gibbor* (strong man) (1 Sam. 17:51) *'Ish-habbenayim* (man between) (1 Sam. 17:4, 23)

In David's day, armies often fought battles by proxy. One strongman stepped forward from each army and they dueled in the no man's land between the front lines. In 1 Samuel 17:4, 23, the phrase *'ish habbenayim* (champion) literally means "a man between." When the Philistines faced Israel, they sent Goliath as their representative. Israel had to produce a suitable opponent or she would lose by default. Only unsuited David had the courage to step forward, represent God and Israel, and become their champion by defeating Goliath. He did so without special weapons or armor but with confidence in the **living God**[566] and "in the name of the LORD of hosts" (1 Sam. 17:45). His confidence came from years of trusting God. By his example, David pointed ahead to Daniel's statement: "The people who know their God will display strength and take action" (Dan. 11:32).

A third Hebrew word can mean "champion." *Rav* applied to captains or chiefs like Rabshakeh. They became commanders because as heroic fighters they had survived brutal battles. Jesus is the champion "gang-response officer" in the operation against Satan. In a prophetic insight into life in Egyptian gang territory, Isaiah called Him **Champion**.

> *In that day there will be an altar to the LORD in the midst of the land of Egypt, and a pillar to the LORD near its border. It will become a sign and a witness to the **LORD of hosts** in the land of Egypt; for they will cry to the LORD because of oppressors, and He will send them a **Savior** and a **Champion**, and He will deliver them.* (Isa. 19:19–20)

Jesus, the Mighty One, bound and plundered the <u>strong man</u> and delivered us from his power. God's Son filled the role of the Champion in the battle; He had the deepest knowledge of and the greatest confidence in His Father.

The progression of the battle is laid out in Daniel 11:36 and elsewhere. At history's end, the Antichrist (Daniel's despicable person who serves Satan) will cast down other gods and their idols and set himself up

> **Lamb**
> Gk.: *To arnion*
> (Rev. 12:10–11;
> 17:14)

as the "true God."[567] When that day dawns, Jesus will return and expose the Antichrist. Satan will be thrown down because of the blood of the **Lamb**.[568] The book of Revelation provides a glimpse of that final victory. "The **Lamb** will overcome them, because He is **Lord of lords** and **King of kings**" (Rev. 17:14). "On His robe and on His thigh He has a name written—King of kings and Lord of lords" (Rev. 19:16).

Special Weapons and Tactics

Meanwhile, the spiritual battle continues. Satan's lying propaganda still pollutes the streets of our cities and our hearts. With his gang graffiti, he attempts to deface the alleys of our minds. He and his gang try to deceive, oppress, afflict, depress, and possess people. So, how do we counter Satan's deceptive intimidation?

Imagine the threats of a nasty bully back at school: "Just wait until school's out." The best defense is to enlist a friend who is two years older and six inches taller than the bully. It helps if the bully has encountered your friend before and doesn't want to meet the person again.

John's first letter tells us how to deal with the spiritual bully. It includes our key point; we should be a people who know God.[569] "We know that the Son of God has come, and has given us understanding so that we may know Him who is true" (1 John 5:20). Knowing we are on His side helps us to be strong, take action, and stand firmly against the enemy.

Jesus is better than a school buddy. Not only do we know Him, but also "we are in Him who is true, in His Son Jesus Christ." Our lives are in Jesus—the safest place possible.[570] When bad things happen to us, we gain a different perspective on them. Satan attacks our mortal lives, but our spiritual lives are eternally secure in God.[571] When Christ and His kingdom are our highest priorities, Satan is hard-pressed to get a grip on us.[572]

The God of gods is poised to eliminate Satan and His gang. In the meantime, He is able to protect everyone who remains in Him. Paul gave us simple instructions: "Be wise in what is good and innocent in what is evil. The **God of Peace** will soon crush Satan under your feet" (Rom. 16:19–20). So, avoid Satan's distractions, don't be intimidated, and "guard yourselves from idols."

Chapter 9

MINISTRY TO
FOREIGN AFFAIRS

If the Father of Spirits, as revealed by Jesus Christ, is not known in these interior wilds of America, they nevertheless often resound the praises of the unknown, invisible great Spirit, as he is denominated by the [Native Americans]. *They are not ignorant of the immortality of their souls, and speak of some future delicious island or country where departed spirits rest.*
—**G. P. Disosway**, *Christian Advocate and Journal*, 1833

Meeting a Muslim in Johnnie Mango's

I never expected to meet a mullah in my favorite restaurant.

Johnnie Mango's was around the corner from my office on St. Croix. It served local dishes for lunch and had a small coffee bar. I was reading my Bible over a mocha when a Palestinian acquaintance entered with an older man wearing a white beard and a distinctive head covering called a *shamuugh*. He introduced his friend as a visiting mullah from Kuwait. Spotting my Bible on the table, the mullah asked about it. Our conversation was an opportunity for me to present him with two items of faith that distinguish Christianity from Islam. The mullah rejected the ideas that God has a Son and that His Son could suffer and die.

Islam is one of the "holiday stamp religions." In the USA, there is a postage stamp for the Eid, as well as for Christmas, Chanukah, and Kwanzaa. Apart from Judaism, Islam is the most similar religion to Christianity. Muslims believe in one, all-powerful creator. Their scriptures, the Qur'an,[573] claim the Holy Spirit's inspiration, and they exhort people to believe in Allah and to live to honor him—rather like the Bible's purpose. The Qur'an even includes statements about resurrection.[574]

Read the *surahs* (chapters) of the Qur'an, and you will find names for Allah that sound similar to God's names. We noted earlier that *Allah* relates to *'Elah*, which is one of God's names. Each surah commences with the best-known names, "*Bismillahi ar-rahmani, ar-rahimi . . .* (In the name of Allah, the Most Gracious, the Ever Merciful . . .)."[575]

Here's a sample of the biblical-sounding names of Allah in the Qur'an:

"Lord" is a common title, as in: Lord of the heavens and the earth, Lord of the mighty throne, and Lord of honor.[576]

Allah is called the All-wise and All-knowing, the All-seeing, and the All-aware.[577]

Other names are: Great Protector, Protecting Friend, Excellent Helper, Grantor of Protection, Acceptor of Repentance, Lord of Beneficence, Omnipotent Sovereign, Master of glory and honor, the Holy, Most High, and Controller of all the affairs of mankind.[578]

Muslims would agree that the similarities between Islam and Christianity don't include the central tenets of the Christian faith. To begin with, Muslims receive the Qur'an as a standard of truth surpassing all other messages, including the Torah (Moses' Law books) and *Injeel* (Gospels). Judgment will fall on anyone who attributes a son to Allah.[579] Muslims deny Jesus' sonship, along with His death and resurrection.[580] Jesus is just another of Allah's messengers, who they believe pointed to Muhammad.[581]

The Supreme Being

People who convert to Christianity from a Muslim background find it appropriate to use the name *Allah* for God, though some call Him "*Allah al Ab*" (God the Father) to highlight an important distinction. There are historical precedents: Paul was quite comfortable applying the Greek names *theos* and *kyrios* to Yahweh.[582] Also, fourth-century Gothic converts embraced the fuller revelation of God's nature that Ulfilas had taught them. His teaching enhanced the meaning of the ancient Gothic word *god*.

More recently, a team of missionaries in Mongolia experienced a church-planting breakthrough in 1994 when they began calling God *Borkhan* instead of *Yurtuntseen Ezen*. *Borkhan* is the traditional Mongolian word for "god." To Mongols, *Yurtuntseen Ezen* (Lord of the Universe) sounded like science fiction. However, the first twentieth-century Bible translator chose *Yurtuntseen Ezen* to avoid any association with Buddhism. Tibetan Buddhists had used *Borkhan* for centuries. As soon as the team said *Borkhan* for "God," conversions increased.[583]

Many cultures have some concept of a Supreme Being who made the universe; many still need to recognize the biblical God as that Being. However, the name that a culture uses for God is not as critical as the characteristics that He is thought to possess. Don Richardson makes this observation:

> There is nothing innately sacred about any particular . . . name for the Almighty. He can have ten thousand aliases, if need be, in ten thousand languages. It is impossible to talk about an uncreated Creator without meaning HIM. Anyone capable of protesting that "some of His attributes are missing" is responsible to fill them in! Any theological vacuum surrounding any culture's concept of God is not an obstacle to the gospel—it's an opportunity![584]

Such opportunities no longer require passports; the world's religions have come to homes and schools near us all. In a barbeque chat with friends from church, comparative religion is a safe topic. Introduce the subject at a coffee table on a multi-ethnic city street, and it can become inflammatory. So, we need to know where the differences lie and how to bridge gaps in understanding.

Colliding Claims

Jesus Himself made a provocative statement that can be interpreted as elitist and exclusive. He claimed, "I am **the way**, and **the truth**, and **the life**; no one comes to the **Father**, but through Me" (John 14:6). His words ensured that the Christian message cannot be swallowed without careful chewing. His claim has a counterpart in the Muslim chant: "There is no god but Allah." Like it or not, the claims collide.

So, how should we relate to those who worship the gods of the world and of our modern society? The bulk of this chapter explores what happened in a city full of idols in a real-life market square confrontation between Paul and worshippers of other gods (Acts 17:16–34). Along the way, we'll learn how to pray for missionaries, befriend people from other religions, and discover more of the depths of God's love as we study one of His more awkward names.

Paul is an example of a man who knew his God, displayed strength, and took action. His life always burned with passion. Initially, he had a passion to persecute the church.[585] After receiving a blinding revelation from God, he directed his zeal to serve God and build up the church. Paul didn't just know about God intellectually from the Old Testament. He had an everyday relationship with God. His passion for God overflowed and changed the world.

Paul's presentation to the philosophers of Athens came from his deep knowledge of God. Paul drew the Athenians' attention to certain attributes of God—attributes that are encapsulated in more names of God. Let's review Paul's encounter using the four broad characteristics of God that were introduced in the last chapter as a framework: creativity, power, love, and life.

Life-Giver (Acts 17:22–29)

The Athenians had an "unknown god" whose identity Paul proclaimed. He began by presenting "God who made the world and all things in it . . ." (v. 24) as the life-giving Creator.

The name **Creator** occurs just twice in the New Testament, though the book of Hebrews also calls God the architect and builder of the heavenly city.[586] But several Old Testament names that identify God as the Maker underlie Paul's statement to the Athenians.

Creator
Gk.: *Ho ktisas*
(Rom. 1:25)
Gk.: *Ho ktistēs*
(1 Peter 4:19)

Amos the prophet waxed lyrical in one description of God. It's too big a mouthful to be an actual name, but he used nouns from three important Hebrew roots, *yatsar*, *bara'*, and *'asah*: "He who forms [*yotser*] mountains and creates [*bore*] the wind . . . He who makes [*'oseh*] dawn into darkness" (Amos 4:13; 9:5–6). The Message Bible neatly paraphrases the first two: "Mountain-Shaper!

Wind-Maker!" Later, Amos called God, "He who made ['*oseh*] the Pleiades and Orion" (Amos 5:8; Job 9:9). Not only did God bring the physical universe into being, but He also made people.

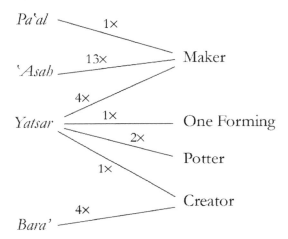

'Oseh points to God as "**Maker**."[587] He is **God my Maker**,[588] **Maker of heaven and earth**,[589] and **Israel's Maker**.[590] He is "**LORD God of Heaven** who made ['*asah*] the sea and the dry land" (Jonah 1:9).

Yotser occurs as "Creator" once, in a warning. Israel's "**Maker** ['*oseh*] will not have compassion on them. And their **Creator** [*yotser*] will not be gracious to them" (Isa. 27:11). *Yotser* is "Maker" four times.[591] *Yatsar* means "to form or fashion," and it describes God as a potter (*yotser*). He rightly asks, "Shall the potter be considered as equal with the clay?"[592] He is also "the **One forming** light and creating darkness."[593] Even the name *'Elohim* carries a note of transcendence above all creation; no one created the Creator.

While *'asah* and *yatsar* are general enough to describe a craftsman fashioning an idol,[594] *bara'* applies only to God's creative work. One commentary explains:

> The word *bara* carries the thought of the initiation of the object involved. It always connotes what only God can do and frequently emphasizes the absolute newness of the object created. The word *asa* is much broader in scope, connoting primarily the fashioning of the object with little concern for special nuances.[595]

God of all flesh
Heb.: *'Elohei kol-basar*
(Jer. 32:27)

**God of the spirits
of all flesh**
Heb.: *'Elohei harukhot
lekhol-basar*
(Num. 16:22; 27:16)

God of the living
Gk.: *Theos zōntōn*
(Mark 12:27 KJV)

**Lord of both the dead
and of the living**
Gk.: *Kai nekrōn kai
zōntōn kyrieusē*
(Rom. 14:9)

Father of spirits
or **Spiritual Father**
(NEB/JB)
Gk.: *Ho patēr tōn
pneumatōn*
(Heb. 12:9)

Bore' is the basis for "Creator" in four verses.[596] God is the "**Creator of the ends of the earth**" and "the **Creator of Israel**, your King." *Bara'* applies to the creation of birds, aquatic animals, humans, wind, the heavens and the earth, Jerusalem for rejoicing, north and south, and a clean heart in a repentant sinner.[597]

The Bible tells us more about God governing life and death.[598] The **God of all flesh** asked, "Is anything too difficult for me?" The New Testament calls Him the **God of the living**, **Father of spirits**, and **God of the spirits of the prophets**. The Hebrew and Greek words for spirit can both mean wind and breath too. God "gives to all people life and breath and all things" (v. 25), so that "in Him we live and move and exist . . . For we also are His offspring" (v. 28).[599]

The Creator also fathered Israel: "Do we not all have one father? Has not one God created us?" said Malachi (Mal. 2:10). Moses called Him the "**Rock who begot you** . . . the **God who gave you birth**" and anticipated His jealousy in the face of idolatry (Deut. 32:18, 21).

Melchizedek's reference to God Most High as "**Possessor** of heaven and

Possessor
Heb.: *Qoneh*
(Gen. 14:19, 22)

Creator (MSG/NIV)
Gk. OT: *Ektisen*
(Gen. 14:19, 22)

earth" (Gen. 14:19, 22) expresses another aspect of God's deep relational commitment to His people. The word for "Possessor" (*qoneh*) has its roots in both commercial transactions and creativity. The picture is of someone doubly invested in an item that he or she has bought and made. The Greek translators of the Old Testament emphasized the creative aspect of the word by selecting *ektisen*. Consequently, some English versions read, "**Creator** of heaven and earth." Craftsmen such as potters love to see their work appreciated and well used.[600] Since He made us, nurtured us, and paid a steep price to redeem us, God is even more interested in having his work appreciated.

Later, the Possessor labeled the newly formed nation of Israel as His own "treasured possession (*segullah*)."[601] He gave them commandments intended to make the relationship flourish, including "You shall have no other gods before [or beside] me." Again, He warned us of His jealous nature (Ex. 20:3–

6; Deut. 5:7–9; 27:15). God transcends our religious structures. He doesn't need temples made by human hands. As His offspring who were made in His likeness, we should know better than to fabricate graven images. He calls us to worship Him alone (vv. 24, 29).

Moses and Aaron understood God's loyalty to His created offspring, Israel.[602] When Korah, one of the priests, incited a rebellion, God sought to destroy the entire nation. Moses and Aaron "fell on their faces, and said, 'O God ['*El*], **God** ['*Elohim*] **of the spirits of all flesh**, when one man sins, will You be angry with the entire congregation?'" (Num. 16:22). Moses was right to appeal to Him; God spared the nation He had birthed and treasured. Using surgical justice, God limited His destruction to the rebellious Korahites.

Laughing God (Acts 17:24–25)

God is so powerful that He laughs at His mocking enemies.[603] Paul pointed to God's sovereignty over everything He made when he declared Him "Lord of heaven and earth" (v. 24). He created and rules both domains. His sovereignty in both domains finds expression in names like **God** (or **Lord) of heaven and earth** and in the statement, "The LORD, He is God in heaven above and on the earth below; there is no other" (Deut. 4:39; see also Gen. 24:3; Josh. 2:11). King Jehoshaphat appealed to God as the ruler of both realms. "O LORD, the **God of our fathers**, are You not **God in the heavens**? And are You not **ruler** over all the kingdoms of the nations?" (2 Chron. 20:6) Jeremiah noted, "You have made the heavens and the earth by Your great power and by Your outstretched arm! Nothing is too difficult for You . . . O great and mighty God. The LORD of hosts is His name" (Jer. 32:17–18).

Several names declare His rule in heaven. Even foreign rulers knew Him as **God of heaven**.[604] He is

Lord of heaven and earth
Gk.: *Kyrios tou ouranou kai tēs gēs*
(Matt. 11:25)

God of heaven and earth
Aram.: '*Elah shemayya' we'ar'a'*
(Ezra 5:11)

God in the heavens
Heb.: '*Elohim bashamayim*
(2 Chron. 20:6)

Ruler
Heb.: *Moshel*
(2 Chron. 20:6; Mic. 5:2 NIV)
Gk.: *Hēgoumenos*
(Matt. 2:6 quotes Mic. 5:2)

God of heaven
Heb.: '*El hashamayim*
(Ps. 136:26)
Heb.: '*Elohei hashamayim*
(Gen. 24:7; Ezra 1:2; Neh.1:4, 5; 2:4, 20; Jonah 1:9)
Aram.: '*Elah shemayya'*
(Ezra 5:12; 6:9; 7:12, 21, 23; Dan. 2:19, 37, 44)
Gk.: *Theos tou ouranou*
(Rev. 11:13; 16:11)

King of heaven
Aram.: *Melekh shemayya'*
(Dan. 4:37)

Lord of heaven
Aram.: *Mare'-shemayya'*
(Dan. 5:23)

Father in heaven
Gk.: *Ho patēr en tois ouranois*
(Matt. 5:45 NIV; 7:21 NAV)

Master in heaven
Gk.: *Kyrios en ouranō*
(Col 4:1)

Ruler of the kings of the earth
Gk.: *Ho archōn tōn basileōn tē gēs*
(Rev 1:5)

King of the nations
Heb.: *Melekh haggoyim*
(Jer. 10:7)
Gk.: *Ho basileus tōn ethnōn*
(Rev. 15:3, saints in KJV)

God of earth
Heb.: *'Elohei ha'arets*
(Gen. 24:3)

God of all the earth
Heb.: *'Elohei khol-ha'arets*
(Isa. 54:5)

Lord of all the earth
Heb.: *'Adon kol-ha'arets*
(Josh. 3:11, 13; Ps. 97:5)

Lord of the earth
Gk.: *Ho Kyrios tēs gēs*
(Rev. 11:4)

also **King of heaven**[605] and **Lord of heaven**.[606] Jesus spoke of His **Father in heaven**, and Paul spoke of our **Master in heaven**. The cryptic periphrasis "Heaven" is another substitute for the God who dwells there and governs all its resources.[607] These names emphasize His transcendence, rather than implying any spatial limitations.

Sometimes, Scripture stresses His other domain. He is **God of all the earth** (another of the seven stated names for God) and **Lord of all the earth** or **Lord of the earth**. Yet His dominion bursts the seams of earth; even heaven cannot contain Him.[608]

Other names also point to God's sovereignty over human political divisions. He is **King of the nations**[609] and **Ruler of the kings of the earth**. He is **Lord of all** or **Lord over all** with respect to the nations.[610] Like a potter, He molds people into wholesome societies.[611] His rule is entirely beneficial and aimed at deepening our relationships with Him. He even delighted to take from among the Gentiles a people for His name.[612]

Jesus, Paul, and the other apostles repeatedly demonstrated the power of God against demonic forces,[613] sickness, and even death. Miracles soften hearts to receive the truth.[614] So, let's pray for demonstrations of God's power when we interact with others. The ministry of the people who know their God should bear the mark of the sovereign God of gods.

Loving God (Acts 17:17–32)

God is not "served by human hands, as though He needed anything, since He Himself gives to all people life and breath and all things" (v. 25). He had nothing to gain from creating and loving us. We can usually detect traces of self-interest in human love, but all His blessings flow from pure love. He is free from partiality and He is immune to bribery.[615] He delights to bless everyone, including the outcasts of society. John Piper says, "God is free to be merciful because he is full and utterly self-sufficient in himself."[616] God's love is of the highest order; it is unconditional and selfless.

One mark of God's love is that He designed us to seek Him; the life-giver implanted a homing instinct in human nature. Paul noted that even His sovereign organization of history facilitates our search for Him. He made nations, "having determined their appointed times and the boundaries of their habitation, that they would seek God, if perhaps they might grope for Him and find Him" (vv. 26–27). We are never satisfied until we discover how much our creating Father loves us.

The marketplace in ancient Athens was a snapshot of a dissatisfied world. Athens exhibited various gods that people encountered on the global quest for the true God. After all of their groping, the Athenians knew something was still missing, so they threw in an undesignated god. How many societies throughout history have done this? Today, many people are looking for spiritual reality, albeit in the wrong places. Many people believe in some kind of spirit world, even if they perceive it wrongly, as the Athenians did.

We are incapable of finding God ourselves, even though "He is not far from each one of us" (v. 27). We might discover certain truths about Him from His creation or because He made us in His image, but we fail to properly grasp Him.[617] One challenge is that Satan, with his gang of demons masquerading as gods and idols, distracts us from worshipping God. Satan's business includes deception.[618] He sows tares in the crop to hinder its growth.[619] The god of this world blinds our eyes to the gospel.[620] He deceives people into thinking that life with one of his disguised agents is good, when in fact it's slavery. Satan flirts with people and seduces them into "foreign affairs"—relationships with gods other than our Creator Father. Sometimes, the lure is blatant idolatry. Historically, it has even involved human sacrifice and cannibalism, but the lure doesn't have to be that extreme. It might be as simple and subtle as materialism. It can be pride in an ideology. It can even be toy train sets. Satan doesn't care, so long as his lure consumes us to the point that we do not worship the true God.

People who are searching for truth are most likely to listen to our message about God's love when our lives are stamped with His loving nature. Paul demonstrated love toward the Athenians; he was respectful and humble. He remained immersed in their culture, visiting their marketplace daily (v.17). He spoke their language and quoted their poetry (even though it honored Zeus). As a result, Paul's religious dialogue in Athens bore fruit.

Intellectual discussion often fails to reach people's hearts, but Paul's audience of Athenian philosophers loved such talk. They invited Paul to the Areopagus, the council that was responsible for investigating religious and moral issues (vv. 19–21).

Paul recognized, as we should, that other religions often contain nodules of truth that are embedded in ignorance or even in dark lies. Because creation points to the Creator[621] and His offspring bear His image, searching hearts can glean nuggets of truth about God from both creation and human nature. The Athenians had three insights: They knew about human origins (v. 28), they were dependent on a higher being (v. 28), and they believed in the existence of an undiscovered god (v. 23). A person's correct insights provide excellent conversation starters.

Hundreds of ethnic groups believe in a supreme god. The practices and stories of some cultures are analogous to certain parts of the gospel message. Don Richardson gives examples of such "eye-openers," or "redemptive analogies."[622] Once missionaries learn the inner workings of a culture and discover these analogies, they can use them to explain the gospel. The analogies function as keys that open spiritual eyes to the truth. It is easier for people to understand the gospel when they hear it explained in terms of familiar stories or practices. The best missionaries are learners before they are teachers; they build relationships and find the keys.

It might be hard to accept, but even Islam makes some valid observations about God. Muslims revere Allah. The Qur'an's emphasis on Allah's sovereignty and his care for his people reflects the character of the True God.

I picked Islam because it resembles Christianity, but nuggets of truth exist in other religions too. Those truths do not validate the religions; neither are they a smorgasbord of religious ideas served up for us to build our own meals of spiritual truth. Without Jesus, those truths can't form complete meals. They serve only as keys for their adherents to find the most essential truth—the way to the Father through the death of His Son. Christians don't have a monopoly on truth, but Jesus and the Bible are the most authoritative statements on God's character and will.

Paul seized his moment. He secured his relationship by acknowledging the religious interest of the Athenians. Then he offered to explain the anonymous god and the enigmatic altar (vv. 22–23).

Locals knew the story of the altar to the unknown god. It had been built centuries before as a plague was decimating Athens. The city elders had made sacrifices to all the gods in an attempt to stem the plague, but to no avail. Epimenides suggested that their sacrifices were ineffective because an undiscovered god, who was responsible for the plague, still needed to be appeased. So, they built the altar and made the appropriate sacrifices, and the plague stopped. The Greeks concluded that they had satisfied the nameless new god. Paul did not suggest that our God had caused the plague, but into their void, he inserted foundational facts about the One true God.

When Paul completed his presentation to the Areopagus, some members chose to pursue their own ways; others continued the dialogue (v. 32). A relationship based on humility and respect can progress; the door remains unlocked and open to more truth.

Living God (Acts 17:28–31)

Paul quoted the poetry of Epimenides: "For in him we live and move and exist" (v. 28). Even though Epimenides spoke of Zeus, Paul saw the glint of truth. God is the source of existence. Then he quoted two more writers: "We also are His children."[623] Again, he applied words about Zeus to God. Paul's logic was that if living and moving humans are God's offspring who were made in His image, He must be a living, active God. He is vastly superior to idols of gold, silver, or stone—even superior to the Greek concept of Zeus (v. 29). A similar appeal to turn to the **living God**, the Creator, came during Paul's visit to Lystra.[624]

For Paul, Jesus' resurrection was the clinching evidence.[625] Resurrection was no theological theory; it transformed lives. The risen Jesus had blazed into Paul's life, dramatically rearranging his misdirected passion to serve His purposes. Now Paul had a deep sense of God's agenda. God wants to create a dynamic body out of those who accept His invitation from every tribe, tongue, people, and nation. Paul described the church as a letter in progress that was written "not with ink but

Living God
Gk.: *Theos zōn*
(Acts 14:15)

Spirit of the living God
Gk.: *To pneuma Theou zōntos*
(2 Cor. 3:3)

with the **Spirit of the living God**" (2 Cor. 3:3). The reborn Paul was zealous to see God's purposes for the church fulfilled.

❦

The character of the god a nation worships profoundly marks lifestyles and whole societies. So, there is value in comparing religions along the lines of the four areas we have just considered. Does the religion cherish life or consider it dispensable? How does it treat those who have less to contribute to society—the needy, the suffering, and the dying? Does their belief system reflect the unconditional love of a god who cares for the weak and the poor? Or does it suggest a god who is interested only in a certain gender, caste, or type of person? Are their gods angry, distant, or aloof? Even if there are displays of power, are they consistent with love and liberty? After all, power can be counterfeited.

Paul did not make comparisons in order to keep score of the Athenians and their objects of worship. Rather, he addressed their emptiness and their nagging question. In place of the unknown, he proclaimed the life-giving God, laughing sovereignly over every enemy and deeply loving His people. He pointed to Jesus as the living representation of the true God (v. 31).

Praying For Missionaries

Paul's presentation to the Athenians suggests seven ways that we can pray effectively for cross-cultural missionaries and for ourselves as we engage in evangelism:

1. Pray for the **reality of the power** of God to protect and equip His ministers. Also, pray that the works of the evil one are destroyed (1 John 3:8).
2. Pray that people encounter the **resurrected life of Jesus** and ask questions.
3. Pray that **respectful relationships** would demonstrate God's love and that keys for presenting the gospel would be discovered. Pray that love would be evident among missionary team members because love shows that we are disciples of a loving Master (John 13:35).
4. Pray for boldness and the ability to give clearly **reasoned presentations** of the gospel.

5. Pray for the Holy Spirit to **reveal truth** to spiritually blind eyes.

6. Pray for the gift of **repentance** to be released so that people will turn away from demons, idols, and gods to the true and living God—from darkness to light (Acts 26:18; 1 Thess. 1:9; 2 Tim. 2:25).

7. Pray that the **Lord of the harvest** will send out laborers to **reap** His harvest (Matt. 9:38; Luke 10:2).

The Unbending Line

Paul continued his presentation: "Therefore having overlooked the times of ignorance, God is now declaring to men that all people everywhere should repent, because He has fixed a day in which He will judge the world in righteousness through a **Man** whom He has appointed, having furnished proof to all men by raising Him from the dead" (Acts 17:30–31).

A Man
Gk.: *Anēr*
(Acts 17:31)

An unbending line divides lives into two periods. On one side are "times of ignorance." On the other side is a time of crucial knowledge about Jesus. The line demands that we decide whether to repent and believe in Jesus or not. When the gospel is proclaimed to someone, they cross the line. Paul implied, "Athenians, your ignorance is over. I have told you about Jesus and His resurrection. Now, how will you respond to His claims?"[626]

In its various forms, the question is the unbending front line of missions. Usually, people reach it through a process, but all true missionaries pray that unbelievers will arrive at the line, choose to accept Jesus' claims, and turn from their distracting idols.

Because of the line, missions and evangelism are provocative. In our cosmopolitan society, which emphasizes tolerance and freedom of choice, we hear objections: "Why do missionaries try to change other people's beliefs? Why can't people be left to their own religions? How could Jesus claim to be *the* way to the Father?"

The answer to those questions lies in the meaning of the most uncomfortable name: **Jealous God**.

A Green-Eyed Monster

More than a hint of jealousy underlies God's command to worship Him exclusively. It is often explicit: "You shall not worship any other god, for the LORD, whose

Jealous God
Heb.: *'El qanna'*
(Ex. 34:14)

name is **Jealous**, is a jealous God" (Ex. 34:14).[627] This is the third time the Old Testament states a specific name for God.

We observed earlier that false gods incite His jealousy.[628] Joshua's parting challenge to Israel was to "put away the gods which your fathers served." He warned that any lapse into idolatry would spark the fiery wrath of the jealous God (Josh. 24:2, 14, 19–20).

What are we to make of His jealousy? Surely, it doesn't suggest that God has a temper tantrum whenever anyone nods at a false god. That might frighten us from idolatry, but it certainly wouldn't inspire genuine adoration of Him. Some people wince at this name of God, yet it occurs in the Old Testament.[629] J. I. Packer summarizes our struggle:

> "The jealous God"—doesn't it sound offensive? For we know jealousy, "the green-ey'd monster," as a vice, one of the most cancerous and soul-destroying vices that there is; whereas God, we are sure, is perfectly good. How, then, could anyone ever imagine that jealousy is found in Him?[630]

The name doesn't imply that kind of jealousy. As Paul explained to the Athenians, God is not "served by human hands, as though He needed anything" (Acts 17:25). Being completely self-sufficient and secure, He delights in our worship, but He does not depend on it. His is another kind of jealousy, which J. I. Packer describes:

> There are two sorts of jealousy among men, and only one of them is a vice. Vicious jealousy is an expression of the attitude, "I want what you've got, and I hate you because I haven't got it." It is an infantile resentment springing from unmortified covetousness, which expresses itself in envy, malice, and meanness of action. It is terribly potent, for it feeds and is fed by pride, the taproot of our fallen nature. There is a mad obsessiveness about jealousy which, if indulged, can tear an otherwise firm character to shreds. . . . What is often called sexual jealousy, the lunatic fury of a rejected or supplanted suitor, is of this kind. But there is another sort of jealousy—zeal to protect a love-relationship, or to avenge it when broken. This jealousy also operates

in the sphere of sex; there, however, it appears, not as the blind reaction of wounded pride, but as the fruit of marital affection.[631]

Packer's description is much closer to God's jealousy—a jealousy for things bought or made that another person steals. He even jealously protects the honor of His name.[632] Applied to His created children, God's jealousy has to do with His affection for them and His pursuit of the very best for them. Our best lies in having intimate relationships with our Possessor (*qoneh*) and Creator. Friendship with the world is spiritual adultery, so God jealously longs for our spirits to find Him.[633]

Jealousy relates to zeal. Out of zeal (*qin'ah*), God sent His governing Child to restore His relationship with all people.[634] Phinehas the priest, who killed an Israelite who had been caught in an adulterous and idolatrous relationship, exemplified God's jealousy. God commended him: "He was jealous with My jealousy among them, so that I did not destroy the sons of Israel in My jealousy" (Num. 25:11).

Zephaniah prophesied of the day of the LORD's judgment from two perspectives: his own day and the future. Upon Christ's return, God's jealous zeal will issue forth in devouring fire. However, that day has precursors—acts of limited judgment that provide opportunities for the humble to turn and take refuge in His name.[635] Remember, God is slow to anger.

The Best Husband

A few of God's names liken His love for His people to marital affection. In the Old Testament, Israel was His bride: "Your **husband** [*Ba'al*] is your Maker ['*oseh*],[636] whose name is the LORD of hosts" (Isa. 54:5).[637]

Hosea dramatically depicted a husband who was betrayed by the beloved wife he had wooed. Hosea took prophetic drama beyond the brief acts of other prophets; Hosea's whole life expressed God's message. God told Hosea to marry a prostitute called Gomer. It paralleled His own love for Israel, who behaved like a harlot, having foreign affairs with Ba'al. Hosea even named his children as statements of God's coming judgment. God sovereignly disrupted the harvest (which was supposedly controlled by Ba'al,

Husband
Heb.: *Ba'al*
(Isa. 54:5)
Gk.: *Anēr*
(2 Cor. 11:2;
Rev. 21:2)

My husband
Heb.: *'Ishi*
(Hos. 2:16)

My Lord/Master
Heb.: *Ba'ali*
(Hos. 2:16)

the god of rain and fertility) to bring Israel to her senses.[638] He wooed Israel back to Himself and provided for her again. It powerfully demonstrated God's faithfulness to His covenant people in the face of their blatant unfaithfulness—His gentle jealousy. Later, Hosea renamed his children to mark God's forgiveness. [639]

Eventually, Israel would start to call God "**My husband**." "'It will come about in that day,' declares the LORD, 'That you will call me *'Ishi* and will no longer call me *Ba'ali*.'" (Hos. 2:16) Remember, "*Ba'al*" suggests possession, ownership, and rule, but it extends to marriage and it can mean, "husband." *'Ish* means "man" and therefore, in some contexts, "husband." God played with words to emphasize that His relationship to Israel is like that of a loving husband, minus any debasing mastery and degrading domination. Submission to God is voluntary, bringing freedom and fulfillment; relationships with Ba'al were life-sapping slavery. God was wooing Israel back, freeing her from any confusion between Ba'al and Himself.

In another prophecy of restoration, God promised new names to Israel. She was no longer "Forsaken" or "Desolate," but "Hephzibah" (My delight is in her). He called the land, "Beulah"[640] (Married). "As the bridegroom rejoices over the bride, so your God will rejoice over you" (Isa. 62:1–5).

The bridegroom's rejoicing extends beyond Israel to every person who returns to Him. God promised the Gentiles, "a memorial, and a name better than that of sons and daughters . . . an everlasting name which will not be cut off." He also made the temple (the center of Jewish worship) "a house of prayer for all the peoples" (Isa. 56:3–7). The one occasion when Jesus displayed what looked like violent anger was motivated by His zeal for God's house.[641] Commenting on that incident, Mark pointed to the promise in Isaiah. In Jesus, God wooed every nation to Himself, and those who share Paul's missionary zeal continue that wooing.

No New Testament writer explicitly called Jesus a "bridegroom," but John the Baptist likened Jesus to one, and Jesus used the picture of Himself.[642] Paul mentioned his own godly jealousy for the church in Corinth, which he described as betrothed to Christ, her **Husband**.[643] In Revelation, the cleansed multitude (the church) is both the bride of the Lamb and the New Jerusalem prepared for her husband.[644]

The Jealous Father

Parents who watch their children drawn away to a wasted life of pain get a taste of God's jealousy. When God breathed His spirit into flesh, He created children; He loves us more than the best father imaginable does. Whenever God sees us lured into damaging behavior, a jealous rage fills His heart. Our loving Father says, "I hate watching my children stray. They are only happy and fulfilled when they have a relationship with Me." His jealousy is a mixture of disappointment and grief.

That same passion should fill our hearts as we interact with wandering brothers and sisters. Understanding the true nature of the Jealous God is vital. Only then can we express His jealous love in a way that correctly represents His character as our Father.

Chapter 10

LIKE FATHER, LIKE CHILD

The reason the mass of men fear God, and at bottom dislike Him, is because they rather distrust His heart, and fancy Him all brain like a watch.
—Herman Melville

Angie changed the subject whenever she heard anyone say, "When I grow up, I want to be like my daddy." She had never known her father. Angie had been conceived in an African police cell. An officer had raped her mother while detaining her overnight on minor charges. Rough justice indeed! Had DNA tests been available in her country, paternity could have been established. That would have meant little to Angie. No one says "Daddy" to a paper certificate. The word usually fits between sobs, giggles, or shouts. A DNA fingerprint cannot compare with strong, warm, reassuring arms wrapped around a little body. A father is much more than a genetic donor; a father is a life invested in a relationship with his child—a life worth emulating. God is a father in both senses—a creator who stays involved.

God is everyone's Father because He spoke a word and created humankind, fashioning us from dust. When the Bible says God made us in His image and likeness, it uses words that allow for a father and child to be similar but to have unique, individual traits.[645] God's name, **Father of spirits**, emphasizes that our spirits originate in Him, not in our natural parents. He is our spiritual Father. Paul called Him, "the Father, from whom every family in heaven and on earth derives its name" (Eph. 3:14–15).[646] Failing human fathers don't define fatherhood—God does.

The first reference to God as Father speaks of the nation of Israel: "Is not He your **Father** who has bought you? He has made you and established you" (Deut. 32:6). Here, we see the same double involvement that we saw in Chapter 9 when we considered His name **Possessor**. He created us and paid a ransom for us. When the Israelites became a nation, they had every reason to be confident in their relationship with their heavenly Father. First, He made them; later, He bought Israel out of slavery in Egypt and declared, "Out of Egypt I called My son" (Hos. 11:1). "The LORD your God carried you, as a father carries his son" (Deut. 1:31 NIV). He chose Israel to be His special, treasured possession out of all the nations on earth. The Israelites had no additional intrinsic value; they did nothing outstanding to qualify, but He chose them nonetheless.[647] Moses hammered the point home for Israel by calling God the **Rock who begot you** and the **God who gave you birth**. The words are graphic. They evoke images of God writhing in pain like a mother in labor. That's the beginning of His love for us.

> **Father**
> Heb.: *'Av*
> (Deut. 32:6)
> Gk.: *Patēr*
>
> ***Abba***
> (Mark 14:36;
> Rom. 8:15; Gal. 4:6)
>
> **Rock who begot you**
> Heb.: *Tsur yeladekha*
> (Deut. 32:18)
>
> **God who gave you birth**
> Heb.: *'El mekholelekha*
> (Deut. 32:18)

The Gap

The world is full of the cries of children like Angie, cries that go unheard because the fathers left their children, perhaps even before birth. For many people, a huge gap separates God's standard for fatherhood and their experiences of it. Their families were far from heavenly. In the absence of a nurturing human father, Angie found it difficult to relate to her heavenly Father. Where there should have been a peg in her life experience on which to hang the truth about her heavenly Father, there was a blank wall. When someone told her God loved her more than the best father ever could, the words fell into a confused heap. Others grow up with fathers around, but their relationships contain painful memories of abuse or impossible demands. Such fathers give little freely or willingly; new bikes have to be earned with grades, and treats feel like tricks. Perhaps the father is unpredictable. The children hardly know what he will do or say. They do not know where they stand with him, so they learn to withdraw. Maybe the relationship is rigid, formal, and characterized by stiff handshakes instead of tender touches. It is no surprise that people with such experiences tend to suspect God of similar coldness, and they approach Him with the same caution.

We perceive life through the grid of previous experiences; this grid is an inner translator of new experiences. For Angie and others like her, any suggestion of intimacy with a father figure triggers a foghorn out of a murky and painful past. It screams a warning: "Relationships are too difficult; you will get hurt if you expose your heart too much."

My own experience was happier. I had less difficulty knowing God as my Father because my natural father, although imperfect, was involved. He attempted to balance his love for his children with his responsibility to provide for us. He worked hard as a schoolteacher, but after facing the challenges of the classroom and a long commute, he was exhausted. To some extent, even the best fathers fail. They can never supply all the love and resources a child can absorb. Human strengths have a downside too. My father excelled at teaching and sometimes he continued to teach at home. During family outings, I often played hooky in my mind while he lectured my brother, my sister, and me on details of British history.

Sadly, I chose to withdraw from my father. It began as petty jealousy (you remember, the "green-ey'd monster") toward my younger brother. I had a sense that he was favored and treated leniently. My gradual withdrawal left me hardly speaking to either of them. Our relationships had plenty of potential for wholeness, but they suffered from my foolish and immature choices. The distance between us continued for several years before healing came.

The nation of Israel behaved worse, despite God's love. We find Him lamenting in Isaiah, "Sons I have reared and brought up, but they have revolted against Me." He continues, calling them "sons who act corruptly!" (Isa. 1:2–4). Jeremiah's prophecy echoes Isaiah's: "Then I said, 'How I would set you among My sons and give you a pleasant land, the most beautiful inheritance of the nations!' And I said, 'You shall call me, My Father, and not turn away from following Me.' Surely, as a woman treacherously departs from her lover, so you have dealt treacherously with Me, O house of Israel" (Jer.

3:19–20). William Barclay called sin a "crime against love. The sinner does not so much break God's law as he breaks God's heart."[648] When rebellion or withdrawal infects a relationship and communications falter, it is hard to stop the gap from widening.

The fact that *'Av* (Father) is used as a title for God only nine times in the Old Testament is symptomatic of the damaged relationship.[649] Descriptions of God's fatherhood are few, and they refer generally to the nation or the race. The only individuals who related to Him as Father were a few kings.[650] His Old Testament reputation as a father is unappealing. He appears to demand honor and respect, and reproof is a sign of His love.[651] We only glimpse His compassion as He mercifully gathers His children and reaches out as a "Father to the fatherless."[652]

The blind spot for the Father carries over to New Testament times; religious Jews refer to God as Father only once in the Gospels.[653] In the Jewish literature of the time, references are sparse. Jews thought of God in terms of obedience to the Law and as Father of the nation, rather than the individual.[654]

The Parable of the Stunted Sons (Luke 15:1–32)

Considering the background, it is interesting to note that one of Jesus' most memorable parables starred two sons and their father. I hesitate to call it "the parable of the prodigal son" because each character teaches us valuable lessons. While the father epitomizes God's Father-heart as he welcomes back his immature and wayward son, the elder brother demonstrates a tragic, stunted sonship. He is not a happy, free child and he fails to be like his father. The family likeness is lacking. The clue to his dysfunction lies in his father's words to him in verse 31: "Son, you have always been with me, and all that is mine is yours."

One day, those words struck me; I realized that they described my background. I grew up with my father at home. I had more than my basic needs supplied. I had known the Lord from childhood, but I still lived in brokenness in three ways, just like the elder son.

Resources

Although the elder son had lived with his father, serving and obeying him, he complained, "You have never given me a young goat, so that I might celebrate with my friends" (v. 29). Apparently, he expected his father to take the initiative to provide a barbeque for him. Even though the father had advanced him his inheritance, something inhibited him from drawing on those resources or asking his father.[655] Yet, Jesus taught that it is good to ask our Father for what we need. Healthy, happy children run to their father, confident that He possesses resources and that he delights in giving His children good things. Asking is normal in our heavenly Father's family.

Relationships

The elder son always resided with his father, but his family ties were weak. His fiercely pointed accusation toward "this son of yours" was gently but firmly met with, "this brother of yours" (vv. 30, 32). In his shrunken and immature sonship, he refused to acknowledge that "all that is mine" included his brother.

Rejoicing

In the absence of a meaningful relationship, the elder son objected to the reunion party. On the other hand, the waiting father, who had scanned the horizon and had run to embrace his lost son, celebrated lavishly.[656] Love that covers a multitude of sins is a family trait—evidence that we are God's children.[657]

These three areas of brokenness in the parable point to immaturity in both players and listeners. In its benign form, immaturity appears in the dry dullness of a dutiful elder brother who is relationally detached and lives in spiritual poverty amid riches. That was my situation. My family was healthy and loving, but I withdrew from having close relationships with some of them through my own wrong choices. Much of Israel was in this condition when Jesus came; after 450 years of prophetic silence, their relationship amounted to dutiful ceremonies. They had little sense of God's blessing on the nation.

Don't forget the third player in the parable, the prodigal son. He typifies people who lose faith in their Father's abundant love. Setting out on a quest for greener grass, they scrape together dry, stringy pods in a kingdom of darkness. They can't imagine that the Father would ever want them back without either subservience or considerable restitution on their part.

But remember, Jesus held up the parable like a mirror to Pharisees and Scribes who were choking on His reception of sinners.[658] He highlighted the worst form of immaturity: religion retching at the idea that bent coins, black sheep, or sin-stained wanderers could have any place in God's family.

Such immaturity is a hideous and shriveled distortion of what God intends for His children.

To each group of immature sons, Jesus addressed not only the parable, but also His life. Revealing God's fatherhood was central to His purpose, so this one name is worth devoting a whole chapter to. The Old Testament concludes with Malachi's prophetic promise about reconciliation between the hearts of fathers and children.[659] That Jesus accomplished a far more important reconciliation is evident from the dramatic increase in the use of the Greek word *patēr* (father) for God. It occurs 168 times in the New Testament, and 94 times in the Gospels alone. Jesus came to show everyone what the Father was really like. He came to bridge the gap and to make a way back to Him. So, let us look at Jesus' mission, which included teaching and modeling relationship with the heavenly Father.[660]

Mission Accomplished

Even as a boy, Jesus knew He belonged in His Father's house.[661] He referred to God as His Father and often spoke of Himself as **the Son**. He said, "I and the Father are one" (John 10:30), yet (this may seem paradoxical) the Father is sovereign over the Son.[662]

Beside the simple name, **Son of God**, Jesus was called **Son of the living God**, **Son of the Father**, and **Son of the Blessed One**.[663] Paul used a phrase that literally means **Son of His love**. A common introduction in the epistles emphasizes their relationship: "the God and **Father of our Lord Jesus Christ**."[664] John spoke of **God the Father** and the **Son of the Father**.[665]

Jesus' relationship with the Father is unique in many ways. It existed before anything else.[666] The degree of mutual knowledge between Father and Son is unmatched.[667] Jesus' name surpasses angelic names precisely because He is His Father's Son, and He sits at His right hand.[668] In the parable of the vineyard, Jesus cast Himself as the ultimate messenger who is superior to both vine-growers and slaves because He

The Son
Gk.: *Ho hyios*
(John 5:22–23; 6:40)

Son of God
Gk.: *Ho hyios
tou Theou*
(Matt. 26:63)

Son of the Father
Gk.: *Ho hyios
tou Patros*
(2 John 3)

Son of the living God
Gk.: *Ho hyios tou
Theou tou zōntos*
(Matt. 16:16)

**Son of the
Blessed One**
Gk.: *Ho hyios
tou eulogētou*
(Mark 14:61)

Son of His love
Gk.: *Ho hyios tēs
agapēs autou*
(Col. 1:13)

is God's beloved Son.[669] From the Father's perspective, Jesus is His **Beloved**, in part because He is the only Son. The fact that Jesus is one of a kind makes Him infinitely precious, and this underlies the name, **only begotten Son**.[670]

Jesus existed eternally with His Father, and the Father sent Him on His special mission.[671] Jesus came and ministered in His Father's name.[672] The Jewish religious system included a chain of authority. Leading rabbis laid hands on their disciples to commission them to continue the work. As Jesus taught in the temple, the Pharisees demanded His credentials: "What right do you have?"[673] The book of Hebrews calls Jesus the **Apostle**, emphasizing that He was sent as an authorized representative. In Jesus' case, the Father was the commissioner.

Beloved
Gk.: *Agapētos*
(Mark 12:6)
Ēgapēmenos
(Eph. 1:6)

Apostle
Gk.: *Apostolos*
(Heb. 3:1)

The paternal character sketch, which was hardly more than a pencil outline in the Old Testament, was colored in by Jesus' example and teachings. Jesus revealed the Father to us so clearly that He could legitimately claim, "If you knew Me, you would know My Father also."[674] For that alone, He deserves the title **the faithful witness**. Jesus showed us what it means to live among all the distractions and temptations of human life while remaining close to the Father.

The Faithful Witness
Gk.: *Ho martys,
ho pistos*
(Rev. 1:5; 3:14)

In Psalm 65:2, King David addressed "**You who hear prayer**." Much of Jesus' teachings on prayer came in the Sermon on the Mount. Jesus describes a Father who is so involved in life that He spots falling sparrows.[675] Jesus speaks of our "Father who sees what is done in secret," readily rewarding our devotion and hearing our prayers.[676] Once, Jesus taught His disciples to pray to the **Lord of the harvest**. Most famously, He introduced us to "Our Father," whose name is hallowed and whose kingdom we should seek.[677] The first two words of the prayer teach volumes about effective prayer—it oozes with relationship. The relationships are vertical with the Father and horizontal within an expanding family of believers. Our Father loves answering prayers, especially those prayed in agreement with others.[678] Meaningless repetitions or "magic-formulae prayers" insult Him.

Lord of the harvest
Gk.: *Tou kyriou
tou therismou*
(Matt. 9:38;
Luke 10:2)

Without a relationship, prayer degenerates to attempted manipulation—a verbal rubbing of the genie's lamp, a babble of abracadabras, or a panic button to press in a crisis. How unnecessary! The Father knows our needs even before we ask.[679] With faith-filled prayer, we place an expectant trust in a Father who loves to give good things to His children because they ask Him.[680] If only the elder son had understood that.

Jesus addressed most of His prayers to "Father."[681] There were two exceptions. First, His agonizing cry on the cross: "My God, My God, why have You forsaken Me?"[682] The cry came right at the point when Jesus felt separated from His Father. The second exception was in the prayer recorded in John 17 when He spoke to "the only true God" (v. 3). The rest of that prayer is typical of His style. Jesus addressed His "Father" six times, including variants like **Holy Father** and **Righteous Father**.

Holy Father
Gk.: *Patēr hagios*
(John 17:11)

Righteous Father
Gk.: *Patēr dikaios*
(John 17:25)

Jesus probably spoke Aramaic, which is similar to Hebrew. So, He didn't say *"Patēr"* but *"'Abba'."*[683] Children of all ages still say *"'Abba'"* in Jewish homes today. It is often the first word a child vocalizes: "Daddy!" Jesus' revelation of His Father was somewhat revolutionary. Not only does the Father desire a deep relationship with His people, He delights in them addressing Him in the simplest and most intimate way. The fact that the Aramaic word, *'Abba'*, crossed the language barrier to enter the Greek New Testament shows how big an impression Jesus made by using it.

Doing the Father's will is another family trait.[684] Jesus submitted to His Father, delighting to obey even when it led to suffering.[685] Obedience took Jesus to the cross to pay our penalty for straying and rebelling. He walked that path in tremendous security because He knew where He had come from and where He was going.[686] Because the Father had shown Jesus His crucifixion in advance, He could look beyond death and feel confident in God's assurance of restored glory.[687] As events tumbled toward the cross, Jesus knew the Father was still in control. Therefore, He maintained His claim to be one with the Father, even though it resulted in His death.[688]

With one last cry, "Father, into Your hands I commit my spirit," Jesus died and completed His redemptive mission (Luke 23:34, 46). He was raised through the glory of the life-giving Father,[689] and He quickly sent a message to

His disciples. Mary delivered the message, and it still reverberates: "I ascend to My Father and *your Father*, and My God and your God" (John 20:17, my emphasis). The ultimate restoration of children to their Father, which Malachi spoke of, had been accomplished. The door was open for all people to be God's children by adoption.[690]

Before He ascended to share His Father's throne, Jesus commissioned us to baptize new disciples in the Father's name.[691] The Father poured out His Spirit to empower us to continue that mission.[692] Now, filled with the **Spirit of His Son**, we too can call on Him in the simple intimacy of Christlike children: "*'Abba'*" or "Dear Father."

Spirit of His Son
Gk.: *To pneuma tou hyiou autou*
(Gal. 4:6)

Decades after the ascension, the disciple John saw a revelation of Jesus and the end times. In it, John glimpsed our own future too. He saw the names of Jesus and the Father written on faithful foreheads as a profound mark of belonging to God.[693]

That sense of belonging has already begun, and it is reflected in the word "Christian."[694] James referred to "the fair name by which you have been called" (James 2:7). The family likeness, which the "fair name" points to, implies increasing love and righteousness, and diminishing sinfulness.[695]

Bridging the Gap

The Father, who Jesus revealed, wants no older sons or prodigals to be away from the heart of the home.[696] He aches to have His children return to receive His welcome. So, what about people like Angie who strain to bridge the gap between their painful experiences of human fatherhood and their developing relationships with the heavenly Father? How can any of us be sure of His love, and how can we exhibit the family likeness? The first letter of John the apostle contains a helpful framework:

> *See how great a love the Father has bestowed on us, that we would be called children of God; and such we are. For this reason the world does not know us, because it did not know Him. Beloved, now we are children of God, and it has not appeared as yet what we will be. We know that when He appears, we will be like Him, because we will see Him just as He is. And everyone who has this hope fixed on Him purifies himself, just as He is pure.* (1 John 3:1–3)

How great is the Father's love for us? Jesus said that someone who has been forgiven much will love much.[697] Some returning wanderers have been so impacted by the Father's unexpected forgiving embrace that they are the ones who find it easiest to live as His children. Now, I'm not suggesting that you go on a binge of sin to maximize your experience of forgiveness. All sin separates us from the Father. He has already extended His forgiveness to each of us. We should reflect on that and on the great investment that He made to adopt us— He gave the life of His sinless only Son.[698]

John emphasized, "such we *are* . . . now we *are* children of God."[699] Our position as God's children is an established fact. Even if a painful experience presents an obstacle to understanding the relationship, our position is still true. It is true because He redeemed us with the blood of His Son. At the end of his prophecy, Isaiah declared, "You, O LORD, are our Father, Our **Redeemer** from of old is your name" (Isa. 63:16). William Barclay summed it up: "In the sense of paternity, we are all children of God; but, in the sense of fatherhood, we are children of God only when He makes His gracious approach to us and we respond."[700]

Isaiah knew that God wanted His family of faith to grow. He promised foreigners "a name better than that of sons and daughters . . . an everlasting name which will not be cut off" (Isa. 56:3–7). We are no longer spiritual orphans or slaves to sin and Satan; we are God's children through faith in Jesus. (John 14:18; Gal. 3:26) The outpoured Spirit, who is called the **Spirit of adoption** and **Spirit of your Father**, guarantees it. No matter what our backgrounds are, accepting Jesus as Lord and Savior by faith makes it a fact—we are God's children.

Spirit of adoption
Gk.: *To pneuma hyiothesias*
(Rom. 8:15)

Spirit of your Father
Gk.: *To pneuma tou patros hymōn*
(Matt. 10:20)

When we bask in that truth, it thaws our hearts. What a relief to be able to drop our guard in the presence of a Father who knows everything about us and still desires our company.

John said, "we love, because He first loved us" (1 John 4:19). As we discover His love for us, love begins to bubble up from us, and it overflows to touch others. We want to "be imitators of God, as beloved children" (Eph. 5:1; see also Matt. 5:16). He is the **Father of mercies**, whose love does not fail even when people are hostile to Him.[701]

Father of mercies
Gk.: *Ho patēr tōn oiktirmōn*
(2 Cor. 1:3)

Our lifelong pursuit of Christlike-ness (the essence of spiritual maturity) begins as a natural and joyful outpouring of our love for God. If we take our eyes off the Father's love for us, the relationship easily deteriorates into a dry, pharisaical ritual. Then most people throw up their hands in resignation to a growing sense that "I will never achieve His standard." Of course, you won't! None of us can.

Maturity lies in a place of balance between God working in us and us allowing Him to. The Father first draws us to Jesus and then keeps us there in His name.[702] But the Father cannot work until we soften our hearts, respond to His wooing, and return from wandering. When required, the **Father of spirits** provides life-giving discipline. A beautiful work begins to mature. In it all, the Father is the **Vinedresser** who cultivates fruit throughout our lives, bringing glory to Himself.[703]

Vinedresser
Gk.: *Geōrgos*
(John 15:1)

Potter (also Creator and Maker)
Heb.: *Yotser*
(Isa. 64:8)

Isaiah portrayed the process using a name that is related to "Creator." "But now, O LORD, You are our Father, we are the clay, and You our **potter**; and all of us are the work of your hand" (Isa. 64:8). The Father who created and redeemed us is a potter as well. Our Creator and Maker stays involved. We can imagine Him squeezing our character as if He were shaping a clay vessel. As we are willing, He molds us into the likeness of His Son. One day, He will complete the process.[704] In the meantime, we are motivated to keep responding to His love, no matter what we face.

The Finish Line

The writer to the Hebrews described our life like a race:

> *Therefore, since we have so great a crowd of witnesses surrounding us, let us also lay aside every encumbrance and the sin which so easily entangles us, and let us run with endurance the race that is set before us, fixing our eyes on Jesus, the author and perfecter of faith, who for the joy set before Him endured the cross, despising the shame, and has sat down at the right hand of the throne of God. (Heb. 12:1–2)*

Our progress toward Christlike-ness is like a school's cross-country race. Often, my classmates and I used to run six or seven miles in the rain, along muddy English farm tracks and even through snow. By the five-mile marker, I was panting clouds of steam, and I had to walk to catch my breath, especially when I was going uphill.

Now, I won't mention names, but some kids cheated—they would tuck their bus passes into their shorts. The course overlapped the bus route in places, so it was easy to ride the bus and alight just before the school gate, hoping the sports teacher wasn't watching. How we would love to do the same in the Christian life.

Honest sportsmen like me had uplifting experiences as we rounded the final street corner. Looking down the road, we could see the school gates. Only four hundred yards! A hot shower, dry clothes, and a chance to go home early awaited us. During competitive runs, a crowd watched and cheered.

Imagine the exhilaration. As we turn the last corner, a final shot of adrenaline propels our aching legs to a glorious sprint finish. It's like the Olympics.

While we run our earthly races with endurance, let's remember that not only a crowd of witnesses is watching. Our Father will be at the finish line Himself to welcome and reward us—not for being perfect, but for running our best, just as Jesus did. Our heavenly Father's welcome won't be a stiff handshake but a warm embrace.

Chapter 11

SATISFIED BY GOD

If I find in myself a desire which no experience in this world can satisfy, the most probable explanation is that I was made for another world.
—**C. S. Lewis**, *Mere Christianity*[705]

C an you think of a time when you were desperately thirsty? My closest call with dangerous dehydration happened on my hike out of 5,600-foot Hell's Canyon. I was fine for a few miles. A tiny creek that drained into the main river trickled near my path, so I drank from it. However, the trail soon veered off and climbed the valley side in seemingly endless switchbacks. An earlier brushfire had consumed all the vegetation, leaving the ground black and dry. A charbroiling, midsummer sun turned the canyon into a vast solar oven, making me sweat like a basted chicken. Now and then, I sipped my rationed water while resting in occasional slivers of shade cast by the trunks of burnt trees. My water was soon gone, so I hiked several miles with nothing to drink. As the sun gave up its torment and set, I finally made my way over the canyon rim onto the plateau. My mouth was dry and my lips were cracked. I had never felt so thirsty. At camp, I immediately poured a huge glass of iced water. Oh, how satisfying! I drank three pints in an hour.

Our worst experiences of physical thirst represent the soul's desire for God. Psalms 42 and 43 talk about soul-thirst.[706]

As the deer pants for the water brooks, so my soul pants for You, O God. My soul thirsts for God, for the living God; when shall I come and appear before God? My tears have been my food day and night, while they say to me all day long, "Where is your God?" These things I remember and I pour out my soul within me. For I used to go along with the throng and lead them in procession to the house of God, with the voice of joy and thanksgiving, a multitude keeping festival.

Why are you in despair, O my soul? And why have you become disturbed within me? Hope in God, for I shall again praise Him, for the help of His presence.

O my God, my soul is in despair within me; therefore I remember You from the land of the Jordan and the peaks of Hermon, from Mount Mizar. Deep calls to deep at the sound of Your waterfalls; all Your breakers and Your waves have rolled over me. The LORD will command His lovingkindness in the daytime; and His song will be with me in the night, a prayer to the God of my life. I will say to God my rock, "Why have You forgotten me? Why do I go mourning because of the oppression of the enemy?" As a shattering of my bones, my adversaries revile me, while they say to me all day long, "Where is your God?"

Why are you in despair, O my soul? And why have you become disturbed within me? Hope in God, for I shall yet praise Him, the help of my countenance and my God. (Ps. 42:1–11)

Vindicate me, O God, and plead my case against an ungodly nation; O deliver me from the deceitful and unjust man! For You are the God of my strength; why have You rejected me? Why do I go mourning because of the oppression of the enemy? O send out Your light and Your truth, let them lead me; let them bring me to Your holy hill and to Your dwelling places. Then I will go to the altar of God, to God my exceeding joy; and upon the lyre I shall praise You, O God, my God.

Why are you in despair, O my soul? And why are you disturbed within me? Hope in God, for I shall again praise Him, the help of my countenance and my God. (Ps. 43:1–5)

Soul Thirst

Comparing his thirst to a deer's, David said, "My soul pants for You . . . My soul thirsts for God, for the living God" (Ps. 42:2). David went straight to the point; he had no illusions that anything else would satisfy his soul the way God did. David's soul-thirst for the living God was passionate. It was not merely a casual desire. He poured out his soul and wept twenty-four-hour tears (Ps. 42:3–4). David wanted God and he wanted Him desperately.

When David described his love for the house of God and the altar of God (Pss. 42:4; 43:4), he did not have a building or a piece of sacred furniture in

God my exceeding joy
Heb.: *'El simkhat gili*
(Ps. 43:4)

My portion
Heb.: *Khelqi*
(Pss. 73:26; 142:5)

Portion of Jacob
Heb.: *Kheleq Ya'aqov*
(Jer. 10:16; 51:19)

Portion of my inheritance
Heb.: *Menat-khelqi*
(Ps. 16:5)

mind. He associated the altar with the presence of "**God, my exceeding joy.**" Joy is better than happiness; what we call happiness tends to be temporary and peripheral. God offers a lasting inner joy that prevails even when life is stormy. David wanted to experience God's presence. He wanted to be with God where He dwells.

Another name, the **Portion of Jacob**, presents God's satisfaction from a different angle.[707] It refers to God as an ample share, or a division of an inheritance. A treasure trove or a lucrative legacy would not provide for us as reliably as God does. God promises that He is the reward in our search for satisfaction.[708] One possible translation of Haggai 2:7 suggests that **Desire of Nations** is a name for the Messiah (though "wealth of nations" is more likely).[709] Jesus is certainly our most valid desire.

David spoke of the **living God** in whose name he had faced Goliath. David's experience went beyond dead religious rituals; his relationship with the living God was relevant to every challenge and decision that he faced.[710]

Living God
Heb.: *'Elohim khayyim*
(1 Sam. 17:26)
'Elohim khai
(2 Kings 19:4, 16;
Isa. 37:4, 17)
'El khai
(Pss. 42:2; 84:2;
Hos. 1:10)

God had helped and delivered him in tangible ways.[711]

Soul-thirst works rather like physical thirst. What makes us drink? Is it a sense of fear or a habit? "I must drink this water or my body will get messed up." Or do we drink because our doctor, our parents, or our spouse prescribe one cup, six or seven times a day? Most of us drink when we are thirsty. It's the same with our souls. Our souls desire to meet with

God, not out of fear or duty but out of a thirst that God put there when He created them.

Why Are You in Despair, O My Soul?

The repeated refrain of Psalms 42 and 43 is, "Why are you in despair, O my soul?" Several causes are possible.

Some people never realize or admit that they even have a soul—an inner life essence. Others deny that their souls need to drink from the Lord's presence. Our fleshy earth-suits are so prominent that we easily forget our souls. However, the soul is our everlasting essence. Either it will wander, forever parched, or it will take the path of eternal relationship with the Lord. We have to care for it.

If we ignore the soul's thirst pangs, its despair becomes deep and its cry grows almost silent. An occasional sense of inner emptiness may be the stifled call of a desiccating soul.

Souls sometimes reach a place of despair because we get too busy caring for the body and its activities, not pausing to quench soul-thirst. Even those like David who "used to go along with the throng and lead them in procession to the house of God," drift into this condition if they don't drink.[712] Satisfaction with God can become a mere memory.

We don't always live on a lush plateau; life has its dry canyons. Abraham spent more than ten years in spiritual aridity, as we will see in the next chapter. Circumstances never prevent us from drinking, but they can make it harder to identify our thirst and find satisfaction. David mentioned several factors that contribute to our spiritual challenges.

In Psalm 42:7–9, David described God's "breakers" and "waves" rolling over him. We don't know the exact circumstances he was referring to, but sometimes life feels like a storm-battered headland, doesn't it? We get overwhelmed as crises break over us—crashing waves of car problems, money shortages, relationship challenges, job demands, and sickness. They can all roll in rapidly, leaving us tottering. The next sneaker wave bowls us over and threatens to suck the last drop of life out.

David mentioned the enemy himself approaching and oppressing him.[713] Usually, we encounter human enemies—people who challenge us. Maybe friends or family members mock, revile, or scorn us. Subtle jabs often hurt more than blatant opposition. Life's circumstances sometimes appear to jeer at us, don't they? Things that don't go smoothly suggest that the flow of

God's blessings is blocked. Is God's power sufficient? Does He care enough to intervene? When goodness is fighting an uphill battle and evil is on a roll, we are taunted by questions: "Where's your God now?" We become sick—"Where is your God?" Our finances are in a mess—"Where is God? Has He forgotten or rejected us?"[714] Under these circumstances, our souls become extra thirsty for the presence of God.

David and the other psalmists were refreshingly honest about their feelings. They poured out their souls to God. And that's the first step to having our soul-thirsts quenched.

Soul Talk

We must not stop at admitting our true condition. We need the discipline of the psalmists to move on; they often spoke to their souls, and they directed them to the Lord. In Psalm 62:5, David instructed his soul to wait on God. Elsewhere, a psalmist said, "I lift up my soul" (Ps. 86:4). A person who has a healthy relationship with God sets aside problems to focus on the Lord. This inevitably results in hope, praise, and rejoicing. In another psalm, David complained about the injustices of life, crying, "O **God of my praise**, do not be silent."[715] By invoking that name, which implies deep thankfulness, he demonstrated his faith. No situation is too hard for God to resolve.

God of my praise
Heb.: *'Elohei tehillati*
(Ps. 109:1)

Habakkuk demonstrated the victory that accompanies a focused lifestyle. He sank to the depths as the gathering storm clouds of an ungodly superpower threatened Israel. Desperate, he asked God to explain. God revealed that He had selected a pagan army as His tool to correct Israel. The answer didn't soften the circumstances. In fact, Habakkuk's body quivered as he waited for the storm to break.[716] He kept his eyes on the Lord, and he chose to exalt Him and rejoice in Him. He sprang out of his canyon of despondency and skipped like a deer on the lush heights of praise.

*I will exalt in the LORD, I will rejoice in the **God of my salvation**. The Lord GOD is **my strength**,[717] and He has made my feet like hinds' feet, and makes me walk on my high places.* (Hab. 3:17–19)

Take Heart from the Hart

In Psalms 42–43, David used the deer to illustrate certain aspects of the soul. It is hard to get close enough to see a deer drinking. They are timid animals, drinking and feeding only when they feel safe. The soul likewise requires inner silence and solitude to meet with God and drink of His presence. Once we learn to focus, it is possible to achieve silence and solitude of the heart with others around. However, it is best to reserve the early morning to be alone with God. Develop the discipline of meditating (thinking deeply) on the Word, expecting God to speak. Such times of quiet can yield delightful discoveries of God's heart, as prayer, worship, and Scripture reading flow back and forth from one to another.

Amazingly, God is more interested in having intimacy with us than we are with Him. David knew God's commitment to draw his soul into His presence, so in Psalm 43:3 he called for God's light and truth to lead him.

What does it mean for the soul to be satisfied, to have its thirst quenched? When we concentrate on God in worship, prayer, or scriptural reflections, we are sometimes flooded with a deep sense of peace, joy, revelation, or understanding that is beyond our natural grasp. It may come as inner warmth, assurance, or calmness about the future—like snuggling in bed under a thick comforter. On other occasions, we experience a connection in prayer or worship; the celestial phone line is clear and we are relieved to find that He hears our hearts crying. He's not offended by our emotions; we can lay them before Him. Fear, anxiety, frustration, confusion, striving—all of these poisons are cleansed by a transfusion of His presence, which brings contentment. It feels as though the heat of a longstanding fever has dissipated and a peaceful coolness has replaced it. What matters most is a deeply satisfying sense of the reality, the greatness, and the love of God.

Deer drink little, but they drink regularly. When they thirst, they know exactly where to find a stream or a watering hole. Theirs is a cycle of thirsting and drinking, thirsting and drinking. Our lives don't have to lurch between high peaks and gaping chasms, especially those caused by denying the existence of our souls or ignoring its need for God's presence. The Lord wants us to adopt the habit of the deer. Thirst a little, and then go to Him to be satisfied.

God Cares

We learn from the psalms that the Lord cares about every aspect of our lives, including the deep canyons. Instead of shaming us by saying, "You shouldn't be depressed or feeling dry," He meets us where we are and comforts us.

God of all comfort
Gk.: *Theos pasēs paraklēseōs*
(2 Cor. 1:3)

Helper (NASB), **Comforter** (KJV), **Advocate** (NIV)
Gk.: *Paraklētos*
(John 14:16; 15:26; 16:7)

Advocate
Heb.: *Sahadi*
(Job 16:19)
Gk.: *Paraklētos*
(1 John 2:1)

Several names of God speak of His comfort. Paul blessed the **God of all comfort**, a name that includes the Greek word *paraklēseōs*. The root literally means "to call alongside," and it reminds us to do just that whenever we are in need. God responds in the form of the *Paraklētos*, the **Holy Spirit**. *Paraklētos* is translated in three ways to reflect the varying aid He brings: **Helper** (NASB), **Comforter** (KJV), and **Advocate** (NIV).

For a short period of time, friends at school rejected me and I felt cut off from God's comfort. A deep but subtle questioning crept in: Did God care for me? Could He do anything? I faced subsequent challenges with my faith undermined by those nagging doubts. Where faith's hands once reached out to grasp answers to prayer, unbelief's hands dropped and hid in my pockets, and I turned away. My doubts made failure inevitable. Months later, when I let the Lord comfort me in my pain, I grew. God soothed me with a sense of His presence. He revealed the truth about what had happened and gave me insight into His purpose in allowing me to feel pain. God healed me with few scars. David said that God is "the help of my countenance." His comfort makes a difference.[718]

Other names of God emphasize His care for every part of our lives: body and soul. Psalm 54:4 calls God the helper and sustainer of the soul. David prayed to the **God of my life**.[719] He is the **God of all flesh**.[720] Although our flesh is temporary, He still watches over it. **Immanuel**, God with us, is intimately involved in the details of our lives.[721] When *Yahweh yir'eh* sees a practical need, He provides.

David spoke of the **God of my strength**.[722] The name tells of a strong place of protection. A similar image appears in another verse, in which David refers to **God my Rock**. The word for "rock" (*sela'*) implies a craggy cliff with large fractures. Moro Rock in King's Canyon National Park is a huge outcrop, but on one side there is a vertical fissure large enough to shelter the mature tree that is nestled there. *Sela'* speaks of security, a handy place to hide in a hurry, and a place of safety from mocking enemies.[723]

There is a Fountain

The descriptive name "rock" (*sela'*) has an interesting double meaning. It is more than a place of refuge. Paul wrote that the rock that split open and gushed water to satisfy Israel's thirst in the wilderness was the spiritual **rock**: Christ.[724] How appropriate! Jesus is the ultimate provision and satisfaction.

Jesus fulfilled yet another name, which Jeremiah spoke prophetically when he warned Israel to turn to the **fountain of living waters** and not to other sources.[725] The word used for a fountain is linked to the idea of digging. Picture a spring. Clear away any debris and dig a channel, then you can collect the water. It needs maintenance to remain accessible. Jesus is such a fountain; He is constant, but we have to cultivate our relationships with Him to stay satisfied.

Rock
Gk.: *Petra*
(1 Cor. 10:4)

Fountain of living waters
Heb.: *Meqor mayim khayyim*
(Jer. 2:13; 17:13)

Jeremiah contrasted the fountain with a cistern. Cisterns are massive and they give the appearance of a secure and reliable source. The cistern at King Herod's winter palace of Masada held a million gallons. Theoretically, that is enough water for a person to drink, cook with, take showers, wash the car, and replenish the goldfish bowl—for life. However, cisterns can have hidden cracks. They depend on rainfall, and the water becomes stale. Natural fountains appear feeble and liable to contamination, but they remain fresh. God is like a fountain. We must trust Him against our normal judgment, using that vital spiritual muscle of faith. Then we find Him to be the most reliable supply.

Another prophecy prepared the world for Jesus, coming as a fountain, cleansing sin and iniquity.[726] During the Jewish Feast of Tabernacles, Jesus dramatically interrupted the temple ritual. He stood and cried out, "If anyone is thirsty, let Him come to Me and drink" (John 7:37). He described a simple process. Faith in Him is the basic condition for Him to quench our thirst. "He who believes in Me, as the Scripture said, 'From his innermost being will flow rivers of living water'" (John 7:38–39). Jesus goes beyond satisfying us; His life overflows. The Spirit in us bubbles out like a spring, forming rivers of living water that flow on to refresh other dusty, dry lives. Jesus might have alluded to any of several Scriptures that speak of the desert being watered.[727] One passage even speaks of a coming king as a desert stream.[728] In Jesus, Yahweh completed the supply of living water. Now it can overflow through us into the spiritually arid world to water others.

Chapter 12

RIDING BY FAITH

Any investigation into His ways assures us that what we see is indeed what we get. But so is what we do not see. The depth of His character stands beyond measure—not as a dark abyss but as a glorious, inexhaustible fount. Although new revelations emerge daily, none is inconsistent with what we have come to know of God's essential person. They are extrapolations rather than inventions. They give us reason to seek the divine unknown rather than fear it.

—George Otis, *God's Trademarks*

God is named after His relationships with a motley array of people. Several names associate God with individuals, groups, and even their hometowns.

Noah blessed the **God of Shem**.[729] The Egyptians understood Him vaguely as the **God of the Hebrews**. The Hebrews took their name from their ancestor, Eber (one who emigrates, wanders, or, crosses over).[730] **God of Israel** was the name used when Moses and the elders saw Him on Mount Sinai. Notice David's words in 1 Chronicles 29:10, "O LORD God of Israel our father."[731] Moses and David knew the Lord as the God of their founding father Jacob, whose

169

God of Shem
Heb.: *'Elohei Shem*
(Gen. 9:26)

God of Elijah
Heb.: *'Elohei 'Eliyyahu*
(2 Kings 2:14)

God of Jerusalem
Heb.: *'Elohei*
Yerushalaim
(2 Chron. 32:19)
Aram.: *'Elah*
Yerushelem
(Ezra 7:19)

God of Hezekiah
Heb.: *'Elohei*
Yekhizqiyyahu
(2 Chron. 32:17)

God of the Hebrews
Heb.: *'Elohei ha'Ivrim*
(or 'Ivriyyim)
(Ex. 3:18; 5:3; 7:16;
9:1, 13; 10:3)

God of Israel
Heb.: *'Elohei Yisra'el*
(Ex. 24:10)
'El Yisra'el
(Ps. 68:35)

name God had changed to Israel.[732] When Elisha took the prophetic mantle from his master, he invoked "the LORD, the **God of Elijah**" and divided the River Jordan just as Elijah had done. The Assyrians and King Artaxerxes of Persia referred to the **God of Jerusalem**. Sennacherib mocked the **God of Hezekiah**.

On one level, the meaning of such names is self-evident; He was the God of those people and He is our God too. There's no great revelation in this. However, profound lessons underlie these names. In the first place, the names don't imply God was an asset they possessed (the God belonging to Israel). Instead, they tell of the God who possessed and repossessed His people. Abraham and Jacob have much to teach us; their relationships with God developed over the years. Through them (and some supporting characters), we'll learn more of what it means to "know God."

God's relational names first appear in patriarchal times because many of His self-revelations came to particular individuals during that period. The names were respectful references to foundations established between God and His people. To understand a name, we must study the individual and ask how God related to that person. Biblical heroes are distant mentors for anyone who wants to grow closer to God. Each one presents a different perspective. Together, they expand our understanding of God.

A Room with a View

Timberline Lodge is six thousand feet up on the slopes of Mount Hood in Oregon. It commands a tremendous view. On clear days, Southern Oregon is visible. When Janet and I eat at the upper restaurant, we hover in the entryway until the diners at one of the tables by the picture window start to leave. Then we dart to the seats before the server has time to clear the table. The window is ten feet long and six feet high. It has a metal brace attached to its center with a rubber pad so that the hurricane force winds that slam into it during storms don't blast it out. From that vantage point, one of us eats lunch looking at mountains in Central Oregon, while the other scans the foothills to the west. Neither of us can see the entire panorama without straining the neck or spilling soup.

What we learn about God from biblical heroes is rather like a view from different seats. Reflect on David's life. Broadly speaking, his window on God opened on His protection and deliverance. God accomplished His purposes for him no matter what the opposition. David experienced His faithfulness, mercy, and forgiveness. He delighted in His approachability. God's presence deeply satisfied David. David's story is the background to the title **God of your father David**, as Isaiah related it to the mortally ill Hezekiah. Facing death, Hezekiah needed to know God just as David had known Him.

> **God of your father David**
> Heb.: 'Elohei Dawid 'avikha
> (2 Kings 20:5; Isa. 38:5)

Nebuchadnezzar blessed the **God of Shadrach, Meshach, and Abednego**, knowing He had saved them from the furnace. Another king, Darius, found inspiration in Daniel's relationship with the **God of Daniel**. Daniel had similar experiences to David, but Daniel also received profound revelations. Daniel's window presents a slightly different angle on God.

> **God of Shadrach, Meshach, and Abednego**
> Aram.: 'Elahahon di-Shadrakh, Meshakh wa'Aved nego
> (Dan. 3:28–29)
> **God of Daniel**
> Aram.: 'Elaheh di-Daniyyel
> (Dan. 6:26)

As we walk through life's challenges, each one is a new opportunity to know God better. What will people learn about God's nature from your relationship with Him? Two words of caution though—just as the window does not create the view, so a person's perspective neither establishes nor changes who God actually is. The Bible is our reference point; it explains the view. The Bible ensures we are not hallucinating, that what we see is not a shifting cloud but mountain-solid truth. Also, our perspective overlaps with that of many others. We need to respect those who know the biblical God in a slightly different way due to their cultural background or the experiences He has brought them through.

In the next chapter, we will look at Jacob's relationship with God and why God changed Jacob's name to Israel. For now, come and peer through Abraham's window on God.

The Family Tree

When Moses encountered the burning bush, he worried that the Hebrews would scoff at his story, dismissing it as a desert mirage or a symptom of sunstroke. Moses needed to know who was speaking to him; he had to provide a name, a reference, if you like. So, God introduced Himself as the **God of your fathers**, and more explicitly the **God of Abraham, Isaac, and Jacob**.[733] The names occur in slightly different forms throughout the Bible. Moses used one after God heard Israel's cries for deliverance from slavery and promised to give them Canaan.[734] The names reminded Israel of God's relationship with Abraham and themselves. As descendants of Abraham, they were also "the people of the **God of Abraham**" (Ps. 47:9). By invoking such names during national crises, they appealed to the covenant promises made with Abraham and reiterated to his son Isaac and grandson Jacob.[735] The introductory names, which God spoke to Moses, told Israel that the patriarchs' God was a God of covenant relationship. The nation was encouraged in one basic item of faith: God looks after His people because they belong to Him.

God of your fathers
Heb.: *'Elohei 'avotekhem*
(Ex. 3:13, 16)

God of our fathers
Gk.: *Ho Theos tōn paterōn hēmōn*
(Acts 3:13; 5:30; 22:14; 24:14)

God of Abraham, Isaac, and Jacob
Heb.: *'Elohei 'Avraham, Yitskhaq weYa'aqov*
(Ex. 3:16)
Gk.: *Ho Theos Abraam kai Isaak kai Iakōb*
(Matt. 22:32; Acts 3:13)

God had established a special relationship with Israel, which gave the name political undertones that surfaced later. Yes, God still loved the descendants of Ishmael and Esau, but their claims on Him were less than Israel's. Hebrews 2:16 restates the long-held belief of the Jewish nation that God "gives help to the descendant of Abraham." One blessing, "May the name of the **God of Jacob** set you securely on high," (Ps. 20:1) appealed to the same long-standing covenant faithfulness.

Just as we often gain insights about God when we reach significant milestones or crossroads in life, so Abraham's relationship with God matured with each momentous event. The highlights, sandwiched between silent decades, pack the pages of Abraham's story in Genesis. At milestones, God often revealed a new name to Abraham. Like an old trunk gradually collecting life treasures, Abraham's understanding of God grew over the years. His legacy is important to us because what God was to the patriarchs, He was to the nation that descended from them, and He is to us. But how can that be, unless we share the tribal blood?

Spiritual descent requires more than lines on a family tree. John the baptizer warned the Jews that being children of Abraham was insufficient. "Bear fruits in keeping with repentance, and do not begin to say to yourselves, 'We have Abraham for our father,' for I say to you that from these stones God is able to raise up children to Abraham."[736] In John 8, Jesus infuriated the so-called "children of Abraham," who already wanted to kill Him. He contrasted their behavior with Abraham's.[737] Far from harboring murderous inclinations like those Jews did, "Abraham rejoiced to see My day" (John 8:56). Answering a question about salvation, Jesus spoke of a narrow door to God's kingdom, which included "Abraham and Isaac and Jacob and all the prophets" (Luke 13:23–28).[738]

So, what was Abraham's relationship with God like? How did it ensure him a place in the kingdom and set him apart from many of his own race? What made him an example for us and makes us like family? Let's climb up to Abraham's attic to unpack that trunk.

Faith Rider

Living a life of faith is like learning to ride a bicycle. After I had mastered the basics on a small bike with stabilizer wheels, my parents bought me a shiny new bike for my seventh birthday. We drove to an abandoned World War II airfield. It was flat and the paved runways made excellent practice grounds, so long as one avoided the occasional potholes that had resulted from twenty years of neglect. My bicycle was too large. The owner of the bike store had promised I would grow into it, but at that point, only one foot could touch the ground at a time.

I did well at first. My wobbles gradually became less dramatic; my nervous curves became more confident straight lines. Then disaster struck. A wobble intersected with a pothole. My toes were too slow to the ground, so my body hit the concrete before them. The crash-landing knocked out my wind and my confidence. I reverted to wobbling around on the soft lawn at home for a week.

The life of our faith-hero, Abraham, was like me on my new bicycle; he wobbled. (Of course, he didn't have a bicycle, but let's assume he rode a camel. They seem like precarious mounts.) In Genesis 12–25, which covers at least thirty-five years, Abraham swung from incidents of astounding revelation into long spiritual doldrums. Even so, Scripture describes his wobbly relationship with God as a friendship and as an example of faith. God revealed some of His most memorable names to Abraham on his shaky faith ride.

When we first meet him, he is called Abram (his name changed later, as we will see). His family left Ur and settled in Haran (Crossroads). Later, the **God of glory**[739] called on the sprightly seventy-five-year-old to make another geographical journey, which was paralleled by a tougher faith journey. Abram had to leave the family home, but God promised him blessings, land, a great name, and countless heirs.[740] God's blessing was two-fold; he would spawn a great nation and the nation would spread the blessing to families everywhere. It is not a picture of self-indulgence or even favoritism—Abram would gain his great name as the blessings flowed out. It's a biblical principle that greatness is a byproduct of blessing others.

Abram relocated in simple, unquestioning obedience. He traveled through the land, eventually settling in the south of Israel. God often places us at crossroads, where we have to choose between a path of His calling and our own way. Abram's bold beginning is highly commendable; don't get stuck like the rest of his family.

During an encounter with the mysterious Melchizedek, Abram identified Yahweh (though he probably had only a rudimentary understanding of that name) with *'El 'elyon*, God Most High, possessor of heaven and earth.[741]

God expanded on His promise of giving Abram descendants as innumerable as the dust.[742] As Abram aged, he contrasted God's promise of an heir with his circumstances. He probably thought about it while he lay awake at night or milked his bad-tempered camels. He had no children. Medical common sense said that he never could. Sometimes, God sets us on a path through life with an initial burst of exciting, prophetic, and visionary guidance. Things start to fall into place; our anticipation grows. However, progress often slows. Why? The vital inner preparations take time—character formation, faith strengthening, and prayer warfare. In Genesis 15, Abram complained to God that the only way he saw his family line continuing was through his slave (vv. 1–3). "So what, if I'm drinking milk and eating honey in the promised land? My wife is barren." Abram tilted and wobbled in his faith.

Far from rebuking Abram for his unbelief, God reassured him. The Creator of the heavens pointed to the unpolluted night sky and again He promised him countless children (vv. 4–5). It was as if God had grasped the reins (or handlebars) to steady him. Right then, Abram must have surged forward in faith because Genesis says, "He believed in the LORD; and He reckoned it to him as righteousness" (v. 6). Abram took God at His word. It was a defining moment, a milestone the Bible keeps returning to. It established Abram as an example of faith.

Sadly, Abram wobbled right back into his doubting questions. When he asked for evidence that he would possess the land, the Lord made a covenant with him (v. 8). Blood covenants, such as the one described in verses 9–18, were the ancient equivalents of legal guarantees or contracts. Typically, the two parties committed their character, reputation, and all their resources. The contract carried a penalty clause. The heifer, goat, and ram, each bloodily severed and arranged on the ground (v. 10), made a statement for both parties: "If I break covenant, may I be mutilated like these animals."[743] In this case, Abram's part was easy. He had nothing to do. In fact, God put him to sleep. The smoking firepot and the flaming torch marked God's presence (v. 17). God committed Himself to unilaterally fulfilling His promise to a wobbly faith walker, while the latter snored.

Covenant makers also ate roast meat together. The meal sealed a new and deeper relationship. It's not clear, but perhaps Abram gained his reputation as a "friend of God" at the forming of this covenant.[744] By now, Abram was sailing down the road—believing that God would give him a son, grasping a watertight covenant promise, and basking in his friendship with God. However, his faith remained vulnerable.

Some people find it easier to trust that God will fulfill unsolicited promises. Begging Him produces a nagging doubt: "Did He only respond because He was sick of my pestering?" Abram failed to grasp that God was doing more than appeasing a nag or favoring a friend in need. God had His own cast-iron reasons to birth a nation through which to bless the world.

If Abram had known God's purposes, perhaps he would have resisted the gust of doubt and temptation that blew on him from Sarai, his wife.[745] We all face peer pressure. Having learned to deal with personal doubts, we often wobble because those closest to us raise new doubts. Sarai suggested that they lend God a hand by appointing Hagar, her maid, as a surrogate mother. At eighty-five years old, Abram decided that this made good sense. But human good ideas often insult the greatness of God. We end up hurting others and ourselves. Abram was blown off course and Hagar got hurt. Her story is worth a detour because she received her own window on God and gave Him another name.

Touched by an Angel (Genesis 16:1–16)

Hagar lived on the edge of society, relationally and spiritually. She was an Egyptian minority in a Hebrew home and a marginalized servant. The surrogate pregnancy gave her a new status. It even offered the luxury of secretly gloating over her barren mistress. She soon discovered how precarious her position was. Sarai reminded her that as a maid she had no legal value or personal rights— hence the exploitative and dehumanizing arrangement. Through no choice of her own, Hagar had become part of a plan that diverted Abram and Sarai from God's way. Hagar did what many of us do when we are living on the edge, especially when that edge crumbles under our feet. In keeping with her name, which suggests "fugitive," she fled.

We meet Hagar at a Bronze Age rest stop (v. 7). Have you ever noticed that rest areas tend to attract, shall we say, unusual people? I have stopped at some and thought I was interrupting a cast reunion of science fiction characters. However, many of them are hurting, lonely, needy, and searching. Like many other travelers, Hagar visited the spring to refuel the camel, rest, and check the maps. The oasis lay on the main highway, "the way to Shur." The road led back to Egypt, her homeland, but away from the family who had exposed her to a life with God. As she glanced back in her mind, perhaps she realized how wholesome her life had been. Yet Abram and Sarai's faith had wavered. This time, their unbelief had entangled and hurt her. So, she had every right to leave, didn't she? What else would a woman in her situation do? She refocused her mind on Egypt. Faith in God's promises and relationships with His people were too hard.

Hagar didn't realize it immediately, but the unusual individual who struck up a conversation with her at the well had been sent by God. God had gone out of His way to speak to her. The opener was simple: "Where have you come from and where are you going?" (v. 8) It paved the way for a message from God. The angel told Hagar to return and submit to Sarai. God would redeem her painful circumstances. She also received a promise that was surprisingly similar to Abram's. God promised her countless descendants.

Amazing things happen when we encounter God. Often, He reveals more of who He is, and sometimes He gives us new identities or senses of purpose.

When God met with Hagar in her crisis, it showed how deeply He cared for her, a low-status fugitive. He revealed more of Himself, the God who hears cries of pain (v.11). God stamped that truth firmly into Hagar's life by telling her to name her son Ishmael, "God hears." While it is not a name of God, it celebrates the wonderful truth that God is deeply and compassionately interested in His people. God reinforced the name several years later. He heard her when she fled; later, He heard Ishmael after their eviction.[746] God hears fugitives and outcasts.

In Moses' time, God comforted the nation, saying that He saw Israel's affliction and attended to her cries.[747] Others called Him the **God of knowledge** and **One perfect in knowledge**.[748] Daniel knew God as **Revealer of mysteries**[749] and God interpreted Nebuchadnezzar's dream to him. So incisive is God's knowledge that it penetrates individual hearts; nothing is hidden from Him. Job 11:11 says, "He knows false men, and He sees iniquity without investigating." Jesus declared, "I am He who searches the minds and hearts."[750] Jeremiah's words fit Hagar's situation, "'Am I a **God who is near**,' declares the LORD, 'and not a **God far off**?'" (Jer. 23:23).[751] Actually, He is both. Psalm 75:1 rejoices, "For Your name is near." Job 34:21 says, "His eyes are upon the ways of a man, and He sees all his steps," including the retreating ones.

God of knowledge
Heb.: *'El de'ot*
(1 Sam. 2:3)

One perfect in knowledge
Heb.: *Temim de'ot*
(Job 36:4; 37:16)

Revealer of mysteries
Aram.: *Galeh razin*
(Dan. 2:28–29, 47)

God who is near
Heb.: *'Elohei miqqarov*
(Jer. 23:23)

God far off
Heb.: *'Elohei merakhoq*
(Jer. 23:23)

As Hagar realized the messenger's full identity (v. 13), she grasped an important truth. God's power is not passive; He keeps His caring eye on us and is poised to act. Hagar felt His loving gaze pierce her pain and shame. Her fears of condemnation and further rejection, which had been reinforced by her years on the edge, evaporated as she became aware of His acceptance.

Relieved, Hagar named Him the **God who sees** (v. 13). It is the first name of God that the Bible declares to be a name. In celebration, she named the well *Be'er lakhai ro'i*, meaning, "Well of the Living One who sees me" (v. 14). Hagar responded to His call for recommitment and submission. The well became a place of turning around. She stopped running and put her faith in

God who sees (me)
Heb.: *'El ro'i*
(Gen. 16:13)

God's promise. Hagar didn't just get water for her camel; she also received a spark for the fire of her life in God.

Spiritual Gatorade (Genesis 17:1–21)

While God was turning Hagar around, He said nothing to Abram. Thirteen tense years pass before we rejoin Abram. Was Ishmael his best hope for an heir after all? Then there was that name! Every time he, Sarai, Hagar, or one of the servants spoke Ishmael's name, it haunted Abram. "Ishmael" (God hears)—was it promise or mockery? Would God hear Abram's heart cry or was God's ear reserved for Hagar alone, as if to spite Abram for his wobbling faith?

Perhaps Abram felt edged out, disqualified by his actions, going through the motions of life as he waited wearily for death. For different reasons, we enter similar seasons—times when our expectations of God meeting us or answering our prayers are low. Take heart from Genesis 17. God took the initiative and appeared to His friend Abram during his crisis. God encouraged Abram and refreshed his understanding of the promise. Ishmael would grow into a great nation, but God's "Plan A" still involved giving Abram and Sarai a natural son (vv. 16–20). Three significant things happened in the meeting:

First, Genesis 17 records the first of several encounters in which God is referred to as *'El shaddai* (v. 1). Later, God reminded Moses of the encounter: "I appeared to Abraham, Isaac and Jacob, as *'El shaddai*, but by My name, *Yahweh*, I did not make Myself known to them" (Ex. 6:3).

God Almighty
Heb.: *'El shaddai*
(Gen. 17:1)

Almighty
Heb.: *Shaddai*
(Gen. 49:25)
Gk.: *Pantokratōr*
(Rev. 1:8; 16:14; 19:15)

Early translators of the Old Testament into Greek (the Septuagint) often picked the word *pantokratōr* to translate *shaddai*. *Pantokratōr* literally means "all power" and led to the English equivalent **Almighty**.[752]

The Hebrew name has several possible derivations. One root associates it with the might of mountains (Akkadian, *shadu*), another with devastating power (*shadad*).[753] With authoritative strength, the Almighty scatters kings and sends destruction on "the day of the LORD."[754] Confusingly, the Septuagint scribes also used *pantokratōr* to translate "LORD of hosts," connecting His might with His armies.

Another possible derivation is the word for a mother's breast (*shad*).[755] One writer called Him "the pourer or shedder forth" of sustenance.[756] Since the Hebrew word *she* means "who" and *day* means "sufficient," perhaps the name emphasizes that He is sufficient to meet all our needs. Five times, Old Testament translators chose the Greek word *hikanos* (sufficient) to emphasize Shaddai's sufficiency.[757]

Rabbis spied an acrostic in the three Hebrew consonants that form the name. The letters *shin*, *dalet* and *yod* suggested the phrase "*Shomer daltot Yisra'el*," which means "Guardian of Israel's doors." Comfortingly, the Almighty is indeed the "One who watches the doors of Israel" and all His people. Today, a slanting tube called a *mezuzah* is often attached to Jewish doorposts; it bears the letter *shin*, which stands for *Shaddai*.

With all the rich meaning packed into the name *'El shaddai*, we can be sure God wanted Abram to know Him as the One whose power was enough to accomplish all His will.

Second, God's dealings with people fit a pattern: when we reach the end of ourselves, the Almighty meets us. While we rely on our own abilities and ideas, we exclude God; when we sprawl helplessly on our faces, we give Him room to work. *'El shaddai* occurs seven times in the Old Testament.[758] The single word *shaddai* occurs forty-one times, thirty-one of which are in the book of Job, the story of a man who hit bottom. God met Paul in trouble and declared, "My grace is sufficient for you, for power is perfected in weakness" (2 Cor. 12:9).

'El shaddai is the name associated with His covenant to Abram's descendants.[759] El shaddai established a central truth about His covenant promises: fulfillment does not depend on our ability but on His resources. God was more than able to produce a son, even a multitude of nations. His commitment to His promises and His miraculous power are so great that He cuts through even the toughest difficulties and silences our unbelieving laughter.[760] Nothing is "too difficult for the LORD."[761]

Third, El shaddai left marks on Abram and Sarai by changing their names (vv. 4–5, 15–16). Abram, the "exalted father," became Abraham, "father of a multitude," emphasizing God's commitment to providing descendants. There may be significance in the insertion of the *h*; it's a sound that uses extra breath, and it is a letter from Yahweh's own name. God's Spirit breathed into Abraham more divine life resources. Similarly, Sarai became Sarah. God also required the circumcision of Abraham and all males in his household (vv. 9–14). It was a physical mark of the covenant, indicating inner transformation and a stripping away of self-dependence.[762] We all need an infusion of the Almighty's life to transform us into new men and women.

The encounter provides evidence that the God of Abraham is utterly competent to fulfill every promise He has ever made.

A Wail of Two Cities (Genesis 18:1–33)

God continued to prepare Abraham, and his "ride" of faith became steadier. He was ready for his next lesson.

> *The LORD said, "Shall I hide from Abraham what I am about to do, since Abraham will surely become a great and mighty nation, and in him all the nations of the earth will be blessed? For I have chosen him, so that he may command his children and his household after him to keep the way of the LORD by doing righteousness and justice, so that the LORD may bring upon Abraham what He has spoken about him." (Genesis 18:17–19)*

God had heard a cry of great sin in Sodom and Gomorrah. It was time to judge and punish them. Abraham felt troubled that God might sweep the righteous away with the wicked (v. 23). He began to appeal to God's justice, saying, "Shall not the **Judge of all the earth** deal justly?" (v. 25).

Abraham secured God's agreement to spare the cities if ten righteous people lived there. This incident teaches us about the effectiveness of prayer, but also about righteousness and justice. Abraham learned of the inherent fairness of God's justice. He also witnessed the importance of righteous living; since fewer than ten righteous people dwelt in the evil cities, God destroyed them. However, God's judgment comes after He provides opportunities for deliverance (God evacuated Lot's righteous family before the firestorm).[763] Scanning the smoking ruins, Abraham was ready to mentor the nation in righteousness and justice. He had watched the rescuing of a remnant from fiery wrath. Now he could teach his descendants about the importance of godly behavior and the nature of just judgment. A righteous and just nation could, in turn, glorify God and bless the entire earth by sharing those truths. Abraham faced one last test.

Dirty Chips (Genesis 22:1–14)

I'm no fan of ordinary potato chips, so my discovery of Dirty Potato Chips came as a pleasant surprise. They serve as a light-hearted illustration to explain how to recognize authentic faith. For years, the people at Dirty said this about the quality of their chips:

Many decades past, all potato chips were made in the old fashioned way. Hand picked potatoes were cooked in open kettles, one batch at a time with a fry master waiting to remove the golden chips at the peak of their flavor. Today, potato chips are made in monstrous fryers with most of the flavor being washed out to prevent the potato slices from sticking to each other. Computers monitor these monsters for efficiency, not for taste or crunch. "Dirty" Potato Chips truly is a giant leap backward in technology! Once again, we select potatoes with the greatest of care, we don't wash the flavor out of the slices, and we cook in small batches using pure peanut oil. A discriminating fry master—not a computer—insures that this bag of "Dirty" Potato Chips will be the crispiest and tastiest you've ever had.[764]

During Abraham's journey the "divine fry master" (a title not found in the Bible) had opportunities to taste his progress. Each time, Abraham had grown a little in his knowledge of God, and he was better prepared to be the father of a multitude. Genesis 22 tells of one final test.

What was the subject of Abraham's test? The grade the angel of the LORD gave him in verse 12 provides the clue. "Now I know that you fear God." God's discerning fry master declared him to be at the peak of his flavor. The test: did Abraham fear God enough to obey Him?

When you read of Abraham's faith, don't switch off, saying, "Abraham is in the Old Testament. He's a 'big potato.' How can I compare with him?" No, remember how like us Abraham was. He embarked on his faith journey with enthusiasm, but he quickly wobbled and fell apart. He tried to birth plans of his own without listening to God. He doubted that God would miraculously give him a son. For thirty-five years, he faltered. However, along his wobbly way, there were enough stretches of confidence in God for him to rank among the great faith heroes.[765] There is nothing to stop you and me from living in faith.

One day, we will all face the discerning fry master. He will ask, "Are you a tasty and crunchy God-fearer?" So, what did the angel mean by "fearing God," and how does it relate to faith?

First, let's consider what fearing God doesn't mean. Vague spiritual quests don't qualify. Worming around in books about spirituality is not enough. A Christian heritage derived from one's family or nation doesn't count. Being a leader or part of the "in" group at church is irrelevant. Good deeds don't cut it either. The listed items sound admirable, but compared with being a truly "dirty" God-fearer they are monster chips, lacking crispness or flavor.

Three things make a God-fearer:

First, Abraham had a relationship with God. When God called his name, he recognized His voice and responded, "Here I am" (v. 1). God's people listen to His voice.

Second, Abraham took God seriously and obeyed His commands in a timely way. Often, we procrastinate or allow other voices of authority to divert us from God's instructions. When God told Abraham to climb Mount Moriah and make a sacrifice, "Abraham rose early in the morning, saddled his donkey . . . and went" (vv. 3–8). His obedience went so far that he drew a knife to pierce his son—a knife that had dissected many animal sacrifices.

Third, Abraham had faith in God. Even though he wobbled, his belief pleased God and "it was reckoned to him as righteousness" (Gen. 15:6).

Jesus said that faith like a mustard seed is enough to move mountains.[766] Many of us hear His words as a nebulous challenge. We have a vague impression of what faith is, and we assume that we will never have enough of it. But Jesus didn't say those words to tantalize us cruelly. Faith is attainable. Abraham provides a real-life example of faith. Like other biblical heroes, he is not remembered for his perfection but for his faith. God knows that we are imperfect and we have nothing in us, but faith has its object outside us. The Lord Almighty, the all-sufficient, is the object of our faith. One writer called faith "the hand of the heart." It reaches out to receive from God, but it can add nothing to His gift.[767] Bent under a bundle of sticks, Isaac walked up the hill and asked his father, "Where's the sacrifice?" Abraham reached for the sufficiency of El shaddai and said, "God will provide for himself the lamb for the burnt offering" (vv. 7–8). If only he had known how prophetic his words were!

Abraham's faith went beyond a confident statement of trust in God's provision. Faith finds expression in words, but more importantly, it results in action—often sacrifice. Abraham had struggled for decades to believe God would provide an heir. Now he had enough faith to relinquish his most precious treasure: his only legitimate son, who represented God's promise that Abraham would have descendants. David Stern explains that James (*Ya'acov* in Hebrew) and Paul (*Sha'ul*) wrote about different sides of the coin of faith: "Ya'acov's point is that if good works are subtracted from genuine faith, what is left is barren and dead. Sha'ul's point is that if legalistic observances are added to or substituted for genuine faith, that result too is barren and dead."[768] Abraham's preparation of Isaac was evidence of authentic faith.[769]

Paul was careful to warn against performance replacing faith (belief). Paul called Abraham "the father of all who believe" (Rom. 4:11–12) because Abraham believed in God's promise before Isaac's birth and before circumcision. Circumcision was the physical mark of the covenant relationship between God and Abraham's clan, a covenant that only God could fully keep. In God's eyes, Abraham's family includes all who put faith in Him. And that answers our earlier question about tribal membership. Faith secures a place in Abraham's multitudinous family, regardless of ethnic background.[770]

God has a "book of remembrance . . . written before Him for those who fear the LORD and who esteem His name" (Mal. 3:16). If being a God-fearer means listening to Him and obeying with practical faith, then surely Abraham's name appears near the front of that book.

Eyes of Faith (Genesis 22:1–14)

Abraham's confidence in God grew as ours does. Abraham's journey began with a single step of faith (Gen. 12:1–6). With each stride of trusting obedience, Abraham experienced God's faithfulness and His all-sufficiency to fulfill His promises. In each chapter of his life, Abraham saw a new vista of God's character and purposes, which were often summed up in a newly revealed name. Finally, a ram caught in a thicket revealed God's provision in a glorious new light. The ram was a practical solution and a prophetic sign—the first substitutional sacrifice (v. 13).

> **LORD will provide**
> (**Jehovah jireh** KJV)
> Heb.: *Yahweh yir'eh*
> (Gen. 22:14)

In response, Abraham named the mountain "the **LORD will provide**" (v. 14). "*Yahweh yir'eh*" does not highlight Abraham's faith trial or his victory; it commemorates God's provision. The name hides a play on words in the original language. It expresses that "the LORD sees and He will provide." God's pre-vision leads to His provision. A similar play on words in English is "God will see to it." This name is related to *'El ro'i*, the name revealed to Hagar, but with the added emphasis that the all-seeing God meets our deepest needs.

The prophetic statement, "In the mount of the LORD it will be provided," echoed around the same mountain for years (v. 14). Study the geographical history of that ridge. One thousand years later, Solomon built the Temple there—animal sacrifices continued.[771] Another millennium passed and a mob arrested Jesus in the thick of Gethsemane. As they marched Him up the same hill, He was bent under His own wooden execution stake. Soldiers laid Him on it and crucified Him—the final sacrifice. Abraham's words are an echo from the Eternal One. The message of the cross reverberates down the passages of time like wind in a flute. Bursting through a finger hole in history which was opened by Abraham's faith, the words pointed ahead to God's costly sacrifice of His **only begotten Son**—prophetic music to our ears.

Where Genesis 22 tells of Abraham's "only" (*yakhid*) son, the Septuagint uses *agapētos* (beloved). The thoughts connect naturally because an only son is especially beloved. God called Jesus His **beloved Son** using the same word.[772]

Only begotten Son
Gk.: *Ho hyios ho monogenos* (uniqueness)
(John 3:16–18;
1 John 4:9)

Firstborn
Gk.: *Prōtotokos* (rights)
(Col. 1:15, 18;
Heb. 1:6)

Scripture also calls Jesus the **only begotten Son** (*monogenēs*) and **firstborn**, but neither name suggests that God created Jesus. The first name speaks of His uniqueness; the latter speaks of the rights and privileges of a firstborn son. Luke used *monogenēs* to describe a dead man as the only son of the widow of Nain.[773] The same word describes Isaac. He was one of a kind—unique—because he alone was the child of promise and miracle.[774] Imagine Abraham's agony when God called him to sacrifice Isaac, the son he had desired for decades. Then reflect on what God endured to offer His perfect and only begotten Son, in place of sinful humans, who had rejected Him.

Zechariah envisioned a day when participants in the crucifixion would "look on Me whom they have pierced; and they will mourn for Him, as one mourns for an only [*yakhid*] son, and they will weep bitterly over him, like the bitter weeping over a firstborn" (Zech. 12:10). Roman lashes tore Jesus apart. Nails pierced God's Son, and a sword severed the **Lamb of God**.[775] Men mutilated Jesus' body like an animal's—a bloody punishment intended for covenant breakers. God made a sacrifice far more costly than the one He had called Abraham to make. God's sacrifice shows how much He loves us. "By this the love of God was manifested in us, that God has sent His only begotten Son into the world so that we might live through Him" (1 John 4:9). And live we can, because Jesus' death restored our covenant with God.

Jesus said, "Abraham rejoiced to see My day, and He saw it and was glad" (John 8:56). It's likely that He had Abraham's prophetic words in mind: "God will provide for Himself the lamb for the burnt offering" (v. 8). In faith, Abraham saw the provision of a sacrifice to end all sacrifices. He also "considered that God is able to raise people even from the dead" (Heb. 11:19). "The **God of Abraham**, and the **God of Isaac** and the **God of Jacob**," who appeared to Moses in the burning bush, "is not the God of the dead but of the living."[776] Abraham rode to the end of his life grasping the hand of *Yahweh yir'eh* and glimpsing resurrection life through the eyes of faith. The God of Abraham loves it when we put our faith in Him.

Chapter 13

GETTING PERSONAL

"Hardly anyone anywhere knows his own name! It would make many a fine gentleman stare to hear himself addressed by what is really his name."

I held my peace, beginning to wonder what my name might be.

"What now do you fancy yours?" She went on, as if aware of my thought. "But, pardon me, it is a matter of no consequence."

I had actually opened my mouth to answer her, when I discovered that my name was gone from me. I could not even recall the first letter of it! This was the second time I had been asked my name and could not tell it!

"Never mind," she said; "it is not wanted. Your real name, indeed, is written on your forehead, but at present it whirls about so irregularly that nobody can read it. I will do my part to steady it. Soon it will go slower, and, I hope, settle at last."

—George McDonald, *Lilith*

Special people get special names. Lovers use pet names. For some reason, they often fall into one of three categories: food, flowers, and cute animals. They might sound strange or trivial to an eavesdropper, but they are names of endearment—names that only the lovers know and understand. The pet name probably began in a joyful and intimate moment; it seals the intimacy.

Relationships don't begin with pet names—they come later. It's easy for relationships to wither early. In the best relationships, after many years together, little remains for couples to discover about each other. The relational learning curve plateaus. It requires extra effort to nurture the relationship, find out new things, enjoy fresh experiences together, and grow closer. Love must be innovative for a relationship to continue deepening.

We can become bored and simply drift along in our relationships with God too. Having read a lot of the Bible, we assume we know what it says. We have heard the sermons before and sung all the good songs. For some people, pain has poisoned the relationship, or frustration about an unmet goal has stifled it. Maybe we think our past sin hinders new depth. It can be hard to find fresh fire in our walk with God.

Abraham faced some of these challenges. He began his relationship with God by having enough faith to step out and say, "I'll obey God and follow Him." Over the years, his faith wobbled. Nonetheless, God faithfully gave Him Isaac. Abraham's confidence in God grew and he testified, "God sees and He will provide."

Abraham's grandson, Jacob, also grew closer to God. For him, what began as a rather distant relationship became more personal.

Abraham's Family Tree

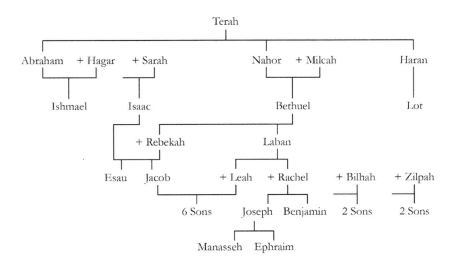

A Hand-Me-Down God

Jacob was younger than his brother, Esau. He was a mommy's boy and a schemer. Jacob's name says it all: "Heel grasper" or "Supplanter." The midwife noticed that Jacob gripped his brother's heel as if to tug Esau back up the birth canal and overtake him as the firstborn. Years later, Rebekah hatched a plan to trick Esau out of Isaac's blessing, a blessing their culture reserved for the firstborn.[777]

When Esau discovered his loss, he vowed to kill Jacob. Rebekah arranged for Jacob to take refuge with her brother, Laban, on the pretext of finding a wife.[778] Blind to the family feud, Isaac ordered, "Jacob, it's time for you to find a wife, but she must come from our clan." He packed Jacob off to Laban, who lived five hundred miles northeast, near the old family home of Haran.

Jacob's journey to Uncle Laban's tent included a night in Luz. He bedded down in a Bronze Age motel we could call Discomfort Inn. The pillows were rocks. Jacob lay down and slept (rather surprisingly). He dreamed of a staircase coming down from heaven bearing angels. Yahweh visited him and declared, "I am the LORD, the **God of your father Abraham** and the **God of Isaac**." Then God repeated to Jacob the same promise He had made to Abraham and Isaac. He promised him descendants as innumerable as the dust, to bless the families of the earth. God also promised to be with him and to bring him home.[779]

God of your father Abraham
Heb.: 'Elohei 'Avraham 'avikha
(Gen. 28:13)

God of my father (Abraham/Isaac)
Heb.: 'Elohei 'avi
(Gen. 31:4–5, 42; 32:9)

God of Nahor
Heb.: 'Elohei Nakhor
(Gen. 31:53)

Fear of Isaac
Heb.: Pakhad Yitskhaq
(Gen. 31:42)

God of my master Abraham
Heb.: 'Elohei 'adoni 'Avraham
(Gen. 24:12, 42, 48)

Jacob responded in two ways. First, he recognized the significance of his encounter, and he changed the place name from Luz to Bethel (House of God).[780] He also made a conditional vow concerning his relationship with God. If God would be with him, keep him, provide for him, and return him safely, then "the LORD will be my God" (Gen. 28:20–21). Before fully committing himself, Jacob was evidently evaluating God and waiting to see how He would perform.

Notice the hand-me-down names of God that Jacob used during this period. Jacob called Him, "the **God of my father**, the **God of Abraham**, and the **fear of Isaac**" (Gen. 31:42, 53). Later, he addressed the "**God of my father**

Abraham[781] and **God of my father Isaac**, O LORD" (Gen. 32:9). Jacob knew God best in reference to His relationship with Abraham and Isaac. It was like hearing about God from TV personalities instead of experiencing Him directly. Despite the distance, Jacob testified that, "the **God of my father** has been with me" (Gen. 31:4–5).

Laban used a similar phrase, "the **God of your father**" and asked "the **God of Abraham** and the **God of Nahor**, the **God of their father**" to judge between him and Jacob.[782] Something similar had occurred a generation earlier, when Abraham sent his servant to find Isaac a bride. The servant called on the "**God of my master Abraham**." Regardless of whether this was a secondhand title, God answered the servant's prayers and led him to Rebekah. Evidently, God does not require a prerequisite depth of relationship before He responds. God answers all those who call on Him in simple faith, even if their faith derives from what someone else has told them. But He wants the relationship to grow.

During the twenty years that elapsed, Uncle Laban tricked Jacob into marrying his eldest and least attractive daughter, Leah, before he could marry his true love, Rachel. Jacob worked for seven years for each sister and six more to acquire a flock. Jacob bred strong sheep, so his flocks grew, while Laban's declined.

In a dream, God directed Jacob to leave Laban and return to Canaan. In relating the dream to his wives, Jacob said that an angel of God had appeared and introduced Himself as the **God of Bethel**.[783] The name stands out among the other names that Jacob used at the time. Jacob knew that God, whom he had met at Bethel, was still watching over him and had not forgotten His promise. The God who is so real to us at key

God of Bethel
Heb.: 'El Bet-'el
(Gen. 31:13)

times in our lives—when we make a life-commitment to Him or when He meets us in a timely way during a crisis—"is the same yesterday and today and forever" (Heb. 13:8). He is not just the God of past experiences, relegated to a memory. He wants us to grow closer to Him in every season of life. As Jacob prepared to return home, the God of Bethel reappeared to jog his memory. The name provided more than a way of reacquainting Jacob with God and reminding him of his encounter with God in Bethel; it pointed to promises that God would faithfully keep over many years. God also called Jacob to fulfill his vow to devote himself to God so completely that he would give one tenth of all he owned.[784]

At times, God reawakens us to things He initiated long ago—things He wants to complete. When Jacob called Him "God of Bethel," the bud of Jacob's spiritual relationship was splitting, ready to blossom.

Wrestling for a Blessing (Genesis 32:1–32)

On the return journey, Jacob's relationship with God deepened. Jacob had noticed a pattern in the way that the "God of his fathers" had dealt with him (vv. 9–10). Realizing God's faithfulness, his heart became tender and open to God's transformation.

Jacob's hard times weren't over, though. He had to face a long-anticipated reunion with his hairy brother Esau. He dreaded the day. The last time Jacob had seen Esau it was just a quick glance over his shoulder as he dodged furtively between the tents, having tricked Esau out of his blessing. Word was out that Esau had a vendetta on him. Now Esau was coming to meet Jacob, accompanied by four hundred friends—hairy and scary. Jacob didn't picture a loving reunion with his brother, but a battle to settle a sore score. Bronze Age Hells Angels come to mind. Jacob feared for his life. Ever the strategist, Jacob schemed to lessen the anticipated blow on his family and fortune; he sent gifts ahead and split his family up. He also called on the God of his fathers because at that moment it would be useful for Him to remember His covenant promises (vv. 9–12).

Having sent all he owned and loved ahead of him as a buffer, Jacob was alone with God (vv. 22–24). It is a good exercise for us to tear ourselves away from life and retreat with God periodically. Jacob's predicament persisted but God met him.

Alone by the stream, Jacob wrestled with God, who took the form of a mysterious man (vv. 24–26). The divine wrestler prevailed by dislocating Jacob's hip, but Jacob held on, desperate for God's blessing.

Life throws us many painful dislocations and heartbreaks. It is easy to succumb to the distractions or to slap a hand on the mat gasping, "I surrender," to self-pity. But God doesn't want us to give up on having a relationship with Him; He wants us to seek Him with all our heart.

Notice that Jacob's opponent appeared as a man. How often do we demand, "God, unless I experience a supernatural visitation, I will not respond"? However, God usually mixes His presence and power with the down-to-earth. It takes a strong sense of desire and humility to meet God on His terms and to admit that an apparently earthy and human vessel is somehow God's face-to-face representative (v. 30). Jacob fought for God in the ordinary.

Jacob's wrestling resulted in his being renamed "Israel" (he who strives with God) (vv. 27–28). It may not seem like a good name to have. Isn't it a bit presumptuous to grapple with God? Nonetheless, the name spotlights a defining quality of Jacob's life. He had wrestled in his relationships with his brother, his father, and his Uncle Laban. He got the better of them, pinning them each down until he wrenched from them a birthright, a blessing, a big flock, and his bride (with a second one thrown in). Finally, God Himself had jumped into the ring and wounded him. Even though he was lame, Jacob wouldn't let go without extracting the blessing he wanted. God blessed him, but Jacob paid the price by accepting his true identity. He owned up to his manipulative nature, and God stamped him with the indelible label, "Israel— He who strives with God . . ."

There is more to the name because God can redeem our worst qualities. Jacob, who strove with people and God in such a sly and underhanded way, became Israel, who so desired God's presence that he hung on for the blessing. "He who strives with God" forever carried a poignant rider ". . . and prevailed." Jacob received his blessing (v. 29).

To cap it all, when Israel limped away from the wrestling match, afraid of what his brother Esau might do to him, he had a pleasant surprise. Esau reached out his hairy arms, not to throttle Jacob but to embrace him.[785]

The God of Israel

Jacob returned home to Shechem. "He erected there an altar and called it 'El 'Elohei Yisra'el [God, the God of Israel]."[786] His simple act reveals a profound change. Jacob had faced himself and accepted God's assessment of him. By humbly admitting his identity, he was able to receive the blessing attached to his new name—God had become more personal to him. The names "Israel" and "Jacob" are often interchangeable in Scripture, so we find his relationship with God celebrated in the names **God of Jacob**, **Mighty One of Jacob**, and **King of Jacob**. The name **Holy One**

Holy One of Jacob
Heb.: *Qedosh Ya'aqov*
(Isa. 29:23)

God of Jacob
Heb.: *'Elohei Ya'aqov*
(Ps. 46:7)

Mighty One of Jacob
Heb.: *'Avir Ya'aqov*
(Gen. 49:24;
Ps. 132:2, 5;
Isa. 49:26; 60:16)

King of Jacob
Heb.: *Melekh Ya'aqov*
(Isa. 41:21)

Portion of Jacob
Heb.: *Kheleq Ya'aqov*
(Jer. 10:16; 51:19)

God of Israel
Heb.: *'Elohei Yisra'el*
(Judg. 5:3, 5;
Isa. 29:23)
Heb.: *'El Yisra'el*
(Ps. 68:35)
Gk.: *Ho Theos tou
Israēl*
(Matt. 15:31;
Luke 1:68)

Mighty One of Israel
Heb.: *'Avir Yisra'el*
(Isa. 1:24)

Rock of Israel
Heb.: *Tsur Yisra'el*
(2 Sam. 23:3)

Stone of Israel
Heb.: *'Even Yisra'el*
(Gen. 49:24)

Glory of Israel
Heb.: *Netsakh Yisra'el*
(1 Sam. 15:29)

King of Israel
Heb.: *Melekh Yisra'el*
(Isa. 44:6; Zeph 3:15)

Holy One of Israel
Heb.: *Qedosh Yisra'el*
(Isa. 41:14; 43:14;
47:4; 48:17;
49:7; 54:5)

of Jacob parallels **God of Israel**.[787] Jacob's altar signified that God was, at last, his God—not just his fathers' God.

Jacob had become Israel. His twelve sons became the twelve tribes. Together, they took the name Israel and were eventually molded into a nation in the oven of Egypt. The Israelites also knew God as their God. Many times, Scripture calls Him the **God of Israel**. Similar names like **Mighty One of Israel**, **Rock of Israel**, the **Glory of Israel**, **King of Israel**, **Hope of Israel**, or **Hope of their fathers** are also used. Six times Isaiah linked the name **Redeemer** to the **Holy One of Israel**. Jeremiah described God as the **Portion of Jacob**, the share or inheritance of His people—better than any earthly treasure.

Isn't it remarkable that God would allow His name to be associated with His people's name? The association is tolerable when Israel aligns herself with God and enjoys His blessing and triumph. However, there was the distinct possibility that after one of Israel's shameful moments someone would sneer at the idea of "worshiping *their* God!" First impressions of God often derive from His people's example. Imagine what Muslims surmise about the God who was represented by the crosses on the battle shields of sword-bearing Christian crusaders. What do our cities learn about God from our churches? What impressions do our friends get of the Jesus we claim as Lord on our car bumpers and T-shirts? It's sobering to consider the messages our lives convey. Why isn't God more careful?

In reality, we do not define God. At best, we are a dim reflection of who He is. He does not change, even if we do.[788] Down through the ages, God continues to be all that He is, whether or not we respond to Him or reflect Him. Jacob's life teaches us that God was always the God of Jacob, even though Jacob spoke of Him as the God of his fathers. God was ever faithful, even though Jacob felt that he had to put conditions on his relationship with the Lord, as if God must prove Himself. God continually watched over His covenant promises, while Jacob thought that his striving helped control the outcome.

Renewed World Order

Where did Jacob's striving originate? The trait dated back to his birth, so it must have had spiritual roots, but cultural norms reinforced it. God's hand was on Jacob's life from the start. God ignored otherwise acceptable human customs and expectations and did something new. In an age when barrenness was shameful, God answered Isaac's prayers for a son. In a culture that typically blessed the firstborn, God said, "The older shall serve the younger" (Gen. 25:21–23). God was perfectly capable of promoting Jacob for the next phase of His plan to form a great nation. God could have done it without Jacob's twenty-year excursion and his nail-biting crisis. Deep inside, Jacob sensed his destiny, but he thought he had to struggle and scheme to beat the natural odds. He expected to fight for blessings. Eventually, Jacob recognized God's deep involvement in his destiny. He realized how tightly God had woven him into His design. That Jacob understood is clear from a footnote to his story. Shortly before he died, Jacob stayed with his son Joseph in Egypt. Jacob blessed his grandsons, Ephraim and Manasseh, starting with the youngest.[789] He blessed them in the order that God preferred—not the order of society.

The story of the nation of Israel repeats certain aspects of Jacob's relationship with God. Jacob likened God to a shepherd. When he blessed his grandsons, he called on "the God who has been **my shepherd** all my life" (Gen. 48:15). Jacob's blessing over Joseph included the phrase, "from the hands of the **Mighty One of Jacob** (from there is the **Shepherd**, the **Stone of Israel**)" (Gen. 49:24). God had been faithful to Jacob, despite his struggles to trust Him while he was hiding from Esau and serving Laban so that he could wed Rachel. Jacob hadn't felt God's hand at the time, but it had been there. He likened it to a strong, caring shepherd's hand. God shepherded Jacob and the Israelites, despite their self-sufficiency and unbelief.

Transformed Destinies

There is even more to God's relationship with His people. God looked beyond Israel as she was, with all her failings. Her potential would be unlocked if only she would allow Him to transform her.

A short letter from Paul to a friend called Philemon provides an example of divine transformation. Philemon's slave, Onesimus, had run away. He might have stolen from his master in the process. In any case, fugitive slaves faced bleak prospects if they were caught. They were punished at their owner's discretion, and that often meant death. Anyway, who could trust a slave with a record? Paul acknowledged that Onesimus was essentially useless to Philemon (vv. 10–11). He had smeared his own name, which literally meant "useful."

In his letter, Paul persuaded Philemon that Onesimus had changed. Paul had seen Onesimus born into a new life in Christ. Onesimus had received a new identity. He had become a spiritual brother to Philemon—not just a slave (vv. 13–16). As a new Christian, he had served Paul well; he would be a great benefit to Philemon. When God transformed Onesimus, He restored his future and his dignity. He gave him the integrity to reconcile with his master in a new, deeper relationship.

What was true for Israel and Onesimus is true for us all—relationship with God is transformational. Consider how early Christians were first described. Initially, people called them disciples, believers, brethren, or those who belong to "the Way."[790] Jesus called His disciples "friends."[791] Many of these terms indicate their relationships with Him and with other followers. Christians were those who "call on the name of our Lord" (Acts 9:14; 1 Cor. 1:2) or who "belong to Christ" (Mark 9:41; 2 Cor. 10:7 NIV). Just as Herodians were followers of Herod, so Christians followed Christ.[792] Briefly, Jews called Christians "the sect of the Nazarenes" and, since the days of the first church, they have called Christians *Notzrim*.[793] Among Gentile nonbelievers, the use of the term "Christian" quickly caught on. It may have begun as a derogatory expression.[794] Only in the late second century did believers call themselves Christians.

James referred to "the fair name by which you have been called" (James 2:7). When Jesus purchased us, we gained His name. Baptism signifies that we belong to His family. Dallas Willard paraphrases Jesus' command for us to baptize new disciples in the name of Father, Son, and Holy Spirit: "immerse them in the Trinitarian reality." He reasons: "The *name*, in the biblical world, is never just words, but involves the thing named. The ritual should be a special moment of entry into the reality, and that was certainly how it was understood in biblical times."[795] With all the cultural and political baggage attached to the word "Christian," wouldn't it be better if we returned to simple terms that emphasize a devoted relationship?[796]

Relationships with God through Jesus are the essence of the Christian life. God counts everyone who is "in Christ" righteous in Jesus. We receive the second most common New Testament designation: "saint." This does not mean that we qualify as models for pieces of medieval art and receive free halos. It means that God has counted us holy; we are set apart in our relationships with Him.[797] Certain names of God emphasize His relationship with His faith family. For instance, He is the **King of saints**[798] and the **Head of the church/body**. Don't let other Christians put themselves down by saying, "I'm no saint." Remind them that when anyone wholeheartedly turns from sin, God forgives that person. Our past cannot disqualify us. God counts us holy in Jesus.

Head
Gk.: *Kephalē*
(Eph. 4:15; Col. 2:19)

Head of the church/body
Gk.: *Kephalē tēs ekklēsias/ tou sōmatos*
(Eph. 5:23; Col. 1:18)

Your Pet Name

Four times in the Bible, God whispered to stumbling, faithless Israel an intimate pet name: *Yeshurun* (Upright one). The fact that this occurred during Israel's lapses provides a powerful lesson for us.

> *Jeshurun grew fat and kicked—you are grown fat, thick, and sleek—then he forsook God who made him, and scorned the Rock of his salvation. They made Him jealous with strange gods; with abominations they provoked Him to anger.* (Deut. 32:15–16)

All of us are marred and unworthy, so it is easy for us to believe that He cannot love us.

The lie takes various forms. At its worst, people are so convinced of their disqualification that they can't stand the self-inflicted pain of pursuing a God who in their minds rejects them anyway. But how did God view Israel? For all her crime and grime, He still saw her as the "upright one." He remained Jeshurun's King.[799]

God is not disappointed in the way that human parents are often disappointed when their promising children fail to live up to their hopes and dreams. God continued to choose Israel, knowing that if she had a relationship with Him, nothing could prevent her from reaching the destiny that He had in store for her.[800] God has long been in the business of helping people mature so that they can fulfill their destinies. The changes that He brings about are marked by changed names. Abram's destiny expanded with the name Abraham; Jacob became Israel. Later, the prophets told of the transformation of entire peoples. People who were once "forsaken" became Hephzibah (My delight is in her).[801] "Not My people" became "My people,"[802] sons of the living God—a prophetic preparation for God's inclusion of the Gentile nations in His family.

God longs to transform us all into His image. The pet name "Jeshurun" singles out one godly quality. The related name *yashar* applies to God—the

Upright One
Heb.: *Yashar*
(Isa. 26:7)

God of Jeshurun
Heb.: *'El Yeshurun*
(Deut. 33:26)

Upright One. He is "a God of faithfulness and without injustice, righteous and upright is He" (Deut. 32:4; Ps. 92:15). Being associated with fallen humans does not tarnish God; His character prevails. On the other hand, He changes us. He patiently woos us and provides a solution for our sins. God's love is so great that He sees beyond our failures, rebellions, and feelings of shame. He sees us made upright again through our faith in Jesus' work on the cross and by the transformation of the Spirit. God sees His saints at the end of time standing around the throne. What a concept—God makes us upright! God views us the way He viewed His restored nation. We are His bride, radiating righteousness and glory like a beautiful royal diadem. "There is none like the **God of Jeshurun**" (Deut. 33:26–29).

The Septuagint translates the name Jeshurun using the Greek word *ēgapēmenos* (beloved). There we come full circle; God's name for His people is also used as a name for Jesus, the **Beloved**.[803] God freely gave His grace to us in His Beloved so that we could enjoy a similar relationship with the Father. Think of it! God loves us so much that He considers us upright and He has a pet name for us: "Beloved."

There is no need to scheme and strive for the name. It is His destiny for us all.

Chapter 14

THE INTERPRETER

*Who has established all the ends of the earth? What is His name or His
son's name? Surely you know!*
—Proverbs 30:4

Glance at a few Christmas cards and you will soon find the name
Immanuel.[804] God first revealed this name to Ahaz. Ahaz is another
example of people like Jacob, to whom God remained faithful
despite their failures to trust Him.

Ahaz, king of Judah, had refused to join Israel and Syria in a three-nation
alliance against Assyria. Israel and Syria besieged Jerusalem, hoping to install
a puppet ruler. God spoke to Ahaz through Isaiah, telling him to trust Him.
God offered a sign of His faithfulness to encourage his trust: "Ask me for a
sign, any sign" (Isa. 7:11). Ahaz declared that he did not want to test God.
His response sounds admirable at first, except that God had told him to
request a sign. Ahaz behaved like people who try to
justify their stubborn unbelief with fake spirituality.
It boils down to disobedience.

God is with us
Heb.: *'Immanu 'El*
(Isa. 7:14; 8:8)

Despite Ahaz's attitude, God still promised the sign—a young woman, a virgin,[805] would bear a child called Immanuel (v. 14). **Immanuel** means "God is with us." It occurs just once more, in Isaiah 8:8. Isaiah 8:10 repeats the phrase "God is with us." The miracle that God promised to Ahaz despite his unbelief was a prophetic statement that God was with Judah; she had no need to fear Israel and Syria. From His heavenly vantage point, God would deal with the earthly enemy. For Ahaz, however, a battalion was a safer bet than a baby, so he cozied up to the reigning heavyweight, Assyria.

God offered Immanuel as the sign of His involvement in Ahaz's immediate crisis, but from that day on, "Immanuel" signified God's desire to be with all His people. Isaiah 7–12 forms a unit that scholars have called "the book of Immanuel." It includes prophecies about the governing **Child**, the **Branch** or **Shoot**, and the second, greater exodus that He would lead.[806]

Pregnancy Crisis

God comes more than halfway to meet people who are stuck between unbelief and faith. He did it for Jacob, Ahaz, and many others. Back in the Christmas cards, we find Mary's betrothed, Joseph, who provides another example. Matthew described Joseph as righteous, but he struggled to believe.[807] We meet him in crisis. Mary was pregnant and he was not the father. The pregnancy tore at his love and his loyalty to Mary. It threatened to ruin his reputation and to rip their relationship apart. He drew his own conclusion and planned his damage control—a relatively painless private end to their betrothal. Joseph saw only a dust cloud that spelled disaster. He had not discerned the wind of the Spirit at work behind it.

God met Joseph in his blinding pain. He sent an angel in a dream to explain, "Joseph, Son of David, do not be afraid to take Mary as your wife; for the Child who has been conceived in her is of the Holy Spirit" (Matt. 1:20). Traditionally, Jews learned to ask three blessings of God: kings, years, or dreams.[808] Joseph's dream signified God's favor and gave assurance. "It's okay, Joseph. It's Me. I'm in control." Out of dust and debris, an outline of God's purpose came into focus.

Joseph received one instruction: "You shall call His name **Jesus**" (Matt. 1:21). Consider the simplicity of some of our divine assignments. Adam gave names to the living creatures.[809] Zacharias, Joseph, and Mary all

Jesus
Heb.: *Yeshua'*
Gk.: *Iēsous*

had similar tasks—to name John and Jesus respectively. Let's not miss the importance of obedience in simple assignments just because we prefer more grandiose tasks.

Of course, the angel used Joseph's native tongue. Jesus' name, *Yeshua'*, is short for *Yehoshua'* (Joshua), meaning, "Yahweh saves." The angel's announcement was significant: "You shall call His name *Yeshua'* [Yahweh saves], for He will save [*yoshi'a*] His people from their sins."[810]

New Testament writers repeatedly highlight the connection between Jesus and Yahweh. In Romans 10:9, Paul declared, "If you confess with your mouth Jesus [*Yeshua'*] as Lord . . . you will be saved." Paul backed up the declaration with a quotation: "Whoever will call on the name of the LORD will be saved" (Joel 2:32; Rom. 10:13). The ordinary Jewish name *Yeshua'* was the ideal incarnation name for God's Son because it expressed His role in Yahweh's salvation.[811]

In the last three chapters, we considered God's relationship with David, Abraham, and Jacob. It is encouraging to see God's faithfulness to weak and failing Old Testament characters. Over their lifetimes, they grew closer to Him. Abraham died expecting resurrection, Jacob recognized God as a caring Shepherd, and David glimpsed His lasting kingdom. As God touched down like a tornado in Joseph's life, He was bursting into history at a new level of involvement. Throughout history, God had persistently pursued humankind and publicized His plan. Now the time had arrived to implement it and to save His people from their sins. God had come to stay.

Hebrews 1 compares the two eras: "God, after He spoke long ago to the fathers in the prophets in many portions and in many ways, in these last days has spoken to us in His Son." The chapter contrasts God's first messengers with the arrival of Jesus.[812] Hebrews 2:10 calls Jesus the **author of their salvation** The breadth of meaning in the name is apparent from the variation in translations.[813] (www.NamesForGod.net/variations lists the main variations on this name.) Hebrews 2:12 expounds on the prophecy of Psalm 22:22, telling of another role of Jesus: "I will proclaim Your name to My brethren." Unlike earlier messengers, the Son of God personally delivered salvation and manifested God's name.

Of Jesus' birth, Matthew said, "All this took place to fulfill what was spoken by the Lord through the prophet: 'Behold, the virgin shall be with child and shall bear a Son, and they shall call his name **Immanuel**,' which translated means, 'God with us'" (Matt. 1:22–23). Jesus' birth to the Virgin

Mary fulfilled Isaiah's prophecy. But the New Testament never refers to Jesus as Immanuel, except in this verse. Fulfillment came as He lived out the meaning of the prophesied name. Jesus left His heavenly vantage point and embedded on the front lines of human life as "God with us" in the flesh. It was essential that He show us what God was like.

God in a Dim Mirror

Humans struggle to comprehend God. Even as His adopted children, our human state limits our relationships with Him. We "see in a mirror dimly" (1 Cor. 13:12), so we easily overlook the Holy Spirit's involvement in our world, just as Joseph did.

Part of the problem is the difference between God and us. God is so glorious and holy that if He fully revealed Himself, it would destroy us.[814] Even with a rudimentary grasp of God's nature, we barely paddle in the vast ocean of who He is. Our brains can't comprehend the Everlasting God, the One without beginning or end. Think about the controversy surrounding the title "Creator." Even though God graciously makes Himself known to us, we sense the limitation of our dim mirror. God often seems distant.

Suffering contributes to our feelings of estrangement. Human misery questions a God who claims the kind of names we have been considering. He calls Himself the gracious and compassionate God, but how do we relate to that when we are distressed? He is the God who heals—sickness challenges that claim. Present the God of justice to refugees and see their response. Many suffering people feel forgotten. What evidence is there of the God of mercy in a cruel world, or of the God who provides in a famine-torn land? Affliction easily skews our views of God.

The separation started in the garden of Eden. That God walked in Eden is a statement of His presence.[815] Adam and Eve faced none of the problems just mentioned. They knew God intimately. Since the fall, when they exercised their free will and chose the wrong way, humans have been unable to fully understand God. We can liken our spiritual condition to the separation experienced by a Hungarian man we'll call Vladik.[816]

Vladik's separation began with a splintering crash, followed by a scream from his mother. Vladik's brother Yuri held onto his jacket sleeve, but it was in vain. Three secret policemen threw Yuri against a closet and then dragged Vladik out through the shattered apartment door. Vladik's last memory of home was of Yuri wrestling to escape his mother's grip and shouting, "Vladi, your ca—"

One minor offense that Vladik committed during the Hungarian uprising resulted in a long Siberian prison sentence. After a few years, the prison guards lost Vladik's papers and forgot his crime. Bureaucrats bounced him between institutions, and eventually abandoned him in a camp where nobody understood his language. Everyone thought that Vladik's Hungarian mutterings were nonsense. One last order transferred him to a mental institution.

Vladik was thousands of miles from home. He was completely misunderstood and isolated from family and friends. He had no idea what was happening to them in Hungary, and he had no way to communicate. Even worse, he felt a nagging bitterness. Why had his brother, Yuri, forgotten his birthday? It seemed trivial but it hurt.

Trapped in the asylum and surrounded by others who really were insane, he struggled to keep his mind. The guards laughed at his mumbled Hungarian. They said, "Crazy old man!" Vladik was forgotten.

In our natural, unredeemed condition, we are cut off from the relationship that God intended for us to have with Him. Most people are unaware of their separation, but God knows. Vladik's pain can be compared with the silent ache of any soul separated from God. His family's grief represents God's broken heart for those who are isolated from Him.

When God promised to send Immanuel, He did it to express His deep desire to see His relationship with His children restored and to end the pain of alienation. The name has three dimensions.

1. God Incarnate with Us

Vladik remained in the Siberian asylum for almost fifty years. For all Vladik knew, his whole family had died. His circumstances changed when an unexpected visitor arrived. On entering Vladik's cell and hearing him speak what the orderlies had labeled gibberish, the visitor recognized Hungarian. The key that unlocked the door to Vladik's freedom was a translator.

God went further. He sent us a translator who knows Him perfectly, because He is one with Him, and who also understands the language of frail humanity. Jesus went beyond words; He demonstrated God in the flesh.

I once attempted something new and complicated on my computer. I began by having a friend explain the software to me on the telephone. He reeled off complex instructions and technical jargon. Without waiting for my reply, he said, "Have you understood so far? Good, because now it gets complicated." I was completely lost. How much easier it was when he came to my house and said, "Let me show you how."

Jesus was Immanuel, God with us, in human form. Hebrews puts it in a nutshell: Jesus "is the radiance of His glory and the exact representation of His nature" (Heb. 1:3). John said, "No one has seen God at any time; the only begotten God[817] who is in the bosom of the Father, He has explained Him" (John 1:18). There is nothing louder and clearer than the living Word, because demonstration is the best translation.

A. W. Tozer noted, "In His incarnation, the Son veiled His deity, but He did not void it."[818] A Christmas carol summarizes Jesus' nature: "Veiled in flesh the Godhead see."[819] Jesus walked under a veil, but He occasionally lifted a corner to reveal glimpses of divinity:

- In His mastery of life, people saw Adonai, the Lord and Master.
- His perfection demonstrated 'El-tsaddiq, the righteous God, and 'Elohim qedoshim, the Holy God.
- Jesus' perception into people's hearts and His care for their pain provided evidence that 'El ro'i is a God who sees and acts.
- He knew people's deepest thoughts and needs exactly. They frequently interpreted His ability as a characteristic of God. How like 'El de'ot, the God who knows.
- A demonized man found deliverance—proof that 'Elohei ha'elohim, the God of gods, had triumphed.
- The healing of the sick was a move of Yahweh rofe'ekha, the LORD who heals you (NIV).
- Five thousand hungry people ate their fill. Yahweh yir'eh, the LORD who provides, was involved.
- The woman who was caught in adultery experienced the gentle touch of 'Eloah selikhot, the God of forgiveness, and the gracious and compassionate God, 'El khannun.
- As Jesus was "moved with compassion" (Matt. 20:34; Mark 1:41), people heard and felt the heartbeat of 'Elohei khasdi, the God of mercy.

- Jesus, "full of grace and truth" (John 1:14), manifested in flesh and blood the grace and truth of *'El 'emet*, the God of truth.
- The transfiguration was like a wind gust blowing aside Jesus' fleshly veil, briefly revealing His divine majesty: *'El 'elyon*, God Most High; *'El gibbor*, the Mighty God; *'El shaddai*, Almighty God; and *'El hakkavod*, the God of glory. The disciples who witnessed the transfiguration grasped some implications of the event and wanted to build a booth to worship Him.

When Jesus raised a widow's son from the dead, onlookers commented, "God has visited[820] His people" (Luke 7:16). He raised His friend Lazarus. Later, through the power of God, Jesus rose from the dead. That miracle demonstrates what Paul said in Colossians 2:9: "In Him all the fullness of Deity dwells in bodily form." As Jesus died, the thick temple veil isolating the Holy of Holies tore. As He rose and ascended, He discarded the veil that had been covering His divinity. His final triumph was the pinnacle of God's communication, but throughout His life, Jesus lived the language of heaven. He demonstrated God's attitude toward us, and He showed us what an unobstructed relationship with the Father can be like.

2. God with Us Again

Jesus also removed the obstruction to relationship by paying the price for our freedom. God "made Him who knew no sin to be sin on our behalf" (2 Cor. 5:21). Without yielding to sin, Jesus took our sin upon Himself. *Yahweh ro'i*, the LORD my Shepherd, came searching for us all. In the same way that Vladik was released, our heavenly translator came to the prison of our mad world to rescue us from captivity.

After Vladik's ordeal ended, he made excited phone calls over a crackly prison phone line to embassy staff members and airlines. After fifty years, he was desperate to locate his family, to see if any of them were still alive.

Vladik's first phone conversation with Yuri involved few words but many exclamations, sighs, and pauses to stifle tears. Later calls were crammed with questions and news. The urgency in Vladik's heart was hard to restrain. "Come on! Can't you speed this process up? Get me a flight to Moscow and on to Hungary."

Immanuel has set us on the path to freedom. Our interpreter opened our prison cell and introduced us to the Father. Compared to our unredeemed lives with their oppressive bondages, we have tremendous liberty. However, a distance remains. None of us has a complete understanding of God or a clear line of communication with Him. We are living like Vladik. We are free, and able to talk, but we are not face to face. What Paul described as seeing "in a mirror dimly" is like a conversation over an old telephone. We are distant from God, yet we can make out His voice. One day, our limited relationship with Him will culminate in a sweet flight home to the mansion He is preparing for us. We will be reunited with our heavenly Father, knowing Him "fully, just as I also have been fully known" (1 Cor. 13:12). The name Immanuel points to the joy of being reconciled with God.

Vladik's emotional reunion with Yuri at Budapest airport drew stares from other travelers. The brothers hugged and planted Slavic kisses on each other's cheeks. In the taxi to the apartment, they hardly paused their conversation, even to breathe. Their first week together was a series of meals, sightseeing walks, and late-night discussions punctuated by short naps. Vladik was grateful that his brother could reminisce about their friends and relatives. They laughed at some memories and wept over the people who would never share the happy reunion. But it was good to be home.

One evening, Yuri returned from his bedroom. "Vladik, I have something for you." He handed Vladik a dog-eared and yellowed envelope. It was addressed, "To Vladi."

The glue had long since disintegrated. Vladik slid out a card with a bright red number twenty-five emblazoned in the center. His hands began shaking. He caught his breath and tears trickled down his cheeks.

"Open it, Vladik. I didn't forget!"

3. God Forever With Us

God has promised never to forget or forsake His people. He made promises specifically to Jacob, Moses, the Israelites, and Joshua.[821] On numerous occasions, He demonstrated His presence by delivering them or providing for them. Finally, the incarnate Son showed what God was like, and He reconciled the entire race to God. Jesus promised His presence with us "always, even to the end of the age" (Matt. 28:20). He sent His **Spirit of truth** to continue His living presence and to interpret truth to us. Appropriately, the Spirit is called a gift.[822] As the **Spirit of grace and supplication**, He manifests God's graciousness to us and assists us in crying out to God. The **good Spirit** expresses God's goodness.[823] The **Spirit of faith** helps us to believe.

The Greek word used to describe the Spirit is *paraklētos*. It means, "One called alongside." The English translation "**Helper**" expresses part of its meaning. Some translations call the Spirit the **Comforter** (KJV). His presence certainly is a great comfort. Two linked names, **Father of mercies** and **God of all comfort**, convey similar ideas.[824] Luke 2:25 speaks of the consolation of Israel but that is unlikely to be a title for Jesus.

When this world ends, other prophecies will be fulfilled. One concerns a city that God showed to Ezekiel. John saw the same city in his vision, and people of faith continue to seek it.[825] Encapsulated in the city's name is that same enduring promise and attribute of God, *Yahweh shammah*, "**the LORD is there**" (Ezek. 48:35). A voice will accompany the city's descent from heaven: "Behold, the tabernacle of God is among men, and He will dwell among them, and they shall be His people, and God Himself will be among them" (Rev. 21:1–3). The essence of the heavenly city is God's intimate presence, which is with us forever.

Spirit of grace and supplication
Heb.: *Ruakh khen wetakhanunim*
(Zech. 12:10)

Spirit of grace
Gk.: *Pneuma tēs charitos*
(Heb. 10:29)

Spirit of faith
Gk.: *Pneuma tēs pisteōs*
(2 Cor. 4:13)

Helper (Comforter KJV)
Gk.: *Paraklētos*
(John 14:16, 26; 15:26; 16:7)

Father of mercies (Father of compassion NIV)
Gk.: *Patēr tōn oiktirmōn*
(2 Cor. 1:3)

God of all comfort
Gk.: *Theos pasēs paraklēseōs*
(2 Cor. 1:3)

The LORD is there
Heb.: *Yahweh shammah*
(Ezek 48:35)

Chapter 15

WELCOMING THE GOOD SHEPHERD

The King of love my Shepherd is,
Whose goodness faileth never,
I nothing lack if I am His
And He is mine forever.
—Henry W. Baker, 1868

A shrill whistle blew in on the wind. Who could make that kind of noise?

Black and white flashed among the shrubs by the stream and caught my eye. Then the whistle came again. This time, I spotted a dog. It was motionless.

Another whistle preceded a series of cries in a language only a dog would understand. The dog seemed to dance with the shouts, rushing forward and crouching, then slinking on his belly like a snake.

"Waaaait!" He froze.

At the sound of a brisk trill, the dog launched toward the heels of two silly, ambling sheep, chasing them uphill.

I witnessed the stupidity of sheep during family holidays in the Brecon Beacons in South Wales. Local farmers used the low mountains to graze sheep. We observed a daily routine. The farmer would ride his horse to the moorside near our campsite, whistling and shouting instructions to his dogs. The dogs drove the sheep from the bottom of the valley, up the hillside, to the ridgetop. Then the farmer and the dogs left.

One day we had the opportunity to ask the farmer about this pattern. He explained that the sheep found it easier to go downhill than uphill. Left to themselves, the flock would gather by the streamside, where they would trample and deplete the grass. Without a shepherd, they would ruin their own pasture. They needed his daily attention because every time he drove them up, they would gradually wander down to the stream again.

The picture of a shepherd with his sheep illustrates the relationship between God and His people because it highlights God's care for us all. In Bible times, everyone in Israel's predominately rural society could understand the picture. Jacob was the first to speak of God as his Shepherd. He blessed Joseph's sons saying, "The God who has been my **Shepherd** all my life to this day . . . bless the lads" (Gen. 48:15–16). Several psalms describe the nation of Israel as God's flock.[826] Psalm 80:1 says, "Oh, give ear, **Shepherd of Israel**, You who lead Joseph like a flock." Ecclesiastes tells us, "The words of wise men . . . are given by one **Shepherd**" (Eccl. 12:11). Then there's the famous psalm that many of us learned as children: "The **LORD** is **my Shepherd**, I shall not want . . ." (Ps. 23:1).

Shepherd
Heb.: *Ro'eh*
(Gen. 48:15; 49:24;
Eccl. 12:11)

Shepherd of Israel
Heb.: *Ro'eh Yisra'el*
(Ps. 80:1)

LORD My shepherd
Heb.: *Yahweh ro'i*
(Ps. 23:1)

The title "shepherd" encapsulates nine interrelated roles that parallel the ways in which God cares for us. God is a living and active personality, so it is unhelpful to dissect or compartmentalize His character. Most of us feel belittled when others try to summarize who we are with a few half-baked statements. We must avoid settling for trite analyses of God that do Him the same injustice. Like any person, all of God's character traits are interconnected. That is why this book interweaves His names. The role of a shepherd blends several different skills. It provides a realistic illustrative framework on which to hang many names of God (some of which appear in more detail elsewhere in this book). This name is where the descriptions we have of Jesus and the Father converge the most—they both relate to us as shepherds.

Provider

The best-known role of the shepherd is to feed and water the flock.

> *The LORD is my shepherd, I shall not want. He makes me lie down in green pastures; He leads me beside quiet waters. . . . You prepare a table before me in the presence of my enemies; You have anointed my head with oil; my cup overflows. Surely goodness and lovingkindness will follow me all the days of my life, and I will dwell in the house of the LORD forever.* (Psalm 23:1–6)

Sometimes certain objects characterize a person. For instance, my binoculars represent part of who I am and what I enjoy doing. When I hike in the mountains, I stop to pick out the details of distant peaks or river valleys. I like to explore, and my binoculars help me plan my route up unfamiliar hillsides. I also use them to watch birds. In a similar way, the shepherd's rod and staff, which are mentioned in the psalm, represent aspects of who God is. A shepherd in Bible times would lean on his staff as he watched the grazing sheep.[827] Later, we will see other ways that the rod and the staff help us understand our Shepherd better.

Other names also present God as a provider. We're shepherded by El shaddai, or God who is sufficient. As El ro'i and Yahweh yir'eh, He attends to our needs in the best possible way. He promises to continue to provide abundantly.[828] Like the Welsh shepherd who daily drove his flock to fresh grazing, our Father sees our daily needs before we even ask.[829]

Jesus also provides living water that goes beyond material needs.[830] Cautioning against anxiety, He concluded, "Do not be afraid, little flock, for your Father has chosen gladly to give you the kingdom."[831] He promised that whenever He sends us out as "sheep in the midst of wolves," the Holy Spirit will provide us with the words to speak.[832]

Pathfinder

The Middle Eastern shepherd is a pathfinder, rather than a driver. In Israel's semiarid landscape, edible vegetation and water are scarce. The shepherd watches for signs of a depleted meadow; he decides when to move on. He finds the best path to the next pasture, where there is fodder to sustain the sheep for a few more days. He guides the flock so they can graze.

We read that, "He leads me beside quiet waters . . . He guides me in the paths of righteousness for His name's sake" (Ps. 23:2–3). God directs us to nutritious food so we can grow spiritually. Sometimes, He even carries us as a shepherd would carry a weak sheep.[833] *Paraklētos*, that hard-to-translate name for the Holy Spirit, pictures us calling Him to come alongside as our **Helper**. The **Spirit of truth** leads us into all truth.[834] Choosing paths of righteousness in every circumstance increases the glory of His name.[835]

During a journey to good grazing, little green sideshows entice the sheep to start nibbling. But the shepherd knows that small patches of thin grass are dangerously short-lived morsels. A tap on the flanks with the staff returns a sheep to the right path whenever it begins to stray.

At other stages of our life journeys we get discouraged. We wonder if something is wrong with us. Why are we no longer in the soft meadows but struggling up a dusty, rocky path through the hills? Is the Shepherd somehow defective if He leads us through places like that? In response to rough, barren periods in life, we may begin to withdraw from the Shepherd and doubt His love. That's when it is comforting to be reminded of His presence, to feel his staff giving us a gentle nudge of encouragement. His voice whispers reassurances that He has us on the right road.

Psalm 23 paints no picture-perfect water meadow. It includes the dark, eerie valley of the shadow of death (v. 4). The Shepherd is there too. Elsewhere, David spoke of **my lamp**, illuminating his darkness. The lamp was no flashlight, though. The tiny, oil-filled clay holder cast a dim aura of light—just enough for a person to take one step at a time. David had known the tough shepherding life. He experienced his Shepherd

My Lamp
Heb.: *Neri*
(2 Sam. 22:29)

guiding him through adversity. After King Saul falsely accused him of treason, David lived as a fugitive in mountain hideouts, where he learned to trust God for protection and provision.

We too can have a relationship that is resilient enough for us to endure hard times with Him while remaining certain that He is still good. He is eminently qualified to lead us through those places. He protects us from thirst, thieves, and thorns along the way. He finds fresh pastures beyond them. In fact, only when we allow Him to shepherd us through life's valleys and deserts do we discover more about His character. Faith grows in such places.

Jesus blazed a trail in other ways, which are expressed by the Greek word *archēgos*. Thomas Dove Keizur illustrates its meaning. He was the pioneer who settled Keizer, the city I live in. Thomas Keizur was born in 1793. He left Independence, Missouri, in 1843 with a group of twenty-three people. He helped lead the wagon train that blazed the Oregon Trail. The Keizur family settled in the Willamette Valley and made some of the first land claims in America under the Donation Land Act.[836] Thomas organized the first militia in the Northwest, which became the Oregon National Guard. The achievements of this short, wiry man who rode a Morgan horse and carried only a rifle and some basic supplies were remarkable. When the city of Keizer unveiled a statue of its founder, 140 of his descendants attended, down to the eighth generation. Greek society used the word *archēgos* to describe men like Thomas Keizur who pioneered routes and founded cities.[837] The word implies originating or initiating something, or taking first place.

Jesus took the lead in salvation, faith, and abundant living. The multiple options for translating *archēgos* are evident in four verses of our English Bible: He is the **author of their salvation**, the **Prince and Savior**, the **author and perfecter of faith**,[838] and the **Prince of life**.

A related word, *archē*, forms part of the descriptive name, "the **Beginning of the creation** of God."[839] It does not imply that Jesus was created first—He existed before all things. Rather, He is creation's source and its beginning. Similarly, the title **firstborn of all creation** emphasizes Jesus' supremacy and preeminence over everything, including the new creation of His followers.[840] Neither Jacob nor Ephraim were the first-birthed, but both are referred to as firstborn because

Author of their salvation
Gk.: *Ton archēgon tēs sōtērias*
(Heb. 2:10)

Prince and Savior
Gk.: *Archēgos kai sōtēr*
(Acts 5:31)

Author and perfecter of faith
Gk.: *Ton tēs pisteōs archēgon kai teleiōtēn*
(Heb. 12:2)

Prince of life
Gk.: *Ton archēgon tēs zōēs*
(Acts 3:15)

Beginning of the creation
Gk.: *Hē archē tēs ktiseōs*
(Rev. 3:14)

Firstborn of all creation
Gk.: *Prōtotokos pasēs ktiseōs*
(Col. 1:15)

First fruits
Gk.: *Aparchē*
(1 Cor. 15:20–23)

Firstborn from the dead
Gk.: *Prōtotokos ek tōn nekrōn*
(Col. 1:18; Rev. 1:5)

they acquired all of the privileges that were normally given to eldest sons.[841] The phrase, **first fruits** speaks of the risen Jesus as the first and finest example of life after death. Calling Him the **firstborn from the dead** implies He took the lead and is the best.

Protector

One winter, I lived in the Judean hills, where shepherds were once a common sight. Hiking through the hills, I had to step carefully to avoid the thorns—nasty, tangled vines whose inch-long spikes lunged at my ankles. At night, I lay awake listening to wolves howling near the village. In the morning, below the hencoops, I would find feathers or severed feet—telltale signs of a predawn raid on the chicken pen.

Shepherds in biblical times had it worse. They had to contend with lions and bears.[842] Robbers would beat a shepherd over the head just for some tough mutton. Diligent shepherds stayed alert. That is what the name **watcher of men** tells us about God.[843]

Watcher of men
Heb.: *Notser ha'adam*
(Job 7:20)

A responsible shepherd had three choices: he could stand in front of the flock to deter attackers. He could actively drive them off, or he could take the brunt of the assault on himself.

References to God as **help**, **shield**, and **strength** reflect His role as our defender.[844] The name *maginni* (my shield) derives from the *magen*, a small and round shield that was used as a defensive cover.[845] The word might also refer to a benevolent ruler who provided for his people and protected them like God does.

The shepherd sometimes used his rod (*shevet*) to fend off wild animals or robbers.[846] *Shevet* refers to the implement used to thresh seeds out of husks. It doubled as a club to swing or throw at assailants. Because it served as an instrument of discipline, it became a symbol of rulership, hence the alternative translation, "scepter."[847] Micah called on God to "shepherd Your people with Your scepter, the flock of Your possession" (Mic. 7:14).

On rare occasions, the shepherd chose to die rather than allow a marauder to take his sheep. Jesus understood the ultimate price of shepherding when He said, "I am the **good shepherd**; the good shepherd lays down His life for the sheep" (John 10:11). Jesus

Good shepherd
Gk.: *Ho poimēn ho kalos*
(John 10:11, 14)

Guardian
Gk.: *Episkopos*
(1 Peter 2:25)

contrasted Himself with a hireling who takes the job seeking a quick and easy paycheck after dozing in the shade while the sheep wander. Hirelings flee when danger looms. The good shepherd remains responsible in every circumstance. Peter echoed what he witnessed Jesus say and do; he called Him the **Shepherd** and **Guardian** of our souls.

Physician

Shepherds once functioned as veterinarians for their sheep. The shepherd would run his staff over the fleece, parting the wool to examine the skin underneath for signs of infection or wounds. He knew where medicinal and nutritional herbs grew. He applied medicine and performed minor surgery to excise diseases.

Jesus surpassed the best physicians when He cured the sick. He predicted that skeptics would mock, "**Physician**, heal yourself!" (Luke 4:23). His miraculous healings fulfilled prophecy[848] and anticipated the greatest remedy, which was administered through His death on the cross.[849] Jesus is a physician

Physician
Gk.: *Iatros*
(Luke 4:23)

for those who are sick with sin or sick of sinning. Peter emphasized that healing happened through the name of **Jesus Christ the Nazarene**.[850] Jesus is the sun of righteousness who rises with healing in His wings.[851] Healing will be available in heaven for the nations.[852]

An incident during the exodus gives prophetic insight into God's healing work. Israel was thirsty and excited to find an oasis, but she became bitterly disappointed. The water was undrinkable. Moses cried to God, who showed him a tree. Moses threw a branch into the bitter water, as instructed, and it turned sweet. The name *Yahweh rofe'ekha* is found in

**The LORD
who heals you**
Heb.: *Yahweh rofe'ekha*
(Ex. 15:26 NIV)

God's conditional promise: "If you listen carefully to the LORD your God and do what is right in His eyes, if you pay attention to His commands and keep all His decrees, I will not bring on you any of the diseases

I brought on the Egyptians, for I am the **LORD, who heals you**" (Ex. 15:22–26 NIV). Later, the Shepherd promised to "bind up the broken and strengthen the sick" (Ezek. 34:16), even though Israel had scattered from Him.

Obedience is always the best preventative medicine, and healing comes through God's word.[853] Sadly, since the time of Adam, humans have often disregarded God's voice. We have strayed into a diseased existence. And so another aspect of the shepherding heart of God comes into play.

Pursuer

God called to Adam, "Where are you?" (Gen. 3:9). The call persists, beating out the heartbeat of a concerned Father seeking His lost child. A rhetorical undertone to the question begs everyone to face his or her own lostness by asking, "Where am I?"

In relation to wanderers, the Shepherd is a pursuer. He comes after everyone. Whatever our reasons are for withdrawing or running away from Him, God pursues His scattered people.[854] Jesus has compassion on shepherdless sheep.[855]

In Matthew 18:12–14, Jesus gives a lovely picture of the shepherd who gives 100 percent for the 1 percent. He reassures us, "It is not the will of your Father who is in heaven that one of these little ones perish." God is utterly loyal and committed to His people.[856] His lovingkindness (His follow-through on His covenant promises) outlasts our lives.[857] He cares for each one so much that He will devote Himself to pursuing us individually.

Two Scotsmen were friends. One was a shepherd whose favorite sheep had slid off a cliff and become entangled. The friend asked him, "Are you going to get your sheep back?"

The shepherd shrugged and said, "Wait a wee while."

Three days elapsed. Each time the friend passed, he saw the sheep below the cliff, struggling to get free. But the shepherd did nothing. Again the friend asked, "Why don't you help your sheep?"

This time, the shepherd explained, "If I reach down to pull my sheep up now, it is still fighting strong. It won't let me get hold of it to untangle it. In a few days, it will weaken and stop struggling. Then I can lower my staff, hook the crook around it, and lift it to safety."

The story describes our own lives. We struggle to unravel our problems, untangle ourselves from the thorns, and extract ourselves from the muddy holes we wallow in. Our efforts often make matters worse. When we cease our self-effort for long enough to allow the Lord to do His work, the **Shepherd** and **Guardian** of our souls can rescue us and restore us.[858] When a sheep returns— and this is an important point in Jesus' parable about lost sheep—there's a big celebration in heaven.[859]

The Bible contains prophecies about God's ultimate pursuit of us as the Good Shepherd. We hear about His coming as far back as Jacob's blessing over Joseph: "His bow remained firm, and his arms were agile, from the hands of the **Mighty One of Jacob** (from there is the **Shepherd**, the **Stone of Israel**)" (Gen. 49:24). Micah 5:2–5, a well-known Christmas passage, points to the One who "will arise and shepherd His flock in the strength of the LORD, in the majesty of the name of the LORD His God."

Israel's kings were viewed as national shepherds. David came to the throne on a promise that he would be a shepherd and a ruler.[860] When the little-known prophet, Micaiah, foretold King Ahab's death, he envisioned "all Israel scattered on the mountains like sheep which have no shepherd" (1 Kings 22:17). Later, God pointed beyond a string of failed kings to another king of the order of David, who cared for God's people: "I will set over them one shepherd, My servant David, and he will feed them" (Ezek. 34:23–24; 37:24). That's exactly what Jesus did when He came as the messianic shepherd.[861]

Jesus took the title **Son of David**, and He fulfilled the roles of humble shepherd and dignified ruler, both of whom used a *shevet*.[862] The **Son of Man** sought and saved the lost.[863] Mark noted that Jesus felt compassion for the great multitude "because they were like sheep without a shepherd," so He taught them and fed them bread and fish.[864] At the end of His life, Jesus

My Associate
Heb.: *'Amiti*
(Zech. 13:7)

embraced Zechariah's prophecy: "'Awake, O sword, against **My Shepherd**, and against the man, **My Associate**,' declares the LORD of hosts. 'Strike the Shepherd** that the sheep may be scattered.'"[865] Jesus identified Himself with the abused Shepherd and prophesied that His own disciples would scatter when He was crucified.[866] However, His costly sacrifice was the ultimate rescue. It threw open a new door, which leads back into the Father's fold.

Portal

In those days, there were two kinds of sheepfold and two types of doors or gates. John 10:1–18 alludes to both of them. Villages had a communal sheepfold near the center. It had a door that was rather like a modern door; it swung on hinges and it had a locking device. A doorman had custody of the sheep overnight. In the morning, the shepherd entered the pen through the door to claim his sheep. He called them to Him, knowing that they would distinguish his voice from a stranger's.[867]

When Jesus said, "I am **the door** of the sheep," He probably spoke of a second type of door that secured pens in the hills. While pasturing sheep away from habitation, shepherds used caves or built rough enclosures with simple low walls or fences. The shepherds from the nativity scene of Bethlehem fit this picture.[868] There was no door; the doorway was a gap in the perimeter. At night, once all the sheep had been corralled into the pen, the shepherd would lay down in the doorway. He kept his rod and staff ready at his side. Anyone who wanted access to the sheep needed his permission. Jesus contrasted Himself with disinterested hirelings, strangers, and exploitative thieves. We can

The door
Gk.: *Hē thyra*
(John 10:7, 9)

paraphrase Jesus' words: "I am the door. Sheep enter my fold by believing in Me. The thief comes to steal, kill, and destroy; I came to give them abundant life." Jesus continued: "I am the **good shepherd**; the good shepherd lays down His life for the sheep" (John 10:9–11). When Jesus died on the cross, He wrested us from the grip of the supreme robber, Satan.

The Jews pictured heaven with doors or gates. When God opened them, blessings and revelations came down. When Jacob saw the ladder at Bethel, he exclaimed, "This is none other than the house of God, and this is the gate of heaven" (Gen. 28:17). Manna fell on Israel in the wilderness through heaven's doors.[869] The heavens opened when John baptized Jesus and the Spirit alighted on Him.[870] Jesus promised Nathanael a view of an open heaven above the Son of Man.[871] In his revelation, John entered heaven through an open door.[872] Jesus continues to provide access to the abundant life that exists under an open heaven where we enjoy God's presence and favor.

In the hearts and minds of Jesus' followers, His death seemed like a door slamming violently shut. However, His death actually shattered another long-locked door. The tearing of the temple veil,[873] which separated men from the holy place where God dwelt, signaled a novel event. The supernatural removal of a large round stone from the entrance to Jesus' tomb was another sign. Jesus had reopened the door to our relationship with the heavenly Father. The gates of hell had not prevailed against Him.

The robber didn't snatch Jesus' life; Jesus chose to make the sacrifice. He had the authority to rise again. He said, "I lay down My life so that I may take it again" (John 10:17–18). Hebrews 13:20–21 proclaims the victory that Jesus won through being raised from the dead: "The **God of Peace**, who brought up from the dead the **great Shepherd of the sheep**[874] through the blood of

**Great Shepherd
of the sheep**
Gk.: *Ho poimēn tōn
probatōn ho megas*
(Heb. 13:20)

the eternal covenant, even Jesus our Lord; equip you." Our Shepherd established lasting peace when He broke Satan's power.

Purchaser

Jesus' death was an act of redemption; He purchased freedom for the slaves of sin. In Chapter 23, we will reflect more on God as the **Redeemer**, the One who ransoms us to bring us into His fold. Jeremiah applied the picture to God as a shepherd. He spoke of God's dual interest in us as the Father and the Redeemer:

> *'I will make them walk by streams of waters, on a straight path in which they will not stumble; for I am a father to Israel, and Ephraim is My firstborn. . . . He who scattered Israel will gather him and keep him as a shepherd keeps his flock.' For the LORD has ransomed Jacob and redeemed him from the hand of him who was stronger than he.* (Jer. 31:9–11)

To build his own flock, Jacob used his staff to segregate his uncle Laban's second-rate sheep. Jesus is not selective; He wants to draw the entire human flock to Himself, having purchased us with His blood. All we have to do is accept His accomplishment by having faith.

Point of Focus

Churchgoers often talk about unity, but we rarely define it. Differences of service style may be symptoms of disunity, but they are more likely to be a refreshing lack of uniformity. There is healthy variety in the larger body of Christ. Of more concern is our inability to present a united front when it comes to social issues, as well as any unloving criticism and sniping. The relationships within a local church can be shallow or easily divided by personal agendas. We live in a society that values individualism and independence. The description of life during the time of the judges is apt for today: "There was no king in Israel; everyone did what was right in his own eyes" (Judg. 21:25). We need a king!

A shepherd's hand feeding his sheep illustrates the most important form of unity. The focus of the flock is visible. They gather as close to the shepherd as they can. Heads point toward him; tails radiate away. If sheep lose either interest or trust in their shepherd, or if they are unable to hear his voice, they stop following and they scatter. The shepherd's presence unites and orders the sheep. The church likewise needs her Shepherd-King. God desires a unity that allows for diversity with regard to style and opinion, but that unity requires a basic agreement about who the Shepherd is and what He has done for us.

Once we are part of Jesus' flock, He applies the metaphor to us differently, as He did to Peter. When Peter returned as a "lost sheep" to Jesus after His resurrection, Jesus instructed him to feed the rest of His sheep and to care for His lambs (John 21:15–17). Jesus wants us to become the shepherds of others. The title "Pastor," which literally means "shepherd," is given to many church leaders.[875] If pastors don't act like Jesus, they might actually drive people from Him.

John wrote a letter about a church control freak called Diotrephes.[876] He wanted first place, and he hindered people who "went out for the sake of the Name" (3 John 7). He behaved like one in the accuser's camp, rather than like a loving shepherd. If we emulate Jesus by shepherding people gladly and selflessly, and by being humble examples to them,[877] then they will hear the Shepherd's voice through us, and they will be united as a flock. To such people Peter promised, "When the **Chief Shepherd** appears, you will receive the unfading crown of glory" (1 Peter 5:4). After that appearing, Jesus will operate in the ninth and final role of the Shepherd.

> **Chief Shepherd**
> Gk.: *Archipoimēn*
> (1 Peter 5:4)

Parter

We saw earlier that God is the **Judge**.[878] When Jesus returns, it will be as a judging king. In a parable, He said, "When the Son of Man comes in His glory, and all the angels with Him, then He will sit on His glorious throne. All the nations will be gathered before Him; and He will separate them from one another, as the shepherd separates the sheep from the goats" (Matt. 25:31–32, 34, 40).

The shepherd used his multipurpose staff to sort through the animals. So, at last, Jesus becomes the Parter of the sheep and the goats. He will base the parting on whether we practically care for the poor and the needy, and whether we share and reflect the heart of our Shepherd.[879]

⳼

The shepherd's nine different roles reflect many different names. The theme runs through the Bible and points us to heaven, where "the **Lamb** in the center of the throne will be their Shepherd, and will guide them to springs of the water of life; and God will wipe every tear from their eyes" (Rev. 7:16–17). God will continue relating to us as a shepherd into eternity. Then Psalm 23 will be true permanently. We will drink from still waters and dwell in the house of the LORD, our Shepherd, forever.

Chapter 16

TWO SIDES OF A COIN

We Jews all expect that the Messiah will be a man of purely human origin.
—**Justin Martyr**, *Dialogue*

The regal Aragorn in J. R. R. Tolkien's *The Lord of the Rings* is a fascinating character with many names and titles.[880] He first appears as a rather sinister cloaked man in a corner of a dark Bree inn. The hobbits treat this ranger, Strider, with great suspicion. It takes a letter from Gandalf, introducing Strider as Aragorn, to reassure them. There is more to Aragorn, son of Arathorn, than meets the eye. He carefully guards his identity and his mission, knowing Sauron's evil eye pierces every shadow.

Aragorn guides the hobbits to Rivendell, the home of the elf king, Elrond. There, Aragorn unveils more of his identity, revealing himself to be Lord of the Dunedain, or men of the west. Elrond had named him Estel, or "hope," to hide his true and more significant identity. In fact, Aragorn was the heir of Isildur, a descendant of the ancient kings of Gondor.

As the adventure unfolds, Aragorn's importance becomes clearer. He finally reveals himself to Sauron as the heir to the throne of Gondor. Then Aragorn boldly challenges Sauron at the gates of his domain, Mordor. This diversion holds Sauron's attention long enough for Frodo, the ringbearer, to slip through Sauron's defenses and destroy the ring of power. The men of Gondor give Aragorn the name Lord Elfstone because he wears a special green stone. The climax comes when Aragorn is crowned King Elessar of Gondor and marries Arwen, Elrond's daughter.

The Authors' Hindsight

Like Aragorn, a plethora of names applied to Jesus, and His true identity was unveiled gradually. His full glory will not become clear until the marriage feast of the Lamb. During His earthly journey, many people misunderstood Jesus, and people continue to misunderstand Him. Nonetheless, John emphasized the importance of believing in His name, since faith averts judgment and makes it possible for us to be adopted as children of God.[881] John could state this confidently because he had the benefit of hindsight when he wrote his gospel.

Jesus faced a challenge as He entered human history. It is mind-twisting, but Jesus emptied Himself to squeeze into human form.[882] The New Testament authors, writing after the resurrection, presented Jesus' nature as two sides of a coin. He was fully man and fully God. The gospels show His heavenly side, but they are frank about His humanity. Jesus experienced human life in most of its dimensions. He was tempted in the same way that we are, yet He never sinned.[883] He was tired, thirsty, hungry, happy, and heartbroken.

The gospel writers blend their hindsight with a record of the raw historical incidents. Their accounts include dialogue, which displays varying degrees of misunderstanding on the part of the participants and the onlookers. It is impossible to know exactly how each person who interacted with Jesus assessed Him at the time. Some incidents are easier to comprehend than others. To some people, Jesus was merely human; to others, He was divine. Opinions ranged between the two. Whether people viewed Jesus as man or God, they found Him to be either refreshingly liberating, or a threat to the status quo. Some grasped who He was immediately; others recognized Him later. Some never grasped who He was at all.

Jesus' dual nature is apparent in the birth narratives, which are packed with different names. Matthew prefaced Jesus' birth story with His family tree, immediately presenting us with the two sides of Jesus' nature. At first glance, many of the names seem ordinary, but there was more to Jesus than met the eye. Despite His earthly roots, He was a shoot from heaven. Let's look at His earthly and heavenly sides in turn.

Earthly Roots

Family trees are interesting. People love to trace their roots. Is there a famous face among the branches? Were any ancestors history-makers? Did they sign the Magna Carta or sail with the Mayflower? In my case, though the historical evidence is inconclusive, an infamous seventeenth-century pirate called John Avery could be one of my ancestors.

Jewish family records are particularly reliable. We already studied Abraham's extended family, which gave rise to the nation of Israel. However, his family tree is really the trunk of a much larger tree, which extends from Adam to David before moving on to the kings and then to Jesus.

In Matthew's genealogy, Jesus Christ is the **son of Abraham** and the **son of David**. His pedigree lies in the tribe of Judah. Jesus was "born of a descendant of David according to the flesh" (Rom. 1:3). He was **the root and the descendant of David**.[884] The genealogy in Luke 3 emphasizes that by direct descent, Jesus was the **son of Adam** (*ben 'Adam*) and the **Son of God**.[885] None of those names necessarily single Jesus out as someone special. Genealogically, all Jews are sons of Abraham. Mary's husband, Joseph, was also a son of David.[886] *Ben 'Adam* is a Hebrew euphemism for being a man. Its meaning is as self-evident as the title of **Child**. Several of these names apply to every human twig of the Jewish family tree.

Son of Abraham
Gk.: *Hyios Abraam*
(Matt. 1:1)

Son of David
Gk.: *Hyios Dauid*
(Matt 1:1)

Son of Adam
Heb.: *Ben 'Adam*
Gk.: *Tou Adam*
(Luke 3:38)

Son of God
Gk.: *Ho hyios tou Theos*
(Matt. 26:63)
Gk.: *Tou Theou*
(Luke 3:38)

Child
Gk.: *Paidion*
(Matt. 2:9–21)

Scripture ascribed the title **Son of God** to Israel and her kings.[887] "Son of" indicated shared characteristics—in this case, with God.[888] Jesus taught us how to be God's children, or "sons of the Most High," by mirroring His unconditional love by loving our enemies.[889] The centurion who watched Jesus die might have said, "This was *a* son of God," meaning, "This man was innocent," which was how Luke reported it.[890] The title, "Son of God," attributed godly characteristics to a person, but it often meant much more, as we'll see.

The name **Jesus** has an ordinary side. The underlying form, *Yeshua'*, was introduced during the exile to Babylon, abbreviating and replacing the older name, *Yehoshua'* (Joshua). "*Yeshua'*" was common in New Testament times, but it had declined in use by the second century.[891] Translators rendered "*Yeshua'*" as "*Iēsous*" in Greek and "Jesus" in English. Jewish custom distinguished Jesus from his namesakes by adding His parentage or hometown to His name. In this vein, people called Him **Jesus of Nazareth** or a **Nazarene**. Once, they called him **Jesus the Galilean**. Acquaintances in Nazareth and Capernaum,[892] who were ignorant of the details of His birth, identified Him by His earthly roots as the **son of Joseph** (or **Joseph's son**) and **son of Mary**.[893] Alternatively, they knew Him by the trade Joseph had taught Him, calling Him **the carpenter's son** or simply **the carpenter**.[894] The term *tekton* can mean a mason, so perhaps Jesus and Joseph were builders.[895]

Even after His resurrection, people continued to address Jesus using everyday names.[896] The risen Jesus introduced Himself to Saul as **Jesus the Nazarene**. This name formed something of a baseline. What people chose to call Him beyond Jesus of Nazareth reveals their bias or their discernment.

The title **son of man** was often used to address ordinary people.[897] It sums up Jesus' human side. One biblical passage in particular tells how Jesus became like us to save us.[898] Of all of His titles, Jesus seemed to prefer this one; the Gospels record Him using it seventy-eight times. Sometimes Jesus Himself substituted this title for the simple personal pronoun "I," but not always.[899] "Son of man" was capable of greater significance, which we will come to.

Several followers called Jesus "**Rabbi**."[900] Rabbi derives from *rav* (great).[901] Initially, it meant "my great one," which was a common, respectful way to address teachers. John the Baptist's disciples also called him "Rabbi."[902] When Mary, by the tomb, realized that the "gardener" who knew her name was Jesus, she exclaimed, "**Rabboni!**" This word reflects the Aramaic that Mary and the blind Bartimaeus spoke.

The Greek word *didaskalos*, **teacher**, indicates a rabbi's main role. *Didaskalos* is a common title for Jesus. The rich young ruler called Jesus, "**Good teacher**." The Qumran sect called their leader the

Heb.: **Rabbi**
Gk.: *Rhabbi*
(Matt. 26:25, 49)

Aram.: **Rabboni**
Gk.: *Rhabbouni*
(Mark 10:51;
John 20:16)

Teacher
Heb.: *Moreh*
(Joel 2:23)
Gk.: *Didaskalos*
(Matt. 26:18;
Luke 22:11)

Good teacher
Gk.: *Didaskalos
agathos*
(Mark 10:17;
Luke 18:18)

Teacher of Righteousness, basing the phrase on a literal reading of Joel 2:23.[903] The title fits Jesus' teaching too. The root verb of *moreh* (*yarah*) describes the shooting of arrows. Teachers aim their students toward targets of knowledge and wisdom. Jesus directed us toward righteousness.

Then there is the word "**Lord**," which was commonly used to address Jesus. One writer noted, "The flexibility of the Greek word 'Lord' must indeed be recognized: not every instance of its use implies a consciousness of divine authority. Not everyone who addressed Jesus as Lord chose the title as the equivalent of deity; it could, as a polite form of address, mean little more than our 'Sir.'"[904] In fact, "sir" is an apt translation in several places.[905] Often, "lord" replaces "rabbi," which, as a Hebrew word, had no meaning in Greek society.[906] Elsewhere, "lord" probably translates the Aramaic "*mari*" (my Lord).[907]

Sarah called Abraham "lord."[908] With fewer rights than they have today, women in first-century society entered into legal contracts by having a *kyrios*, who was rather like a guardian, sign for them. In Greek, *kyrios* applied to slave masters, property owners, and heads of households with whom Paul compared God, our **Master in heaven**.

Lord/Sir/Master
Gk.: *Kyrios*
Aram.: *Mare'*

Master in heaven
Gk.: *Kyrios en ouranō*
(Col. 4:1)

Two other words with ordinary meanings, *despotēs* and *epistatēs*, are used to describe Jesus as **Master**.[909] *Despotēs* speaks of ownership, and is also used to call God **Lord**.[910] Jesus' followers called Him "Master" during His early ministry; later they called Him "Lord." Ten lepers used the same mode of address.

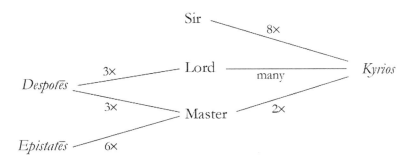

Notice that Jesus accepted such ordinary names. He never sought the inflated adulation or human fanfares often attached to titles like "Rabbi" and "Lord." In fact, He warned His disciples not to revel in human accolades or to use titles like "Rabbi" or "Leader/Guide" (unlike the Pharisees), especially if they were undeserved. Jesus alone exemplified the roles of **Teacher** and **Leader**.[911]

When Jesus wrapped a towel around His waist to wash His disciples' feet at the Last Supper, He demonstrated a deep sense of security. That security freed Him to do the job of the lowest servant. In the process, He reconfigured the disciples' understanding of ordinary roles.[912] He was not above menial tasks. Serving didn't lower His self-esteem. Limited or inaccurate labels didn't inhibit Him as they do some of us. Rather, Jesus fulfilled humble roles in an exemplary way. By embracing these roles, He elevated them. Simple service became honorable because Jesus did it. That is the pattern with Jesus' names and titles. He defined or redefined them; they did not shape Him.

Leader/Guide
Gk.: *Kathēgētēs*
(Matt. 23:10)

Even Pilate's wife, who referred to Jesus as "that **righteous Man**," apparently recognized something special about Him that went beyond ordinary manhood. Certainly, New Testament writers who used those simple words, "**the Man**," knew their fuller meaning—but that was post-resurrection. When Pilate said, "Behold, the Man," was there more on the tip of his tongue? Could he not articulate it, or did he lack the courage to express what he sensed in Jesus? We will never know, but perhaps Pilate glimpsed an otherworldly dimension to Jesus—another side to the coin of His nature.

Righteous Man
Gk.: *Ho dikaios*
(Matt. 27:19)
The Man
Gk.: *Ho Anthrōpos*
(John 19:5;
1 Tim. 2:5)

Heavenly Shoot

To passersby, the babe lying in the feeding trough of a dark Bethlehem inn was just a human baby named **Jesus**.[913] However, the details of His birth cast Him in a different light. He was a unique baby. Mary and Joseph, who witnessed the responses of various visitors, had much to ponder as He grew up—mysterious angelic messengers usually get people's attention. The nativity angels claimed that Jesus fulfilled prophecies about God's **Son**.[914] Eastern astrologers were convinced of His royalty. Glorious messengers stunned some shepherds by announcing the advent in the city of David of "a **Savior**, who is **Christ** the **Lord**" (Luke 2:11). The devout elders, Simeon and Anna, declared the arrival of the long-awaited **Christ**, God's **Salvation** and His **light of revelation**.[915] Each nativity detail bears heaven's signature, but "Savior" could have been underlined and in bold capitals. Even the name "*Yeshua'*," which God gave to Jesus, meant, "Yahweh is salvation."[916] God had a purpose for this baby.

Convinced that God had sent Jesus, John the Baptist said, "**He who comes** from above is above all." A little phrase, *ho erchomenos*, underlies the highlighted words. It often stands as a codename for God's agent. Elsewhere, it is translated as "**He who is coming**" or "the **Expected One**." We will explain this cryptic phrase later, but John knew that Jesus had a special assignment.

Gk.: *Ho erchomenos*

He who comes
(John 1:15, 27; 3:31)

He who is coming
(Matt. 3:11)

Expected One
(Matt. 11:3;
Luke 7:19–20)

When we closely investigate the names that we considered earlier, we find that many of them display a heavenly side too. Take **Son of Adam**, for a start. Jesus' descent from Adam was natural. However, the title hints that Jesus fulfilled the prophecy that God spoke to Eve, which stated that her **seed** would bruise the serpent's head, end his regime, and begin a new kingdom.[917] Paul stressed the contrast between the first man, Adam, and Jesus.[918] While the former was entirely of earth, Jesus—the **last Adam** and the **second Man**—was human but emphatically from heaven. Watchman Nee's assessment underlines this dichotomy and the transition from one era to another. "As the last Adam, Christ is the sum total of humanity; as the second Man He is the Head of a new race. . . . As the last Adam He wiped out the old race."[919]

Seed
Heb.: *Zera'*
(Gen. 3:15)
Gk.: *To sperma*
(Gal. 3:16)

Last Adam
Gk.: *Ho eschatos Adam*
(1 Cor. 15:45)

Second Man
Gk.: *Ho deuteros anthrōpos*
(1 Cor. 15:47)

The title **Son of Abraham**, when used to describe Jesus, is not just a common-or-garden way of referring to a Jew. It has overtones of the specially-cared-for promised seed that passed through Abraham and germinated to bless all nations.[920] Balaam spoke of the seed of Jacob and a descendant king with vast dominion.[921] The seed continued through David and on to Jesus, who crushed the serpent's head.[922]

Even the seemingly inconsequential word "**Child**" has its roots in a prophecy: "For a child will be born to us, a son will be given to us; and the government will rest on His shoulders; and His name will be called **Wonderful Counselor**, **Mighty God**, **Eternal Father**, **Prince of Peace**."[923] The governing Child, who shares the names and attributes of the Mighty God Himself, will know "no end to the increase of His government or of peace." He will sit

Wonderful Counselor
Heb.: *Pele' yo'ets*
(Isa. 9:6)

Mighty God
Heb.: *'El Gibbor*
(Isa. 9:6)

Eternal Father
Heb.: *'Avi'ad*
(Isa. 9:6)

Prince of Peace
Heb.: *Sar-shalom*
(Isa. 9:6)

on "the throne of David and [rule] over his kingdom, to establish it and to uphold it with justice and righteousness from then on and forevermore" (Isa. 9:6–7).

Matthew said that by being called "a **Nazarene**" (*nazoraios*) Jesus fulfilled prophecy.[924] Of which prophecy was Matthew thinking? One suggestion is Judges 13:5, which tells of Samson the deliverer who was a Nazirite (someone who vowed extra devotion to God). However, there is no sign that Jesus took such a vow. *Nazoraios* is more likely to be a play on two words. The first word occurs in a prophecy about a sprouting branch (*netser*) from David's line. Second is the Hebrew word for Jesus' hometown, *Natseret*.[925]

If Matthew had no particular prophecy in mind, perhaps he spoke of the prediction that people would despise God's servant just as they ridiculed Nazareth.[926] After Jesus was arrested, the High Priest's servant girl used the word "Nazarene" contemptuously, as if He had been "born on the wrong side of the tracks."[927] Pilate penned a sign, "Jesus of Nazareth, King of the Jews," and then pinned it to the cross. Perhaps he was deliberately capturing the irony of a king coming from Nazareth, of all places.[928]

That title "king" caused problems. Ordinary Jews became overexcited when they heard it. Religious Jews reacted with suspicion, and rulers responded in whatever way was politically expedient at the time. The titles Lord, Son of God, Son of David, and Son of Man all connect to kingship. They all have layers of meaning. In the next chapters, we must pry apart the layers to explain why reactions to Jesus were so strong and why He was so misunderstood. Our goal is to grasp the heavenly sides of these highly charged titles in the same way that the first witnesses did once they believed the reports that Jesus had risen from the dead. However, in the absence of faith, the political meaning of the titles stole the headlines. So first, let's take a trip to the news archives.

Chapter 17

HARK THE HERALD ANGEL

The Messiah was this man.
—Flavius Josephus

The cross had a powerful message for a desperate Jewish shepherd called Athronges. Long before it became an item of jewelry, Romans used the cross as an execution device. Crosses delivered strident warnings. Crosses with bodies still nailed to them made the best deterrents for troublemakers. They said, "Resistance is futile. Surrender or die." If Athronges and others planned to rebel, they had better be determined; if they failed, they would face an excruciating death. The cross only made Athronges angrier. It tried to dictate what he and his people could and could not do.

For most of Israel's history, shepherding had been a respected profession. King David had been a shepherd and Scripture called God, "Shepherd of Israel." However, by Jesus' time, shepherds had a reputation for dishonesty. In a society that lived under crushing oppression, shepherds were among the poorest and most exploited people. They were inclined to cause trouble.

That oppression explains why Athronges, crowned like a king, led a futile revolt against Herod Archelaus and the Romans in 4 BC, shortly after King

Savior
Heb.: *Moshia'*
(Isa. 43:11; 45:15, 21;
Hos 13:4)
Gk.: *Sōtēr*
(Luke 1:47; 2:11)

Lord
Heb.: *'Adonai/'Adon*
Aram.: *Mare'*
Gk.: *Kyrios*
Eng.: **Messiah**
Heb.: *Mashiakh*
(Dan. 9:26)

Herod the Great died. Athronges and his brothers died in a failed attempt to restore Israel's dignity. Athronges makes a brief appearance in the historical record,[929] but he is typical of several freedom fighters who lived around Jesus' time. Each of them considered himself to be God's Messiah, anointed to lead Jewish armies to victory. Every uprising ended with nothing but bad news: harsh Roman punishment on the offenders' villages, grieving wives and mothers, and many orphaned children.

Considering the mess that their world was in, it is no wonder that a band of shepherds grabbed their staffs and ran to investigate the nativity angel's news of "a **Savior**, who is **Christ** the **Lord**" (Luke 2:11). Could this be the one?

Messiahs in the News

Each of the three short titles that the angel mentioned has a deep meaning. We will continue to explore them from different angles in the coming chapters. "Christ" is the English equivalent of the Hebrew word "*Mashiakh*," which means "anointed." King David was called the "Lord's anointed," so "Messiah" was a politically emotive word for the Jews of Jesus' time. "Messiah" has different connotations for Christians because Jesus redefined messiahship. Jesus was not the only one who claimed to be a messiah, but He was unique.[930]

To understand the various reactions to the titles in the angelic announcement properly, we need to know how the Jews expected a messiah to save them and what they expected him to save them from. So, here is a brief synopsis of Israel's complicated history around the time of Jesus. It is interspersed with what an imaginary news media might have written about key events. (For information about the historical documents of this period see www.NamesForGod.net/jewish-literature.)

In the sixth century BC, Israel returned from exile in Babylon, a shadow of her former glory.[931] In 332 BC, Alexander the Great swept in and conquered the region. So began over two centuries of Greek domination. The Greeks' Hellenistic culture infiltrated Jewish society, threatening to swamp Judaism.[932]

Sold to the Highest Bidder!

In a shameful twist of events, the high priesthood has changed hands again. Three years ago, Jason bribed Antiochus Epiphanes for the office of High Priest, which was previously held by Jason's brother, Onias III. This week, Jason lost the office when his courier, Menelaus, "donated" an undisclosed sum to Antiochus. Commentators expect High Priest Menelaus to erode Jewish religion more than Jason did.

Jerusalem Shofar. 172 BC

What a Swine!

Antiochus Epiphanes caused unspeakable offense yesterday by erecting an altar to Zeus and sacrificing a pig on the holy altar of the temple in Jerusalem. He also banned all Jewish sacrifices, and circumcision. Leaders across the board have condemned his anti-Jewish actions. Many are predicting a violent response.

December 9, 167 BC
Jerusalem Shofar

Wanted, Dead or Alive   167 BC Judean Times

Soldiers on a routine law-enforcement assignment met with an unexpected outburst this week in the mountain village of Modiin. One soldier and a resident died. The incident occurred when troops tried to enforce Antiochus' orders that Jews perform Greek sacrifices. A local priest named Mattathias refused. When an unnamed Jew stepped forward to obey, Mattathias cried out, "Whoever is zealous for the laws of our country and the worship of God, follow me!" Unsheathing his knife, he murdered the villager and a soldier, and then he fled. A manhunt is underway for Mattathias and his five sons.

Maccabeans Taking Ground
166 BC Judean Times

Hopes are rising in Israel. After several months of hammering by guerrilla units in the Judean hills, Greek forces sound less confident that they can swiftly end the Maccabean uprising. Judah Maccabaeus, son of Mattathias of Modiin, is proving to be an effective leader. His followers call themselves Maccabees, or hammers. Sympathizers report miraculous interventions. Certainly, the success of untrained men tackling Greek soldiers is surprising. Military analysts say that the tide turned when the Maccabees made the unprecedented decision to fight in self-defense on the Sabbath.

Temple Purified, Sacrifices Restored

Judah, leader of the Maccabean rebellion, secured his place in Jewish history yesterday. His forces recaptured the Temple Mount from Greek troops. In a hasty but reverent ceremony, they built a new altar and relit the sacred menorah, which symbolizes God's glory. The temple cleansing comes three years after its desecration by Antiochus Epiphanes. Observers say this is the best news Israel has heard for several centuries.

December 164 BC
Jerusalem Shofar

Even successful campaigns of the most popular political candidates sometimes lead to disillusionment. The Maccabean brothers quickly disappointed the nation, and their dynasty reverted to embracing Hellenism.[933]

139 BC - Roman Times

Simon Acknowledged as Jewish Leader

Caesar recognized Simon Maccabaeus as king of the Jews yesterday. Simon and his delegation are visiting Rome from Judea. He became king and high priest in 142 BC after Jonathan's assassination. Jewish leaders confirmed him in those offices in 140 BC. Simon is a controversial leader at home because, like his brother before him, he combines the offices of king and high priest.

134 BC - Jerusalem Shofar

King David's Tomb Pilfered

John Hyrcanus abused his position as high priest by taking three thousand talents from King David's tomb this week. John used the money to buy off Antiochus VII, whose siege of Jerusalem has reduced the city to starvation. Hyrcanus has ruled Judea since the assassination of his father, Simon Maccabaeus, in February. Once again, Judea faces the prospect of Greek occupiers exploiting them further. Criticism of the Maccabeans is at an all-time high.

The Maccabeans left a mixed legacy. It included a collection of war stories and Maccabean heroes for people to emulate, but they also left a divided and compromised nation. When they installed their king as the High Priest, many devout Jews distanced themselves.

One emerging group was the Pharisees.[934] They worked for change within the system, while waiting for God to free their nation. They permitted religious practices outside of the temple, and they developed an oral Torah that was relevant to ordinary Jewish life. They believed that national purity and piety would usher in Israel's redemption, so in the Gospels they seem like religious monitors of cleanliness and the Sabbath. On occasion, because of their zeal for Law and their nation, the Pharisees rebelled against corrupt rulers or those they saw as heretics.[935]

Perhaps in response to the Pharisaic movement, aristocratic priests formed another association, the Sadducees.[936] They included most of the twenty thousand priests. In general, ordinary Jews preferred the Pharisees to the wealthier and stricter Sadducees. However, real power lay with the priests.[937] The Sadducees were the majority in the seventy-one-member Sanhedrin, the judicial council that the High Priest presided over. Inevitably, despite some dissenting Pharisees, the Sanhedrin supported whoever governed at the time.

In the same period, disgruntled priests formed a mysterious breakaway sect called the Essenes. Josephus says there were thousands of them.[938] Like the Pharisees, they did not believe in forcing political change, but they were even more zealous for the Law. The Essenes believed God had appointed their group as His new, covenant people, and He would soon reveal them to the world. In their eyes, their strict communities had replaced the temple. Their codes, beliefs, and lifestyles are preserved in the ruins of Qumran and in the Dead Sea Scrolls, a collection of literature that was found hidden in surrounding caves. They expected two messianic figures to come: an Aaronic high priest (the Interpreter of the Law) and a warrior-king who was descended from David.[939] Calling themselves the Sons of Light, they were a righteous community that was led by the Teacher of Righteousness[940] and pitted against the Sons of Darkness. The scrolls tell of two opponents—their archenemy the Wicked Priest, which is probably a reference to the current, illegitimate high priest, and the Romans (Kittim).[941] The Essenes expected to prevail and receive God's vindication.[942]

Judea Annexed
63 BC Roman Times

Our esteemed consul, Pompey, took the bold but necessary step of annexing Judea this week. Years of squabbling between Pharisees and Sadducees have left the nation in chaos. Judea is now a client state of the empire; Jews will only rule at Rome's pleasure. The response around the empire has been enthusiastic because the food supply, for which the region is vital, comes under direct Roman control. However, experts on Jewish affairs predict a backlash once the new subjects experience imperial taxation. Advisors warn that added tax burdens increase poverty and banditry. Bandits pilfer from property owners and justify their criminal actions as a redistribution of wealth. Pompey has promised to respond with harsh punishments, including crucifixion.

Roman Times, 36 BC

Herod Confirmed as King of the Jews

The Senate has voted Herod in as king of the Jewish nation, thereby replacing the fractured leadership. While Jewish leaders complain that Herod is from neighboring Idumea and is not a Jew by birth, most people believe his leadership strengths will more than compensate.

+ Jerusalem Shofar, 20 BC

Priests to Renovate Temple

In a move widely interpreted as a political stunt, King Herod announced a massive expansion of the temple. Royal funds will pay for it, while priests will do the work. Temple rituals will continue as normal during construction, which may take decades. Cynics claim that this is merely another attempt on the part of Herod to win favor with the Jews, just like his marriage to the Maccabean princess Mariamne. They maintain that Herod is modeling his project on David and Solomon's glorious temple construction. An Essene spokesman is quoted as saying, "Only a true Jewish king can rebuild it—not Herod!" The temple is the latest of several extravagant projects, including the fortification of the desert butte, Masada, as his winter palace.

Jerusalem Shofar
Sometime between 6 and 4 BC

Rachel Wails for Her Children

Last night, a squadron of Herod's troops slaughtered young children in and around Bethlehem. A stunned silence hangs over the city as the community tries to recover from this brutal act. Anonymous palace workers report that King Herod succumbed to paranoia following a visit by Eastern astrologers. The sources say the visit concerned the bright new star that has recently been visible in our skies. The astrologers claim that the star heralds a royal baby. Herod's action was a precautionary measure to prevent rebels from exploiting hopes of the imminent fulfillment of Micah's prophecy. Herod is well known for ruthlessly eradicating enemies and rivals, including sons and one wife.

Herod was a severe ruler. He had spies everywhere and he punished dissent harshly. His leadership style, which was reinforced by Roman troops who maintained a watchful eye from Syria, kept full-scale rebellions in check. Nonetheless, trouble brewed. Everyone resented taxation. Religious leaders pointed fingers at each other's failings. In the people's eyes, few of them held office legitimately. No one had forgotten the success of the Maccabean heroes in throwing off Antiochus' yoke. All the ingredients were in place to spur men like Athronges to rebel. Whenever a messianic leader stepped forward, claiming to have the vision and the competency to fix the social and political mess, there were ready followers. Self-appointed messianic saviors abounded, and all of them sought autonomy for Israel.[943] Notably, they wanted a legitimate priest to run the temple, and they wanted a Davidic king to rule with God's authority. [944]

March 14, 4 BC
Jerusalem Shofar

More Protests in the City of Peace

Two Pharisees, Judas and Matthias, incited a serious disturbance yesterday by the temple gate. Shouting that pagan images defile God's city, protesters tore down the ornamental eagle from above the gate. Soldiers detained the ringleaders, and the ailing Herod ordered them burned. More rebellion is anticipated as Herod's health deteriorates.

Roman Times. April 4 BC

Herod the Great Dead at 70

King Herod, the longtime friend of Caesar Augustus, has died in Jerusalem, following a protracted illness. Legions based in neighboring Syria are on high alert in case disaffected parties take advantage of the resulting transition in leadership. Augustus will probably grant Herod's request for his son Archelaus to succeed him.

Judea Named a Province of the Empire

Rome has made Judea a separate province, following Caesar Augustus' removal of Herod Archelaus as king. Augustus plans to appoint a governor soon. Jewish reactions are muted. Most Jews viewed Archelaus as a Roman puppet anyway. Roman Times AD 6

Jerusalem Shofar. AD 6
Census Objectors Rebel

Violence erupted yesterday over the recent Roman census. Judas the Galilean, from Gamla, accompanied by a Pharisee called Zaddok, led the uprising. Witnesses heard the crowds chanting, "No king but God." Critics claim censuses serve to maximize tax revenues and are "tantamount to slavery." This is the latest upsurge of insurrection since Herod's death.

Jerusalem Shofar. AD 30

Baptizer Beheaded

Herod Antipas has executed John the Baptist in the citadel of Machaerus. Herod imprisoned him, fearing he would incite a rebellion. John had been critical of Herod's recent marriage to his brother's wife, Herodias. His death comes as a surprise because Herod was mildly interested in John's teaching

Popular Galilean Crucified

Under strange circumstances, Jesus of Nazareth, the much-loved teacher and miracle worker, was crucified Friday, along with two bandits. Details remain unclear, but after soldiers arrested Jesus, Jewish and Roman officials interrogated him overnight. Sympathizers claim that Jesus did not deserve crucifixion and that Pontius Pilate's decision was unexpected. Witnesses say that Pilate offered a prisoner exchange as a goodwill gesture to the crowd, but the crowd opted to have the murderous insurrectionist Barabbas released instead.

Jerusalem Shofar.
Sunday, April 5, AD 33

AD 54 or 56 - Roman Times

Former Pharisee Leader Arrested in Temple

The Pharisee-turned-ringleader of the Nazarene sect, Paul of Tarsus, remains in prison in the Caesarea garrison. Soldiers arrested him in the Jewish temple on suspicion of starting a riot. Paul claims that he is innocent and that he was mistaken for an Egyptian terrorist. The Egyptian led the Sicarii, a group that carries concealed daggers and is notorious for stabbing Jews who are loyal to the empire. According to rumors, Paul will represent himself in court and he might appeal to Caesar.

Our readers will note that the current prolonged period of increased banditry and activism is due in part to a recent famine and popular resistance to taxation. Many will remember Theudas, the prophetic rebel leader who was beheaded ten years ago. Shortly afterward, Tiberius Alexander crucified Jacob and Simon, sons of Judas the Galilean. Roman leaders remain determined to extinguish every revolt, using whatever force is necessary.

AD 66 - Jerusalem Shofar

Legitimate High Priest Installed

Yesterday, Jewish fighters successfully delivered the holy Temple and restored the high priesthood to the Zadokites. They also captured the adjacent fortress. To the cheers of the common people, one of their first defiant acts was to burn the records of individual debt. Meanwhile, correspondents report that brigand bands, the largest of which is led by John of Gischala, are fleeing Galilee ahead of Titus's army.

Spring, AD 69, Jerusalem Shofar

Trouble Brewing between Competing Factions

The charismatic guerrilla leader, Simon bar Giora, entered Jerusalem yesterday with ten thousand fighters. Crowds welcomed him enthusiastically, hoping he would deliver the city from the two smaller rival Zealot groups, which are led by John of Gischala and Eleazar ben Simon, respectively. For three years, their factions have bitterly divided the city.

Summer, AD 66, Jerusalem Shofar

Messiah Murdered by Rival Cousin

This week, Eleazar, the temple captain, tortured Menahem ben Judah to death. Ben Judah is famous for aiding the Zealots in recapturing Jerusalem. Ben Judah's Sicarii plundered weapons at Masada and brought them to assist in the battle for the city. His regal entry to Jerusalem made a strong impression. Ben Judah was descended from Judas the Galilean, who rebelled against a census sixty years ago

Late AD 70 Roman Times

Jewish Insurgent Simon bar Giora Dead

The climax of Caesar Vespasian's triumph ceremony was the execution of Simon bar Giora, a so-called messiah of the Jewish War. Following the recent surge in troops, legions re-entered Jerusalem. They captured bar Giora and Zealot leader, John of Gischala, and they crucified thousands of Jewish rebels. One commentator reflects, "The Jews were stirred to war by a vague prediction that someone from their land would rule the world." Bar Giora disappointed them.

Since the siege ended, the legions have been destroying Jewish national symbols, including the temple and the city wall. Caesar's policy is to quash Jewish nationalism. The priesthood has scattered. Eleazar ben Ya'ir leads the most notable pocket of resistance. He fled to the royal palace of Masada, seizing it as Sicarii headquarters.

April 18, AD 74 or May 4, AD 73 Roman Times

Mass Suicide Reported

Runners arrived early today with welcome news from Masada. The siege has ended. Soldiers of the Tenth Legion stormed the desert palace two days ago, meeting no opposition. Instead, they found the bodies of 960 Jews and a handful of survivors. It appears the rebels committed mass suicide. This is good news for Rome. No serious resistance remains in Judea.

Good news for Rome was terrible news for the Jews. The absence of temple, priesthood, and city forced Judaism to change direction. The Pharisaic movement morphed into rabbinicism. Jewish religion refocused on the study of the Torah in local synagogues. A subdued peace prevailed for a while.[945]

AD 132, Roman Times

Bar Kokhba to Produce New Coin

Jewish rebel leader Simon bar Kokhba recently announced plans to produce his own coins. They will be date-stamped starting with "The first year of Israel's liberation." Bar Kokhba assures his followers that this is the long-awaited new age for Israel. This move celebrates recent successes against imperial forces. Bar Kokhba, born Simon ben Kosiba, became a prominent messianic leader when he rallied an army against Roman authorities. He objected to Emperor Hadrian's ban on circumcision, as well as the founding of a new city over the ruins of Jerusalem and an altar to Zeus on the temple mount. In intercepted correspondence, he calls himself "Prince over Israel."

Ben Kosiba gained the support of Rabbi Akiva, who proclaimed him "King Messiah" and dubbed him, "bar Kokhba" (Son of the Star). This title derives from a passage in the Jewish Scriptures that states, "A star shall come forth from Jacob, a scepter shall rise from Israel."

AD 135, Roman Times

Rebellion Crushed

Emperor Hadrian is victorious. The bar Kokhba revolt is over. To eliminate any possibility of further trouble, the emperor has ordered the dispersal of Jews throughout the Roman Empire.

The three hundred complicated years between the Maccabean uprising and the crushing of bar Kokhba were filled mostly with bad news for the Jews. "Israel's sovereignty was denied and her very existence threatened by the imperial combination of Hellenistic culture and Roman military power."[946] The Jews were desperate for God-appointed rulers who would establish justice and prosperity. Almost anyone with an ounce of charisma could rally followers who sought a liberating messiah. It helped if these charismatic leaders were descended from King David. Jesus was born in the middle of political tension and heated debate about the Messiah. Jesus' words and actions were surprisingly relevant to the political situation. However, the kingdom lifestyle that He taught, especially in the Sermon on the Mount, transcended other agendas. As N. T. Wright says, Jesus had "a revolutionary way of being revolutionary."[947]

The Messianic Hopes of Israel

Having scanned the noteworthy news clippings, we need to summarize the main patterns in the messianic expectations. What did the Jews hope for in the Messiah?

Israel was God's covenant nation, but the people acknowledged their imperfections and expected judgment.[948] They felt that their sins explained why God continued to subject them to pagan rulers. If people would behave themselves as God had commanded in the Torah, then God would save the nation. He would intervene, punishing and driving out the occupiers. He would renew His covenant with Israel and rule via His appointed king. That king would properly restore the temple and the priesthood.

In the Jewish concept of salvation, God Himself would intervene as their Savior. However, most Jews expected God to send a human Messiah (some of them even expected two messiahs), rather than a transcendent or divine one.[949] Thus, the Messiah depicted in the Psalms of Solomon is human, "the exalted instrument of the Divine Will."[950]

The Jews did not expect the world to end. Instead, they believed in a massive regime change, whereby God would replace the present evil age with the age to come[951]—His kingdom of restored and revived covenant people. God would rule His kingdom through a descendant of David and a priest who had descended from Aaron.[952] The anticipated change was so drastic that writers described it like a cosmic cataclysm.

Peace, prosperity, justice, and love would mark the kingdom age. Popular literature of the time oozes with syrupy descriptions:[953] men sitting in the shade of their fig trees or vines,[954] mountains dripping wine,[955] and the dead rising *en masse* to enjoy the utopia. All creation would celebrate.

The essential identifying mark of God's covenant people, the true Jews, was that they observed the Torah. This set Israel apart from other nations. They did not focus on performing in order to earn salvation; sacrifices were intended to deal with failures and restore their relationship with God.

Religious debates raged over the details of conformity to the Torah. The hottest topics were circumcision, Sabbath, purity, and kosher regulations. It seemed essential to get them right. If they succeeded, God would free the nation as promised; if they failed, their subjection would continue. No wonder the Sadducees, the Pharisees, the Essenes, the Zealots, and other like-minded groups were so intense. No wonder they were upset by sinners and anyone who led people astray.

Determining who was a sinner was an important issue. Most parties agreed that the present religious and royal leaders who were in collusion with the Romans deserved to be judged. Everyone, however, disagreed about who else had crossed the line and to what extent they had done so. The Essenes, for instance, included even the Pharisees, and called them "speakers of smooth things."

The Jews were less clear about the fate of pagan nations. Some thought that the Gentiles would observe the blessings of life in God's new kingdom from the sidelines. Perhaps they would visit as pilgrims or even convert to Judaism.[956] Others expected and wanted the Gentiles to be punished, destroyed, or at least pruned.

The Jews believed that God's reign would commence with afflictions that they called the "travail [birth pangs] of the Messiah,"[957] or the "day of the LORD." The latter phrase originated with the prophets.[958] It denoted a day of judgment that would be marked by cosmic and social disorder. After the dust settled, God's kingdom would envelope the world.

The idea of the Jewish God having dominion over the world infuriated the Romans. After all, at that time, they ruled it.

Clearly, by the time of Jesus' birth, many Jews had focused their messianic hopes on political outcomes. Most messiahs had overt nationalistic agendas, and the authorities responded by unleashing their political machinery. However, the angelic herald's message for the shepherds had a different focus. Angels certainly aren't politicians.

Chapter 18

FOUR THREADS IN AN EMBROIDERY

Wishing to appear openly to those who seek Him with all their heart and hidden from those who shun Him with all their heart, He has qualified our knowledge of Him by giving signs which can be seen by those who seek Him and not by those who do not. There is enough light for those who desire only to see, and enough darkness for those of a contrary disposition.
—**Blaise Pascal**, *Pensées*

G od does embroidery with prophecy. For centuries, God stitched prophetic threads into the mesh of Israel's culture, especially into Scripture. His embroidery presented His loving plans for His people and introduced His Messiah, though mostly in other guises. The Jewish people, to whom Jesus first came, should have been able to recognize Him from the pattern, but because of their nationalistic bias, few of them did.

God didn't ignore the political arena. His Messiah is an answer for every issue facing every human social group. The answer begins with changed individual hearts, and it proceeds to transform the world on every level. Jesus even revolutionized the highest human office—that of the king.

Three of the titles we mentioned earlier (Son of David, Son of God, and Son of Man) have to do with God's king. They are three threads in God's complex embroidery. A fourth thread is the suffering servant, a concept that radically altered the idea of kingship. The overall pattern is hard to discern because, over the years, the threads intertwined and wove in and out of sight. In this chapter, we will tease apart the strands to see God's plan more clearly. Most messianic titles for Jesus, including "Christ," can only be understood properly in the context of all four threads.

When the angel announced "Christ the Lord" to the Bethlehem shepherds, he used their language.[959] The English word "Christ" translates the Greek word "*Christos*"; the Hebrew title *Mashiakh* underlies C*hristos*.[960]

The Hebrew verb for anointing or smearing with oil is *mashakh*; *christos* is the equivalent Greek adjective for "anointed."[961] The angel had declared the arrival of Yahweh's **Messiah**—the LORD's anointed.[962] But, what did "messiah" mean to the shepherds beyond its revolutionary connotations?

Anointed
(Ps. 2:2)
Heb.: *Mashiakh*
Gk. OT: *Christos*

Christ
Gk.: *Christos*
(Matt. 1:18)

Messiah
Gk.: *Messias*
(John 1:41; 4:25)

Few Old Testament verses mention the Messiah,[963] but it was part of the culture to anoint people with oil. The list of specific ingredients reads like a recipe for a fancy Italian dressing. Sometimes the mixture was applied lavishly.[964] Priests often received anointing, and prophets occasionally did.[965] Kings began their reigns after they had been anointed.[966] The psalms often call David "anointed."[967]

Jesus fulfilled all three anointed roles. As a priest, He mediated between God and the people. He also fulfilled the central messianic role—the king to which the three royal threads pointed.[968] However, according to N. T. Wright whose writings provide fascinating perspective on this period, "Jesus' public persona within first century Judaism was that of a prophet."[969]

In Psalm 2:2 "Anointed" is capitalized as a title because it can indicate the Messiah. "Why are the nations in an uproar and the peoples devising a vain thing? The kings of the earth take their stand and the rulers take counsel together against the LORD and against His **Anointed**." Initially, this psalm might have been a coronation song because it continues triumphantly, "I have installed My King upon Zion, My holy mountain" (Ps. 2:1–2, 6). By Jesus' time, people read the psalm as a prophetic pointer to the anointed Messiah.[970] Luke interpreted it as a reference to Jesus.[971]

Son of David

The first thread is anchored in God's promise to King David: "I will raise up your descendant [literally "seed"] after you . . . and I will establish his kingdom . . . . Your house and your kingdom shall endure before Me forever" (2 Sam. 7:12–16). The theme of an enduring Davidic house reappeared often in Jewish history.[972] It spawned two important titles, **Son of David** and **King of Israel**.[973] Let's follow the thread chronologically.

Son of David
Heb.: *Ben Dawid*
Gk.: *Hyios Dauid*
(Matt. 1:1)

King of Israel
Heb.: *Melekh Yisra'el*
Gk.: *Basileus tou Israēl*
(John 1:49; 12:13)

When David uttered his last recorded words, he expressed confidence that God would keep His promise about his house. "Will He not indeed make it grow [*yatsmiakh*]?" (2 Sam. 23:5) The word that is translated as "grow" literally means, "sprout or spring up," and it is used in a similar way for the growth of "horns," which symbolize power and leadership.[974] Hannah ended her thanksgiving for Samuel's birth by saying that God "will give strength to His king and will exalt the horn of His anointed" (1 Sam. 2:10).[975] Other verses repeat the expectation. "I will cause the **horn of David** to spring forth ['*atsmiakh qeren leDawid*]." Also, "On that day I will make a horn sprout ['*atsmiakh*] for the house of Israel" (Ezek. 29:21). The prophecies all point to an irrepressible bursting forth of a leader from David's line.

Horn of David
Heb.: *Qeren leDawid*
(Ps. 132:17)

At the bottom of my garden is the rotten stump of an old maple tree. The previous owner felled the tree decades ago. Most of the gnarled stump is decayed and soft, and it is covered with fascinating fungi in the fall. Squirrels use it as a workbench to break their nuts on or store them under. Every year, the stump amazes me by sprouting vigorous suckers. Some shoots can grow four feet in a year, and they block my shed door if I do not prune them back.

My maple stump does what the verb *yatsmiakh* describes; it sprouts new growth. For the prophets, this word was initially a verbal concept, but it became a messianic title (*tsemakh*) that they applied to a member of the Davidic line, "the **Branch of the LORD**."[976] In Chapter 16, we mentioned a different word for branch (*netser* in Isa. 11:1–5); the word-picture is similar.[977]

Branch of the LORD
Heb.: *Tsemakh Yahweh*
(Isa. 4:2)

An immediate fulfillment of the promise came when David's son Solomon succeeded him. However, shortly after Solomon's death, the kingdom divided and it began to decline and disappoint. Descriptions of the messianic age are reminiscent of the glorious years in which David ruled Israel.[978] The idea that a Davidic Messiah might again rule Israel appealed to the national nostalgia, especially during the years of weak kings, puppet rulers, and exile.

Branch
Heb.: *Tsemakh*
(Zech. 3:8; 6:12)
Heb.: *Netser*
(Isa. 11:1)

Righteous Branch
Heb.: *Tsemakh tsaddiq/
tsedaqah*
(Jer. 23:5; 33:15)

As each of the Jewish kings took the throne in turn, the people hoped they would save the nation from its troubles. Will this one usher in a revival and return Israel to the greatness of David's days? Most kings failed and hope was relegated to the future.

After Assyria and Babylon axed the monarchy like a troublesome tree, leaving just a dead-looking stump, there were no more kings.[979] Nonetheless, God said He would cause the stem, which was rooted in David's father, Jesse, to sprout a new shoot. It was a powerful prediction of a radical new start: "A shoot will spring [*yatsa'*] from the stem of Jesse, and a branch [*netser*] from his roots will bear fruit" (Isa. 10:33–11:1). The human shoot would grow up like a young plant and bear the fruit that God intended. Such is the origin of the names, **root of Jesse**, **root of David**, **shoot**, and **branch**.[980]

Root of Jesse
Heb.: *Shoresh Yishai*
(Isa. 11:10)
Gk.: *Hē rhiza tou Iessai*
(Rom. 15:12)

Root of David
Gk.: *Hē rhiza Dauid*
(Rev. 5:5; 22:16)

Shoot
Heb.: *Khoter*
(Isa. 11:1)

A related title is found in Matthew's précis of Micah's prophecy: "Out of you [Bethlehem] shall come forth [*yetse'*] a **ruler** Who will shepherd My people Israel" (Matt. 2:6; Mic. 5:2–5). Several times, the Davidic Messiah is pictured as the shepherd of the Israelite flock.[981]

The final king, Zedekiah, whose name meant "Yahweh my righteousness," sat unrighteously on an ever-weakening throne. Jeremiah pointed beyond Zedekiah to a **righteous Branch** sprouting from David's house, the **LORD our righteousness**.[982] According to Jeremiah, the Lord would lead a second exodus that would be so far-reaching that it would surpass the first Exodus in the collective memory.

When Ezekiel prophesied that the ruins of Zedekiah's monarchy would endure "until He comes whose right it is, and I will give it to Him" (Ezek. 21:27), he probably echoed the ancient prophecy about a ruler arising from Judah. "The scepter shall not depart from Judah, nor the ruler's staff from between his feet, *until Shiloh comes*, and to him shall be the obedience of the peoples" (Gen. 49:10, my italics). Some scholars prefer to translate the phrase in italics, "until he comes to whom it [rulership] belongs"—a rendering which Ezekiel's words would certainly support.[983]

Shiloh
Heb.: *Shylh*
(Gen. 49:10)

During the return to Judah following the exile to Babylon, another prophet, Zechariah, spoke of "**My servant** the **Branch**."[984] Historically, the phrase probably applied to Zerubbabel, the governor who descended from David and organized the rebuilding of the temple. Even he disappointed, and revival never came to the nation. People still awaited a Davidic Messiah who would accomplish God's purposes.

A few decades before Jesus' birth, the thread reappears in a pharisaic work.[985] It foretells a Son of David, reigning as King of Israel and judging sinners and aliens. It says he will break them with a rod of iron, just like God's anointed son did in Psalm 2.[986]

A rod-wielding king who would smash pagan occupiers and their temple-defiling idols was just what many Jews wanted, but no exact template existed. "Messiahship, it seems, was whatever people made of it."[987] Nonetheless, "the king was the focal point of the dream of national liberty."[988] Rebel leaders of Jesus' time often masqueraded as kings. Some of them wore royal robes, while others headed to the temple because good kings stood up for God's house.

Horn of my salvation
Heb.: *Qeren-yish'i*
(2 Sam. 22:3; Ps. 18:2)

Horn of salvation
Gk.: *Keras sōtērias*
(Luke 1:69)

King
Gk.: *Basileus*
(Matt. 21:5)

King of the Jews
Gk.: *Basileus tōn Ioudaiōn*
(Matt. 2:2)

Even Herod's temple-renovation project might have been a laughable messianic claim.

The royal thread surfaces in the events surrounding Jesus' birth. John the Baptist's father, Zacharias, celebrated the raising of "a **horn of salvation** for us in the house of David His servant" (Luke 1:68–71). The insightful, stargazing magi recognized the birth of the **King of the Jews**. King Herod, influenced by a hunted Satan, connected the title with the **Christ**. Paranoia drove him to attempt the extermination of the messianic King.[989] Herod held the throne legally, and he had the power to defend his claim. The coordinates of the messianic **ruler**'s birthplace were just as Micah had recorded them: Bethlehem, the city of David.[990] So, that was where Herod deployed his troops.

During Jesus' ministry, blind men and a Canaanite woman with a sick daughter appealed to the **Son of David** for help.[991] Perhaps those desperately needy people clung more tightly than others to the hope that a Davidic savior would come with the authority to dispense God's promised healing.[992] Paul turned to Isaiah's prophecy that the **root of Jesse** would be a signal for the nations. He pointed to mass Gentile conversions as the fulfillment of the prophecy.[993]

The clearest reference Jesus made to Himself as "Lord" included a comparison with David. It came in response to Pharisees who criticized the disciples for plucking grain on the Sabbath. Jesus pointed to a precedent that David had set while he was anointed, yet opposed prior to his enthronement. Who else could act like David and the priests and also be greater than the temple?[994] "The Son of Man is **Lord of the Sabbath**," was a messianic claim.

Jesus' entry into Jerusalem on a colt a few days before His crucifixion demonstrates the popular confusion over His identity. The event is packed with meaning. The Gospel writers explain that it fulfilled Isaiah and Zechariah's prophecies about a coming gentle (or meek) **King**.[995] At the time, the city wondered, "Who is this?" (Matt. 21:10) To some, He was "the **prophet** Jesus, from Nazareth in Galilee" (Matt. 21:11). Others in the crowd cried, "Hosanna to the **Son of David**; blessed is **He who comes** in the name of the Lord."[996] John recorded extra words: ". . . even the **King of Israel**" (John 12:13).

"Hosanna" transliterates the Hebrew *hoshi'ah na'*, "Save please!" The crowd was shouting a bold and politically incorrect prayer: "Save us please, Son of David!" Even the throwing of garments in Jesus' path was reminiscent of Jehu's ascension to the throne eight centuries earlier.[997]

The Gospels do not specify which gate Jesus entered Jerusalem through. However, since the east gate faced the Mount of Olives, perhaps Jesus used that gate to fulfill Ezekiel's prophecy of the coming **prince**.[998] The event returns us to the ancient passage about the arrival of the One to whom rulership belongs, who "ties his foal to the vine, and his donkey's colt to the choice vine" (Gen. 49:10–11; Matt. 21:2).[999]

Prince
Heb.: *Nasi'*
(Ezek. 44:3)

Oh, how the religious leaders hated the suggestion that this Jesus, so contrary to their own expectations, was the messianic King.[1000] Their murderous scheming intensified.

Son of God

To begin with, God referred to the nation of Israel as His son.[1001] Representing Israel to God, Israel's kings bore the title **Son of God**. Royal descendants of David, from Solomon on, were God's sons: "I will be a father to him and he will be a son to me."[1002] The coronation psalm continues: "I will surely tell of the decree of the LORD: He said to Me, 'You are **My Son**, today I have begotten You. Ask of Me, and I will surely give the nations as Your inheritance, and the very ends of the earth as Your possession'" (Ps. 2:7–8).[1003] The psalm prophesied about the Messiah.[1004] God said more about the Davidic Messiah: "I also shall make him my **firstborn**, the highest of the kings of the earth."[1005]

Son of God
Gk.: *Ho hyios tou Theou*
(Matt. 26:63)

My Son
Heb.: *Beni*
(Ps. 2:7)

Firstborn
Heb.: *Bekhor*
Gk.: *Prōtotokos*
(Ps. 89:27)

When the angel Gabriel announced Mary's conception of "the **Son of the Most High**," he interwove the royal threads: "The Lord God will give Him the throne of His father David; and He will reign over the house of Jacob forever, and His kingdom will have no end" (Luke 1:31–33).[1006] Jesus' kingdom will be infinitely more extensive and enduring than David's kingdom.

Son of the Most High
Gk.: *Hyios hypsistou*
(Luke 1:32)

Prior to Jesus' resurrection, sonship was a secondary thread that was intertwined with the royal messianic thread.[1007] No one thought about the full implications of being God's son. However, Jesus certainly understood His unique relationship with the Father. His claims offended the Jews, who presented them as evidence at His trial.[1008] After the resurrection, the implications became clear to His followers, as we shall see in Chapter 22.

Son of Man

Political overtones tainted the first two royal messianic threads. "Jesus' conception of His messianic role was so much at variance with the popular connotations of *christos* that He preferred to avoid the title."[1009] Instead, Jesus called Himself "**Son of Man**." He spoke it mostly to His followers or to religious opponents to whom it had greatest relevance.[1010] The only time that ordinary people used the title, they seemed puzzled by it.[1011]

Son of Man
Heb.: *Ben 'Adam*
Aram.: *Bar 'enash*
(Dan. 7:13)
Gk.: *Ho hyios anthrōpou*
(Matt. 9:6)

It's a puzzling title. Except for its use in the book of Daniel, "Son of Man" is not an Old Testament messianic title, although it does occur in a few inter-testamental messianic passages.[1012] Jesus' frequent use of the title was unique in His day. A study of the parallel passages shows that Jesus sometimes adopted it instead of the personal pronoun "I."[1013] He used it to equate Himself with God and alongside titles like Son of God, Christ, and King of Israel. So, it was clearly messianic.[1014] Beyond the Gospels, the title hardly occurs in the New Testament.[1015] Once Jesus' glory was evident, the umbrella titles, "Christ" and "Lord," superseded it.

Sometimes Jesus' words about the Son of Man sound like a reference to a third person. However, that was His way of explaining aspects of His messianic ministry. The Son of Man came to save people, and He demonstrated His authority to forgive sins, most notably when He healed a paralytic.[1016] Forgiveness is an option for any judge, but the religious watchdogs didn't expect it of the Messiah. They bayed for retribution. Ironically, the crowd responded by praising God for giving authority to a man, instead of recognizing the implication that Jesus was no ordinary man. Jesus also used this title to speak of His resurrection.[1017] Most significantly, He told of His imminent suffering.

This title also helped distinguish between His present and future roles.[1018] Jesus implied that His messianic role spanned the ages between present initiation and future completion. He came first to restore our relationships with the Father, and He will return to judge our response to His invitation. Full-scale judgment is kept on ice, waiting for a later day for its conclusion. That day is the setting of the parable of the sheep and the goats, which portrays the Son of Man, who is King alongside His Father, judging flocks of humanity.[1019]

"The sign of the Son of Man" will precede Jesus' return (Matt. 24:30). Perhaps it will be a blazing light like the one that was prophesied in Isaiah.[1020] At His second coming, our decayed world will be replaced by God's kingdom in its full glory.

This third thread originates in Daniel's vision of "one like a **Son of Man**." The vision has a lot to do with the kingdom, confirming that this is another royal title.

*I kept looking in the night visions, and behold, with the clouds of heaven
One like a Son of Man was coming, and He came up to the Ancient of Days
and was presented before Him. And to Him was given dominion, glory
and a kingdom, that all the peoples, nations and men of every language
might serve Him. His dominion is an everlasting dominion which will
not pass away; and His kingdom is one which will not be destroyed.*
(Daniel 7:13–14)

The Son of Man appears in the vision as a welcome contrast to four bestial
kings. That Daniel saw no mere human is clear from what happens in the vision.
The Son of Man travels in clouds—Yahweh's mode of transportation.[1021] From
the **Ancient of Days** He receives dominion, glory and an eternally indestructible
kingdom that He shares with the saints. God passes judgment in favor of His
faithful people—the Son of Man and the saints that He represents.[1022] He
and they receive worldwide dominion forever from God, while their beastly
enemies are condemned. The passage gives hope that God will vindicate His
people after they have been persecuted; it encouraged Jews to remain faithful
through their sufferings.

In light of the above, when Jesus evoked the image of "the Son of Man
coming on the clouds," He was using shorthand for vindication by God,
a vindication that opponents and followers alike would witness in their
lifetimes.[1023] Jesus' resurrection and ascension (in a cloud),[1024] as well as the fall
of Jerusalem to Roman armies, proved that He was the Messiah; His prophecies
had come true.[1025] Jerusalem's fall was God's wrath on the nation; the majority
of Jews had refused to pursue Jesus and His way of peace. Instead, they had
followed freedom fighters.

Suffering Servant

Suffering preceded vindication. Jesus' most common message reads like a
formula predicting His fate. He foretold betrayal, condemnation, mockery,
scourging, crucifixion, and ultimately resurrection. All of these events had a
purpose. As the Son of Man was lifted up from the earth, He became a banner
for spiritual healing and God's glorification.[1026]

The interweaving of all four threads began after Peter confessed that Jesus
was the Christ.[1027] Jesus promised Peter the keys to His kingdom, and He talked
of His coming in glory for that kingdom. Then He predicted His suffering. Jesus

took Peter up a mountain, where Jesus was gloriously transfigured and affirmed by His Father: "This is **My beloved Son**, with whom I am well-pleased; listen to Him!" (Matt. 17:2, 5; Mark 9:3, 7) Luke's account links another messianic word to the Son, "This is My Son, My **Chosen One** [*eklektos*]" (Luke 9:35). Luke combined two important verses about God's son and servant:

*You are **My Son**, today I have begotten You.* (Psalm 2:7)

*Behold, **My Servant**, whom I uphold; **My chosen one** in whom My soul delights. I have put My Spirit upon Him.* (Isaiah 42:1)

The Father had identified His Son as His chosen servant, the Messiah.[1028] When Jesus stated, "the Son of Man did not come to be served, but to serve, and to give His life a ransom for many," He linked messiahship with service and suffering, and He redefined kingship.[1029]

Prior to departing for Jerusalem, the disciples did not understand how suffering fulfilled messianic prophecy.[1030] They were not alone. Little evidence exists that anyone noticed a suffering and serving Messiah on the radar screen.[1031] No other aspiring Messiah put that spin on his campaign. It drew no crowds. Of all of Jesus' messianic redefinitions, this was the biggest bombshell.

Yet we can discern a subtle blending of the threads in Scripture. First Samuel 2:35 hints at a coming servant priest. Prophecies of the Messiah predicted the paradox of a ruler serving as a shepherd: "Then I will set over them one shepherd, My servant David, and he will feed them . . . and My servant David will be prince among them" (Ezek. 34:23–24).[1032] Zechariah heralded, "My servant the Branch" (Zech. 3:8).

The fullest descriptions of **My Servant** occur in Isaiah's four prophetic songs.[1033] They culminate in the suffering described in chapters 52–53. Scripture calls several individuals "servant of the LORD" (*'eved Yahweh*), including prophets. So, who best fits Isaiah's description?[1034] None of the historical contenders, not even Isaiah, is convincing. King Jehoiachin, the last hope of an exiled nation, and Zerubbabel, the governor after the exile, both failed to accomplish much.

The songs display both individual and collective elements, just like many messianic titles. Isaiah referred to Israel as God's servant. He may have intended Israel as an ideal, or a faithful "Israel within Israel," a group credited with living up to the ideal. The worthiest segments, in that case, were the priesthood or more likely the prophets. However, Isaiah pointed beyond any group to an individual servant, and Jesus best fulfills the servant songs.

Matthew viewed Jesus' healing miracles as a direct fulfillment of the predicted removal of infirmity by the Servant.[1035] Jesus' desire to avoid publicity fulfilled prophecy.[1036] He was the **despised One**, the **Servant of rulers**. Before His accusers, Jesus remained silent as a lamb led to slaughter.[1037] Quoting Isaiah, Jesus said that people would number Him with transgressors.[1038] His death between two criminals fulfilled that Scripture.[1039] Jesus interceded for His executioners.[1040] Lashes scarred His body.[1041] They buried Him in a rich man's tomb.[1042] When a eunuch asked to whom Isaiah 53:7–8 referred, Philip said Jesus.[1043] His suffering had a purpose: He bore the sins of many, and He "was delivered over because of our transgressions, and was raised because of our justification."[1044] A slightly longer version of Isaiah, which was found among the Dead Sea Scrolls, seems to foretell His resurrection: "After he has suffered, he will see the light of life and be satisfied" (Isa. 53:11 NIV).

Despised One
Heb.: *Bezo-nefesh*
(Isa. 49:7)

Servant of rulers
Heb.: *'Eved moshelim*
(Isa. 49:7)

All of the verbs of Isaiah 53:1–9 are in the "prophetic past" tense, in which the future is so certain that the prophet stated it as though it had already been accomplished. Jesus fulfilled all of the prophetic details; He is the ultimate Servant of the LORD.

Although no one called Jesus "servant" during His lifetime, one old man said some profound words. Emotions must have run deep when Jesus' parents took Him as a baby to the temple for the first time. From among crowds of worshipers, an elderly man slowly but deliberately approached them. "Could I hold the baby?" With trembling voice, Simeon began to bless God. He had been waiting decades for that day. With his dream fulfilled, he could die in peace. Surely, there were tears in everyone's eyes.

Sunrise from on high
Gk.: *Anatolē ex hypsous*
(Luke 1:78)

Sun of righteousness
Heb.: *Shemesh tsedaqah*
Gk. OT: *Hēlios dikaiosunēs*
(Mal. 4:2)

Among Simeon's pronouncements was the title, **light of revelation**. It derived from the servant songs, one of which said the servant would be "a light of the nations so that My salvation may reach to the end of the earth."[1045]

The subject of illumination reconnects the servant thread to the royal thread. Zacharias prophesied that his son, John the Baptist, would prepare the way for the **Sunrise from on high** to shine on those in darkness.[1046] His words probably derive from Malachi's rising **sun of righteousness**.[1047] In Greek, "sunrise" is *anatolē*. Translators also chose it for the Hebrew *tsemakh*—the sprouting Davidic branch.[1048] The **Child**, coming to reign on David's throne, would illuminate the world.[1049]

Child
Heb.: *Yeled*
(Isa. 9:6)
Servant
Gk.: *Pais*
(Acts 3:13, 26)
Holy Servant Jesus
Gk.: *Ho hagios pais*
(Acts 4:27, 30)

The book of Acts contains the first instance of Jesus being called **Servant**. The apostles spoke with significance of "Your **holy servant Jesus**, whom You *anointed*."[1050] Paul noted, Jesus "did not regard equality with God a thing to be grasped, but emptied Himself, taking the form of a bond-servant . . . . He humbled Himself by becoming obedient to the point of death, even death on a cross" (Phil. 2:6–8).

Radically Redefining Royalty

Although most aspiring messiahs risked death on a Roman cross, none of them included it on their campaign "to do" list. The vast majority of messiah-watchers sought a competent warrior-king. Jesus, however, expected to be crucified.

Suffering did have a small place in Israel's hope of salvation; occasionally, people suffered vicariously to pay off the debts of other people and to free them.[1051] Nonetheless, occupied Israel believed she had to suffer for her own sins to pay off her debt and go free. God had another way—a servant suffering and dying for the sin of the world.

The embroidery of Scripture included those subtle details, especially in Isaiah's final song, in which the suffering servant became the offering for guilt.[1052] Jesus pointed to the thread. He taught that in His kingdom leadership was about service.[1053] He demonstrated "royalty beyond earthly measure"[1054] by serving His people as the ultimate sacrifice. Service and suffering were His concealed weapons. He used them to deal a fatal blow to the real enemy, Satan. But before they realized the victory that this astonishing King had won, Jesus' hopeful fans found His suffering and death devastatingly disappointing.

Chapter 19

A DISAPPOINTING MESSIAH

There are two ways to be fooled. One is to believe what isn't true; the other is to refuse to believe what is true.

—Søren Kierkegaard, *Works of Love*

Here's a recipe you won't want to cook up! It's a simple recipe for misunderstanding God:

Take some Scriptures out of context, add your favorite interpretations, and let them stew for a few centuries.

Most Jews of Jesus' time cherished messianic expectations that were like bad home cooking. It was hard for them to relinquish their long-held interpretations. Inevitably, Jesus disappointed folks.

God knew exactly how to deliver people, but people had cooked up their own job descriptions for the Messiah, and they had established their own requirements. Few people viewed Jesus as a viable candidate. It takes humility to abandon our cherished perspectives and accept God's. Over the centuries, the threads in God's embroidery had been misinterpreted.

When the eternal God, for whom a thousand years are as one day, tells human beings about His plans, He challenges comprehension.[1055] Bible prophecies that take just hours to read may require millennia to be outworked. Some aspects of God's purposes are already in motion, but they will not reach completion until the end of time. Malachi delivered the last Old Testament prophecy about 450 years before Jesus. During the intervening years, people reinterpreted and embellished God's words. Wishful thinkers attached their hopes and dreams to the variations, and those dreams caught and colored hungry imaginations. In their political and economic situation, it was easy to misinterpret prophecy. When Jesus arrived on the scene, He encountered a plethora of inaccurate expectations with which people would contrast Him.

As we read of the reactions to Jesus in the Gospels, we have to inquire about the set of expectations that people were comparing Him with. Jesus could draw a crowd, but He died deserted by everyone except for a handful of loyal but disillusioned friends. Why were people so disappointed?

See How They Run

In some circles, especially early on, there was considerable excitement about Jesus. Multitudes swarmed to His miracles and authoritative teaching. He sweetened His stories with witty illustrations and laced them with sharp criticisms of misguided leaders. When Jesus cleansed people from leprosy or bleeding, made bodies whole, and forgave sinners, those outcasts could immediately rejoin God's family. They were pure again. The exorcisms that Jesus performed demonstrated His dominion over hell as well as earth. Jesus' miracles indicated that God's kingdom had arrived, and a kingdom implied there was a king.

A huge crowd that Jesus had just fed became so excited that they desperately wanted to make Him king of Israel. Jesus perceived their nationalistic expectations, but he refused. Shortly thereafter, the same people drifted away; they resented Him for claiming a heavenly origin. They deserted Him when He instructed them to eat His flesh and drink His blood.[1056]

Tax collectors tried to trick Peter into incriminating Jesus by presenting their bill. It was an excellent opportunity for passive resistance—a non-violent tax-revolt. But Jesus miraculously produced a coin from a fish and paid up.[1057]

Other Jewish officials tried to spring a similar trap: "Whose law should we obey when it comes to imperial taxes?"[1058] Jesus replied, "Bring me a denarius."

The little coins bore Caesar's title and image. Images and foreign taxes offended the Jews. There was no king but God, yet the empire demanded tribute. Where did a good Jew's loyalty lie? With a few wise words, Jesus swerved around their trap and avoided collisions with Rome and Jerusalem. He had a solution that was better than either compromise or revolt: "Render to Caesar the things that are Caesar's, and to God the things that are God's."[1059]

Certain Jewish messianic expectations conflicted with common knowledge about Jesus' life. In Jerusalem, a dispute arose because most people knew of Jesus' Galilean roots, while the Messiah was supposed to have originated in Bethlehem (or to have had an obscure origin). Few people knew enough of the details of Jesus' nativity to know that they fulfilled messianic prophecies.[1060]

The leaders, of course, were suspicious. Anyone who attracted a crowd was dangerous, so the Scribes and Pharisees kept Him under surveillance. They were unofficial monitors of religious compliance. Miracles were not the issue. Everyone knew God performed miracles through His prophets, but false prophets performed miracles too. So, was Jesus leading the people astray? For sure, Jesus praised the Law and talked of perfection, but He also questioned the Pharisees' application of the Torah, and He prescribed heart-change, rather than scrupulous legalism.[1061] Jesus was not replacing old ways, but His teaching suggested, "Certain commands would become redundant, like candles in the sunrise."[1062]

The Pharisees became agitated whenever Jesus healed people on the Sabbath, touched sick people, or interacted with sinners. Surely, everyone understood that it was vital to the national cause to observe the Torah in great detail. The Maccabees died rather than eat pork, but Jesus let His disciples eat with unclean hands. "Jesus' zealous contemporaries would have said: Torah provides the litmus test of loyalty to Israel's god and to his covenant. Jesus said: what counts is following me."[1063] Jesus riled the Jewish leaders even more by claiming God as His Father; they tried to stop Him or stone Him.[1064] If

Deceiver
Gk.: *Planos*
(Matt. 27:63)

Jesus were misleading people, perhaps he fitted the Torah's description of a **deceiver** and therefore deserved death.[1065]

Jesus was used to being misunderstood and slandered. Upon witnessing Jesus deliver a blind-mute from a demon so that he could see and speak again, the crowds wondered, "This man cannot be the Son of David, can He?" The Pharisees retorted that Beelzebul, ruler of demons, empowered Him.[1066] Apparently, someone had mockingly called Jesus "**Beelzebul**." Jesus predicted that His followers would be slandered in the same way. It was just one of a string of names that they called Jesus. "The Son of Man came eating and drinking, and they say, 'Behold, a gluttonous man and a drunkard, a **friend of tax-collectors and sinners!**'"[1067] Like arrows, the words were designed to hurt, but they unintentionally advertised the wide embrace of God. As Jesus reached out His hand to sinners, an accusing finger pointed straight at His cold-hearted, self-assured opponents. He proclaimed woes on them.

Beelzebul
Gk.: *Beelzeboul*
(Matt. 10:25)
Friend of tax collectors and sinners
Gk.: *Philos telōnōn kai hamartōlōn*
(Matt. 11:19;
Luke 7:34)

In Jesus' reckoning, the Gentiles would condemn Israel.[1068] God's judicious pruning would include the Jews; fruit-bearing repentance was the key to salvation.[1069] Jesus' indictment pierced every heart, but His solution went further. Jesus forgave sinners and Gentiles, who had been written off by the establishment, and He welcomed them into God's family.

While Jesus spoke against pagan politics, He also condemned violent reactions to paganism. Repentance included a renouncing of revolutionary aspirations and it required faith in Jesus. The nation was rushing blindly down a broad path leading to unspeakable destruction, and Jesus was not afraid to say so.[1070]

Placing faith in Jesus presented a huge challenge to Judaism. It meant substituting the ancient symbols of Jewish faith. "Jesus was replacing adherence or allegiance to Temple and Torah with allegiance to Himself."[1071] Repentance provided an entrance into the kingdom of God—the new age that the Jews so longed for. Repentance still involved turning *from* sin, but it also meant turning *to* Jesus. Jesus had the effrontery to declare that the kingdom of God was at hand. The age of the new covenant, which was written on human hearts, had come—and it had come in an unorthodox way.

Faith in Jesus defined the new covenant community of Abraham's children that God was raising up.[1072] The church that Jesus' followers would establish would be a living temple dwarfing Herod's grand project. God's kingdom was more extensive than the nation. Israel had received her invitations first, but Jesus was gaily passing them out to the whole world, demonstrating His agenda by performing miracles for foreigners. What right did He have to redefine

God's people? Such teachings threatened Judaism and invited persecution on the part of the authorities.

Jesus didn't even look like a messiah. He used no reverberating sound system, and He had no majestic appearance that would make Him attractive to the real kingmakers.[1073] Plenty of leaders did mount appealing publicity campaigns, but Jesus shunned such methods. He redefined lordship by modeling meek and gentle servant-hood, rather than being an aloof and steely ruler. Although Jesus acknowledged His authority to judge, He deferred judgment.[1074] Instead of condemning people, He emphasized the Son of Man's authority to forgive sins.[1075] He also taught about His need to suffer and His expectation of betrayal.[1076]

When betrayal resulted in arrest, Jesus' friend Peter drew a sword and slashed out in defense. The best of us are tempted to adopt militant methods when we are cornered. This must be the moment for action. This must be the moment when God will intervene and rout the opposition. Surely, this was the signal for Jesus to launch His military campaign. But it was not. The One with God's hosts at His disposal renounced the sword.[1077] Jesus rebuked Peter, and He allowed Roman soldiers to nail Him to a cross.

How foolish. Jesus couldn't possibly be the Messiah.

How to Make Enemies and Irritate People

The Pharisees were Jesus' main opponents, but they were relatively moderate, falling between violent brigands and isolated Essenes. Among the crucifixion players, the Roman authorities were reluctant executioners and the Pharisees played a secondary role—the priests arranged the crucifixion.

Toward the end, when Jesus relocated His ministry from Galilee to Jerusalem, He was preparing for a showdown. The raising of Lazarus galvanized Jewish leaders under the High Priest to eliminate Him.[1078] His king-like entry into Jerusalem further infuriated them.[1079]

When Jesus flipped over the traders' trestles in the temple, He cried, "You are making it a robbers den."[1080] His action doubled as a prophetic statement. Because of the topsy-turvy tables, the escaping doves, and the evicted merchants, it appeared as if a hurricane had devastated the ordered world of the religious hierarchy. Jesus' action was reminiscent of what the Maccabees had done when they had wrested the temple back from the Greeks. By all appearances, Jesus had directly challenged the priesthood, which managed temple affairs.

In part, Jesus' action fulfilled the prophecy that there would "no longer be a Canaanite [merchant] in the house of the LORD of hosts" (Zech. 14:21). Those words are associated with a bigger concept a few verses earlier: "The LORD will be king over all the earth; in that day the LORD will be the only one, and His name the only one" (Zech. 14:9). Jesus surgically removed decay to restore the temple as a prayer house for all nations, not just Israel.[1081]

The cleansing had a darker side; it dramatized future Roman military action. When the legions razed the temple in AD 70, they proved that Jesus had been right. Resisting God's plan for salvation did result in destruction.

Jesus upset more than tables. He overturned concepts about the temple, and He proclaimed God's love for the nations. The kingdom of the world was becoming the kingdom of God. It felt incredibly uncomfortable, but Jesus was actually turning the world right side up.[1082] Drastic measures were required on the part of Jesus and the powers that be.

Tying the Threads to the Trial Scene

During Jesus' trial, the opinions of the Jewish religious authorities clashed with Jesus' view of Himself. Sparks flew. The High Priest who presided over the ruling council (Sanhedrin) made two blunt demands, which Matthew and Mark combined: "'Tell us whether You are the Christ, the Son of God.' Jesus replied, 'You have said it yourself; nevertheless I tell you, hereafter you will see the Son of Man sitting at the right hand of Power, and coming on the clouds of heaven.'"[1083] Jesus answered the priest's question in the affirmative; the barb was His quotation of two verses:

The first said, "The LORD [*Yahweh*] says to my Lord ['*Adoni*]: 'Sit at My right hand until I make Your enemies a footstool for Your feet'" (Ps. 110:1). Although the Pharisees expected the Messiah to be a son of David who was enthroned at Yahweh's right hand, they were infuriated by the idea that He could be David's superior "Lord" and that they were God's enemies.[1084]

The second verse was Daniel 7:13. Jesus identified Himself with the Son of Man, who had approached on the clouds. According to some rabbis, he had taken a throne next to God.[1085] Remember, the imagery of the verse was shorthand for God vindicating His people after suffering, by judging their enemies and initiating the kingdom of His true people. By combining the two verses, Jesus acknowledged His messianic role and claimed that God would vindicate Him. The priests judged His comments to be blasphemous, and they said that he deserved to die.[1086]

To achieve their goal, the Jews had to convince the Roman leaders of Jesus' guilt. Luke recorded the political accusations that the Jews presented to Pilate. Jesus was misleading the nation, inciting a tax revolt, and claiming to be Christ, a king.[1087] Pilate questioned Him about that last charge: "Are you the King of the Jews?" Like King Herod at Jesus' birth, Pilate had to assess the implied threat to Rome. Reassuringly, Jesus declared, "My kingdom is not of this world. If My kingdom were of this world, then My servants would be fighting" (John 18:36–37).

Although Pilate pronounced Jesus innocent, political pressures prevailed. Jesus had been heralded at birth as **King of the Jews**; now, using the same title, Pilate mocked and presented Him to the people.[1088] The sign that the soldiers nailed on the cross above Jesus' head was like an indictment. It read, "Jesus of Nazareth, King of the Jews." It appears in religious artwork as the Latin acrostic, INRI (*Iesus Nazarenus Rex Iudaeorum*). Even a criminal recognized it as a messianic title.[1089] Pilate let the title stand as written. Perhaps he was mocking Israel's representative king by saying, "Look, I'm crucifying your last hope." [1090] Jesus was so clear about being the messianic king that He willingly accepted the charges, suffered, and died. Whether or not Pilate was aware, Jesus had not made an empty claim.

Another One Bites the Dust

For Jesus' enemies, the shameful execution of the latest messianic claimant came as a relief. The deaths of other wannabe messiahs had proved them to be frauds.[1091] The charismatic insurgent Simon bar Kokhba (son of a star) died in battle a century after Jesus. After Simon died, cynics altered his title to bar Kozeba (son of a lie/deceit).[1092] Centuries passed before the Jews seriously considered an individual messiah again.

Many people thought that Jesus' career had met a similar fate.[1093] The same mocking name-calling went on: "He saved others; let Him save Himself if this is the Christ of God, His **Chosen One**" (Luke 23:35). As far as they were concerned, His claims were empty. He had failed to free Israel, and He had never built a new temple. His opponents resorted to calling Him a **deceiver**, which was the opposite of what He really was. He was the Way, the Truth, and the Shepherd of straying sheep.[1094] N. T. Wright emphasizes that,

The violent execution of a prophet . . . still more, of a would-be Messiah, did not say to any Jewish onlooker that he really was the Messiah after all, or that YHWH's kingdom had come through his work. It said, powerfully and irresistibly, that he wasn't and that it hadn't.[1095]

The Coming Messiah

During Jesus' life on earth, the paths of messianic expectations divided.[1096] The Jews had not believed Moses and the prophets; most people would not believe that Jesus was the Messiah even when He rose from the dead.[1097]

The Jewish messianic ideal continued to develop. Two of the eighteen daily prayers, which are in use today but date from the fall of the temple, are pleas for the Messiah to come.[1098] Maimonides (AD 1135–1204) included this expectation in his thirteen articles of faith. This belief continues among Orthodox Jews today. Conservative and Reform Jews work toward a future messianic age, while others talk of a Messiah who is embodied collectively in a reformed society. Over the years, different groups have indulged in varying degrees of mysticism surrounding the Messiah and God's names.

On the other hand, people who have met the risen Jesus, either in the flesh or in faith, already have the Messiah and a taste of His kingdom in their hearts. Faith makes sense of God's four threads. All that remains is for the Son of Man to return in glory, bring the deferred judgment, seal history, and fully institute the kingdom of God.[1099]

Revelation 19:11–21:8 tells of Jesus' end-time messianic function—the conqueror smiting the nations with the sword of His mouth and a rod of iron, just like the anointed Son of Psalm 2.[1100] Jesus declares, "I am the **root and the descendant of David**" and wields authority symbolized by the key of David (Rev. 3:7; 5:5; 22:16).

Long before bar Kokhba's shameful death, the church recognized Jesus as the true **bright morning star**. Jesus is the One "who is and who was and who is to come" (Rev. 1:4, 8; 4:8). "**He who is coming**" is a fulfilled title, but in another sense Jesus is still coming. As the appointed or foreordained Messiah, Jesus will return, restore everything, and end tribulation once and for all.[1101]

The Real Battle

The disciples continued to express their disappointment after Jesus was crucified: "We were hoping that it was He who was going to redeem Israel"

(Luke 24:21). The amazing experience of meeting the risen Jesus failed to reform their entrenched expectations completely. Following His resurrection, they still pressed Him about political freedom.[1102]

However, Jesus' messiahship soon came into focus. Having spent time explaining the Scriptures to His disciples, Jesus ascended to the Father in a cloud.[1103] God had vindicated His Son, as Daniel had indicated He would. The Holy Spirit alighted. The church began and grew.

The fall dulled human discernment of what God does and says. Like the disciples, we all need the illumination of the Holy Spirit. The disciples' memories of Jesus' messianic acts, His claims to John the Baptist (we will consider Matthew 11 later), and His death as a fulfillment of messianic prophecies all became clear at Pentecost.[1104] His followers finally understood the importance of suffering, and they recognized Jesus as Messiah according to God's definition rather than that of the Jewish revolutionaries.[1105] They saw the pattern in the prophetic threads of God's embroidery. It was astonishingly beautiful and glorious.

Instead of tackling petty puppet rulers with swords and daggers, Jesus pulled off the greatest act of subversion. He redefined the battle. By choosing suffering and death in place of a sinful world, which included misguided Jewish revolutionaries, Jesus had accomplished the redemption that He had hinted at when He exorcized demons. He freed the world from Satan, who was the biggest of the oppressing giants, and He released us from death, the ultimate prison.

By binding the strongman, Jesus had made it possible to put the whole house in order. Satan has no legal toehold left in the entire universe, and everyone who trusts in Jesus can walk free. Our freedom is more than spiritual; it touches all the ills of society that zealous Jews longed to see corrected. In a sense, Jesus did have a political agenda because politics concerns people's lives. The New Testament is full of practical instructions for living in healthy relationships on every level: marriage, family, employment, commerce, government, and church. In Him, the barriers between the sexes, races, and generations come down. Jesus established new standards for earning, owning, and distributing property. The power of sin is broken in every sphere of life. Jesus' salvation is broad and deep. And that is really good news.

Chapter 20

WHO DO YOU SAY THAT I AM? (Matt. 16:15)

We are talking about God; so why be surprised if you can't understand? For if you understand, it isn't God. Let us rather make a devout confession of ignorance, instead of a brash profession of knowledge.
—Augustine of Hippo

The ways in which people introduce Jesus in the Gospels are instructive. Several incidents remind us of a bumbling master of ceremonies introducing a celebrity guest. Disciples, crowds, and a Samaritan woman—friends and enemies alike—all acted as if they had inadequate bios of Jesus. They were slow to grasp His true nature, and they had partial and inaccurate perceptions. The clearest declarations of who He was came from spiritual beings in both camps (angels and demons). We benefit from the hindsight of the New Testament writers. In this chapter, we will tie up some loose ends by surveying the most important introductions and the names and titles of Jesus that are associated with each of them. But like the blundering

MC, we should step aside to let Jesus speak. So, space is reserved for His self-introductions.

John the Bulldozer

John the Baptist was expecting the Messiah. John played a vital role in introducing "**He who is coming** after me" (Matt. 3:11; John 1:15, 27; Acts 19:4). When priests and levites questioned John, he used Isaiah's words to describe his role as preparing a highway for the Lord—leveling valleys, mountains, and rugged places like a gigantic prophetic road grader. Isaiah had spoken of Yahweh; John bulldozed for Jesus.[1106]

Malachi prophesied that the Messiah would mediate a new covenant between God and humans. An Elijah-like forerunner would prepare the way for "the **messenger of the covenant**, in whom you delight, behold, He is coming" (Mal. 3:1).[1107] So, was John the new Elijah, or not? John denied that he was the fulfillment of Malachi's prophecy, yet Jesus quoted it specifically to affirm John's preparatory role.[1108] The perspectives of Jesus and John reconcile when we distinguish between a reincarnation of Elijah (which John was not) versus John coming in the same spirit as Elijah (which he did).[1109]

> **Messenger of the covenant**
> Heb.: *Mal'akh habberit*
> (Mal. 3:1)
>
> **Bridegroom**
> Gk.: *Nymphios*
> (John 3:29)

John also subscribed to the view that the Messiah's coming signaled His marriage to the people of Israel. He spoke of Jesus as the **Bridegroom**.[1110] Jesus gave a nod to this imagery,[1111] though His wedding parable pointed to His second coming.[1112]

John railed at the religious leaders, warning them to repent because he expected God's wrath to begin once the Messiah arrived. He anticipated "He who is coming after me" pruning with an axe, threshing and winnowing the chaff, and lighting a big bonfire.[1113] John foresaw the Messiah judging dead religion, among other things.

Under duress, we often question our faith. In his imprisonment, John questioned whether Jesus really was the coming One. He asked cryptically, "Are you the **Expected One**?" (Matt. 11:3; Luke 7:19–20) Jesus responded with a résumé of His miracles; they fulfilled three passages in Isaiah pertaining to the Messiah or to the restoration of God's people.[1114] Matthew pointedly called them "the works of Christ" (Matt. 11:2), although miracles rarely authenticated Jesus as the Messiah.[1115] Mark recounted the healing of a deaf man with a speech impediment (*mogilalos*) using the same word that is found in a messianic prophecy in Isaiah.[1116] Jesus' account of the highlights of His miracles reads as if He were checking off completed items from a messianic job description. Certainly, He was the Messiah.

One item remained unchecked: judgment. All three passages in Isaiah mention it. Jesus was challenging John not to stumble while justice delayed.[1117] He would complete His messianic task in stages; freedom for some captives would have to wait. Judgmental wrath would come much later than expected.

John's double announcement at Jesus' baptism launched His public ministry: "Behold, the **Lamb of God** who takes away the sin of the world," and "This is the **Son of God**" (John 1:29, 34, 36).[1118]

Lamb of God
Gk.: *Ho amnos tou Theou*
(John 1:29, 36)

Our Passover
Gk.: *To pascha hēmōn*
(1 Cor. 5:7)

As Lamb of God, Jesus most radically shattered the mistaken pictures about the messianic king. Like a sacrificial lamb, His bloody death provided cleansing from sin. Jesus' atonement was so complete it ended the need for any further animal sacrifices.[1119] In his gospel, the disciple John presents Jesus as the Passover lamb. By some reckonings, John's gospel implies that Jesus died at the same time that Jewish families sacrificed their lambs in the temple. Paul also identified Jesus as **our Passover**. Philip explained to the Ethiopian that Isaiah's prophecy, which described the servant suffering as a lamb, referred to Jesus.[1120] Jesus' death was foreshadowed in the earliest sacrifices, including the time when *Yahweh yir'eh* provided a ram in place of Abraham's son.[1121]

"But how could a sovereign God allow His son to die?" Muslims and others exclaim. How do we reconcile a sacrificial lamb with a messianic ruler whose eternal kingdom includes victory over His enemies and justice for His people? The book of Revelation provides a perspective that resolves the confusion arising from the unexpected combination of names and roles. In His incarnation, Jesus stooped from His throne to serve as a sacrifice to reconcile us to God. His baptism and transfiguration provided glimpses of deity. Although Jesus had all the dignity of a king and all the power of the Almighty, a spotlight focused on His deep love for humanity, which was demonstrated most fully in His death on the cross. Other aspects of His divinity remained veiled. John's vision of heaven revealed the same eternal combination of attributes, but with the balance of the lighting restored.

That light results in the most powerful paradox in the Scriptures. The angel told John to "behold, the **Lion** that is from the tribe **of Judah**, the **Root of David**." However, John turned and saw "a **Lamb** standing, as if slain" (Rev. 5:5–6).[1122] There, in a triumphant heaven that was filled with the might and majesty of God, we find the marks of sacrifice displayed. If this doesn't show that costly love is central to God's eternal nature, I don't know what does.

Lion of Judah
Gk.: *Ho leōn ho ek tēs phylēs Iouda*
(Rev. 5:5)

Heaven's Lamb receives worship, shares the glory of God, and presides as the victorious judge of enemies who fear His wrath.[1123] He also has a book of life like the typical membership lists that the kings of that period maintained. "The Lamb who was slain, the Lamb who is the irresistible conqueror, and the Lamb who shares the throne of God are all one."[1124] In the throne room, our spiritual necks no longer have to strain to capture the full extent of His glory and to reconcile what to us are conflicting extremes. His glory is exquisitely condensed in the Lamb who is also a conquering lion. We must toss out the clutter of our small opinions of God to make room for this gigantic truth.

20/20 Vision

Immediately following John's baptism of Jesus, when God so clearly affirmed Jesus, the devil deliberately targeted their Father-Son relationship. Twice, he suggested that Jesus should use it to His own advantage. "If you are the Son of God . . ." (Matt. 4:3, 6; Luke 4:3, 9).

It wasn't a question. Like God's angels, Satan and his hordes have 20/20 vision in the spiritual realm in which they exist. Legion, the man who was possessed by many unclean spirits, immediately recognized Jesus as **Son of God** or **Son of the Most High God**.[1125] Similarly, a man in the Capernaum synagogue who was possessed by an unclean spirit, blurted out with demonic insight, "What business do we have with each other, **Jesus of Nazareth**? Have You come to destroy us? I know who you are—the **Holy One of God**!" (Mark 1:24; Luke 4:34) Mark and Luke identified a pattern: demons equate "Son of God" with "Messiah."[1126] In the spirit world, some things are crystal clear. Demons know Him, but they tremble.[1127]

A Rousing Speech

When Jesus introduced His own ministry in His hometown synagogue, giving what amounted to His inaugural speech, He quoted part of His job description from Isaiah: "The spirit of the Lord is upon Me, because He *anointed* me to preach the gospel" (Isa. 61:1–2; Luke 4:16–20). In what ways was His introduction significant?

Isaiah had described the Spirit resting on the **shoot** and **branch** of Jesse (King David's father).[1128] Later, Peter pointed to miracles, like those that Isaiah foretold, as evidence of Jesus' anointing with the Holy Spirit.[1129] Jesus' words also echoed Psalm 2, which tells of God's anointed Son.[1130] Jesus was claiming to be the Davidic Messiah whom God's Spirit had anointed.

The members of the Nazareth congregation, many of whom were acquainted with Jesus, allowed their down-to-earth impression of Him to override His new twist on the old passage. They asked, "Is this not **Joseph's son**?" (Luke 4:22). Until then, they had missed His veiled claim to messiahship. Their unbelief paraded in an agreeable-sounding admiration for their hometown boy's nice words.

Moments later, Jesus drove His point home and they flew into a murderous rage. He even predicted their cynicism and their challenge for Him to apply His power to Himself: "**Physician**, heal yourself!" (Luke 4:23) While Jesus Himself did not use that title, He certainly lived out the role, healing the physically and spiritually sick.[1131] But miracles like that couldn't happen in Nazareth because of their unbelief and because, "no **prophet** is welcome in his home town" (Luke 4:24; Matt. 13:57; Mark 6:4; John 4:44).

Assessing the Prophet

Jesus seemed comfortable being called a **prophet**. He spoke of Himself that way one other time: when predicting a prophet's fate for Himself.[1132] Ordinary people persisted in using the title right up until Jesus entered Jerusalem, but how did the title apply to Him?[1133]

Prophet
Heb.: *Navi*
(Deut. 18:15–19)
Gk.: *Ho prophētēs*
(John 6:14; 7:40–41)

Early in Jesus' ministry, *"people were saying, 'John the Baptist has risen from the dead, and that is why these miraculous powers are at work in Him.' But others were saying, 'He is Elijah.' And others were saying, 'He is a prophet, like one of the prophets of old.' But when Herod heard of it, he kept saying, 'John, whom I beheaded, has risen!'"* (Mark 6:14–16)[1134]

This passage contains three opinions. Evidently, King Herod subscribed to the extreme first notion that Jesus was John, risen from the dead—God's vindication of His righteous servant.

Although most references attribute the role of a returning Elijah to John the Baptist, a second group cast Jesus in the role of the Messiah's forerunner.[1135]

According to a third view, Jesus was simply an extension of the line of Old Testament prophets, named or otherwise. When Jesus asked His disciples at Caesarea-Philippi, "Who do people say that the **Son of Man** is?" their polls reflected this view.[1136] G. Vermes says that the Galileans venerated certain righteous miracle workers who, like Elijah, prayed and performed miracles.[1137] He claims that Jesus was just another "holy man"—the latest member of the prophetic club. The evidence in the Gospels is more complex. Jesus' ministry actually resembled that of several Old Testament prophets, who demonstrated God's power and declared His standards. However, Jesus' ministry was different.

In addition to the expectation that Elijah would return as the prophetic forerunner of the Messiah, the Bible uses the term "prophet" to describe the Messiah himself. This use stems from Moses' words: "The LORD your God will raise up for you a prophet like me from among you" (Deut. 18:15–18).[1138] A Levite's questions to John the Baptist demonstrate the distinction between the two anticipated prophets.[1139]

So, was Jesus the ultimate Mosaic messianic prophet? Jesus said that Moses had written about Him.[1140] Certainly, both Jesus and Moses performed miracles. Both of them were instrumental in revealing God in a greater dimension, and they both mediated covenants. A careful comparison shows that Jesus' ministry surpassed that of every previous prophet. That is not surprising, considering He was the Messiah.[1141]

Peter and Stephen said that Jesus had fulfilled Moses' messianic prophecy.[1142] However, they said this after Jesus' resurrection. Weeks before Peter and Stephen's speeches, two devastated disciples reminisced about their dead leader as they walked to Emmaus. Their evaluation of their crucified leader stopped short at "a prophet mighty in deed and word in the sight of God and all the people" (Luke 24:19).

So what did people see? Their responses to Jesus' miraculous deeds formed a pattern. They often compared Him to great prophets who had done similar things.

The pattern is clear in one of Jesus' early encounters. Upon meeting a woman at the well of Samaria, Jesus acted in two prophetic ways. He supernaturally saw her promiscuous affairs, and He confronted her about her sin. She concluded, "Sir, I perceive that You are a prophet" (John 4:19).

Samaritan religion derived from Judaism. In the eyes of true Jews, who despised Samaritans, foreign influences had polluted their beliefs. Samaritans had messianic expectations that were similar to those of the Jews, but theirs centered on Mount Gerazim, rather than Jerusalem.[1143] They revered the five books of Moses, but they did not recognize any prophets beyond Moses, other than the Messiah.[1144]

In the context of her Samaritan beliefs, the woman eventually recognized the full implications of Jesus' statements. She introduced Jesus to the people of Sychar with a question: could Jesus really be the **Messiah**?[1145] Later, the townsfolk agreed, saying, "This One is indeed the **Savior of the world**." This sidelined sect was the first to grasp the idea that God offered salvation to a world that included them.

Savior of the world
Gk.: *Ho sōtēr tou kosmou*
(John 4:42)

The pattern recurred each time that Jesus miraculously provided food, just as Moses and Elijah had done.[1146] The crowd interpreted one incident as a sign of the fulfillment of Moses' prophecy in Deuteronomy, and they concluded that He was the coming prophet.[1147] They saw messianic implications in the miracle, and they wanted to make Him king.

When Jesus raised the widow's son at Nain, the multitude concluded that Jesus was a "great prophet" like Elijah or Elisha, who had both resurrected dead sons.[1148] The miracle in Nain preceded John the Baptist's question about Jesus' identity. Jesus' résumé-like answer to John included a reference to raising the dead—something that had not been mentioned in the prophecies of Isaiah that Jesus had referred to.[1149]

When Jesus spoke of Himself as the source of living water, perhaps He was referring to either Moses or Elisha, both of whom had miraculously provided water.[1150] The crowd drew varied conclusions. Some said, "This certainly is the prophet." A few recognized Him as the Messiah, but others questioned His origins.

Healing a man who had been born blind was an unprecedented miracle that was perhaps in the vein of Elijah's healing of leprous Naaman in the River Jordan.[1151] The healed man first took Jesus to be a prophet from God. The man's parents leaned toward acknowledging Him as the Messiah, but they were afraid to say so. After a further conversation with Jesus, the man's own belief in the Son of Man came into focus.

Even the disciples, who interacted with Jesus more than anyone else, were unsure about what Jesus' prophetic behavior implied. Once, when a Samaritan community rejected Jesus and His entourage, James and John thundered about commanding fire from heaven to consume the village.[1152] After all, Moses and Elijah behaved similarly.[1153] But Jesus stressed how different His prophetic ministry was. The Son of Man had come to save rather than destroy.

The possibility that Jesus was the Messiah-prophet raised a question for the disciples. Roughly put, "If you are the Messiah, what happened to Elijah who was supposed to come first?" (Matt. 17:10; Mark 9:11) In reply, Jesus educated them about the functions that underlie names. "Elijah already came, and they did not recognize him" (Matt. 17:12). In other words, John the Baptist had come "in the spirit and power of Elijah" (Luke 1:17) and prepared the way. "More than a prophet," John fulfilled the forerunner's job and was the "prophet of the Most High" (Matt. 11:7–14; Luke 1:76).

The religious leaders labeled John as demonized because he didn't fit their expectations of the pre-messianic Elijah.[1154] Similarly, because "the **Son of Man** came eating and drinking," they dubbed Him "a gluttonous man and a drunkard, a friend of tax-collectors and sinners!" (Matt. 11:19) Then He suffered at their hands.[1155] After all, prophets would behave with the utmost dignity; they'd recognize and avoid sinners, wouldn't they?[1156] Jesus raised the bar. He was not a prophet who was itching to dispense fiery judgment on sin. His death made a way for sin to be eradicated, rather than just condemned. He had the authority to forgive sin and embrace some surprising people. The borders of His kingdom extended far beyond the religious maps of the leaders.

A Rising Tide of Faith

Jesus' disciples provide our best example of people who struggled to grasp who He really was. They came to know Jesus gradually, rather as Abraham's faith had grown centuries before. Some of the early disciples understood, at least in rudimentary terms, that their **Rabbi** was the **Messiah**. Philip introduced **Jesus of Nazareth**, the **son of Joseph**, as the One Moses and the prophets had spoken of. After a brief but insightful conversation with Jesus, Nathanael concluded, "Rabbi, You are the **Son of God**; You are the **King of Israel**." For

Philip and Nathanael, Jesus was special but hardly divine. Nonetheless, Jesus affirmed Nathanael in his faith by declaring that he would see a new Jacob's ladder surpassing that of the patriarchal Israelite. The **Son of Man** Himself would be the stairway to heaven.[1157]

Simon Peter's rising faith is the most instructive; he admitted they *came to know* Him as the **Holy One of God**—faith involved a process.[1158] Caesarea-Philippi marked a high tide in Peter's faith. Jesus shrugged off public opinion and pointedly asked the question of the ages: "Who do *you* say that I am?" Peter put his faith on the line, declaring that Jesus was more anointed than any prophet: "You are the **Christ**, the **Son of the living God**" (Matt. 16:16; Mark 8:29) or "the **Christ of God**" (Luke 9:20). It was the first time that Peter made that declaration, but his walk on the water with Jesus had similarly impressed other disciples.[1159] Peter still saw Jesus squarely within the concept of a national hero. He vehemently opposed any suggestion that his Christ should suffer. Nonetheless, Jesus noted the faith milestone by changing Simon's name to Peter, which meant "rock," just as God had marked similar steps in the lives of Abraham and Jacob.[1160]

Six days later, Peter's rock of declared faith was cemented in place as he observed the transfiguration of Jesus. The phenomena he witnessed were reminiscent of other appearances of God's shekhinah presence. They also fulfilled a prophetic passage about the Branch of the LORD coming in glory.[1161] As Jesus' "face shone like the sun, and His garments became as white as light," men again heard God's voice from a cloud: "This is My Son, My **Chosen One**" (Matt. 17:2; Luke 9:35). Did the disciples miss the baptism? Or did God need to repeat His words because of their slowness to grasp His true identity?

Jesus' first followers have a lesson for us. Even when we struggle with doubts and questions, as John the Baptist and Peter did, Jesus patiently disciples us. Some people accept Jesus' claims quickly and early on; others come to faith in Him more slowly. It is not all that important how or when we put our faith in Him, so long as we do.

Who Do I Say That I Am?

Well, it's time for the blundering emcees to step aside so we can see see how Jesus introduced Himself. The basis for the seven self-introductions that John recorded is an emphatic Greek phrase, "*egō eimi*—— (I am——)." This phrase prefaces seven word-pictures: bread, door, light, resurrection, etc. Each one illustrates some aspect of the relationship between God and us. Other chapters provide more detail for some of them. This is a summary:

- Jesus multiplied bread and fish for a crowd, then said, "I am **the bread of life**." The Jews expected the Messiah to feed people as Moses (and Elijah) had done. Jesus tweaked their mindset by acknowledging God as the primary source of the manna and likening Himself to our divine sustenance. According to the Jews, manna was angel-food, varying in taste according to need.[1162] Jesus supplies exactly what we require. Like the bread of the Lord's Supper, His body was broken to satisfy our most profound spiritual need.

- Jesus claimed, "I am **the door**," providing access to the Father's fold and protection from the enemy.

- Jesus also said, "I am **the good shepherd**." He displayed selfless devotion to His flock and identified Himself with the Shepherd of Israel[1163] and the Davidic shepherd-servant-king.

- Jesus' statement, "I am **the true vine**," rested on several Old Testament images, including one that likens God's people to a vineyard.[1164] He promised meaningful connection with God. The **vinedresser**'s pruning promotes spiritual vigor.

- When Jesus said, "I am **the light of the world**," He claimed to be our illumination and guidance. Later rabbis thought Isaiah 60:1 implied that "light" was another name for the Messiah.

- Similarly, "I am **the way, and the truth, and the life**; no one comes to the Father but through Me" asserts an exclusive access to God.[1165]

I AM
Gk.: *Egō eimi*
(John 8:58)

Bread of Life
Gk.: *Ho artos tēs zōēs*
(John 6:35, 48)

Door
Gk.: *Hē thyra*
(John 10:7, 9)

Good Shepherd
Gk.: *Ho poimēn ho kalos*
(John 10:11, 14)

True Vine
Gk.: *Hē ampelos hē alēthinē*
(John 15:1)

Light of the World
Gk.: *To phōs tou kosmou*
(John 8:12; 9:5)

The way, the Truth and the Life
Gk.: *Hē hodos kai hē alētheia kai hē zōē*
(John 14:6)

The Resurrection and the Life
Gk.: *He anastasis kai hē zōē*
(John 11:25)

- Jesus capped those words with "I am **the resurrection and the life**." He is the instrument of our own resurrected life.[1166]

But did Jesus claim far more by employing the *egō eimi* construction? Jesus' Hebrew (or Aramaic) words underlie the Gospel records. Perhaps the words were the everyday expression, "*'ani hu*" (I am He). God used "*'ani*" or "*'ani hu*" in several significant statements.[1167] God declared Himself to be the absolute deity: "See now that I, I am He [*'ani hu*], and there is no god besides Me; It is I who put to death and give life" (Deut. 32:39). His reiterations of the covenant promises to the patriarchs included "*'ani*," and a related word, "*'anokhi*," introduced the Ten Commandments.[1168]

In some cases, the name that God told Moses at the burning bush, *'ehyeh* (I AM), might underlie Jesus' "*egō eimi*." *'Ehyeh* may be either present or future tense ("I am" or "I will be"), thereby adding to the sense of His timelessness. That is exactly how Yahweh revealed Himself to Moses. The Septuagint translated it, "*egō eimi ho ōn*" (Ex. 3:14), which meant, "I am the Being." Was Jesus deliberately adopting Yahweh's words?

Jesus used "*egō eimi*" when He walked across the water. Mark tells us "He intended to pass by them" (Mark 6:48).[1169] The disciples thought they were seeing a ghost, but Jesus reassured them, "It is I [*egō eimi*], do not be afraid" (Mark 6:50; Matt. 14:27; John 6:20).

Perhaps the woman at the well of Samaria spotted the clue that Jesus gave: "I who speak to you am He [*egō eimi*]" (John 4:26, which is close to God's words in Isa. 52:6).

When Jesus appeared after His resurrection, He spoke the words again.[1170] They are part of the promise of His presence, "I am with you always" (Matt. 28:20; Acts 18:10), echoing Yahweh's own pledge.[1171] Jesus warned that false messiah's would imitate His claim by saying, "I am He."[1172]

Four uses are even more pointed. John recorded it as an item of faith to believe that "**I am** [He]."[1173] The words resulted in a dramatic reaction when the posse came to arrest Him. They fell to the ground as people had fallen before Yahweh in the Old Testament.[1174] Jews screamed "Blasphemy!" at Him when He deliberately mixed His tenses, saying, "Before Abraham was born, **I am**" (John 8:58). Lastly, at His trial, Jesus included the words in His response to the High Priest.[1175] Remember, one Jewish tradition said that only the Messiah would be able to pronounce the name of God.

The book of Revelation reverberates with God's words from Isaiah, "I am He, I am the first, I am also the last" (Isa. 41:4; 44:6; 48:12; Rev. 1:17; 2:8; 22:13). This phrase is part of Jesus' application of God's titles to Himself—titles that span past, present, and future.[1176]

Everyman's Messiah

As we conclude these four chapters, a broader perspective on Jesus as the Messiah is necessary. The concept of the messiah has held these chapters together because Jesus' Jewish society longed for a messiah. Our Bible is rooted in Jewish culture, so we benefit from viewing His messianic names through the lens of Jewish titles and terms. Jesus came first for His own people as a "**servant to the circumcision**." Those who recognized that Jesus fulfilled what God had said of His Messiah could respond to Him positively. For the Jews, His messiahship was and is essential to faith in Him.

> **Servant to the circumcision**
> Gk.: *Diakonos peritomē*
> (Rom. 15:8)
>
> **Lord of all**
> Gk.: *Kyrios pantōn*
> (Acts 10:36;
> Rom. 10:12)

But Jesus was also the servant of the Gentiles.[1177] Both Paul and Peter emphasized that Jesus is **Lord of all**, both Jews and Gentiles.[1178] The Jewish race accounts for just part of the world He came to save. The question of messianic fulfillment, which is so pertinent to Jews, is a more technical and culturally specific version of the faith question that everyone faces. Gentiles can certainly profit from understanding Jesus as the Messiah. Grasping that background enriches our reading of the Bible, but faith is a simpler matter. It is critical for us to believe that Jesus is and was fully God, yet fully man, and that He paid the penalty for our sins by dying on the cross. Jesus' many names do more than present Him as Messiah; they present Him as the fullness of God's glory and as our Savior.

Personal faith rarely depends on one item of evidence. Rather, our faith is like a planet in a solar system; it is held in orbit by the gravitational pull of a sun and other planets. Our faith balances between several things that we find compelling. Each element supports our faith to a different degree. Scripture is vitally important. Our personal and collective experience of His risen presence comprises one giant "planet." We see Him working in verifiable ways through healings, revelations that only He can give, and tangible actions in the lives of our friends and ourselves. The evidence ranges from objective observations to subjective senses of His presence. Even the subjective is valuable to the individual. It is a valid piece of the evidence undergirding our faith. Anchoring all those interacting forces and greater than them all, is one central "sun"—the historical bodily resurrection of Jesus.

The New Testament writers documented the responses of witnesses to Jesus' resurrection. It is to the resurrection, and to the names connected with it, that we must turn. The resurrection is the linchpin of our faith. As a prelude, let's examine the first announcement about the risen Jesus.

Pointing beyond the Empty Tomb

The beautifully sensitive introduction that an angel gave at the empty tomb must surely round off our survey of the names of Jesus the Messiah. The angel said to the spice-bearing women, "Do not be amazed; you are looking for **Jesus the Nazarene**, who has been crucified. He has risen; He is not here" (Mark 16:6). Perhaps the very ordinary title "Jesus the Nazarene" was all that He remained to those traumatized women who had witnessed His crucifixion and His burial. In their pain, they yearned for their earthly friend. The angel tenderly indulged them, but he directed their gaze upward, from a Nazarene called Jesus, to the crucified One, and then beyond to the risen One.

Living One
Gk.: *Ho zaō*
(Luke 24:5; Rev. 1:18)

According to Luke, it was blunter. Angelic watchers applied another of Yahweh's names to Him: "Why do you seek the **living One** among the dead?" (Luke 24:5)

It is God's nature to surpass our expectations of Him in extraordinary ways. The resurrection demonstrates that. Having burst from the grave, how much more is Jesus able to accomplish His purposes in our lives?

Chapter 21

A MATTER OF
LIFE AND DEATH

Many a man lives a long life through, thinking he believes *certain universally received and well established things, and yet never suspects that if he were confronted by those things once, he would discover that he did not* really believe *them before, but only thought he believed them.*
—Mark Twain, *Roughing It*

Nancy had never had so much money at her fingertips. Now, right when she had a chance to double it, indecision paralyzed her. Conscious of the cameras, Nancy managed to resist biting her nails, but perspiration wasn't optional. What would her husband, Hugh, advise? If only she could ask him. Near the front of the studio audience, his mouth moved like that of a fish in a school of other fish, but a roar swamped his voice. "Answer the question!" "Take the money!" A dozen variations on those themes blended into another wave of muddled noise from the audience, adding to her confusion. Should she risk tripping over the mystery question in the sealed box and losing everything, or should she settle for her

272

accumulated winnings? Then she imagined what her new life would be like if she answered correctly.

"Nancy Parker, you have five seconds to make your decision," the host announced cheerily.

Waiting for Glory (John 11:1–57)

A life of faith is similar to that quiz show. Every challenge to our faith is an opportunity to "open the box" for God to work and thus build faith, which is our spiritual capital. Or we can settle for life as usual, and plateau. However, true faith contains no element of chance, and we have nothing of value to lose.

John 11 tells of a highly charged faith challenge. It happened shortly before Jesus' crucifixion, and it forms the backdrop to His death and resurrection.

Jesus was on a ministry trip when word arrived that Lazarus, His good friend, was sick in Bethany. As Jesus responded, He interacted with several groups of people facing a tomb-shaped "box" that contained a body. Some were disciples; others were friends. A few folk had gathered to sit *shivah*. They considered the Jewish mourning custom their social responsibility. Another set resented Jesus' intervention, and they reacted with hostility. For each group, Jesus' actions and words challenged them to have deeper faith in Him. As we survey the crowd, we should ask which players we identify with. Most important, how is Jesus challenging us to grow in our faith?

When the gathered disciples heard the news, they were afraid (vv. 4–16). The rumbles of opposition to Jesus had grown ominous. If Jesus wasn't careful, they could die by stoning or suffer another gruesome fate. They preferred to stay thirty miles from the epicenter that was Jerusalem, on the safe side of the Jordan river. "If Lazarus is asleep, he is going to wake up soon," they reasoned. "So, you don't need to go there, Jesus!" But Jesus called His loyal followers to deeper faith. His purpose was for God to be glorified and for their faith to increase (vv. 4, 15, 40, 42).

Why does God sometimes keep us waiting until the last minute before He responds? Why did Jesus wait two more days before going to Bethany? Like a friend withholding a long-awaited present, He seems to tease out our love until the last possible moment. The anticipation grows. When the gift is finally unwrapped, joy and amazement reach their peaks. When God responds at the last minute, His timing proves that He did it, and our faith and love grow. Jesus' delay produced the maximum glory for God.

Stepping Stones of Faith

Enter Martha, a woman of faith.[1179] She welcomed Jesus, confident that if He had been around, Lazarus would not have died because Jesus would have healed him. Others in the crowd, who were sitting *shivah*, shared her faith. "Could not this man, who opened the eyes of the blind man, have kept this man also from dying?" (v. 37)

It is hard to fault even limited faith; after all, Jesus commended mustard seed faith. However, Jesus doesn't let us settle with trusting Him to heal us, provide for us, protect us or perform other miracles. He used the death of Lazarus to take onlookers a step further. We can expect to encounter new, more challenging "boxes"—opportunities for our faith to progress. But we don't like challenges, do we? Being stretched is uncomfortable.

Nonetheless, Martha reached out in faith: "Even now I know that whatever You ask of God, God will give You" (v. 22). Her faith in Jesus' healing was a stepping-stone to greater faith. Jesus saw her reaching out, and He cheered her on. "Your brother will rise again" (v. 23). The implied challenge: "Martha, you believe in My healing power. Now trust Me to resurrect Lazarus."

Martha's response exemplifies another position we might take: "I know that he will rise again in the resurrection on the last day" (v. 24). Like others of her time, Martha believed in resurrection.

The Old Testament says little about resurrection, though Daniel 12:2 and other writings show that Jesus' contemporaries had a concept of it.[1180] Martha had perused the books in the Jewish bookstore, and she had heard it on Radio Judea. Preachers had bellowed it from pulpits, and she had shouted "Hallelujah" and "Amen" to encourage them. She had read the stories about dead boys who had been raised by the prophets: Elijah in Zarephath and Elisha in Shunem.[1181] She had kept newspaper clippings about a widow's son, whom Jesus had raised moments before he was buried in a tomb in tiny Nain.[1182] She had heard the flashy news of Jairus' daughter, whom Jesus had lifted off her deathbed in Galilee.[1183]

Martha knew the names **Living God, Creator,** and **God of the spirits of all flesh.** Perhaps she had even heard Jesus say that the dead would hear His voice and live because "just as the Father has life in Himself, even so He gave to the Son also to have life in Himself" (John 5:25–29). Her doctrine was as sound as it could be.

This was different though. Martha said, "This is my brother and he hasn't just died; he's been dead four days. Mary and I wrapped his body in grave clothes and sealed it in that mountain tomb." The nice Bible story had leapt from the book right into her living room. It beckoned Martha to get up from her recliner, become part of a new miracle, and go deeper in her faith.

It is not enough to hold religious opinions about life after death. If resurrection were just a doctrinal crutch to get through life and if the grave actually ended conscious existence, then it wouldn't matter what we believe. Paul addressed such speculations, listing witnesses and concluding that resurrection is real: "Christ has been raised from the dead, the **first fruits** of those who are asleep" (1 Cor. 15:12–20). Resurrection refuses to be mere theory. Our eternal destiny depends on faith in Jesus' historical resurrection. The miracle in Bethany prepared His followers to believe in that.

Each opportunity to grow in faith tends to come as a statement about God followed by a demonstration of that truth. Jesus said, "I am the **resurrection and the life**," (v. 25). It was an invitation to step onto a solid rock of fact and to experience the results. When Jesus calls us to deeper faith, He does not point to things that we can have or to what He might do. No, He points to Himself. Jesus is the object of faith—not His miracles, provisions, or plans for us, but Him. Jesus is the only hope for eternal life. So, "he who believes in Me will live even if he dies" (v. 25).

The Resurrection and the Life
Gk.: *Hē anastasis kai hē zōē*
(John 11:25)

Martha responded to His challenge, saying, "Yes, Lord; I have believed that You are the **Christ**, the **Son of God**, even He who comes into the world" (v. 27). But would she put all her weight on her stepping-stone of established belief and cross into a new dimension of faith that lay beyond her present crisis?

Bread of Life
Gk.: *Ho artos tēs zōēs*
(John 6:35, 48)

Living Bread
Gk.: *Ho artos ho zōn*
(John 6:51)

A similar challenge faced those who had witnessed Jesus miraculously multiply food for a multitude.[1184] He said, "I am the **bread of life**; he who comes to Me will not hunger, and he who believes in Me will never thirst." Judging from Jesus' explanation, belief meant

Living Father
Gk.: *Ho zōn patēr*
(John 6:57)

ingesting the very flesh of the **living bread**. Somehow, life flows from the **living Father**, via Jesus, to the believing partaker. Perhaps Jesus' explanation was a reference to taking the bread and wine of the Lord's Supper. Certainly, He emphasized how central to life faith should be.

Going Deeper

Mary and Martha had no time to adjust their ideas; the demonstration had begun. Approaching the tomb, Jesus ordered, "Remove the stone" (v. 39). The words immediately tested their precarious-looking stepping-stones, which had been laid on a slender understanding of resurrection and of who Jesus was.

We can sense their paralysis when they said, "But Lord!" Like the quiz show audience, some bystanders might have shouted: "Open the tomb! Roll away the stone!" Others would have played it safe. Lazarus had been in the grave for four days. The implications of moving the stone were huge, yet someone had enough faith to obey Jesus.

We can make four observations about faith that is growing:

First, growing faith requires practical decisions. Faith is not just a theory or an opinion; it results in action and change. It does not settle for life as usual or allow fear of the unknown to win. In Bethany, someone strained and moved a heavy stone.

The call of Jesus includes enough practical applications to last a lifetime. We make every turn from sin believing that God offers something better than sinful earthly pleasure. Obeying His command to love one another requires faith that, even if others do not return our love, His love for us is enough. When we embrace His commission to "Go, even to the ends of the earth and make disciples," we have faith that His purpose for our lives surpasses our own ambitions.

Second, deepening faith challenges common sense—in this case, the sense of smell. Bodies decay fast in a hot Mediterranean climate. It was the Jewish custom to visit a grave for three days after a burial, partly to ensure they had not buried a comatose patient. By the fourth day, decay would have set in, removing any doubt as to whether the spirit had left. Lazarus was dead. He had been dead for longer than the widow's son or Jairus' daughter; no one had buried them. Lazarus was already in the grave, and Mary and Martha's hopes were dead too. What a stink there would be if they moved the stone.

Some ancient spectators at the faith-challenge game show might well have shouted, "Don't open the tomb! Take the truth you already know and move on. Settle for Jesus as a nice man, a good teacher. Be grateful He's a healer. Let's develop our theory of a future resurrection, but we must not open the grave!" Common sense grimaced, urging Mary and Martha not to open the tomb because "by this time there will be a stench, for he has been dead four days!" (v. 39)

Third, it's natural to want evidence. Our inclination is to assess the "contents" before we act. Now, it's fine to gather facts, but the flow of evidence often runs dry before we are satisfied. At some point, Jesus calls time on our analyses. "You have all the evidence that you need. Take the step." As faith deepens, we accept the point when we must open the box.

In the story, the crowd by the tomb witnessed Martha and Mary make their decision. In some people, perhaps an excitement rose. "Open the tomb. Jesus can do this." As we face our faith challenges, words of encouragement strengthen us so that we can experience more of Jesus' power.

One note of caution, though. There is a difference between faith and presumption. Faith challenges typically start with God speaking, and His voice is always consistent with Scripture. It helps to keep notes of what God says in each big decision so that we have something to refer to. Presumption has no record to point to.

Lastly, with a growing faith, we experience increased blessings. Martha believed in a resurrection, although it was a distant one. She had not considered resurrection in the here and now, made possible by the One who is the Resurrection and the Life. The disciples believed Jesus was extraordinary, yet Thomas settled for pessimism about a premature death (v. 16). However, as their faith deepened, they enjoyed more of God's blessings—in the case of the sisters, they saw their brother restored to life.

Jesus looked on and said, "Did I not say to you that if you believe, you will see the glory of God?" (v. 40) Everyone saw God perform a mighty miracle. Despite their initial fears and low expectations, their faith grew and they witnessed more of God's glory.

Compelling Evidence

"So, they removed the stone" (v. 41). Jesus prayed and then "cried out with a loud voice, 'Lazarus, come forth'" (v. 43). One commentator said that if Jesus had not specified "Lazarus," all the tombs would have emptied of bodies, so authoritative was His command.

Just then, the crowd understood the words, "the **resurrection and the life**," in the most down-to-earth way. They also witnessed a fulfillment of other names that speak of God's power and might. It was a great miracle of the **God who works wonders**.[1185] When God snatched Lazarus back from death, He exercised His authority as the **God of all flesh**, **Lord both of the dead and of the living**, and the **Eternal God**.[1186] The **Creator** and the **Author of life** re-created life and raised the already decomposing body of Lazarus. It was a foretaste of "the **last Adam**" becoming "a life-giving spirit"

Author of Life
Gk.: *Archēgos tēs zōēs*
(Acts 3:15 NIV)

(1 Cor. 15:45). The strange sight of mummy-like Lazarus waddling stiffly from the tomb prepared onlookers to believe in Jesus' own resurrection and to understand His oneness with the un-decaying King.[1187] The **word of life** had issued a command to a dead man. The result spoke for itself.

The evidence convinced one significant group, while another group missed the point. "Many of the Jews who came to Mary, and saw what He had done, believed in Him. But some of them went to the Pharisees and told them the things which Jesus had done" (vv. 45–46). The first group understood the implications of the miracle: "Jesus raised a corpse, so He must be God." The second group was so preoccupied with politics that they reported Jesus to the religious authorities. For them, Jesus' earlier words proved true, even a resurrection would not sway some people.[1188]

Considering how compelling the raising of Lazarus must have been, the disciples' reactions on the first Easter morning are interesting. Surely, they should have believed the reports of Jesus' resurrection. Yet Mark said of some, "They were afraid." Of others, he said, "They refused to believe it." Of another group, he said, "They did not believe them either." When Jesus came to the gathered disciples, He "reproached them for their unbelief and hardness of heart, because they had not believed" (Mark 16: 8–14). Given what the religious and political leaders had done to eliminate Jesus, the disciples thought they would lose everything if they started claiming that Jesus had risen from the dead. It was no light matter.

However, the experiences of seeing, touching, and hearing their risen Master were more convincing than secondhand reports. The disciples soon testified boldly to the resurrection. Their encounters with the risen Jesus propelled them like rocket fuel, and their eyewitness accounts form the basis for our own faith. Will we accept the evidence for Jesus' resurrection? Our lives depend on it!

Eternal Life

Why is belief in the resurrection of Jesus a matter of life and death? Before Jesus' rendezvous with us, we are all spiritually dead and in various stages of decay. We have rotten thoughts, bad habits, decayed relationships, broken-down marriages, and decomposed families. The concepts that we absorb into our brains and the chemicals that we suck into our bodies corrode our lives. More seriously, without Jesus, sin separates us from the living God, and judgment follows death. Belief in Jesus' resurrection is essential if we are to live—to really live.

"If you confess with your mouth Jesus as Lord, and believe in your heart that God raised Him from the dead, you will be saved" (Rom. 10:9). Jesus saves us from death and gives us eternal life. "Eternal life means knowing Me and the Father who sent Me."[1189] Paul summarized the present and future dimensions of the new life: "For you have died and your life is hidden with Christ in God. When Christ, who is our life, is revealed, then you also will be revealed with Him in glory" (Col. 3:3–4). Eternal life is a quality of life in relationship with God. It begins the moment we accept Him and it continues forever. When we believe in Jesus' resurrection, we get a bonus—the assurance that Jesus has made us right with God and that He will raise our bodies too.[1190] We are equipped to overcome sin and given the power for ministry.[1191] It is a gloriously abundant life.

Opening Other Graves

Much of the time, the Gospels give us a sense that Jesus was the most socially skilled and likeable guy around. However, occasionally He struck His own culture as offensively inappropriate. He had conversations with women of questionable repute, allowing one to cover His feet with tears, ointment, and kisses.[1192] He hiked unperturbed through a pig farm, vandalized a temple court, and even touched unclean lepers and a coffin—without gloves!

If anyone else had approached a funeral party and begun talking about faith and resurrection, burly men would have escorted that person from the room.

"Can't you see how distraught his sisters, Mary and Martha, are?"

"This is painful enough for us. Stuff your religious idealism!"

"What right do you have? For goodness sake, leave us alone to mourn."

You and I would probably have heeded the early warnings and tiptoed around everyone's feelings, but Jesus knows exactly when it is right to slice through taboo. Many of His greatest miracles and most memorable messages unfolded in delicate moments. If He had not boldly broken several of the rules of His time, we would have no model for loving and accepting a sinner while clearly rebuking the sin. We would have no sense of how precious even the most infected of us are to Him. We would be unable to point to His power over a whole legion of demons. Jesus knows when to touch a tender heart, when to expose an unjust custom, and how to bring glory to God out of the darkest pits.

The raising of Lazarus was a high point in a string of miracles. It declared Jesus' authority over death. It paved the way for us to have faith in His own greater resurrection. It heralded His impartation of eternal resurrection life at the last trumpet to those who believe in Him. It gives us confidence that if Jesus can raise dead bodies, He can resolve our most entrenched and entangled situations. It showed that the impact of His salvation on our lives is limitless.

Where does human pain lie? Often, we keep it wrapped in bandages, buried deep within the walls of our hearts. One or two people might be mourning with us, reliving our memories. Frequently, the pain is a private, sealed subject. Even our closest friends and family members can't find the right words to say. For human pain to be healed, a qualified comforter must enter those dark places.

The story of Lazarus helps us to recognize Jesus for exactly who He is, and to welcome Him as He approaches the recesses of our lives. Don't be put off by His directness. His touch is life-giving. He can resuscitate dead dreams. He can restore relationships. He can open doors for those who are buried in dead-end jobs, or those who live under mountains of debt or regret. He is the one who revives dead wombs, turns mourning into gladness, and births new beginnings. Jesus does all of this because He is God.

Chapter 22

DOMINOES TO DOMINION

A man who was merely a man and said the sort of things Jesus said would not be a great moral teacher. He would either be a lunatic—on the level with the man who says he is a poached egg—or else he would be the Devil of Hell. You must make your choice. Either this man was, and is, the Son of God, or else a madman or something worse. You can shut him up for a fool, you can spit at him and kill him as a demon or you can fall at his feet and call him Lord and God, but let us not come with any patronizing nonsense about his being a great human teacher. He has not left that open to us. He did not intend to.

—**C. S. Lewis**, *Mere Christianity*[1193]

Most of us have stood dominoes on end in a row and enjoyed tapping the first domino to begin a chain reaction. Serious domino topplers design elaborate and artistic cascades. The dominoes split into multiple rows, climb slopes, turn corners, and then converge in a dramatic finale. The world record stands at over 4.4 million dominoes toppled.[1194]

Jesus' resurrection caused misunderstandings about Him to tumble like cascading dominoes. Long-held yet inaccurate ideas about God's Messiah yielded to eternal truth. The evidence compelled many people to become followers, and many followers gave their lives for the new faith. A vibrant church burst into life. Within thirty years of the resurrection, Paul and other leaders wrote letters that present us with the early church's view of Jesus. They had recognized Jesus' heavenly side.

The resurrection shouted that everything about Jesus was bigger and better than anyone had thought. No contemporary Jewish text suggested that the Messiah would rise from the dead (after all, the Messiah was not supposed to die), yet Jesus appeared to over five hundred people.[1195] That Jesus could step from the grave three days after His excruciating death on a Roman cross demonstrated that God had vindicated His claims. That vindication flattened any suggestion of Him being a deceived dreamer. Jesus was no wannabe messiah; He was the true Messiah—and what a Messiah!

A dynamic new concept of messiahship overrode the popular Jewish image of a militant messiah. This messianic Son of David came as a new kind of King for an expanded Israel. The horrendous flogging and crucifixion failed to silence Jesus. Instead, at the resurrection, God's purpose for Jesus' suffering and death became clear. He had taken sin on Himself as our substitute.

What of the mass resurrection the Jews expected? That expectation was replaced by a new understanding among Christians: Jesus is the **first fruits**, the **firstborn from the dead**. Those who are still dead await a later resurrection.[1196] God's kingdom is here, but it is not yet complete; it is coming in stages. Jesus is the heavenly king who will return to conclude what He began. Then the dead in Christ will rise.

Angel Eyes

It was easy for the angel to herald Jesus as Savior, Lord, and Christ. He knew Jesus was one with Yahweh, sent as His anointed deliverer. To Jesus' contemporaries, "Son of God" did not imply that Jesus was the second person of the Trinity; calling Jesus "Lord" did not equate Him with Yahweh. Those truths were veiled to all but the angels. Before the resurrection, most people were being polite when they called Jesus "Lord," and they were being political when they used the royal title "Son of God." Nonetheless, the truth of Jesus' divinity is eternal. After the resurrection, it became clear to His followers. Two titles in particular gained greater significance: Son of God and Lord.

Thomas provided the first example of the conclusion that followers began to draw. When Jesus invited Thomas to finger His resurrected scar tissue, Thomas exclaimed, "My Lord and My God" (John 20:28). Jesus' disciples finally began to comprehend the full import of the angel's proclamation to the shepherds. Jesus was *the* Lord.

This chapter explores the titles **Son of God** and **Lord** from the newly grasped heavenly perspective. What impact did this understanding have on the new Christians, and how did it sit with the current rulers, the Romans?

The Learning Curve

What was plain to angels took a few years to settle in human hearts and minds. The distribution of the titles in the New Testament reflects the learning curve.

The name "**Jesus**" occurs on its own 605 times in the Gospels, but it hardly occurs at all (seventy-five times) in the rest of the New Testament. Instead, it forms part of about two dozen different combinations of titles that distinguish the extraordinary Nazarene with the common Jewish name. (www. NamesForGod.net/names-of-jesus provides a summary of the combinations, and comments on their distribution.)

The title "**Christ**" is uncommon in the Gospels;[1197] in the remainder of the New Testament, it is abundant. Most writers refer to Jesus as Christ in most of the combinations. The claim that Jesus was indeed the promised Messiah was an important theme of the first evangelistic messages, and it was central to Paul's "gospel of Christ."[1198]

The Gospels often use "Lord" to indicate Yahweh (e.g., "the glory of the Lord" in Luke 2:9) and when quoting the Old Testament.[1199] Jesus referred to Himself as Lord only once—when He pointed out "the Son of Man is **Lord of the Sabbath**" and demonstrated it with a Sabbath healing (Matt. 12:8–14). "**Lord Jesus**" occurs just twice in the Gospels,[1200] but it occurs thirty-eight times elsewhere in the New Testament. Beyond the Gospels, the New Testament boldly states that Jesus is God's Son, Savior, Christ, and Lord.

Greetings

The triple title **Lord Jesus Christ** seems to be the fullest and most formal title for Jesus because it often features in the beginnings and endings of New Testament letters.[1201]

A typical greeting mentions Jesus and the Father together and calls for grace from both:

> *Grace to you and peace from* **God our Father** *and the* **Lord Jesus Christ**. (1 Cor. 1:3)[1202]

There are interesting variations. In his letters to Timothy, Paul modified his opening to, "Grace, mercy, and peace from God the Father and **Christ Jesus our Lord**."[1203] Writing to Titus, he said, "Grace and peace from God the Father and **Christ Jesus our Savior**."[1204] Paul was the only New Testament author to use the doublet **Christ Jesus**;[1205] all others stuck to **Jesus Christ**.

God our Father
Gk.: *Theos patēr hēmōn*
(1 Cor. 1:3)

John used a similar style of introduction, but he emphasized that Jesus was the Son of God:

> *Grace, mercy and peace will be with us, from God the Father and from Jesus Christ, the* **Son of the Father**, *in truth and love*. (2 John 1:3)

Many greetings present Jesus alongside God, sharing His divinity.[1206] "Lord" is ultimately a divine title.

The Lordship of Jesus

Concluding an important declaration to the Philippians, Paul pronounced Jesus' exaltation.

> *God highly exalted Him, and bestowed on Him the name which is above every name, so that at the name of Jesus every knee will bow, of those who are in heaven and on earth and under the earth, and that every tongue will confess that Jesus Christ is Lord, to the glory of God the Father.* (Phil. 2:9–11)

That declaration of bowed knees to Jesus the Lord comes from Isaiah 45:23–25, in which Yahweh was the subject.

Many New Testament passages, including those that call Jesus "Lord," share an underlying theology—Jesus and Yahweh are equivalent.[1207] Nonetheless, Jesus is clearly subordinate and has a distinct role.[1208]

Jesus shared in creating the universe alongside Yahweh.[1209] Later, God sent Jesus into the world to conquer sin.[1210] Paul equated calling on the name of Yahweh for deliverance with calling on the Lord Jesus for salvation.[1211] He also called Jesus "**Our great God and Savior**," and Peter called Him "**Our Lord and Savior**." Jesus and the Father are both responsible for salvation.[1212] Together, they minister grace and peace.[1213]

Our great God and Savior
Gk.: *Ho megalos Theos kai sōtēr hēmōn*
(Tit. 2:13)

Our Lord and Savior
Gk.: *Ho kyrios hēmōn kai sōtēr*
(2 Pet. 1:11; 2:20; 3:2, 18)

In some verses, the Old Testament "day of the LORD" becomes the "day of Christ," which is a joyful day for Jesus' followers.[1214]

Lord of glory
Gk.: *Ho kyrios tēs doxēs*
(1 Cor. 2:8)

The crucified one is the **Lord of glory** or **glorious Lord Jesus Christ**, and of course, God Himself is **God of glory**.[1215] Jesus' Lordship and His descent from David soon became tenets of the faith, and the early church worshipped Jesus as God.[1216]

Glorious Lord Jesus Christ
Gk.: *Ho kyrios Iēsous Christos tēs doxēs*
(James 2:1)

Jesus debated Psalm 110 with the Pharisees,[1217] and He quoted it at His trial. It begins, "[*Yahweh*] says to my Lord ['*adoni*]." Peter pointed to those words and said of Jesus, "God has made Him both Lord [probably meaning '*Adon*] and Christ" (Acts 2:34–36). In Malachi 3:1–2 "['*Adon*], whom you seek" seems to herald Jesus. The Aramaic cry "*Marana' tha*," which is derived from "*mare*'" (Lord), is probably in the future imperative, "Our Lord, come!" as Revelation 22:20 implies.[1218] John used "Alpha and Omega" for both God and Christ.[1219] The title **LORD of lords**, which first applied to Yahweh, was given to Jesus: "One who is identical with Yahweh and yet distinct."[1220]

That brings us to the doctrine of the Trinity, for which the end of one well-known letter is important because it includes all three persons.

The grace of the Lord Jesus Christ, and the love of God, and the fellowship of the Holy Spirit, be with you all. (2 Cor. 13:14)

Luke mentioned all three persons of God when he reported the conspiracy of world rulers who were behind the crucifixion.[1221] Once, the **Holy Spirit, Spirit of Jesus,** and **God** all get credit for guiding the disciples.[1222] The names **Spirit of Christ** and **Spirit of God** occur together.[1223] Several names for the

Holy Spirit reflect God's triune nature: **Spirit of our God**, **Spirit of the living God**, **Spirit of Jesus Christ**, **Spirit of the Lord**, **Spirit of your Father**, and **Spirit of His Son**.[1224]

The Son's Divinity

Mark introduced Jesus as the "**Son of God**," and throughout his Gospel, he presented evidence of the title's truth.[1225] Luke concurred that by the supernatural conception of the Holy Spirit, Jesus was Son of God.[1226] We don't know what eyewitnesses concluded as they saw Jesus minister and heard Him speak—the title's full meaning only became clear after the resurrection. However, the Gospel writers had hindsight (and the Holy Spirit's illumination). They recognized Jesus' heavenly side, and they grasped all of the implications. Their new understanding flavors the Gospels.

Jesus calmed a storm in a way that reminds us of psalms about God's power over tempests.[1227] When the disciples saw Jesus walk on water, the title "Son of God" flew from their tongues, but they most likely had the Jewish messiah in mind.[1228] Jesus so impressed Peter that he exclaimed, "You are the Christ, the **Son of the living God**" (Matt. 16:16). Jesus called to His Father at the tomb of Lazarus and received glory as God's Son when the dead man emerged.[1229] Even before it happened, Martha, the sister of Lazarus, said, "You are the **Christ**, the **Son of God**, even **He who comes** into the world" (John 11:27). John frequently inserted insights about Jesus' divine status into his Gospel, including the fact that Jesus knew that as the Son of God His voice brought life.[1230]

The Gospels certainly affirm Jesus' divinity, but I must emphasize that no one connected the title Son of God to divine Lordship immediately. "Without the resurrection story, this faith has not reached full expression, not least because until Easter the grounds for it are not fully secure."[1231] The empty tomb changed that.

When God commissioned Paul to bear His name to the Gentiles, Paul did not hesitate to proclaim Jesus as the Son of God.[1232] Both he and the book of Hebrews state that Psalm 2:7 spoke of Jesus.[1233] Romans 1:3–4 tells us He was "declared the Son of God with power by the resurrection from the dead, according to the **Spirit of holiness**, Jesus Christ our Lord."[1234] Some passages that speak of the everlasting kingdom equate the Son with God, the Father; they share Kingdom rule.[1235] John wrote his Gospel because he wanted his readers to believe that Jesus was God's Son and Messiah.[1236] It remains an essential part of our faith.[1237]

That faith is founded on the resurrection; it proves Jesus is divine in origin and in person. Jesus is LORD and Son of God—heaven's answer to the emperor.

The Rolling Stone

Let's pick up a tiny Roman coin again, like the one Jesus asked to see. Among the many coins circulating at the time were several denarii struck by Caesar Augustus and his son Caesar Tiberius. A denarius was the wage for a day's labor. Everyone knew Caesar's claim because around his image the coins boasted his title in bold letters: "Son of god." The empire had no room for another son of god. A collision between Jesus and Rome was one inevitable result of the truth cascading from the resurrection.

Historians tell us that Roman emperors were gradually elevated from being first citizens. For some years, loyal subjects believed Caesar became deified at death.[1238] Eventually, citizens honored them as gods while they were alive. Luke gave us a glimpse of Festus calling Nero (AD 54–68) "my lord."[1239] Nero's titles included "Lord of all the world," which in this case connoted majesty but not necessarily deity. Domitian (AD 81–96) reigned as the New Testament period ended. Imperial documents called him *dominus et deus* (our lord and god). The danger of a clash with Rome intensified. Annually, each citizen had to offer a pinch of incense and make the declaration, "Caesar is lord." Christians died rather than make that statement. No, Jesus is Lord!

One response of the church is especially interesting; Christians began to employ the Greek word, *ichthus* (fish). Perhaps you have the bumper sticker version. Originally, it was an acronym: I-Ch-Th-U-S. It functioned as a defiant, perhaps secret, sign that Christians used to identify each other. It stood for "Jesus Christ, Son of God, Savior."

Luke's Acts of the Apostles describes what God's messengers faced as the kingdoms collided. Acts doubles as a guidebook of Middle Eastern prisons. Paul was the supreme missionary jailbird. He spent many years "on trial for the hope and resurrection of the dead," kept in chains for the gospel (Acts 23:6; 26:6–8). He persisted with his message and carried the news of "another king" right to Caesar's doorstep (Acts 17:7; 28:16, 30–31).

Another word used as a name for God rolls into place here. Scripture calls God the **Stone of Israel**, using the word in parallel with *'avir* (mighty). *'Even* refers to a simple lump of, say, river rock. It is not a demeaning description. The river rock edging my flowerbeds took hundreds of years to wear smooth. It's tough!

Stone of Israel
Heb.: *'Even Yisra'el*
(Gen. 49:24)

Stone
Heb.: *'Even*
(Ps. 118:22; Isa. 28:16; Dan 2:34–35)
Gk.: *Lithos*
(Acts 4:11)

Chief Cornerstone
Heb.: *Ro'sh pinna*
(Ps. 118:22)
Gk.: *Kephalē gonia*
(Luke 20:17; Acts 4:11; 1 Pet. 2:7)

Cornerstone
Heb.: *Pinna*
(Isa. 28:16)
Gk.: *Akrogoniaios*
(Eph. 2:20; 1 Pet. 2:6)

In Daniel's explanation of Nebuchadnezzar's dream, the stone was a picture of God's Kingdom rumbling irresistibly down through history. The stone toppled earthly dominions, pulverizing them like brittle dominoes: Babylonia, Persia, Greece, and so on.[1240] Jesus cited Psalm 118:22: "The stone which the builders rejected has become the **chief cornerstone**." He hinted that He was the Landowner's rejected Son, the Stone.[1241] This stone, one way or another, gains dominion. Either a person falls on Him voluntarily or the stone crushes the un-submissive to dust.

Peter explicitly identified Jesus as the **Stone**.[1242] Elsewhere, Peter joined the words from Psalm 118 to two verses from Isaiah.[1243] His point was that contrary to human opinions Jesus is God's chosen foundation for His spiritual house. That house grows as other "living stones" are added to it through their choices of faithful obedience.[1244] The context of Isaiah 28:16 indicates that the cornerstone is part of the foundation, while Psalm 118:22 literally says the "head corner" and implies some kind of capstone. All these words point to the importance of Jesus' Lordship. He must be both the foundation of our lives and the conclusive goal we build toward. Without Him, everything is shaky, liable to subside or to collapse in on itself.

The Roman Empire, which was founded on myths and capped by men who aspired to be gods, began to crumble shortly after Jesus' time. Its demise is an object lesson that teaches us that any attempt to promote humans as gods will eventually fail. The Divine master plan, executed by God-become-human, will prevail. The life and fruit of the heavenly shoot will never cease.

Prostrated Tyrants

Emperors are no more, but we all love to be in control of something—partners, families, finances, careers, countries, and even ourselves. Every social grouping is as wholesome as the sum of the men and women who run it.

When the first tyrant—self—surrenders to the Lord's agenda, the change in that person cascades through his or her sphere of influence. As each follower takes the good news to the end of his or her piece of earth, God's kingdom grows. More people bow their knees to Him, and justice, righteousness, and joy spread. In the meantime, believers who live under evil regimes receive grace to endure injustice and oppression, knowing that God will one day hold such rulers accountable.

Signs will herald the King's return. One sign will be the fullness of the harvest of the Gentiles. Gentiles will join Jews in bowing to Jesus, their common Messiah and Savior.

Chapter 23

GOD'S SAVING ART

God is the Savior God; Jesus Christ did not live and die to change the attitude of God to men; he lived and died to demonstrate what that attitude is.

—**William Barclay**, *Jesus as They Saw Him*

Thump! I crashed to the ground, gashing my arm on a thorny vine. I pulled my leg from the hidden crack in the lava and checked it for injury. Apart from a bruise, I was fine, but I knew I was in trouble.

I had hiked around the rim of the Kilauea volcano in Hawaii, and I had decided to cut across country for about three miles to a road. At first, the going was easy, but then I encountered tall grasses and dense shrubs. Although I knew my approximate location and where I needed to head, I was exhausting myself trying to plow through the vegetation. In every direction, I found worse thickets and dangerous cracks concealed by dead grass. My water had run out (yet again) and there was potential for the situation to deteriorate. So, I began praying.

To keep track of the time, I had packed my cell phone. As I prayed, it occurred to me that 9–1–1 might still be available, even though my provider had no coverage in Hawaii. I dialed and a woman answered. In another situation, when she asked, "Which service do you need?" I might have responded, "A large, deep pan, bacon, and pineapple pizza, please." But I meekly said, "I'm lost and I need rescuing."

The dispatcher connected me to a National Park ranger. Using my phone signal to calculate my GPS coordinates, two rangers eventually hiked in to lead me out. Meanwhile, his simple instruction was to stay right where I was. "Don't move!"

I learned three useful tips about salvation from that hike:

1. Resist pride, which stops us from crying out for help. The embarrassment of needing help and the fear of ridicule could easily have inhibited me.

2. Don't wait until a situation becomes dangerous before seeking assistance. In my case, I was able to sit calmly in the shade and watch birds while I waited for the rangers. I made the right choice, and I phoned before I became the subject matter for a six o'clock news segment.

3. Never dictate how to be helped. I had hoped for a helicopter rescue. After all, it would have spared the two rangers a four-hour hike through the worst terrain I had ever seen (it was only one mile each way). I even checked out landing areas and had my camera ready for aerial shots of the volcano. No, a humble person lets the rescuer do what is best and stays still until told otherwise.

Beyond those three tips was a more important lesson. I was facing a tough situation at home. While hiking, I had spent time praying about it. The ensuing drama provided an object lesson that answered my prayers. God used my hiking adventure to prompt me to find practical human help with my home situation before it deteriorated.

Salvation as an Art

Salvation happens when something moves a person from a situation of distress to one of safety and relief. When we feel trapped and unable to move, it is hard to believe our destiny is bigger and better than the jaws of the trap suggest. But faith looks beyond overwhelming circumstances with no clear solutions to God

My Salvation
Heb.: *Yish'i*
(Ps. 27:1)
Heb.: *Yeshu'ati*
(Ps. 62:2, 6; Isa. 12:2)
Heb.: *('Adonai) teshu'ati*
(Ps. 38:22)

the Savior. Faith calls out an SOS. God's solutions might involve everyday resources or they might appear right out of the blue, counterintuitive and miraculous. The nativity shepherds probably expected the heralded Savior to eliminate injustice and liberate Israel, but Jesus' salvation is far broader. Each act of salvation is like a work of art.

The Italian artist Leonardo da Vinci created many inspiring works of art. Near the end of his life, he produced his masterpiece, the *Mona Lisa*. It is a mysterious painting. Who was the woman and what does her simple facial expression indicate? Every collector would love to display the painting, but it is far too valuable for France to part with. It remains in the Louvre behind sophisticated security sensors and a sea of visitors. Like most tourists in Paris, Janet and I made a beeline for it.

God's acts of salvation are like the works of a great artist. He saved and delivered in a multitude of ways throughout history. While His saving work is consistently perfect, over time, alert people saw the pattern and anticipated an even greater deliverance. The day came when God created His masterpiece: the crucifixion.

God's saving acts are collected in Scripture rather like pieces of art in a Leonardo da Vinci gallery. Let's take a tour around the biblical exhibits and view the names connected with salvation.

The Entrance Lobby

Psalm 79:9 makes a good introductory piece for the exhibition lobby: "Help us, O **God of our salvation**, for the glory of Your name; and deliver us and forgive our sins for Your name's sake."[1245] Notice the close relationship between deliverance and salvation. Notice that they always glorify God.

Salvation so characterizes God that the psalmist described Him as "**God our Savior**" in parallel with "**God of deliverances**." He bears our burdens and rescues from death.[1246] Sometimes He is referred to as **my help**: "I am afflicted and needy; hasten to me, O God! You are **my help** and **my deliverer**; O LORD, do not delay."[1247] Often the Bible simply calls God "**Savior**."[1248] Isaiah foretold that even Israel's archenemy, Egypt, "will cry to the LORD because of oppressors, and He will send them a **Savior** and a **Champion**, and

He will deliver them" (Isa. 19:20). No other god can save: "I, even I, am the LORD, and there is no savior besides Me. It is I who have declared and saved and proclaimed . . ." (Isa. 43:11–12; Hos. 13:4).

The biblical catalogue lists many subjects for His art. God delivers us from spiritual darkness, and He saves us from uncleanness, from danger and distress, from this perverse generation, and from illness.[1249] The book of Esther (the only biblical book lacking a name of God) is about the rescue of Jewish refugees from genocide. The New Testament mentions salvation with respect to a storm, illness, persecution, tribulation, and death.[1250] Each time God intervened to save His people, it was as if He had created another piece for His collection.

God of my salvation
Heb.: *'Elohei yeshu'ati*
(Ps. 88:1)

God our Savior
Heb.: *'El yeshu'atenu*
(Ps. 68:19 NIV)
Gk.: *Ho Theos ho sōtēr hēmōn*
(1 Tim 1:1; 2:3)

God of deliverances
Heb.: *'El lemosha'ot*
(Ps. 68:20)

My Deliverer
Heb.: *Mefalti*
(Pss. 18:2; 40:17; 70:5; 144:2)

My Help
Heb.: *'Ezrati/'Ezri*
(Pss. 40:17; 70:5)

My Helper
Heb.: *'Ozer li*
(Pss. 30:10; 54:4)

Savior
Heb.: *Moshia'*
(Isa. 19:20; 43:11; 45:15)
Gk.: *Sōtēr*
(Luke 1:47)

Snapshots from the Battlefield

Among God's deliverance names, military images abound. Israel's history was one of conflict and oppression. She lay sandwiched between large, cruel empires. Egypt lay to the south. To the east and northwest lay Assyria, Babylon, Persia, Greece, and Rome. Neighbors seeming like military giants often threatened the tiny nation of Israel. From her earliest days, Israel cherished memories of God's salvation from regional thugs, so this category dominates the biblical collection.

Many psalms belong in this wing. They tell us that God saves us "from our enemies, and from the hand of all who hate us" (Luke 1:71; see also Ps. 106:10). "Save us, O **God of our salvation**, and gather us and deliver us from the nations, to give thanks to Your holy name, and glory in Your praise" (1 Chron. 16:35). "Wondrously show Your lovingkindness, O **Savior** of those who take refuge at Your right hand from those who rise up

God of our salvation
Heb.: *'Elohei yish'enu*
(1 Chron. 16:35)

against them" (Ps. 17:7). No opposing people or their gods can resist Him. "There is none who can deliver out of My hand" (Isa. 43:13; 45:15–17).

Shield
Heb.: *Maginnenu*
(Pss. 33:20; 115:9–11)

My strength
Heb.: *'Uzzi*
(Ps. 28:7; Jer 16:19)
Heb.: *Ma'uzzi*
(Pss. 31:4; 43:2)
Heb.: *Kheyli*
(Hab. 3:19)
Heb.: *Khizqi*
(Ps. 18:1)

My Strong Fortress
Heb.: *Ma'uzzi khayil*
(2 Sam. 22:33)

Tower of deliverance
Heb.: *Migdol yeshu'ot*
(2 Sam. 22:51)

My Stronghold
Heb.: *Misgabi*
(Pss. 62:2, 6; 144:2)
Heb.: *Ma'uzzi*
(Jer. 16:19)

My Fortress
Heb.: *Metsudati*
(Pss. 31:3; 71:3;
91:2; 144:2)

My Refuge
Heb.: *Menusi*
(2 Sam. 22:3;
Jer 16:19)
Heb.: *Makhsi*
(Pss. 46:1; 91:2, 9;
Isa. 25:4)

As you read the following passages, put yourself in the position of a photojournalist documenting weapons and shields in an armory and surveying defensive positions.

God is my **help** and my **deliverer**. The word *'ezrati* (my help) is related to *'azar*, which connotes military help and evokes a picture of armies of angels massed for deployment.

A horn symbolizes power. The "**horn of my salvation**" is a phrase that reminds us that God has the power to deliver.

Psalm 33:20 uses a defensive military image, calling God "our **help** and our **shield**." The word *magen* typically refers to a small, round battle shield that the infantry used. Stepping between danger and us, God takes the blows.[1251]

Psalm 28:7 adds "**my strength**" to "**my shield**." The root word for strength (*'oz*) is often used to describe God.[1252] A synonym, *khayil*, refers to physical strength and efficiency like that of an army. Habakkuk 3:19 says, "*Yahweh 'adonai* is my strength."

Jeremiah combined **my strength** (*'uzzi*), with a related epithet, **my stronghold** (*ma'uzzi*).[1253] David used *ma'uzzi* as a component of names like **God my strength**.[1254] It denotes a place to run quickly to hide—a defensive bolthole.[1255] Proverbs 18:10 tells us "the name of the LORD is a strong tower; the righteous runs into it and is safe."[1256] Again, David said, "God is **my strong fortress** . . . He is a **tower of deliverance**[s] to His king." In verse 3, he used another word (*manos*), meaning a place of escape: "my **refuge**; my **savior**, You save me from violence" (2 Sam. 22:3, 33, 51).

God is also "**my refuge** and **my fortress**, My God, in whom I trust" (Pss. 91:2, 9; 71:7; 142:5; Joel 3:16). *Makhaseh* often denotes natural hill shelters, convenient hideouts for guerrillas. *Metsudah* applies to mountain summits, ideal sites for impregnable castle strongholds.[1257] King Herod built his winter palace, Masada, on a 1,300-foot butte. In AD 73, it took thousands of Roman legionnaires five months to build a siege wall and a ramp to penetrate the fortress, which 960 Jews had occupied. A similar idea is contained in the word *misgav*, which tells of an inaccessibly high place. When the psalmist said God's name is exalted, that was the picture.[1258] In the same sense, "the **God of Jacob** is **our stronghold**" (Ps. 46:7, 11). God is better security than all the refuges described by these words.

The Bible often presents names like these alongside descriptions of God as a rock or cliff. In Psalm 42:9, David, whose "window" on God included numerous experiences of God's salvation, spoke of **God my rock**. He chose a word that implies a rock with a fissure that was large enough to hide a person.

More common is the word *tsur*. It indicates a crack-free rock or a solid mountain. In strength, endurance, and reliability, God is like three-thousand-foot high El Capitan in Yosemite National Park. Using the same word, *tsur*, He is the **Rock**, **Everlasting Rock**, **Rock of my salvation**, **Rock of Israel**, and **Rock of my refuge**.

Since her early days, Israel was known for her special experience of God's deliverance: "Blessed are you, O Israel; who is like you, a people saved by the LORD, who is the **shield of your help**, and the **sword of your majesty**! So your enemies will cringe before you, and you will tread upon their high places" (Deut. 33:29).

All the resources we need are in God. He fights for us. He defends us. He is like an impenetrable rocky place for us to shelter in.

God my Rock
Heb.: *'El Sal'i*
(Ps. 42:9)

My Rock
Heb.: *Sal'i*
(Pss. 31:3; 42:9; 71:3)
Heb.: *Tsuri*
(Ps. 18:2)

Everlasting Rock
Heb.: *Tsur 'olamim*
(Isa. 26:4)

Rock of my strength
Heb.: *Tsur-'uzzi*
(Ps. 62:7)

Rock of my salvation
Heb.: *Tsur yeshu'ati*
(Deut. 32:15;
Ps. 89:26)
Heb.: *Tsur yish'i*
(2 Sam. 22:47;
Ps. 95:1)

Rock of Israel
Heb.: *Tsur Yisra'el*
(2 Sam 23:3;
Isa. 30:29)

Rock of my refuge
Heb.: *Tsur makhsi*
(Ps. 94:22)

Rock of your refuge
Heb.: *Tsur ma'uzzekh*
(Isa. 17:10)

Shield of your help
Heb.: *Magen 'ezrekha*
(Deut. 33:29)

Sword of your majesty
Heb.: *Kherev ga'avatekha*
(Deut. 33:29)

David's Memory Book

David's songs provide a large archive of imagery. He experienced God's deliverance while he was shepherding, facing Goliath, fleeing from King Saul, and ruling as king of the expanding nation. Psalm 18 could be his pocket album displaying names that highlight God's protection and deliverance. Many of the above epithets are compiled into beautiful images of God.[1259]

> I love You, O LORD, **my strength** [*khizqi*]. The LORD is **my rock** [*sal'i*] and **my fortress** [*metsudati*] and **my deliverer** [*mefalti*], My God, **my rock** [*tsuri*], in whom I take refuge; **my shield** [*maginni*] and the **horn of my salvation** [*qeren-yish'i*], **my stronghold** [*misgabi*]. I call upon the LORD, who is worthy to be praised, and I am saved from my enemies. (Ps. 18:1–3)

In the psalm, as God arrives to rescue His people, multiple phenomena signal His presence: smoke, fire, darkness, clouds, wind, hail, earthquake, thunder, and lightning.[1260]

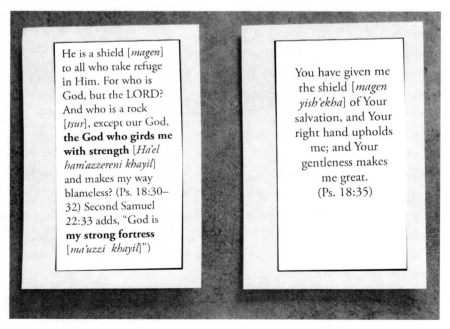

> He is a shield [*magen*] to all who take refuge in Him. For who is God, but the LORD? And who is a rock [*tsur*], except our God, **the God who girds me with strength** [*Ha'el ham'azzereni khayil*] and makes my way blameless? (Ps. 18:30–32) Second Samuel 22:33 adds, "God is **my strong fortress** [*ma'uzzi khayil*]")

> You have given me the shield [*magen yish'ekha*] of Your salvation, and Your right hand upholds me; and Your gentleness makes me great. (Ps. 18:35)

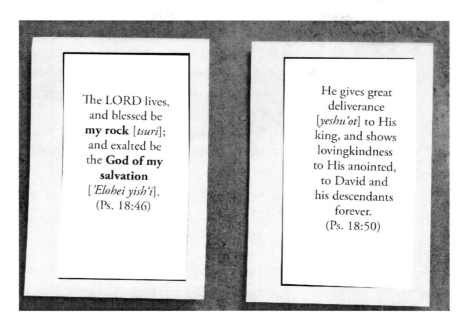

> The LORD lives, and blessed be **my rock** [*tsuri*]; and exalted be the **God of my salvation** [*'Elohei yish'i*]. (Ps. 18:46)

> He gives great deliverance [*yeshu'ot*] to His king, and shows lovingkindness to His anointed, to David and his descendants forever. (Ps. 18:50)

Multiple experiences of salvation produced a plethora of metaphors. No wonder Jews called Him **my hope**, the **Hope of Israel**, or the **Hope of their fathers**. *Miqweh* indicates an object of eager expectation.[1261] Observant people recognized the pattern of God's deliverance, and they put their hope in Him. David urged his soul to "hope in God, for I shall again praise Him for the help of His presence" (Pss. 42:5, 11; 43:5). At the time, he wanted God to end his spiritual dryness.

The prophet Micah was confident too: "I will watch expectantly for the LORD; I will wait for the **God of my salvation**. My God will hear me. Do not rejoice over me, O my enemy; though I fall I will rise. Though I dwell in darkness, the LORD is a light for me" (Mic. 7:7–8). Hope was infectious; it eventually spread to the nations.[1262] He is the **Savior of the body**, but He is also the **Savior of all men**.

My hope
Heb.: *Tiqwati*
(Ps. 71:5)

Hope of Israel
Heb.: *Miqweh Yisra'el*
(Jer. 14:8; 17:13)
Gk.: *Tēs elpidos tou Israēl*
(Acts 28:20)

Hope of their fathers
Heb.: *Miqweh 'avotehem*
(Jer. 50:7)

God of my salvation
Heb.: *'Elohei yish'i*
(Mic. 7:7)

Savior of the body
Gk.: *Sōtēr tou sōmatos*
(Eph. 5:23)

Savior of all men
Gk.: *Sōtēr pantōn anthrōpōn*
(1 Tim. 4:10)

Flooding Pharaoh

One ancient classic deserves room to itself: the Passover night. The setting was Goshen, the Hebrew area of Egypt. That particular night's miracle concluded a series of works described in the early chapters of Exodus. Nine plagues had displayed God's power, emphasized God's faithfulness to Israel, and prepared Pharaoh for a warning: "If you do not let my people go, you will suffer the death of the firstborn in your land and your family." Pharaoh stubbornly disregarded the warning.

Each Jewish household sacrificed a lamb in place of their firstborn, then ate it. That night, the Jewish people left Egypt and marched toward promised freedom. Pharaoh finally relinquished his pursuit when the Red Sea, which had parted for Israel to cross safely, engulfed his army. The exodus was so significant that Isaiah said it made a glorious, everlasting name for God, our **Father** and **Redeemer**.[1263] It established His reputation as a deliverer, and today it remains the centerpiece of Jewish history.

Forgetting the Savior

Despite God's faithfulness, Israel turned away. Just weeks after the Passover, while camped at Sinai, the people sculpted a golden calf idol and "forgot **God their Savior**, Who had done great things in Egypt" (Ps. 106:21). "Jeshurun grew fat and kicked—you are grown fat, thick, and sleek—then he forsook God who made him, and scorned the **Rock of his salvation**" (Deut. 32:15). Later, Isaiah and Jeremiah pronounced the same indictment: "You have forgotten the God of your salvation and have not remembered the rock of your refuge" (Isa. 17:10). "We have sinned against You. O **Hope of Israel**, its Savior in time of distress" (Jer. 14:7–8). Their fickleness resulted in God's discipline.

> **God their Savior**
> Heb.: *'El moshi'am*
> (Ps. 106:21)

I notice a discipline cycle in my own life. It's not an exercise bicycle. It's a circuitous route that I take in my relationship with God. I begin drifting from Him, hardly realizing my condition until life no longer runs so smoothly. Often, I'm the one messing things up. When I admit my drifting and pursue God again, life improves.

The cycle was pronounced during the time of the judges. God disciplined Israel for her sin by allowing enemies to rise up against her. Each time, the people of Israel cried out to Him. Then He sent a judge to lead them to victory and return them to freedom and prosperity.[1264] Scripture sometimes refers to the judges as deliverers.[1265]

God's salvation can penetrate hearts that are stuck in the worst downswings and ravaged by the blackest guilt. After committing adultery with Bathsheba, David pleaded, "Deliver me from bloodguiltiness, O God, the **God of my salvation**" (Ps. 51:14) and God forgave him. David still had to face consequences (his child became sick and died), but he immediately experienced freedom from guilt. God is able to clean the dirtiest hands and the grimiest hearts, imputing righteousness to those who seek Him.[1266] None of life's paths takes us beyond God's reach.

The psalms of David that celebrate his experience of God's mercy hang, as it were, in one of the hallways leading to the main exhibit. These sung stories are preludes to a more extensive forgiveness. Prophetic pieces also line the corridor like paintings, depicting scenes that only the Master's time-piercing eye could see back then. They are visions of the coming of salvation and righteousness (Isa. 51:5–8; 56:1). Job's confident statement is another piece: "As for me, I know that my **Redeemer** lives, and at the last He will take His stand on the earth" (Job 19:25).

Stepping Up to the Masterpiece

Predictive prophecies are like recessed spotlights. The lights themselves are incidental, and they should be inconspicuous. The studio designer intended them to shine on an object so that it would be easily recognized and clear. When a display stand is empty, spotlights have no subject to illuminate, so the beams fall on odd places like the wall or the floor. If we look directly at the lights, they dazzle and confuse us. As Jesus stepped onto the stage of history, the purpose of the diverse prophetic beams became evident. They shone on Him.

Matthew pointed out two prophetic beams converging on Jesus as He rode into Jerusalem just before His crucifixion.

Say to the daughter of Zion, 'Behold your King is coming to you, gentle, and mounted on a donkey, even on a colt, the foal of a beast of burden.' (Matt. 21:5)

Isaiah had proclaimed, "Say to the daughter of Zion, 'Lo, your salvation comes; Behold His reward is with Him, and His recompense before Him'" (Isa. 62:11). Zechariah had said, "Rejoice greatly, O daughter of Zion! Shout in triumph, O daughter of Jerusalem! Behold, your king is coming to you; He is just and endowed with salvation, humble and mounted on a donkey, even on a colt, the foal of a donkey" (Zech. 9:9). The two prophets' spotlights converged on Jesus as He entered Jerusalem. In *Yeshua'* (Yahweh is salvation), salvation was embodied and ready to do a work surpassing all others.[1267]

Jesus' work was so consequential that the writer of Hebrews celebrates Him as the originator, or **Author of their salvation**.[1268] The Gospels call Jesus "**Savior**" only twice,[1269] but the rest of the New Testament often gives the name to Him.[1270]

Jesus had already packed His earthly ministry with the same variety of salvation works that we considered earlier. At first, perhaps, our eyes find them more colorful and attractive than the masterpiece. He healed a woman from a hemorrhage, gave sight to a blind man, delivered people from demons, raised the dead, cleansed lepers, and deeply touched individual hearts by forgiving sins. All of these miracles came with a flourishing statement like, "Your faith has saved you."[1271] Each miracle gave a taste of the supreme act that forever saved humans from the problem of sin.

The Masterpiece

We come hushed, to the most important work of God. The masterpiece is a stark cross holding the bloody sacrifice of God's own Son, Jesus.

Graphic Art

Unlike the *Mona Lisa*, the subject is no great mystery; it crowns a series of graphic artworks. The earlier pieces, which are woven into the fabric of Jewish society and recorded in the Old Testament, anticipate the details of the masterpiece. All the Old Testament pictures of salvation were like a national gallery for the Jewish people. New Testament writers referred to the pieces in that gallery when they wrote about Jesus' saving work.

The popular theology that talks about being "saved from sin" can sound trite and theoretical. Jesus' central work was gruesome. Many of the Old Testament rituals form a backdrop that helps make the shocking comprehensible. We need to study nine pieces as an explanatory set. They involve more names of God, and they are essential for grasping the full significance of the masterpiece.

There is a Redeemer

Redemption is an important concept to understand because **Redeemer** is another specific name of Yahweh, the Father. God said comfortingly, "'Do not fear, you worm Jacob, you men of Israel; I will help you,' declares the LORD, 'and your Redeemer is the **Holy One of Israel**'" (Isa. 41:14). Again, He stated, "I, the LORD, am your Savior, and Your Redeemer, the Mighty One of Jacob" (Isa. 49:26; 60:16). Yet another reason for blessing the Lord's name is that He "redeems your life from the pit" (Ps. 103:4). So, what does a redeemer do?

Redeemer
Heb.: *Go'el*
(Ruth 4:14; Job 19:25)

Close relative
Heb.: *Go'el*
(Ruth 2:20; 3:9, 12; 4:1)

Avenger
Heb.: *Go'el*
(Num. 35:12, 19; Deut. 19:6, 12; Josh. 20:3, 9)

The story of Ruth helps answer that question. It works rather like one of England's most important historic relics—the Bayeux tapestry. I'm not sure why the English cherish it so much, since it depicts William the Conqueror defeating England. The two-hundred-foot embroidered tapestry is comprised of a series of panels. Each panel depicts one episode of the invasion. It ends with the Battle of Hastings, the death of King Harold, and the victory of the Normans. The tiny book of Ruth is like a romantic tapestry panel telling how a Jew called Boaz became a redeemer and married a young widow called Ruth.

Ruth was a foreigner from neighboring Moab. She married into a Jewish family. When her husband died, she demonstrated her love and loyalty by accompanying her widowed mother-in-law, Naomi, as she returned to Bethlehem. In those days, widows struggled to survive, unless they had capital or they could remarry. Naomi's wealthy relative, Boaz, eventually saved Naomi by buying her land. But there was a problem.

Ruth had planned to glean a living from Boaz's fields, but the strategy developed to the point of wooing Boaz, who eventually married her. However, Boaz was not the first in line. By law, the closest relative (*go'el*) had to redeem Naomi by paying off her debt.[1272] In the ensuing negotiations, Boaz pointed out that the land came with the responsibility to produce children for Naomi's dead husband so that his name would be preserved.[1273] Ruth would bear those children. Marrying Ruth was part of the package, an added responsibility. Knowing that, the closest relative lost interest and relinquished his right. Boaz had all the resources he needed to pay Naomi the redemption price of the land and to support Ruth as his wife. Redeemer Boaz paid a price to transfer Ruth out of destitution and into her new destiny as his wife and as the great-grandmother of King David.

Naomi's friends made one of the last comments in the book. Perhaps they had gathered in the shade at the village well to hear her recount how God had arranged everything. They said, "Blessed is the LORD who has not left you without a redeemer" (Ruth 4:14).

Our own Redeemer "rescued us from the domain of darkness, and transferred us to the kingdom of His beloved Son, in whom we have redemption, the forgiveness of sins" (Col. 1:13–14). Jesus paid the price with His life.

Broken Sacrifices

Ruth's story is consistent with other descriptions of God, the Redeemer, who watches out for the fatherless and demonstrates practical concern for justice. He also deals with trespassers and boundary movers (Prov. 23:10–11). Redemption from sin comes at a higher price. The Old Testament drums home the problem of being separated from the Holy One because of sin and the need to repair the fractured relationship.[1274] God's temporary solution included atonement through a system of sacrifices that were detailed in long, seemingly dry chunks of the Old Testament. Sometimes, ransom money would suffice.[1275]

The Hebrew noun for atonement is *kippur* (Yom Kippur is the Jewish Day of Atonement).[1276] It is related to the verb *kipper*, which means, "to make atonement by offering a substitute" or "to cover." Another noun,

Hebrew	English	OT Greek	NT
Kipper	To make atonement /cover (87X)	Exhilaskomai	-
Kippurim	Atonement (8X)	Hilasmos	Propitiation (I John 2:2; 4:10)
Kofer	Ransom (11X)	Lytron	Ransom (Matt. 20:28; Mark 10:45)
Khatta't (not related above)	Sin offering (116X)	Hilasterion	Sacrifice of atonement (NIV) Propitiation (Rom. 3:25 NASB)

kofer, indicates the payment of a penalty price to match the offense so that justice will be done. The Septuagint translated *kofer* with *lytron*, which means "ransom" and approaches the original meaning. It certainly isn't a fortune paid to Satan to secure our freedom, as if some diabolical pirate were holding us hostage. We sin against God and He requires the ultimate penalty: the forfeiting of an unblemished life (blood is equivalent to life). Paul named the price: "the wages of sin is death" (Rom. 6:23).

The sacrificial system was ineffective. Unblemished animals were not enough, and fallen people could never atone for themselves.[1277] Yet the imperfect system functioned for over a thousand years. During that long season, God was patient with sin and kept His wrath in check. Meanwhile, He hinted that the system would change one day, saying, "You were sold for nothing and you will be redeemed without money" (Isa. 52:3), thereby pointing ahead to His precious and perfect Son.

In the Old Testament, various sacrifices were necessary to cover the gamut of uncleanness, guilt, and sin. The suffering servant became an offering to remove guilt.[1278] The New Testament says that Jesus' death fulfilled the most important redemptive sacrifices: the Passover sacrifice, the sin offering,[1279] and our "sacrifice of atonement" (*hilastērion*).[1280] The book of Hebrews presents Him as a covenant-inaugurating sacrifice and the substitutional sacrifice made on the Day of Atonement.[1281] His death on the cross was clearly a redemptive act.[1282]

Jesus said of Himself, "Even the Son of Man did not come to be served, but to serve, and to give His life a ransom for many" (Mark 10:45; Matt. 20:28).[1283] Peter's first letter tells us, "You were not redeemed with perishable things like silver or gold from your futile way of life inherited from your forefathers, but with precious blood, as of a lamb unblemished and spotless, the blood of Christ" (1 Peter 1:18–19).

Passed Over

Paul declared, "Christ, **our Passover lamb**, has been sacrificed" (1 Cor. 5:7 NIV), connecting Jesus' death to the sacrifice of the first Passover lambs *in lieu* of the firstborn.[1284] Jews smeared the blood on their doorframes to signal to God that they had made a substitutionary sacrifice. The marked home would be passed over and spared from the last plague, the death of the

Our Passover lamb
Gk.: *To pascha hēmōn*
(1 Cor. 5:7 NIV)

firstborn. Jesus died as our substitute on the cross.[1285] When we accept that truth by faith, His blood protects us from God's wrath against our sin.

A Curse

Christ also "redeemed us from the curse of the law, having become **a curse** for us" (Gal. 3:13).[1286] This is a good place to recall the graphic covenant scene in Abram's vision in Genesis 15. Participants cut animals in half to demonstrate what would happen to either party if they broke covenant; the dissection portrayed a gory penalty clause in the covenant. In a sense, Jesus received fatal

> **A curse**
> Gk.: *Katara*
> (Gal. 3:13)

wounds for our unfaithfulness to God. The offended One took our punishment on Himself.[1287]

But we mustn't take the idea of an angry God who needs to be appeased too far. God provided atonement for sin out of love for us (1 John 2:1–2; 4:9–10). His compassion for all His people and His commitment to them motivated Him to save us. Isaiah noted, "'In an outburst of anger I hid My face from you for a moment, but with everlasting lovingkindness I will have compassion on you,' says the LORD your Redeemer" (Isa. 54:8). "For He said, 'Surely they are My people, sons who will not deal falsely.' So He became their Savior. In all their affliction He was afflicted, and the angel of His presence saved them; in His love and in His mercy He redeemed them" (Isa. 63:8–9).

A Fragrant Aroma

Again, on the theme of sacrifices, Paul said Jesus gave Himself up for us as "an offering and a sacrifice to God as a fragrant aroma" (Eph. 5:2). He chose Greek words that, in the Old Testament, stood for various sacrifices and offerings, all of which were necessary to maintain relationship with God. On the cross, Jesus covered our foul sins with His sweet sacrifice.

The Avenger

The kinsman redeemer *(go'el)* had another role beyond the one in Ruth's story. In the event of an unjust slaying, the kinsman had the right or duty to avenge his relative. In such cases, the kinsman was the "avenger of blood."[1288]

David pictured God like that, saying, "The LORD lives, and blessed be my rock; and exalted be God the **rock of my salvation**, the **God who executes**

vengeance for me, and brings down peoples under me, who also brings me out from my enemies" (2 Sam. 22:47–49).[1289] Satan binds people, robbing them of the abundant life that God intended. Jesus, the conquering champion, dealt with our enemy.[1290] He set us free from Satan's power.[1291]

Shadow Sculpture

The book of Hebrews indicates that everything in the tabernacle and temple— each furnishing and every ritual—was a shadow of a greater reality that exists in heaven. In Chapter 4, we saw that the "mercy seat" (*kapporet*) covered the ark where God's presence resided with His people. Annually, on the Day of Atonement, the High Priest approached the mercy seat to make atonement with the blood of bulls and goats. *Kapporet* indicates the covering where atonement happened. The English phrase reminds us that people appealed to God's mercy by sprinkling animal blood on that lid. The cross, on which Jesus' blood was shed, fulfilled and surpassed the Jewish Day of Atonement; the cross is eternity's highpoint.

Hebrew	English	OT Greek	NT
Kipper	To make atonement /cover (87X)	Exhilaskomai	-
Kofer	Ransom (11X)	Lytron	Ransom (Matt. 20:28; Mark 10:45)
Kapporet	Mercy Seat (27X) (Cover of the ark)	Hilasterion	Mercy seat (Heb. 9:5)

God arranged Old Testament sin offerings on something like a sliding scale of fees. No one got off free, but individuals offered what they could afford. Priests offered a bull for themselves, and rulers provided male goats, while ordinary folks brought lambs or female goats. Poor people could bring a dove. If they lived in extreme poverty, they could bring a measure of flour. The system tells us that God did everything possible to make reconciliation accessible.

At the top of the scale, as it were, the supreme sacrifice of a goat on the Day of Atonement provided outward cleansing annually for the entire nation. Jesus' atoning death extended the scale to cover every degree of sin, for everyone, forevermore. The most poverty-stricken in spirit gained access to the kingdom of heaven. Jesus' death cleansed consciences eternally and globally.

The imagery goes further. The mercy seat covering supported the King of glory's throne, or His seat. According to this imagery, the priests sprinkled the atoning blood at the base of His throne, or His "footstool." Because of Jesus' blood, we can "draw near with confidence to the throne of grace, so that we may receive mercy and find grace to help in time of need" (Heb. 4:16).

There is more because, "The LORD says to my Lord: 'Sit at my right hand until I make Your enemies a footstool for Your feet'" (Ps. 110:1). This verse portrays the enemies of God bowing finally at the feet of the King on the throne. Probably our most worshipful position is a voluntary prostration before Jesus' cross, which is the equivalent of the mercy seat.

The Highest Priest

An anonymous prophet first heralded the Messiah's priestly role: "I will raise up for Myself a faithful priest[1292] who will do according to what is in My heart and in My soul; and I will build him an enduring house, and he [or it] will walk before My anointed always" (1 Sam. 2:35). Jesus is the only priest who remained perfectly faithful to God's will.[1293] Today, the church of His followers is the enduring house that will walk before Him forever.

Hebrews draws much imagery from the Jewish sacrificial system. The book paints Jesus into the picture to make clear how extensively He fulfilled the images. Hebrews repeatedly calls Him **High Priest**, and it refers to him once as the **Great Priest** (a more literal expression of the Hebrew term for the High Priest, *hakkohen haggadol*).[1294]

In Old Testament times, priests made sacrifices. The priests came exclusively from the tribe of Levi and were consecrated for the task. Only the High Priest could perform the supreme sacrifice on the Day of Atonement.

Great Priest
Gk.: *Hiereus megas*
(Heb. 10:21)

High Priest
Gk.: *Archiereus*
(Heb. 3:1; 4:14;
8:1; 9:11)

**Minister in
the sanctuary**
Gk.: *Tōn hagiōn
leitourgos*
(Heb 8:2)

The scene is graphic. Very reverently, the High Priest passed through the heavy curtain veil, carefully carrying a bowl containing the sacrificial blood. He gingerly approached God's presence above the mercy seat, between the extended wings of the two cherubim. As he sprinkled the blood on the mercy seat, the nation's worship reached its yearly climax. The blood atoned for Israel's sin.

Hebrews describes Jesus' work in terms of the Day of Atonement. He is not only the sacrifice; He is also "a merciful and faithful **High Priest**" (Heb. 2:17) and a **minister in the sanctuary** (Heb. 8:2). The latter phrase emphasizes the temple service of the priests. Jesus' priestly offering of His own life is the perfect sacrifice for our sins.[1295] Even His passage through the heavens is noted.[1296] He continues to intercede for us as Priest.[1297]

The writer of Hebrews stressed how special Jesus is to God. "Son" is a better name than the angels have.[1298] His sonship underlies His position as **High Priest**. He is the fulfillment of Psalm 110, in which the messianic Son of God was designated as a priest by divine edict: "You are a priest forever according to the order of Melchizedek" (v. 4). Hebrews connects Him to another tribe—the tribe of Judah, rather than that of Levi. The change of order indicated a change in the priestly system. Hebrews states His qualifications. He is completely human yet perfectly divine. Like Melchizedek (Abram's mysterious guest), He did not receive the office by birth but by divine appointment. Representing a different tribe, He instituted a new, adequate priesthood.[1299] Unlike the former priests, Jesus had no sin of His own to atone for; His substitutionary death ransomed all comers for all time.[1300]

The Mediator

The title, **Mediator**, applies to Jesus in two ways, both of which depend on Jesus' death and His dual nature—divine and human. No angelic or earthly agent could take His place. Only He could represent both sides. Paul explained Jesus' mediation in terms of His ransom: "There is one God, and one mediator also between God and men, the man Christ Jesus, who gave Himself as a ransom for all" (1 Tim. 2:5–6). Paul also described atonement's effect on our relationship with God as a reconciliation of enemies.[1301] Jesus' role as **advocate** is similar; He draws alongside as our helper, having paid our penalty (*hilasmos*).[1302]

Mediator
Gk.: *Mesitēs*
(1 Tim. 2:5)

The book of Hebrews mentions the **mediator of a new covenant**. Jesus sealed the better covenant with His own blood,[1303] thus triggering the fulfillment of Jeremiah's prophesied new covenant: "They will all know Me, from the least of them to the greatest" (Jer. 31:31–34).

In another sense, as the Servant of Yahweh, Jesus was a living "covenant to [or of] the people," as Isaiah said He would be (Isa. 42:6; 49:8).

Appraising the Masterpiece

Jesus' crucifixion deserves the accolade "masterpiece" because in every way it is history's highpoint. Two forces that had never converged before met on the cross: God's requirement for justice and His love for humankind were both expressed there. His wrath against sin, which had been restrained for millennia by His patience, was unleashed. Motivated by love and a desire for reconciliation, Jesus paid our penalty, satisfied justice,[1304] and reconciled us to God, all in one act.

Now "the righteousness of God [is] through faith in Jesus Christ for all those who believe . . . being justified as a gift by His grace through the redemption which is in Christ Jesus" (Rom. 3:22, 24). Humble confession of sin releases the cleansing that Jesus' blood accomplished.[1305] Since Jesus fulfilled every aspect of the gory sacrifices and complex laws, those things are no longer required for us to have relationships with God.

In the nine explanatory pieces we scanned, God often has two roles. The Father provided the sacrifice and accepted it as atonement. Jesus served as the priestly **mediator** and victim.[1306] He was also the propitiator and the propitiation.[1307] In Jesus, God could "be just and **the justifier**" (Rom. 3:26; see also Rom. 4:5; 8:33). The Father is the redeemer; Jesus is our ransom. Yeshua is the artist and the art.

> **The Justifier**
> Gk.: *Ho dikaiōn*
> (Rom. 3:26; 4:5; 8:33)

Peter made it clear: "There is salvation in no one else; for there is no other name [Jesus Christ] . . . by which we must be saved" (Acts 4:12). It sounds exclusive until we realize that He is the real deal. His is no quick fix or imitation salvation that is partially effective and wears off like a dental anesthetic. Jesus, the perfect Son of God, was the only one who could properly satisfy God's requirements for justice.

In the past, salvation appeared to focus on one nation, Israel. Now, everyone is clearly on God's invitation list. At the cross, salvation became available to "everyone who calls on the name of the Lord" (Acts 2:21, quoting Joel 2:32). "The LORD has bared His holy arm in the sight of all the nations, that all the ends of the earth may see the salvation of our God" (Isa. 52:10; see also Ps. 67:1–2). "There is no other god besides Me, a righteous God and a Savior; there is none except Me. Turn to Me and be saved, all the ends of the earth; for I am God, and there is no other" (Isa. 45:21–22). The story of Ruth, the Moabite, demonstrated that God wanted to save the entire world. No work will ever penetrate as deeply or extend as broadly or as far as God's *pièce de résistance*, which is the atoning work of Jesus.

The Artist's Studio

The cross is pivotal to our relationship with God, and the salvation of our souls is the most important transaction we can ever enter into. However, it is by no means God's only act of deliverance in our lives. Let me illustrate it this way:

On August 16, 1986, Janet and I got married. That day was certainly a high point in our lives, but we continue to have an ongoing relationship. We look at our wedding photographs and share fond memories, but we've had other experiences. Jolts, as well as joys, helped us grow closer.

Our relationships with the Savior are the same. Salvation often refers to the supreme transaction affecting the soul, but our experience of salvation develops because of His lifelong acts of practical deliverance. Having seen the masterpiece, we can anticipate the finished quality of works in progress.

Great art has a price tag. Unfortunately, we cannot experience God's deliverance from distress unless we get into distress. Naturally, we dislike difficulty, let alone danger. Everything in us hunts for the quickest way out of a crisis. I did not enjoy getting lost in Hawaii, but the rangers rescued me and I learned valuable lessons. Our predicaments are the raw materials that God transforms into amazing works of salvation. If we resist the inclination to run, and lay them like a piece of canvas before a painter, He will turn what look like dirty messes into personalized memorabilia. So, let's cultivate lifestyles that allow Him to create more saving art to display on the walls of our lives.

To understand the artist at work, let's look at another piece in the exhibition.

Singing of Salvation

The song with the lyrics recorded in Exodus 15 soared up the charts shortly after Israel crossed the Red Sea. Perhaps that triumphal song's depiction of drowned Egyptians captures our attention:

*I will sing to the LORD, for He is highly exalted; the horse and its rider He has hurled into the sea. The LORD is **my strength and song**, and He has become my salvation.* (Ex. 15:1–2)

My Strength and Song
Heb.: *'Ozzi wezimrat*
(Ex. 15:2; Isa. 12:2)

It describes the climactic act of God's destruction of Israel's Egyptian oppressors. To the Israelites, it didn't seem so wonderful in the making.

Exodus 14 tells the story. Having grabbed their bags and fast food on the first Passover night, the Israelites soon found themselves cornered (vv. 5–10). Pharaoh's intimidating forces had followed them. Trapped between a chariot regiment and the Red Sea, they were terrified.

Israel's first response was her best. The Israelites cried out to the Lord (v. 10). Our 9–1–1 call to Him is a basic expression of our faith in Him and a humble admission that only He can save us. Our cries lay the canvases of our crises before God and commission Him to paint another salvation work of His own design into our lives.

All battles are hard, but battles that follow months or years of relentless opposition are the greatest tests of our readiness to trust in God's saving power. Israel was tested. The people had three choices, just as we have when we feel overwhelmed.

Their cries to the Lord (if they ever were that) became complaints to Moses. "Is it because there were no graves in Egypt that you have taken us away to die in the wilderness?" (vv. 10–12) They compared their present predicament with the past, and they concluded that the past was better. Their first choice was to return to Egypt. Israel had lost sight of God's purposes. Forced labor in Egypt was not God's will for them. God had called them out of slavery and promised them a fulfilling destiny. However, they focused on the bittersweet security of their familiar fiend, Pharaoh.

It is tempting to bolt the door on unmanageable and unpredictable situations. The Israelites wanted to retreat from their challenging situation. They turned in an application for early retirement, telling Moses, "Leave us alone that we may serve the Egyptians" (v. 12).

Option two was to deal with Pharaoh in their own strength. For a group of unarmed, runaway slaves who were being pursued by disciplined charioteers, it was not much of an option. However, we are often tempted to rely on our self-efforts.

Moses demonstrated his leadership ability by refocusing the people on the best option: God's help. We need to take His simple exhortation to heart: "Do not fear! Stand by and see the salvation of the LORD which He will accomplish for you today" (vv. 13–14). Obeying that instruction is better than panicked running or frantic striving. We all need a faith-filled Moses who knows God's capability and will point us to God's help.

Moses' advice was good. Often, the best response is to resist fear and prayerfully wait for the Lord to act. Sometimes we can do nothing practical. In Moses' case, even his short sermon was too long. The Lord interrupted Moses: "Why are you crying out to Me?"

God gave some simple directives: "Tell the sons of Israel to go forward. As for you, lift up your staff and stretch out your hand over the sea and divide it." Then He told of His own part, saying, "I will harden the hearts of the Egyptians" (vv. 15–17).

Sometimes, God gives us specific instructions. So we must listen to Him in every new situation. Our part is usually quite simple (Moses probably didn't think so), and it seems entirely insufficient. God's part is the miracle. Thankfully, Israel stepped forward in obedience. Oh, I know it was wavering, but they chose right and God acted.

The nation drew breath as Moses raised his staff. Then the people picked up their luggage, took their children's hands, and walked toward the sea. A new wind blew up and the waves began parting. Did Egypt massacre the people? No. Did the sea drown them? No. They passed through to the other side, looked back, and saw God complete the salvation He had begun in Goshen (v. 30). As Moses reached out once more, they witnessed the Egyptian team making the first attempt at underwater chariot races and unsynchronized swimming. It never caught on, of course. The people burst into the song of Exodus 15. God's latest picture, which had been born in such tension, was complete.

Springs of Salvation

The exodus was such a historic work that a few lyrics from Exodus 15 were reused.[1308] Jews still recognize its importance; Exodus 15 remains part of daily morning prayers. In his final blessing, Moses reminded the tribes about God's salvation.[1309] When Isaiah prophesied a second exodus from captivity in Assyria, he said, "Behold, God is my salvation, I will trust and not be afraid; for the LORD GOD is **my strength and song**, and He has become my salvation. Therefore you will joyously draw water from the springs of salvation" (Isa. 12:1–3). What lovely imagery! It was as if Isaiah were pointing to the most celebrated work in the national gallery of the time and saying, "What God did in the exodus is more than history. He will repeat it!" Experiencing God's deliverance in one situation increases our confidence for future trials.

The prophet Habakkuk knew about God's pattern of dependability. Foreboding disaster and destitution, his book ends on an upbeat note as he faithfully exalts in the "God of my salvation" (Hab. 3:17–19).

God's exhibition of salvation assures us that His saving work, which climaxed on the cross, will continue. The Old Testament gallery that served as a rich reference for New Testament writers still inspires people of faith, but God continually adds to the collection. Springs of salvation consistently issue forth from God's heart, which gushes with new works. The centerpiece of our lives is, of course, Jesus crucified. However, lives that draw joyously from the springs of salvation will see more examples of the Savior's art. He will complete personalized works, pieces for groups, and even some magnificent masterstrokes on the national and historical scale, including the Jews.

The two prophetic spotlights that shine on Jesus in Matthew's account of His triumphal entry also point forward through history. They hint at His

Deliverer
Gk.: *Rhyomenos*
(Rom. 11:26)

second coming as King. He will have worldwide dominion, and He will bring rewards and recompense.[1310] Following an outpouring of the **Spirit of grace and supplication**, Israel will recognize her crucified Messiah.[1311] Paul predicted that Israel would partially harden until other nations came to faith.[1312] Then he said, "The **Deliverer**[1313] will come from Zion, He will remove ungodliness from Jacob. This is My covenant with them, when I take away their sins" (Rom. 11:26).[1314]

The whole exhibition will culminate in the events that the book of Revelation describes. We will stand before another sea—the glassy sea. As we reflect on our lives and review God's works throughout history, we will burst into song. John gave credit for the song to Moses and to the Lamb.[1315] The victory song celebrates the King's eternal reign over the nations and His marvelous works and righteous acts, including many acts of salvation.

THE LONG HALLELUJAH

Crown Him with many crowns, the Lamb upon His throne.
Hark! How the heavenly anthem drowns all music but its own.
Awake my soul, and sing of Him who died for thee,
And hail Him as thy matchless King through all eternity.
—Matthew Bridges

I turned to see the voice that was speaking with me. And having turned I saw seven golden lampstands; and in the middle of the lampstands [I saw] one like a son of man, clothed with a robe reaching to the feet, and girded across His chest with a golden sash. His head and His hair were white like white wool, like snow; and His eyes were like a flame of fire. His feet were like burnished bronze, when it has been made to glow in a furnace, and His voice was like the sound of many waters. In His right hand He held seven stars; and out of His mouth came a sharp two-edged sword; and His face was like the sun shining in its strength. When I saw Him, I fell at His feet as a dead man. And He placed His right hand upon me, saying, "Do not be afraid; I am the first and the last, and the living One; and I was dead, and behold, I am alive forevermore, and I have the keys of death and of Hades." (Rev. 1:12–18)

I n heaven, all eyes will be on God—not on us. John was drawn by His voice and stunned by His appearance; lavish lampstands could not compete for John's attention. No, what arrested John's eye was the revelation of "one like a son of man."

From his unique, visionary vantage point, John witnessed the full breadth of the identity of the **Son of Man** in a way that was not possible on earth. Jesus spans the entire range of meaning in the title Son of Man. He was incarnated, and He remains recognizable in human form, yet He displays all the glory and majesty of deity. The Son of Man shares the characteristics of the enthroned Ancient of Days who Daniel saw. In heaven, God's laser of glory is unshielded and fully ablaze.

Daniel saw the Son of Man approaching the Ancient of Days with the clouds to receive glory and a kingdom.[1316] With its crescendo of seals, trumpets, and bowls, the book of Revelation elaborates on the final investiture. It describes more details of the court scene that Daniel only glimpsed: the King's final triumph, the beastly enemy slain and burned, and open record books. The book of life is the most prominent book. It contains the names of the faithful. The list is long and the crowd is massive.[1317]

A Big Crowd and a Big Question

Gradually, Abdullah's eyes grew accustomed to the strangely diffuse yet bright light. It emanated from a magnificent throne beyond a mirror-like basin. A rainbow surrounded the throne. Its dominant color was emerald. In front of the basin, stretching out of sight, stood a crowd that focused on the enthroned One. The crowd matched in number the sand grains on earth's shores and the stars in the sky. Abdullah's name appeared in the book; he stood in the multitude. Abdullah's descendants clustered excitedly around him, glad that their ancestor had chosen ridicule and persecution as the price for following Isa (Jesus). He had discovered God as his Father. They were Abdullah's legacy.

Abraham stood near the front of the assembly. The great God-fearer had demonstrated practical faith by his willingness to sacrifice his most precious and promising treasure: his son. Abraham had trusted God above all others. He had become the father of a multitude of faithful people. The people among the vast throng had numerous stories of similar choices. More diverse than the crowd who witnessed Pentecost, they came from every tribe, tongue, and nation. Every skin color, hair type, and eye shape was represented. Tens of thousands of people groups, once ignorant of any name beyond those of their primeval gods, had called on the Lord before the last day. All were grateful that someone had taken the time to point them to the right choice.

The fatherless Angies of the world were scattered among the crowd. In faith, they had reached out to snuggle in the healing embrace of the heavenly Father at the finish line of life's race.

Will we stand in the crowd? Do our names appear in the book of life? That all depends on our choice of owner. The crack of a whip tells stock animals, like camels, to whom they belong. We select our masters and then those owners brand us. Will we bear Jesus' name and, with His help, become like Him? Or will we bow to a lesser god?

The choice begins with the question of the ages. Who do we say Jesus is and how do we respond to Him? We can promote His name or our own names. Either people admit their need for His salvation and bow to His Lordship, or they pursue a smorgasbord of what appear to be tastier options. The book of Revelation frames these questions in terms of whose mark we bear. Is it a beastly god's mark or the Lamb's mark? The Lamb's name and His Father's name are inscribed on the foreheads of the faithful.[1318]

Since the fall, God has been renaming men and women and reforming them in His image. It is one of several biblical subplots that are revisited in the book of Revelation. Abram became Abraham. Jacob received the name Israel. God renamed His forsaken people "My delight is in her" and "Beloved."[1319]

In messages to seven churches, Jesus promised new names to overcomers.[1320] For believers in Pergamum, the new name is written on a stone and known only to the recipient. Philadelphian overcomers receive "the name of My God, and the name of the city of My God . . . and My new name" (Rev. 3:12). Until heaven, people will not know what their new names are. They might be unique to the individual or the name "Jesus" or His own, still-secret name.[1321]

God's Brand

Regardless of the exact details of our new names, the transformation confirms our devotion and indicates God's ownership of us, which in turn guarantees His protection. The renamed ones are sealed (*sphragisōmen*) and molded into His likeness.[1322] The process seems slow on earth, but John promised that "when He appears, we will be like Him, because we will see Him just as He is" (1 John 3:2). His image is our destiny.

The enemy has his own fallen and twisted version: a name and a number. Satan's mark (*charagma*) will appear on hands and foreheads, perhaps to mock Jewish phylacteries.[1323] Those who choose to worship the beast's image will bear the mark.[1324] Such people blaspheme God's name, just as the beast does.[1325] By contrast, those listed in the Lamb's book of life, including the martyrs, will escape the mark.[1326] The "seal of the living God" will protect the faithful from judgment.[1327] The beast's mark will bring judgment on its bearers.[1328] Make no mistake; the choice of marks is critical and our eternal destiny depends on it.

Revelation describes the battles that will occur at the final colliding of kingdoms. The outcome is crystal clear. The woman bearing the name, "Babylon the great," will collapse and burn.[1329] The "great harlot," who is the ultimate personification of world orders that are opposed to God, represents Satan and his evil, self-seeking dominion. At her fall, a jubilant, "Hallelujah," will erupt and another cry will announce, "The kingdom of the world has become the kingdom of our Lord and of His Christ; and He will reign forever and ever" (Rev. 11:15).

Four Hallelujahs (Revelation 19)

The cry, "Hallelujah" (Praise *Yah*), occurs four times in the New Testament, all of them in Revelation 19. A great multitude shouts the first two hallelujahs to celebrate the judgment of the "great harlot," Babylon, and her eternal burning.[1330]

The third hallelujah is an enthusiastic echo of the multitude's shouts by twenty-four elders and four living creatures worshipping God. We can imagine them holding their collective breath throughout history while generations of humans reach a crossroads. Would a promising, golden cup of pleasures lure people down a wide thoroughfare, or would they pursue a narrower path of faith accessed through a difficult gate of humility? Would they resist the enemy and invite God to mark them? Earlier crowds had gathered on plains to build towers promoting humanity or to bow to a supposed ruler-savior like Nebuchadnezzar; the crowd on heaven's plain will delight in honoring God. The third hallelujah serves as a sigh of relief for the multitude's wise choices.

The last hallelujah in the Bible is a loud one. It sounds like the cheers of an earthly crowd, mingled with roaring waters and reverberating through the sky like mighty peals of thunder. That fourth and final hallelujah will surely last the longest because "the Lord our God, the Almighty, reigns," and will continue to reign forever (v. 6).

What will we call Him then? All God's names are forever appropriate because He never changes. He will always be holy, righteous, true, and glorious. He will forever possess all knowledge and wisdom. He will be the source of light, satisfaction, and joy forevermore. Perhaps heaven's citizens will speak His personal name, *Yahweh*. However, the main significance of most biblical names will be historical, reminders of His work on earth:

The people that God once comforted will no longer have sorrow and tears. His forgiveness, mercy, and redemption will no longer need to be extended because His people will nevermore be lost. A people who have forever been made whole will no longer need His healing. God will no longer have to shield the prey from their enemies; those enemies will have been reduced to a mere memory.

He will remain almighty as the LORD of hosts, but names that contrast Him with usurpers will no longer be necessary. In heaven, His name will be the only one.[1331] In heaven, every knee will bow and swear allegiance to the One whose name is above all other names.[1332]

His earthly, messianic, mediatory, and priestly names reflect His accomplishments. Names of suffering, sacrifice, and resurrection will endure like golden trophies. The Judge's punitive work will be complete, though His justice will endure. The Shepherd-Lamb will be heaven's focal point. He will still be the all-sufficient provider, but all other pastoral roles will have been fulfilled. The New Jerusalem will be the Creator's final flourish.

It is as **Father** and **King** that He will function forever. It is as the reigning King that heaven's inhabitants will praise God eternally.

Following the last Hallelujah, John witnessed a white horse bearing the victorious Lord. Jesus, the "Faithful and True . . . the Word of God," wears a blood-dipped robe with a title draped over it that says, "King of kings, and Lord of lords" (vv. 11–16). The Revelation party is for Him. It celebrates the beginning of His uncontested reign and the final judgment of Satan. But first, the jubilant crowd anticipates the marriage supper of the Lamb (vv. 6–9).

A Heavenly Wedding

Using the same word that John used in Revelation, Paul described another sealing. It is a sealing that prepares us for the heavenly wedding. When we surrender to Christ, we are "sealed [*esphragisthēte*] in Him with the Holy Spirit of promise, who is given as a pledge [*arrabōn*] of our inheritance" (Eph. 1:13–14; 4:30; 2 Cor. 1:22; 5:5). *Arrabōn* was a deposit on a purchase, earnest money that guaranteed full payment later. Similarly, the Holy Spirit's presence with us on earth assures us that we will know God fully in heaven, just as we are fully known. The Spirit gives us a taste of that profound relationship.

In Modern Greek, *arrabona* means "engagement," a commitment to marriage. The pledge of the Spirit, reminds us that our destiny lies in intimacy. Believers from every tribe, tongue, people, and nation will be part of the bride of Christ, His beloved people. We will join God in an intimacy that is only tasted on earth in blissful marriage. "As the bridegroom rejoices over the bride, so your God will rejoice over you" (Isa. 62:5).

Later, Revelation likens the bride to the city, New Jerusalem.[1333] She will be the ultimate dwelling of God with people. She will need no temple because "the Lord God the Almighty and the Lamb are its temple" (Rev. 21:22). The city will be shadowless because the glorious presence of God will illuminate it.[1334]

The intimate relationship will exclude all pain. Instead, healing will be readily available.[1335] People will see God's glorious face and live as they have never lived before. The kings of earth will return to Him the glory He loaned the nations.[1336]

Having filled the earth with the knowledge of God's glory, His people will finally enjoy their destiny. They will be like a typical Jewish bride of Jesus' time. An escort of her lamp-bearing friends will sweep her along to a new mansion, which her groom will have built as an extension of his father's house.[1337] Her wait will be over. Her ecstasy will begin. She will bear His name, shine with His likeness, and enjoy His presence forever.

Writing a Review or Sharing about *The Name Quest*

If you enjoyed *The Name Quest* please spread the word so that other people can be blessed. Honest book reviews play a big part in helping a book succeed. Posting reviews on sites like Amazon.com and Goodreads.com is relatively simple. You can write one review and post it in several places. Just find *The Name Quest* on the site and then find the place to paste your review. Also, why not paste your review into your favorite Social Media or include it in an e-mail to friends with a link to www.NamesForGod.net?

In order of priority, I would appreciate posts to the following. Please remember to give the book a star rating:

Amazon.com
*Shelfari.com (if you have an Amazon account, the login is the same)
Barnes and Noble.com
*Crossreads.com
Other reader sites that you know of.

*Goodreads.com

Books.google.com
*LibraryThing.com

Sites marked * require that you set up a simple free account.

Arise

John had fallen face down before the Son of Man. His encounter ended with a simple gesture. Characteristic of Jesus' life mission and the tenor of His kingdom, the Son of Man extended a hand and an invitation to a man groveling in the dust.[1338] John had no reason to be afraid. On the contrary, Jesus enables everyone to rise above his or her trampled image and to be transformed into the fullness of glory—the image of God.

ABOUT THE AUTHOR

John Avery is a trained teacher with over thirty years experience as a Bible teaching pastor, small group leader, and missionary. He has lived in England, Israel, Africa, and the Caribbean, ministering with Youth With A Mission (YWAM) and local churches. He and his wife, Janet, now make their home in Oregon. John likes to hike, snowshoe, and cross country ski. John writes a regular Bible devotional on www.BibleMaturity.com and maintains a comprehensive resource for all the names of God at www. NamesForGod.net.

ENDNOTES

Prologue

1   This quotation is often wrongly attributed to Mark Twain.

2   Wikipedia article on Babylon. Sadaam Hussein began reconstruction of Babylon in 1983. It is now a World Heritage Site.

Introduction

3   YHWH, *Yah*, *'El ro'i*, Jealous, Redeemer, Lord of Hosts, the Lord our righteousness, and God of all the earth. The Encyclopedia Judaica lists *'Adonai*, *'El*, *'Eloah*, *'Elohim*, *Yhwh*, *'El 'elyon*, *'El 'olam*, *'El shaddai*, *'El ro'i*, and *'El berith* as names of God and says the rest are descriptions of His nature rather than true names. Hartman, Louis F., *et al.* "God, Names of." *Encyclopaedia Judaica*. Ed. Michael Berenbaum and Fred Skolnik. 2nd ed. Vol. 7. Detroit: Macmillan Reference USA, 2007. 672–678. *Gale Virtual Reference Library*. Web. 6 Apr. 2012.

4   Throughout this book, the first mention of a name of God and important subsequent mentions are in bold. Scripture references and the Hebrew or Greek words often appear in a sidebar.

5   E. Peterson, *The Jesus Way* (Wm. B Eerdmans Publishing Co. 2007), p. 25–26.

6   In her classic devotional on the Song of Songs, Jeanne Guyon (1648–1717) identified the Bridegroom with the "Rose of Sharon" and the "Lily of the Valley." In fact, it is more likely they are the words of the bride about herself. Some other writers have continued to apply the names allegorically to Jesus.

7   James 2:19 and Mark 12:29 quote Zech. 14:9 and the Jewish "*Shema*" of
       Deut. 6:4. Some people take *'El 'ekhad* as a title of God. See Marvin R.
       Wilson, *Our Father Abraham* (Wm. B. Eerdmans, 1989), p. 125 and *NTPG*
       p. 259.

8   Other examples are the "one day" of Gen. 1:5, "one flesh" of a couple in
       Gen. 2:24, "a cluster of grapes" in Num. 13:23, "one assembly" of Ezra
       2:64, and a joined stick in Ezek. 37:17.

9   Throughout the book, I will use the capitalized "LORD" to indicate that
       the underlying word is *Yahweh*, just as the NASB does (Chapter 2 explains
       this more).

10   E.g. *Yahweh 'Elohim* (LORD God) in Gen. 2:4; 3:23 and *'El 'Elohim
       Yahweh* (the Mighty One, God, the LORD) in Ps. 50:1.

11   Wayne Grudem points out that God is not a collection of attributes but
       a singularity. Wayne Grudem, *Systematic Theology* (Inter-Varsity Press and
       Zondervan Publishing House, 1994) p. 177–180.

Chapter 1

12   Num. 26:53.
13   Isa. 4:1.
14   Abraham is an example in Gen. 12:2; 17:4–6.
15   Gen. 22:14; 33:20; Ex. 17:15; Judg. 6:24; Ezek. 48:35.
16   1 Chron. 17:23–24.
17   Ex. 9:16; Josh. 9:9; Neh. 9:10; Isa. 63:12–14; Rom. 9:17. For other
       examples, see 1 Chron. 17:21; Pss. 79:9; 102:18–22; 142:7.
18   Pss. 30:4; 97:12; 102:12; Hos. 12:5.
19   Ex. 3:15–16 and Hos. 12:5, where KJV has "memorial."
20   Isa. 26:8; see also Ps. 135:13; Prov. 10:7.
21   Ex. 20:7.
22   Lev. 19:12; 22:32.
23   Gen. 48:16.
24   2 Sam. 18:18; see also Ps. 49:10–11.
25   Nah. 1:14; see also Deut. 7:24.
26   Deut. 29:20; Ps. 9:5; Isa. 65:15.
27   Jer. 23:16–22.
28   Ex. 5:23; 1 Chron. 21:19; 2 Chron. 33:18; Jer. 20:9; 44:16; James 5:10.
29   Deut. 18:18–22; Jer. 14:14–16.
30   Acts 19:13–15.
31   Pss. 44:5; 118:10–12.
32   In 2 Chron. 14:11 King Asa appealed to God for help on that basis. The
       sense of serving in His name, as the priests did, is similar (Deut. 21:5).
33   1 Sam. 17:45–47.
34   Mic. 4:5.
35   Josh. 7:8–9; 1 Sam. 12:22.
36   Deut. 28:9–10.
37   Jer. 15:16.
38   Matt. 7:21–23.
39   Ps. 118:26; Matt. 21:9.

40   John 10:25.

41   Mark 16:17–18.

42   John 14:13–14; 15:16; 16:23–24.

43   1 Cor. 1:10.

44   2 Thess. 1:11–12.

45   Because "testament" doesn't mean much these days, and since it is preliminary rather than "old," I would prefer to call it the "book of the foundational covenant." However, because that is clumsy, I will continue with the convention of using "Old" and "New" Testaments. Biblical covenants were like ancient legal contracts.

46   Rev. 19:12–13.

47   1 Cor. 1:2.

48   A possible Akkadian root of the name means, "To be weak."

49   Ex. 34:5; Ps. 124:8.

50   Gen. 12:8.

51   John 1:12; 3:18; 20:31; Acts 4:12; 1 John 3:23.

52   Ps. 33:21; 1 John 5:13.

53   Matt. 18:20.

54   Ps. 61:5; Rev. 11:18; see also Mal. 3:16; 4:2.

55   Joel 2:32; Acts 2:21; 10:43; Rom. 10:13.

56   Acts 3:6, 16; 4:7; 10, 30; James 5:14.

57   Luke 10:17; Acts 16:18.

58   2 Kings 2:24.

59   Ps. 116:4, 13, 17.

60   Ps. 54:1; Acts 4:12.

61   Zeph. 3:9–12.

62   John 17:11.

63   Pss. 9:10; 33:21.

Chapter 2

64   Gen. 4:26; 5:3, 6.

65   Deut. 32:18; Hos. 11:1. Strictly speaking, they were the Hebrew people. Later, they took the name Israel from Abraham's grandson.

66   The words "faith" and "belief" mean essentially the same thing in the Bible, especially in the New Testament where they are from the same Greek word. They are active and practical.

67   Ex. 2:11–15.

68   M. Buber, *Moses* (East and West Library, Oxford, 1946) p. 48.

69   The three names occur together in Ex. 34:23.

70   Dan. 2:47; 4:19; 24; 5:23 all have the Aramaic alternative, *mare'*.

71   Gen. 18:12; 24:9–10.

72   2 Sam. 11:9; 1 Kings 18:7.

73   Prov. 25:13; Isa. 26:13; Jer. 27:4. In Amos 4:1 *'adonim* is translated "husbands."

74   Ps. 123:2.

75   Mal. 1:6.

76 T. E. Lawrence, *Seven Pillars of Wisdom* (Penguin MC, Estate of T. E. Lawrence 1926, Reprinted 1964), p. 41.

77 www.etymonline.com "God," 2001–2012 Douglas Harper.

78 Ps. 89:7 has "Greatly feared." For the rest, see Deut. 7:21; 10:17; Neh. 1:5; 4:14 (said of Adonai); 9:32; Dan. 9:4.

79 Compare with Matt. 27:46, probably quoting Ps. 22:1, which prophetically portrayed Jesus' suffering.

80 The derivation is disputed, but J. B. Scott, TWOT p. 41, says this is more likely.

81 R. B. Girdlestone, *Synonyms of the Old Testament* (Hendrickson Publishers, Inc. 2000), p. 34.

82 I have inserted the English form of the Hebrew names in several of the following passages.

83 Other examples of plural pronouns with *'Elohim*: Gen. 3:22; 11:7; Isa. 6:8. Plural verbs with *'Elohim*: Gen. 20:13; 35:7; 2 Sam. 7:23; Ps. 58:11. Plural adjectives with *'Elohim*: Josh. 24:19; Ps. 149:2; Eccl. 12:1; Isa. 54:5.

84 *Mere Christianity* by C. S. Lewis, copyright © C. S. Lewis Pte. Ltd. 1942, 1943, 1944, 1952. Extract reprinted by permission.

85 By the Masoretes, who made copies of the Old Testament in the 7th – 10th centuries AD.

86 Raymond Martin, *Pugio Fidei*, AD 1270, p. 559. This name appears in the KJV Ex. 6:3; Ps. 83:18.

87 For example, Theodoret's *Exodum* and Clement of Alexandria's *Stromata*; see also the Greek Dead Sea Scroll 4Q120, frag. 20:4, which renders *YHWH*, *IAŌ*.

88 Num. 13:8, 16.

89 Ps. 115:18.

90 In this combination, *YHWH* has the vowel points of *'Elohim*. The English capitalization indicates the underlying *Yahweh*.

91 Ex. 6:3; 15:3; Deut. 28:58; Ps. 83:18; Isa. 42:8; Jer. 16:21; 33:2; Hos. 12:5; Amos 5:8; 9:6.

92 According to Jewish tradition, the number of divine names that require the scribe's special care is seven: *'El*, *'Elohim*, *'Adonai*, *YHWH*, *'Ehyeh 'asher 'ehyeh*, *Shaddai*, and *Tseva'ot*. H. Lockyer, *All the Divine Names and Titles in the Bible* (Zondervan Publishing House, 1975), p. 191. *Soferim* iv (8th century AD) gives a Jewish interpretation of Deut. 12:3–4.

93 The priests spoke it in the daily blessing of Num. 6:27 and ten times on the Day of Atonement (Ecclus. 50:20–23; *Tosefta Yoma* ii. 39b).

94 The vowel points did not provide the missing vowels to guide pronunciation, contrary to what those who believe that "Jehovah" is the correct pronunciation suppose.

95 Mark 14:61–62.

96 Dan. 4:26; Matt. 26:64; Mark 14:62; Luke 22:69.

97 2 Peter 1:17.

98 Heb. 1:3; 8:1.

99 Mighty One: Gen. 49:24; Ps 132:2, 5; Isa. 1:24; 49:26; 60:16. Fear of Isaac: Gen. 31:42, 53.

100   Targ. Ex. 19:17 (the people meet the *memra'*); *Targum Deut.* 9:3 (the *memra'* is the consuming fire).
101   CD Geniza A Col. 15:1–2 in Michael Wise, Martin Abegg Jr. and Edward Cook, *A New Translation, The Dead Sea Scrolls* (Harper One, 2005), p. 68. Italics original.
102   Acts 5:41; 3 John 7.
103   When Simeon the Righteous died (*Tosefta Yoma*).
104   Ex. 3:2.
105   Gen. 32:29 is another example of God's representative withholding his name. The word *pele'*, translated "wonderful" or "incomprehensible," is part of the name "Wonderful Counselor" (Isa. 9:6).
106   Ex. 33:14; Isa. 63:8–9.
107   W. Grudem calls him a theophany or appearance of God and lists His appearances. W. Grudem, *Systematic Theology* (Inter-Varsity Press and Zondervan Publishing House, 1994), pp. 189, 229, 401.
108   J. A. Motyer, *Introducing the Old Testament* (Church Pastoral-Aid Society, 1960) p.11.
109   Ex. 3:4.
110   *Yahweh* is found in Genesis 165 times and is used by the patriarchs at least 45 times. Much of the following section is based on J. A. Motyer, *The Revelation of the Divine Name* (Tyndale Press, 1959).
111   Gen. 12:1, 4, 7; 15:1.
112   Abraham's servant (Gen. 24:12, 27), Laban (Gen. 24:31, 35, 40, 44, 50, 51; 30:27; 31:49), Lot (Gen. 19:14), Sarah (Gen. 16:2, 5), and Rachel and Leah (Gen. 29:32–35; 30:24).
113   Gen. 4:26.
114   Gen. 14:18–23.
115   Gen. 16:13.
116   Gen. 21:33.
117   Gen. 28:21; 31:13; 33:20.
118   Gen. 22:14.
119   Gen. 17:1; 35:11; 48:3.
120   Gen. 28:3; 43:14; 49:25.
121   Ex 6:3 (NIV).
122   The Septuagint, a translation of the Old Testament made 300–200 BC by seventy scribes for Greek-speaking Jews in Egypt and popular throughout the region during New Testament times. It is often abbreviated with the Roman for seventy, LXX.
123   Reprinted by permission. *Searching for God Knows What* p. 147, Donald Miller, 2004, Thomas Nelson Inc. Nashville, Tennessee. All rights reserved. (Italics original).
124   J. I. Packer, *God's Words* (InterVarsity Press, 1981), p. 46.
125   Ex. 3:5.
126   J. Barton Payne in *Theological Wordbook of the Old Testament* Ed. R. Laird Harris (Moody Press, 1980), p. 211
127   Ex. 4:1–9.
128   J. I. Packer, *God's Words* (InterVarsity Press, 1981), p. 47.

129   J. I. Packer, *God's Words* (InterVarsity Press, 1981), pp. 47–48.
130   Ex. 3:11; 4:1, 10, 13.
131   Ex. 3:18; 5:2–3; 9:1. Later, settlers in Samaria call Yahweh "the **god of the land**" (2 Kings 17:26–28).
132   See also 2 Sam. 7:22–23; Jer. 16:14–21; 32:20; Dan. 9:15.
133   Ex. 14:4.
134   Ex. 15:1–21.
135   Ex. 20:1–2; Deut. 4:34–35.

Chapter 3

136   Dan. 5:23.
137   Isa. 24:16 uses another word, *tsevi*, (also meaning, beauty and honor) "Glory to the Righteous One." The name **Glory of Israel** (NIV, NASB), Pre-eminence of Israel (YLT), or Strength of Israel (KJV) is *Netsakh Yisra'el* (1 Sam. 15:29).
138   Gen. 31:1 (KJV); Isa. 8:7.
139   In Gen. 13:2, the related word, *kaved*, describes Abram as "rich."
140   Col. 1:11; 2 Thess. 1:9.
141   S. Aalen, "Glory, Honour" in *Dictionary of New Testament Theology*, Ed. Colin Brown (Zondervan, 1986) 2:44–48. *Doxa* is where the English word "doxology" (words of praise) comes from.
142   H. R. Jones in *New Bible Commentary* (Inter-Varsity Press, 1970), p. 117.
143   E. F. Harrison, Glory in *Evangelical Dictionary of Theology*, Ed. W. A. Elwell (Baker Books, 1984), p. 443.
144   Ex. 13:21; 16:7, 10; Num. 12:5; Deut. 31:15.
145   Ex. 24:15–18.
146   Ex. 24:17–18; Judg. 13:20; 1 Kings 18:38. 1 Tim. 6:16 says that God lives in unapproachable light (*phōs aprositon*)—the same expression Philo used for the glory on Mount Sinai.
147   Earthquake or shaking (Ex. 19:16–20; Judg. 5:4–5; Pss. 68:8; 77:18; 97:1–6; 114:4, 7; Rev. 15:8), darkness (1 Kings 8:12 especially NIV and KJV), tempest (Nah. 1:3), trumpet (Ex. 19:16, 19; 20:18), at the end time (Matt. 24:31; 1 Cor. 15:52; 1 Thess. 4:16), and falling (Josh. 5:13–15; Ezek. 1:28; 3:23; 44:4; Dan. 8:17; Rev. 1:17; 19:10). Heb. 12:18–19 lists various signs, all linked elsewhere with His presence. See also Deut. 4:11.
148   Isa. 6:1–5; see also Ezek. 9:3; 10:18–19.
149   John 12:41.
150   2 Sam. 6:2.
151   Ezek. 10:4.
152   Taken from *Systematic Theology* p. 220 by Wayne Grudem. Copyright © 1994 by W. Grudem. Used by permission of Zondervan. www.zondervan.com and Inter-Varsity Press.
153   *Khanaf* is also translated "fold" (Hag. 2:12), "corner" (Num. 15:38; Deut. 22:12), and "edge" (1 Sam. 15:27; 24:4, 5, 11; Ezek. 5:3).
154   In classical Greek, the word refers to Venus.
155   Rev. 2:28.

156   From Wayne Grudem, *Systematic Theology* (Inter-Varsity Press and Zondervan Publishing House, 1994), pp. 219–221. He also describes beauty as the corollary of perfection.

157   Isa. 9:2; 42:6; 49:6; 60:1–3.

158   Ezek. 1:26–28. The bright figure on the throne appeared in the clouds overhead, suggesting a circular rainbow surrounding the throne rather like the halo that is sometimes seen around the sun or moon when they are behind high clouds.

159   Isa. 43:20–21.

160   Ps. 8:1–9; Acts 14:17; Rom. 1:20.

161   See also 1 Chron. 16:23–29; Ps. 72:18.

162   Judg. 13:18 uses the word *feli'*.

163   Ex. 8:19; 31:18; Deut. 9:10; Luke 11:20.

164   Isa. 53:1; 63:12; John 12:38.

165   Either His voice thundering or His voice manifested in the crashing of a thunderstorm.

166   Heb. 4:12.

167   Gen. 1:1–3, 6, 9, 11.

168   Ps. 107:20.

169   Gen. 27:33, 38–40.

170   Isa. 55:11.

171   The word *aphthartos* means un-decaying and imperishable in contrast to men who do perish and decay.

172   The idea is alluded to in Titus 2:14; 1 Peter 2:9.

173   Rom. 2:29 may include a play on the words.

174   See also Rom. 9:4–5.

175   Ps. 86:9.

176   Ps. 96:3.

177   Ezek. 10:3–4,18–19; 11:22–24.

178   Ezek. 28:22.

179   Ps. 79:9 says help, deliverance, and forgiveness bring Him glory too.

180   Ezek. 43:1–5; 48:35.

181   Ezek. 20:9; 36:20–22.

182   Matt. 1:20; Luke 1:11, 20, 26, 41, 67.

183   See also Matt. 17:1–8; Mark 9:2–8.

184   Prov. 8:12, 22–31. The Greek-speaking Jewish philosopher Philo identified wisdom with *logos*. Memra' (word) is a circumlocution for "God" in Aramaic Scriptures. See also *NTPG* p. 413–4 on Ecclus. 24:1–23.

185   Rom. 16:27; see also (in KJV) 1 Tim. 1:17 and Jude 25.

186   Prov. 8:1, 22–36; 9:1–6; Matt. 12:42; 1 Cor. 1:24, 30. In Matt. 23:34 Jesus said, "I am sending . . ." but in Luke 11:49 "the wisdom of God said 'I will send . . . .'"

187   Mark 4:21.

188   Rev. 19:12–15.

189   Num. 9:15–22; 1 Kings 8:10–11; 2 Chron. 5:13–14.

190   John 2:11.

191   Ps. 96:3.

192   See also Matt. 9:8; Luke 5:25–26; 13:13, 17; 17:15; 18:43; Acts 4:21.
193   John 11:4–6, 40.
194   John 7:39; 12:16, 23–28; 13:31–32; 1 Peter 1:11, 21.
195   Heb. 2:10.
196   Rom. 8:17–18.
197   2 Cor. 4:17.
198   John 21:19.
199   Acts 1:9–11.
200   Mark 8:38; 13:26; Luke 21:27; 2 Thess. 1:10; Titus 2:13; 1 Peter 4:13; 5:1.
201   Rev. 21:23.
202   Col. 3:4; 1 Peter 5:4.
203   Ezek. 37:27; Zech. 2:5; Rev. 7:15.

Chapter 4

204   Ex. 25:8; 29:45–46.
205   Lev. 9:6, 23–24; Num. 20:6.
206   Rom. 1:20.
207   Heb. 8:5. The Law was a shadow of good things to come (Heb. 10:1–2).
208   Pss. 11:4; 22:3; 103:19; 113:5; 123:1.
209   2 Sam. 6:2; 2 Kings 19:15; 1 Chron. 13:6; Pss. 80:1; 99:1; Isa. 37:16.
210   Pss. 89:14; 97:2; Isa. 66:1; Matt. 5:34–35.
211   1 Chron. 28:2.
212   Ps. 99:5.
213   Rom. 3:23.
214   Gen. 3:24.
215   Ex. 33:7.
216   Deut. 12:5, 11; 1 Kings 8:10–21.
217   Ex. 29:43; 40:34–35.
218   1 Kings 8:18; 48–49; 9:3; 2 Kings 21:4; Ps. 122:3–4; Isa. 18:7.
219   1 Kings 8:11; 2 Chron. 7:1–3.
220   Isa. 60:13.
221   Ps. 29:9; Hag. 1:8.
222   1 Sam. 4:4–7; Pss. 80:1; 99:1; Isa. 37:16; Ezek. 10:1–4.
223   The first five books of the Old Testament are called the *Torah*, which means "instruction."
224   Lev. 9:6.
225   No one (Ex. 33:20), Jacob (Gen. 32:30), Moses (Ex. 3:6), Elijah (1 Kings 19:13), and Samson and his parents (Judg. 6:22–23; 13:22).
226   Lev. 9:21–24; Num. 14:14.
227   Ex. 24:9–11.
228   Deut. 4:12; 5:22–27.
229   Deut. 18:15–19.
230   See also Deut. 34:10. Num. 12:8 uses the expression, "mouth to mouth."
231   Ex. 33:18–20; John 1:18; 1 Tim. 6:16.
232   Ex. 33:7–10.
233   Ex. 33:12–17.

234 *'Akhor* is not an anatomical term; it is not meant to contrast with "face." Rather, *'akhor* is a directional word, speaking of what came behind God, rather like a wake following a boat (R. L. Harris, TWOT, pp. 33–34).

235 V. P. Hamilton in *Theological Wordbook of the Old Testament* Ed. R. Laird Harris (Moody Press, 1980), p. 727.

236 Jonah 1:3.

237 Ex. 33:19.

238 H. R. Jones in *New Bible Commentary* (Inter-Varsity Press, 1970), p. 138.

239 The collection seems important, it is repeated in different forms several times through the Old Testament (Num. 14:17–18; Deut. 4:31; 2 Chron. 30:9; Neh. 9:17, 31; Pss. 86:5, 15; 103:8; 111:4; 116:5; 145:8; Joel 2:13; Jonah 4:2).

240 Isa. 49:15. *Rakhem* denotes a deep inward feeling of loving concern, usually of a superior for an inferior. Pity, compassion, and mercy are all part of it (L. J. Coppes, TWOT 2:841–3).

241 Pss. 86:15; 145:8–9.

242 In 2 Cor. 1:3 *oktirmos* means "pity" or "compassion," hence "Father of compassion" in the NIV.

243 *Khannun* is sometimes translated "mercy" but the emphasis is on the graciousness with which that mercy is extended (E. Yamauchi, TWOT 1:303–4).

244 Ex. 33:19; see also Rom. 9:14–16.

245 Ex. 32:10, 12.

246 Jer. 31:3.

247 Pss. 57:10; 108:4.

248 John 18:36–37.

249 Pss. 57:10; 108:4.

250 Deut. 32:4; Lam. 3:23; Isa. 49:7; Hos. 11:12.

251 Rom. 3:3–5.

252 1 Kings 1:36.

253 2 Cor. 1:20.

254 Isa. 53:4.

255 So do Ps. 86:5 and Dan. 9:9 speaking of Adonai.

256 Num. 14:10–12; Ps. 99:8.

257 Gen. 4:14; Deut. 31:17–18; Isa. 59:2.

258 The context is God raising up an enemy king, Cyrus, to repatriate the Jewish exiles. See also Isa. 8:17.

259 John 1:18; 6:46; 1 John 4:12.

260 Ex. 34: 5–17.

261 Ex. 34:29–35. The word for Moses' veil is different from the temple veil.

262 Rick Searfoss was pilot of Colombia (STS-58), launched October 18, 1993, Atlantis (STS-76), March 22, 1996, and commanded Colombia (STS-90), April 17, 1998. www.wikipedia.org/wiki/Rick_Searfoss.

263 H. C. G. Moule says *Theotēs*, the word for Deity, refers to the totality of God, His entire Nature. H. C. G. Moule, *Colossian Studies* (New York: Hodder and Stoughton, 1898), p. 144.

264 John 17:11–12.

265   KJV has "Son."
266   John 3:16–17 my paraphrase.
267   2 Cor. 4:4.
268   Heb. 2:10.
269   Dr. Ken Blue, counselor, teacher, and author, at a conference in Salem
       October 2004.
270   Eph. 1:12, 14; Rev. 7:9.
271   John 12:20–23.
272   Rom. 11:25; 16:25–27; Eph. 3:2–9.
273   Phil. 2:10–11.
274   Ex. 34:29–35. It is not clear where Paul got the idea that the glory on
       Moses' face faded (2 Cor. 3:13).
275   The word *katoptrizomenoi* could also mean, "reflecting."
276   *Metamorphoō* is also the root verb for "transfigured."
277   In Col.1:26–27 Paul uses a plural "you," this could refer either to
       individuals who comprise the church, or to the Spirit of Christ dwelling in
       His body as a whole, in Colossae and elsewhere. Both are true.
278   1 Cor. 3:16; 6:19.
279   Hag. 2:5–9.
280   Eph. 5:26–27.
281   Rev. 1:10–17.
282   2 Thess. 2:14.
283   John 5:44; 7:18; 8:50.
284   Luke 4:6–8.
285   Heb. 5:5–6.
286   John 17:1–5.

Chapter 5

287   Lev. 20:3; 22:2; 1 Chron. 16:10, 35; 29:16; Pss. 30:4 (using *zekher*); 33:21;
       97:12 (using *zekher*); 103:1; 105:3; 106:47; 111:9; Isa. 57:15; Ezek. 20:39;
       36:22; 39:7, 25; 43:7–8; Amos 2:7.
288   Matt. 6:9; Luke 11:2.
289   Lev. 22:32.
290   Alan F. Johnson, taken from "Revelation" in Vol 12 *The Expositor's Bible
       Commentary* Ed. Frank E. Gaebelein Copyright © 1981 by The Zondervan
       Corporation p. 463. Used by permission of Zondervan. www.zondervan.
       com
291   Donald Guthrie, *New Testament Theology* (Inter-Varsity Press, 1981), p. 99.
292   Isa. 5:16; Hab. 1:13.
293   The Holy Spirit is only mentioned in the Old Testament this way three
       times (Ps. 51:11; Isa. 63:10, 11). Rom. 1:4 is near the Hebrew expression.
294   Josh. 24:19.
295   Taken from *Walk Leviticus* by Jeffrey E. Feinberg. Copyright © 2001, p.54.
       All rights reserved. Used by permission of Messianic Jewish Publishers, 6120
       Day Long Lane, Clarksville, MD 21029. www.messianicjewish.net.
296   Ex. 19:16; 24:17; Deut. 5:25–27.

297   1 Sam. 5:1–12.

298   In Jer. 3:12 it translates into God's claim, "I am gracious."

299   John 17:11, 25.

300   Acts 2:27, 31–32; 13:35; see also Rev. 15:4; 16:5.

301   Hab. 1:13.

302   Rom. 3:25.

303   Ezek. 36:22–23; 39:7, 25.

304   J. I. Packer, *God's Words* (InterVarsity Press, 1981), pp. 171–2.

305   Eph. 3:19; see also 2 Peter 1:4.

306   Isa. 40:6–8.

307   War: Lam. 2:3; Joel 2:1–5, God's tongue: Isa. 30:27, 30.

308   Deut. 9:3–4.

309   Deut. 4:23–24.

310   Matt. 25:41.

311   Job 9:2 asks a similar question: How can a man be right before God?

312   Jer. 51:56 is literally "God of recompenses."

313   Judg. 11:27; Job 23:7; Pss. 50:6; 58:11; 75:7; 94:2.

314   Hos. 11:9.

315   Gen. 18:25; see also Heb. 12:23.

316   Ps. 7:9.

317   Pss. 89:14; 97:2; 119:137; see also Deut. 32:3–4.

318   Acts 10:42; see also 2 Tim. 4:1–2.

319   1 Peter 1:15–17; 2:23.

320   Luke 18:1–8.

321   Matt. 25:31–46; John 3:17; Acts 17:30–31.

322   Ps. 94:1 is literally "God of vengeances."

323   Elmer B. Smick in *Theological Wordbook of the Old Testament* Ed. R. Laird Harris (Moody Press, 1980), p. 599.

324   Gen. 3:10.

325   In Jer. 32:40, the same fear helps men to stay within the new covenant relationship.

326   Prov. 9:10; Mic. 6:9.

327   W. Barclay, *New Testament Words* (The Westminster Press, Philadelphia, 1974), p. 232

328   See also Deut. 7:21; 10:17; Neh. 4:14; 9:32; Ps. 99:3. *Yare'* is the root of both "fear" and "awesome."

329   Neh. 1:11; Isa. 50:10.

330   Ps. 86:11; Mic. 6:9; 1 Tim. 6:1–2; 2 Tim. 2:19.

331   2 Chron. 6:24–27; Mal. 1:6–7; Rev. 2:13; 3:8.

332   Lev. 22:31–33; Ps. 74:10, 18.

333   Lev. 24:10–23.

334   Mal. 2:2.

335   Nathan Stone, *The Names of God* (The Moody Bible Institute of Chicago, 1944), p. 113.

336   In Josh. 22:34 the men of Reuben built an altar as a witness of their devotion to Yahweh.

337   Ex. 34:5–8.

338   Isa. 57:15.

339   Rom. 11:22–23.

340   Lev. 9:24; 1 Kings 18:38; 1 Chron. 21:26; 2 Chron. 7:1. *'Akhal* means, "To eat up." Each time God dramatically sent fire from heaven, a significant sacrifice was happening.

341   Ex. 31:13; Lev. 20:8; Ezek. 20:12; 37:28.

342   Nathan Stone, *The Names of God* (The Moody Bible Institute of Chicago, 1944), p. 103.

343   Ezek. 37:26–28.

344   Isa. 41:14; 43:14; 47:4; 48:17; 49:7; 54:5 (once He says He is Savior Isa. 43:3).

345   O. Chambers, "It is Finished" in *My Utmost for His Highest* (Barbour and Company, Inc. 1963), p. 326 (Nov 21 devotion).

346   Isa. 51:22; Matt. 26:39.

347   Mark 1:24; Luke 4:34. So did Simon Peter in John 6:69.

348   Acts 3:14; see also Isa. 24:16; Acts 7:52; 22:14; Heb. 1:8–9.

349   Gal. 3:10–13; Deut. 21:23.

350   Ps. 85:8–10.

351   John 14:27; Rom. 5:1; Phil. 4:7; Col. 1:19–23.

352   W. Kaiser, *The Messiah in the Old Testament* (Zondervan Publishing House 1995), pp. 52–53 offers an alternative meaning for the word **Shiloh**: "peacemaker" (Gen. 49:10; Ezek. 21:27).

353   Rom. 15:33; 16:20; Phil. 4:9; 1 Thess. 5:23; Heb. 13:20.

354   John 12:47–48.

355   Hence, NIV translates *hilasmos* "atoning sacrifice."

356   I. H. Marshall, *The Epistles of John* in New International Commentary (Grand Rapids, Eerdmans, 1978), p. 118.

357   Lev. 16:14–15.

358   See also 1 Cor. 1:30 and Heb. 10:22.

359   Rev. 7:14.

360   Eph. 5:25–27.

361   Heb. 10:10, 14.

362   J. I. Packer, *God's Words* (InterVarsity Press, 1981), p. 177.

363   Jer. 23:6; 33:16.

364   Rom. 8:1; 2 Cor. 5:21.

365   1 Thess. 5:23.

366   Josh. 24:19; Luke 1:78–79.

367   Luke 7:40–50.

Chapter 6

368   Isa. 47:4; 51:15; 54:5; Jer. 32:18; Amos 4:13. **God of hosts** is also said to be His name in Amos 5:27.

369   King: Jer. 46:18; 48:15; 51:57, God of Israel: Isa. 48:2, Redeemer: Isa. 47:4; Jer. 50:34, Creator: Isa. 54:5; Jer. 10:16; 31:35; 51:19.

370   The translation was available to the New Testament writers and the first church.

371   Confusingly, they also used *pantokratōr* to translate *shaddai* (discussed in Chapter 12). So in the English Old Testament, "Almighty" can indicate *Shaddai* or *Yahweh tseva'ot.*

372   2 Cor. 6:18 may quote 2 Sam. 7:8, which, in the Greek, says that *Kyrios pantokratōr* spoke to David.

373   Rev. 1:8; 4:8; 11:17; 15:3; 16:7, 14; 19:6, 15; 21:22.

374   Rev. 19:6 but there is no difference in the Greek or Latin to justify a different translation from other verses. In fact, *omnipotens* is only used to translate *shaddai* in the Latin Old Testament, never for *tseva'ot.*

375   Rom. 9:29 (which quotes Isa. 1:9) and James 5:4.

376   Taken from *The Names of God* © Copyright 1967 by Andrew Jukes p. 63. Published by Kregel Publications, Grand Rapids, MI. Used by permission of the publisher. All rights reserved.

377   Never lies (Num. 23:19; Heb. 6:18; Titus 1:2), denial (2 Tim. 2:13), temptation (James 1:13), shuns evil (Hab. 1:13 NIV), unchanging (Heb. 13:8 and Heb. 1:11–12, which quotes Ps. 102:25–27).

378   Ps. 24:8.

379   Deut. 7:21; Neh. 1:5; 4:14; 9:32.

380   Ps. 40:16.

381   Josh. 7:9; Ezek. 36:23.

382   Ps. 8:1, 9; see also Jer. 10:6 (where "might" is *gevurah*) and Mic. 5:4 (where *ge'on* meaning "exaltation" is translated "majesty").

383   Josh. 22:22; Ps. 50:1.

384   Power (Matt. 26:64; Mark 14:62; Luke 22:69 NIV has Mighty God), Majestic Glory (2 Peter 1:17).

385   David H. Stern has *HaG'dulah BaM'romim* in his *Jewish New Testament Commentary* (Jewish New Testament Publications Inc. 1992), p. 664.

386   1 Cor. 1:24.

387   Titus 2:13.

388   Ex. 38:8; Num. 4:23, 35, 39, 43; 8:24; 31:14.

389   Created things (Gen. 2:1; Ps. 33:6), celestial bodies (Deut. 4:19; Isa. 40:26).

390   Amos 4:13; Isa. 37:16; 54:5; Jer. 10:16.

391   Pss. 103:20–21; 148:1–2; Luke 2:13; Matt. 26:53.

392   1 Kings 22:19; 2 Chron. 18:18.

393   Ex. 6:26; 12:41; 1 Sam. 17:45.

394   Isa. 13:1–5.

395   Eph. 6:12.

396   Jer. 10:11–16.

397   Isa. 31:1–5.

398   Kay Arthur, *Lord I Want to Know You* (Multnomah Books, 1992), p. 156.

399   Ps. 46:7–11.

400   *Sar* (captain) can also mean "commander" or "prince." It is similar to the Aramaic word in Dan. 8:11.

401   Deut. 25:17–18.

402   Ex. 17:16.

403   1 Sam. 1:3, 11; 4:4; Ps. 99:1.

404   1 Sam. 4:5–11, 21–22; Ps. 78:61.

405	1 Sam. 2:13–14, 22.
406	1 Sam. 5:1 – 6:12.
407	Isa. 6:3–5; Rev. 4:6–8.
408	Isa. 6:6–7.
409	Isa. 6:9–10; Matt. 13:14–15.
410	2 Sam. 11:1–27. David's house stood at the top of Mount Zion, other houses were squeezed below on the steep hillside.
411	Num. 21:6–9.
412	Isa. 11:1–2, 10–12.
413	John 3:14–15; 12:32–33.
414	Eph. 1:19–22; Col. 2:14–16.
415	1 Sam. 13:14.

Chapter 7

416	From p. 53, *The Knowledge of the Holy* by A. W. Tozer, © 1961 Aiden Wilson Tozer. Reprinted by permission of HarperCollins Publishers.
417	This is the one psalm attributed to Moses, not David.
418	Ps. 90:12; see also Ps. 39:4–5.
419	Psalm 8 is another meditation on the smallness of man contrasted with the endlessness of God.
420	Isa. 40:26.
421	*Shabbath*, 55a.
422	Ps. 117:2.
423	Ps. 31:5 and descriptively in Ex. 34:6; Pss. 57:10; 108:4.
424	Isa. 26:4; see also Hab. 1:12.
425	Rom.1:20–23.
426	Dan. 7:9–10; Rev. 1:9–18.
427	John 14:6; Col. 1:16–18.
428	See also John 17:24.
429	Gen. 9:16; 17:7; 1 Chron. 16:17, 34, 41; 2 Chron. 5:13; Ps. 136:1–36.
430	Ps 111:3 (using *'ad*); Prov. 8:23; Isa. 51:6, 8.
431	See also Ps. 45:6 (using *'olam wa'ed*). On His reign, see Ex. 15:18; Ps. 10:16 (using *'olam wa'ed*); Ps. 145:13; Isa. 9:7; Dan. 4:3, 34; 7:14, 27; Matt. 25:34; 2 Peter 1:11.
432	Some manuscripts end with "guide us forever."
433	Num. 23:19; 1 Sam. 15:29; Ps. 119:160; Heb. 13:20.
434	Eph. 3:9–11; see also Hab. 3:6.
435	See also Eph. 1:11.
436	From p. 47, *The Knowledge of the Holy* by A. W. Tozer, © 1961 Aiden Wilson Tozer. Reprinted by permission of HarperCollins Publishers.
437	Theologians debate whether man has two or three parts and how "soul" and "spirit" fit. There are verses that seem to support both views. The Bible uses the words "spirit" and "soul" somewhat interchangeably.
438	During lunar night, the moon's surface is a frigid -153 °C.
439	Titus 1:2.
440	Matt. 7:13–14.

441 Eccl. 12:7; see also Gen. 2:7.

442 Pss. 104:29; 146:4.

443 Fire (Matt. 18:8; 25:41; Jude 7), punishment (Matt. 25:46), judgment (Mark 3:29; Heb. 6:2), and destruction (2 Thess. 1:9; Pss. 9:5–6; 92:7). Theologians views on eternal punishment range from eternal conscious torment to annihilation.

444 Isa. 56:5.

445 Ps. 139:24.

Chapter 8

446 Dan. 2:37; Ezek. 26:7; see also Ezra 7:12 where King Artaxerxes of Persia used the title for similar reasons.

447 Dan. 2:44–45.

448 Matt. 4:17; 24:14; Mark 1:14–15.

449 Dan. 11:21.

450 Rev. 11:15.

451 *New College Standard Dictionary* (Funk & Wagnall's Company, 1947), p. 505.

452 The word does not occur in the Hebrew text but is implied and appears in italics in the NASB.

453 See also Deut. 4:39; 32:37–39; Jer. 2:11; 5:7. Luke 10:17, 20 equate demons and spirits.

454 1 Cor. 8:4–6; 10:14–22.

455 Ps. 106:34–39.

456 Rom. 1:24–25.

457 Col. 3:5.

458 Reprinted by permission. *Blue Like Jazz* p. 87, Donald Miller, 2003, Thomas Nelson Inc. Nashville, Tennessee. All rights reserved.

459 Phil. 3:18–19. The word translated "appetite" is literally "belly."

460 James 1:13–14.

461 1 Cor. 10:14.

462 Matt. 6:19–34 (MSG).

463 Reprinted by permission. *Blue Like Jazz* p. 93–4, Donald Miller, 2003, Thomas Nelson Inc. Nashville, Tennessee. All rights reserved.

464 Gal. 4:3, 8–11; Col. 2:8, 20–23.

465 2 Chron. 33:22; Ps. 97:7; see also 2 Kings 19:17–18; 2 Chron. 13:9; Jer. 16:10–20.

466 1 Chron. 16:25–26; Ps. 96:4–5. "Idols" (*'elilim*) are "worthless," and perhaps, "deficient," godlets.

467 *Rab* is a prefix meaning "captain" or "chief."

468 In 2 Chron. 32:19 Sennacherib's servants used the name. In Ezra 7:19 the Persian king, Artaxerxes used it.

469 Ps. 106:35–37; Ezek. 16:20; Hos. 4:14.

470 1Kings 18:28.

471 The kings Nebuchadnezzar and Belshazzar were named in recognition of their supposed dependence on the gods Nebo and Bel (Isa. 46:1). Nebo was

the god of wisdom. Bel is another name for Ba'al and the word means "lord" or "master."

472   2 Kings 1:1–6, 16.
473   Matt. 10:25; 12:24–27; Mark 3:22–26; Luke 11:15, 18–19 (KJV has "Beelzebub" in all three). Satan's names are underlined throughout this chapter to give an idea of how many names even he has.
474   His Greek title "*Theos Epiphanes*" means "the god manifest."
475   As in Dan. 11:31; 12:11; 1 Macc. 1:54–64. Notice the similarity between *shamayim* and *shomem*.
476   Mark 13:14; Matt. 24:15.
477   Luke 21:20.
478   See also Jer. 10:3–7, 14–16.
479   Eph. 5:5.
480   Matt. 25:41.
481   John 12:31; 14:30; 16:11; Eph. 2:2. The word *archōn* means "ruler" or "prince."
482   Dan. 10:12–21. The passage also calls Archangel Michael a prince.
483   Rom. 8:38–39; Eph. 6:12; Col. 2:15.
484   Rev. 9:1, 11.
485   In 1 Tim. 4:1 (KJV/NEB) demons are called "devils," but the Greek makes a consistent distinction and states there is only one devil.
486   Mark 13:22.
487   Dan. 7:1–8, 23–28.
488   Rev. 13:1–2; 17:3.
489   Rev. 13:11–18. The word "mark" (*charagma*) is used of inscribing and engraving.
490   Rev. 13:18. The number in the manuscripts varies. Likely candidates are Nero (emperor AD 54–68) who called himself "Savior of the world," or perhaps Domitian (emperor AD 81–96). Alan F. Johnson, "Revelation" in Vol 12 *The Expositor's Bible Commentary* Ed. Frank E. Gaebelein (The Zondervan Corporation, 1981), pp. 533–536.
491   In Rev. 2:17; 3:12; 7:2–4; 9:4 the "seal" (*sphragis*) was used to indicate ownership. The early church spoke of baptism by water and the Holy Spirit as a seal.
492   Rev. 1:4, 8; 4:8; 11:17; 16:5 cf. Rev. 17:8, 11. My italics.
493   1 John 2:18–22; 4:1–3; 2 John 7.
494   The title "son of destruction/perdition (*apoleia*)" is the same one that Jesus used to describe Judas in John 17:12, consequently, some have mistakenly equated Judas with the Antichrist.
495   2 Thess. 2:8–9.
496   And perhaps false prophets (*pseudoprophētai*) and false Christs (*pseudochristoi*).
497   Isa. 14:12–17; Ezek. 28:1–19.
498   Ezek. 28: 13–14, 17.
499   Isa. 14:14.
500   Isa. 14:12 (KJV).
501   Num. 22:22; 1 Kings 11:14; Ps. 109:6.

502   Zech. 3:1–2; Rev. 12:10.
503   1 Peter 5:8.
504   Job 1:6–12; 2:1–7.
505   1 John 2:2; 4:10 (NIV has "atoning sacrifice," NASB/KJV have
        "propitiation"). Isa. 53:11; Rom. 3:26; 4:5; 8:33 mention His justification.
506   1 Chron. 21:1; Matt. 4:1–11; 1 Thess. 3:5.
507   Unclean (Mark 1:27), infirmity (Luke 13:11, 16, KJV), dumbness (Mark
        9:17, KJV), divination (Acts 16:16), false prophecy (1 John 4:1–6).
508   1 Tim. 4:1–4; 2 Tim. 2:24–26.
509   2 Cor. 10:3–5 (NIV).
510   2 Cor. 6:15. Richard N. Longenecker, "Acts," in Vol 9 *The Expositor's Bible
        Commentary* Ed. Frank E. Gaebelein (The Zondervan Corporation, 1981),
        p. 315 lists apocryphal names for Satan (adversary): Asmondeus, Semjaza,
        Azazel, Mastema, and Belial (perhaps Beliar). The 8th century *Targum
        Yerushalmi* mentions Sammael.
511   In particular, the *War Scroll* (1QM) and the *Community Rule* (1QS).
512   In Deut. 13:13, for instance, "worthless men" is literally "sons of Belial."
513   Matt. 13:19; Mark 4:15; Luke 8:12; 2 Thess. 3:3.
514   John 10:10.
515   Matt. 13:38–39; 1 John 3:10.
516   John 8:44; 1 John 3:8.
517   Tricks (2 Cor. 2:11; Eph. 6:11), snares (1 Tim. 3:7; 2 Tim. 2:26).
518   Gen. 3:1–15; 2 Cor. 11:3; Rev. 12:9.
519   Rev. 12:3, 8–9, 15–16; 20:2.
520   Sin (missing the mark, Rom. 7:14) and iniquity (unrighteousness, Acts
        8:23) both bind people.
521   Judg. 2:2–3.
522   Rom. 8:21–23.
523   Gal. 2:4; 4:3, 9. The "elemental things" that threatened to enslave the
        Galatians were Jewish religious rules superimposed on their newfound faith.
524   E. Peterson, *The Jesus Way* (Wm. B Eerdmans Publishing Co. 2007), p. 230.
525   Matt. 28:18–20; Mark 16:15–18; Acts 1:8.
526   Jude 9.
527   Many of God's names reflect His creativity; we will look at them in the next
        chapter.
528   Col. 1:16.
529   John 10:10.
530   Pss. 2:4; 59:8–9.
531   Mark 1:23–26; 5:2–13.
532   1 Sam. 20:42.
533   Gen. 40:17; Deut. 26:19; Ps. 89:27.
534   Num. 24:16; Deut. 32:8; 2 Sam. 22:14; Pss. 9:2; 18:13; 21:7; 46:4; 50:14;
        73:11; 77:10; 78:17; 82:6; 83:18; 87:5; 91:1, 9; 92:1; 107:11; Lam. 3:35,
        38. Satan used it in Isa. 14:14.
535   G. Lloyd Carr, TWOT, p. 669.
536   Gen. 14:18–22.
537   Mark 5:7; Luke 1:32, 35, 76; 6:35; 8:28; Acts 7:48; 16:17; Heb. 7:1.

538   *Yahweh* (Pss. 18:13; 21:7; 83:18), *'El* (Num. 24:16; Ps. 107:11), *Shaddai*
        (Num. 24:16; Ps. 91:1).
539   Ps. 83:18.
540   Root words added in parentheses. Numerous passages repeat one or more
        words of the triplet: Deut. 7:21; 10:17–18; Neh. 4:14; 8:6; 9:32; Pss. 45:3;
        89:8; Isa. 10:21, 34; Jer. 32:18.
541   Ps. 76:1; Mal. 1:11 (among nations); Jer. 10:6.
542   Isa. 10:34.
543   Isa. 33:21.
544   1 Kings 8:41–42.
545   Isa. 10:21; Jer. 32:18.
546   Gen. 49:25.
547   Ex. 15:11; see also 2 Chron. 2:5; Ps. 135:5.
548   Ps. 96:4.
549   Titus 2:13.
550   Jesus claimed to exorcize demons with the same authority (Ex. 8:19; cf.
        Luke 11:20).
551   Judg. 6:31.
552   1 Sam. 5:7.
553   1 Kings 18:20–40.
554   2 Chron. 32:13–19.
555   1 Kings 20:28.
556   Job 1–2. The evil spirit could only afflict Saul because God sent it,
        presumably as punishment (1 Sam. 16:14–23); see also Luke 22:31–32.
557   Ps. 56:8.
558   2 Chron. 6:14.
559   Ps. 115:3–8; Isa. 46:5–7.
560   Isa. 37:4, 17.
561   Isa. 7:14; 9:6 (*'El gibbor*).
562   William Barclay, *The Gospel of Matthew* Vol 2 (Westminster John Knox
        Press, 1975), pp. 133–135.
563   2 Tim. 1:10; Heb. 2:14.
564   1 Sam. 17:25.
565   1 Sam. 17:51. *Gibbor* means "strong" or "mighty," as in the name Mighty
        God, *'El gibbor*. See also Jer. 20:11 where God is likened to a "dread
        champion" and Zeph. 3:17 where He is a "victorious warrior."
566   1 Sam. 17:26, 36.
567   2 Thess. 2:3–4.
568   Rev. 12:7–12.
569   1 John 5:18–21.
570   John 10:27–29.
571   Ps. 91:14; John 8:51; Rom. 8:38–39.
572   Gal. 2:20; Phil. 1:21–24; Col. 3:1–4.

Chapter 9

573   The name of the book can also be spelled "Koran" in English. Non-biblical references in this chapter are to the Qur'an.

574   Inspiration (16:101–104; 53:1–4), belief (5:54), and resurrection (2:259–260; 16:38–39).

575   Note the linguistic similarities with *'El rakhum*, Merciful God.

576   13:16; 9:129; 40:1.

577   6:83; 10:1; 11:1; 12:1.

578   Protector (6:165; 8:69), friend and helper (8:40), Lord of beneficence (40:3), sovereign (54:55), master (55:78), holy (62:1), most high (87:1), and controller (114:2).

579   6:101; 19:88–92; 72:3; 112:3.

580   Sonship (18:4–5), death and resurrection (2:72–73; 3:27; 4:157–159; 5:17).

581   2:253; 4:171; 5:75; 61:6, 14.

582   "Zeus" was not appropriate because he was offspring of Cronus and Rhea and therefore not a supreme god in Greek thinking.

583   Brian Hogan, *There's a Sheep in my Bathtub* (Asteroidea Books, 2008), pp. 106–7.

584   Don Richardson, "Redemptive Analogy," in *Perspectives on the World Christian Movement, A Reader* Ed. Ralph D. Winter and Steven C. Hawthorne (William Carey Library, 2009), p. 435.

585   Acts 8:1–3.

586   Rom. 1:25; 1 Peter 4:19; Heb. 11:10.

587   Job 36:3. The word *po'ali* only occurs here.

588   Job 35:10.

589   Pss. 115:15; 146:5–6 (NIV).

590   Pss. 95:6; 149:2 (a plural "makers"); see also Prov. 14:31; 17:5; Isa. 51:13; 54:5; Hos. 8:14.

591   Isa. 45:9, 11; Jer. 10:16; 51:19.

592   Isa. 29:16; 45:9; 64:8.

593   Isa. 45:7, 18; Amos 4:13. He also formed man from dust (Gen. 2:7).

594   Isa. 44:9–19.

595   Thomas E. McComiskey in *Theological Wordbook of the Old Testament* Ed. R. Laird Harris (Moody Press, 1980), p. 701.

596   Eccl. 12:1(a plural, "creators") and Isa. 40:28; 43:1, 15.

597   Heaven and earth (Gen. 1:1; Isa. 65:17), Jerusalem (Isa. 65:18), birds and fish (Gen. 1:21), humans (Gen. 1:27; Deut. 4:32; Ps. 89:47), north and south (Ps. 89:12), wind (Amos 4:13), and a clean heart (Ps. 51:10).

598   Deut. 32:39; Job 12:10.

599   The first words are from *Cretica* by the Cretan poet Epimenides (c. 600 BC). The second line is probably from *Phaenomena* 5 by Cilician poet Aratus (c. 315–240 BC) or perhaps from *Hymn to Zeus* by Cleanthes (c. 331–233 BC).

600   Jer. 18:6.

601   See Chapter 3 for the significance of this word in Ex. 19:5–6. See also Deut. 7:6; 14:2; 26:18; Ps. 135:4; Mal. 3:17.

602   Num. 16:22; 27:16.

603   Ps. 2:1–4.

604   Cyrus (Ezra 1:2), Darius (Ezra 6:9), Artaxerxes (Ezra 7:12, 21, 23); see also Gen. 24:7; Neh. 1:4, 5; 2:4, 20; Ps. 136:26; Dan. 2:19, 37, 44; Jonah 1:9.

605   Nebuchadnezzar in Dan. 4:37.

606   Dan. 5:23 uses the Aramaic, *mare'*, for Lord.

607   Dan. 4:26; Luke 15:18, 21; John 3:27.

608   1 Kings 8:27; Jer. 23:24.

609   Jer. 10:7; Rev. 15:3. Some manuscripts have "ages" (reflected in NIV, 1984), and one has "saints" (reflected in KJV).

610   Acts 10:36; Rom. 10:12 (KJV) has the latter name. Rom. 9:5 (NIV) calls Jesus **God over all**.

611   Jer. 18:6–11.

612   Acts 15:14.

613   Eph. 6:12.

614   1 Cor. 2:4–5; 1 Thess. 1:5, 9.

615   Deut. 10:17–19.

616   John Piper, *Let the Nations be Glad* (Baker Books, 1993), p. 30.

617   Rom. 1:18–25.

618   Gen. 3:13; 1 Tim. 4:1; Rev. 20:10.

619   Matt. 13:25, 39.

620   2 Cor. 4:3–4.

621   Pss. 8:1–9; 19:1–6; Acts 14:17; Rom. 1:20.

622   Don Richardson, *Eternity in their hearts* (Regal Books, 1981).

623   Aratus of Cilicia, *Phenomena* 5 and Cleanthes, *Hymn to Zeus* 4.

624   Acts 14:15–17.

625   Acts 17:18, 31.

626   Of course, there is still a measure of judgment of those who have not heard the gospel (Rom. 1:18–20).

627   See also Ex. 20:4–6; Deut. 4:24, 39; 5:7–11; 6:14–15; Nah. 1:2 (*'El qanno*).

628   Deut. 32:21.

629   Ex. 34:14; see also 1 Cor. 10:22 (*parazeloo*) and James 4:5 (*phthonos* is "envy") where the context is also idolatry or lust.

630   J. I. Packer, *Knowing God* (Hodder and Stoughton, 1975), p. 186. Reproduced by permission of Hodder and Stoughton Limited.

631   J. I. Packer, *Knowing God* (Hodder and Stoughton, 1975), p. 189. Reproduced by permission of Hodder and Stoughton Limited.

632   Ezek. 39:25.

633   James 4:4–5.

634   Isa. 9:6–7.

635   Zeph. 1:18; 3:8–9, 12 where *qana'* is the root of both jealousy and zeal.

636   Both words are plural: "husbands" and "makers."

637   See also Isa. 62:5 and Jer. 3:14 (NIV/KJV); 31:32.

638   Hos. 2:5–6, 8–15.

639   *Lorukhamah* (She has not obtained compassion) became *Rukhamah* (She has obtained compassion). *Lo'ammi* (Not My people) became *'Ammi* (My people). See Hos. 1:4–10; 2:1, 23.
640   From the same root as *Ba'al.*
641   John 2:13–17 (quoting Ps. 69:9 which uses *qana'*); Mark 11:17.
642   John 3:29 (*nymphios*); Matt. 9:14–15; 25:1–13; Mark 2:18–20; Luke 5:34–35.
643   2 Cor. 11:2.
644   Rev. 19:7; 21:2, 9–10.

Chapter 10

645   Gen. 1:26; 5:3.
646   The Greek word *onomazetai* means, "is named."
647   Deut. 7:6–8.
648   William Barclay, *Jesus as They Saw Him* (William B. Eerdmans Publishing Company, 1978), p. 257.
649   Deut. 32:6; Pss. 68:5; 89:26; Isa. 9:6; 63:16 (twice), 64:8; Jer. 3:4, 19.
650   2 Sam. 7:14; 1 Chron. 17:13; 22:10; 28:6.
651   Mal. 1:6; 2:10; Prov. 3:12.
652   Pss. 68:5; 103:13; Jer. 31:9–10, 20 .
653   John 8:41.
654   Joachim Jeremias, *The Central Message of the New Testament* (Fortress Press, 1981), pp. 14–16.
655   Luke 15:12.
656   Luke 15:20–32.
657   1 Pet. 4:8; 1 John 4:7.
658   Luke 15:2. The parable comes after two others (the lost sheep and the lost coin), which make a similar point.
659   Mal. 4:6.
660   Matt. 11:25–27; Luke 10:21–22.
661   Luke 2:49.
662   Matt. 20:23; 24:36; Mark 13:32; John 14:28; Acts 1:7.
663   The latter in an accusing question from the High Priest.
664   Rom. 15:6; 2 Cor. 1:3; Eph. 1:2–3; Col. 1:3; 1 Peter 1:3.
665   2 John 3.
666   John 17:5, 24; Col. 1:13–17.
667   Matt. 11:25–27; Luke 10:21–22; John 10:15.
668   Heb. 1:4–14.
669   Mark 12:1–12 and parallels.
670   John 3:16–18; 1 John 4:9.
671   John 3:17, 35–36; 5:36–37; 6:57; 10:36; 12:49–50; 16:28; 17:1–5; 20:21; Rom. 8:3; Gal. 4:4–7; 1 John 4:9–10, 14.
672   John 5:17–26, 43; 10:25.
673   Matt. 21:23–27; Mark 1:21–27. The practice became official in the 2nd century AD under R. Johanan be Zakkai.
674   John 1:14, 18; 6:46; 8:19; 10:38; 14:6–11.
675   Matt. 10:29.

676   Matt. 6:1, 4, 6, 18.
677   Matt. 6:9; Luke 11:2; John 16:23–27.
678   Matt. 18:19; John 15:16; 16:23.
679   Matt. 6:7–8, 26, 32; Luke 12:30, 32; John 6:32.
680   Matt. 7:11; Luke 11:13; John 14:16, 26; 15:26.
681   Matt. 11:25–26; Luke 10:21. Also, in Gethsemane (Matt. 26:39, 42; Luke 22:42), on the cross (Luke 23:34, 46), at the grave of Lazarus (John 11:41–42), and speaking to His disciples (John 12:27–28; 14:16).
682   Matt. 27:46; Mark 15:34 quoting Ps. 22:1.
683   Mark 14:36. *JVG* pp. 648–9 argues that Jesus used it as a representative of Israel, the son of God.
684   Matt. 12:50.
685   Matt. 26:39, 42; Mark 14:36; Luke 22:42; John 8:28–29, 38; 12:27–28; 18:11.
686   John 13:1–3; 16:10, 28.
687   Matt. 20:18–19; John 5:19–20; 8:28–29.
688   Luke 22:70; John 5:18; 10:30–33; 19:7.
689   John 5:21; Rom. 6:4.
690   John 1:12–13; Rom. 8:14–15, 19; Gal. 3:26; 4:6–7; Heb. 12:6; 1 John 2:29; 3:1–2.
691   Matt. 28:18–19; John 20:21; Rev. 3:21.
692   John 14:16, 26; 15:26; Acts 1:4; 2:33.
693   Rev. 14:1.
694   First used in the New Testament in Acts 11:26.
695   1 John 2:29; 3:9–10; 4:7–8.
696   Matt. 18:14.
697   Luke 7:40–48.
698   2 Cor. 5:21.
699   Emphasis mine.
700   W. Barclay, *The Letters of John and Jude* (Westminster John Knox Press, 2002), p. 82.
701   Matt. 5:44–48; Luke 6:36.
702   Matt. 16:17; Luke 10:21; John 6:37, 40, 44–45, 65; 10:29; 17:6, 11, 26.
703   John 15:1; see also Isa. 27:2–3.
704   Phil. 1:6; 1 Thess. 5:24.

Chapter 11

705   *Mere Christianity* by C. S. Lewis, copyright © C. S. Lewis Pte. Ltd. 1942, 1943, 1944, 1952. Extract reprinted by permission.
706   The lack of heading to Psalm 43 and the refrain that is common to both psalms suggest these two psalms were originally one. See also Pss. 63:1–3; 84:1–4; 143:5–8.
707   Ps. 16:5 mentions God as a calculated portion and inheritance (*menat*).
708   Gen. 15:1; Heb. 11:6.
709   Hag. 2:6–9 (KJV). An argument for this is found in W. Kaiser, *The Messiah in the Old Testament* (Zondervan Publishing House 1995), pp. 207–8.

710   Ps. 43:3.
711   Pss. 42:5, 11; 43:1.
712   Ps. 42:4.
713   Ps. 43:1–3, 10.
714   Pss. 42:9; 43:2.
715   See also Deut. 10:21. The book of Psalms is called *Tehillim* in Hebrew.
716   Hab. 3:16.
717   The word for "my strength" (*khayli*) emphasizes God's resources, be they wealth, power, or efficiency.
718   Pss. 42:11; 43:5.
719   Ps. 42:8.
720   Jer. 32:27.
721   Matt. 1:23.
722   Ps. 43:2.
723   2 Sam. 22:2–4, 33; Pss. 18:1–3; 31:1–5; 42:9; 71:3.
724   Ex. 17:6; Num. 20:8–11; Ps. 105:41; 1 Cor. 10:4.
725   Jer. 2:13; 17:13. Even the word *miqweh*, translated "hope" in the second passage, can have the meaning "pool."
726   Zech. 13:1.
727   E.g. Isa. 41:17–20; 43:19–20; 44:1–4; 55:1; 58:1–12; Ezek. 47:1–12; Joel 3:18.
728   Isa. 32:1–2.

Chapter 12

729   Gen. 9:26. Shem was Noah's son.
730   Gen. 10:21–25. "*Ever*" (Eber)and "*Ivriyyim/Ivrim*," the word for the tribe, are related in Hebrew. Eber was father of the nation and representative of them in Num. 24:24. D. J. Wiseman, *The Illustrated Bible Dictionary* (Intervarsity Press, 1980) Vol 1, p. 405.
731   See also 1 Chron. 17:24.
732   The Hebrew people became the nation of Israel—twelve tribes descended from the sons of Jacob. Later, ten tribes broke away from the tribe of Judah (Benjamin did not, 2 Chron. 11:1, 3, 12, 23). The ten kept the name "Israel," the other two, "Judah." Sometimes the Bible continues to refer to them jointly as "Israel."
733   Ex. 3:13, 16; 4:5.
734   Deut. 1:21; 26:7–9.
735   1Kings 18:36; 1 Chron. 29:18; 2 Chron. 30:6.
736   Luke 3:8 In Hebrew there is a word play between *ben* (son) and *eben* (stone).
737   John 8:39–40.
738   See also Matt. 8:10–11.
739   Acts 7:2.
740   Gen. 12:1–9.
741   Gen. 14:17–22.
742   Gen. 13:16.

743	Jer. 34:17–20.
744	2 Chron. 20:7; Isa. 41:8; James 2:23. Jeremiah called God "**friend of my youth**" (Jer. 3:4).
745	Gen. 16:1–2. Later God changed Sarai's name to Sarah.
746	Gen. 21:14–21.
747	Ex. 2:23–25; 3:7.
748	"Take notice" in Ex. 2:25; 3:7 is from the same root (*yada'*) as *de'ot*.
749	Dan. 2:28–29, 47; see also Job 12:22.
750	Rev. 2:23; see also 1 Sam. 16:7 and John 2:25.
751	See also Deut. 4:7.
752	Latin translators used *omnipotens*, which also means "all powerful."
753	Jer. 5:14–17; Amos 4:13.
754	Ps. 68:14; Isa. 13:6; Joel 1:15.
755	Gen. 49:24–25; Isa. 60:15–16.
756	Taken from *The Names of God* © Copyright 1967 by Andrew Jukes p. 66. Published by Kregel Publications, Grand Rapids, MI. Used by permission of the publisher. All rights reserved.
757	Ruth 1:20–21; Job 21:15; 31:2; 40:2.
758	Gen. 17:1; 28:1–4; 35:9–15; 43:14; 48:3–4; Ex. 6:3; Ezek. 10:5.
759	Gen. 28:1–4; 35:9–15; 48:3–4. *Ba'al berit* and *'El berit* are titles for *Ba'al* in Shechem (Judg. 8:33–34; 9:4, 46).
760	Gen. 17:17–21; 18:9–15.
761	Gen. 18:14. The word *peli'*, meaning "difficult," relates to "wonderful."
762	Rom. 4:11; Col. 2:11.
763	Gen. 19:27–29; 2 Peter 3:9.
764	www.dirtys.com used with permission.
765	Heb. 11:8–12.
766	Matt. 17:20.
767	F. Godet, *Commentary on the Epistle to the Romans* (Edinburgh: T. & T. Clark, 2 Vols. E.T. 1883–84).
768	Commenting on James 2:17–26. Taken from *the Jewish New Testament Commentary* by David H. Stern. Copyright © 1992. All rights reserved. Used by permission of Messianic Jewish Publishers. www.messianicjewish.net
769	James 2:21–23.
770	Rom. 3:25–30; 4:1–25; 9:6–8; Gal. 3:6–9; Heb. 2:16.
771	2 Chron. 3:1.
772	Matt. 3:17; 17:5.
773	Luke 7:12.
774	Heb. 11:17.
775	John 1:29, 36; 1 Peter 1:19.
776	Ex. 4:5; Matt. 22:32; Luke 20:37–38; Acts 7:32; Rom. 14:9. *RSG* pp. 415–426 explains that the patriarchs are alive, awaiting resurrection.

Chapter 13

777   Gen. 27:1–40. Earlier, Jacob had seized an opportunity to snap up Esau's birthright (Gen. 25:29–34).

778   Gen. 27:41–46; 28:1–2.

779   Gen. 28:13–15.

780   Gen. 28:16–19; 35:7.

781   We would say Jacob's grandfather Abraham.

782   Gen. 31:29, 53. According to Josh. 24:2, Terah, and perhaps his sons, followed other gods. But, both brothers knew the name *Yahweh* (see Chapter 2). Nahor was Abraham's brother.

783   Gen. 31:11–13. In Gen. 35:7 the name is given to the place.

784   Gen. 28:20–22.

785   Gen. 33:4.

786   Gen. 33:18–20 (my italics and brackets).

787   Isa. 29:23.

788   James 1:17.

789   Gen. 48:10–20.

790   Disciples or believers (Acts 2:44; 5:14; 6:1; 14:21; 2 Cor. 6:15; 1 Tim. 4:10, 12), belonging to the way (Acts 9:1–2; 19:9, 23; 22:4; 24:14, 22), brethren (Acts 18:27 is just one example of this, the most common term for Christians).

791   John 15:15.

792   Mark 3:6; 12:13 cf. Acts 26:28; 1 Peter 4:16. N. T. Wright's translation of 2 Cor. 1:21 shows the verbal connection: "The one who strengthens us with you into the anointed one and anointed us is God." N. T. Wright, *Climax of the Covenant* (Fortress Press, 1992), p. 48. Used with permission.

793   Acts 24:5. The Talmud and modern Jews call Jesus *Yeshu haNotzri* (*Berakhot* 17b, *Sotah* 47a). The twelfth benediction of the *Shmoneh Esreh* (Cairo Geniza text) calls Christians *Notzrim*. The expression indicates that Christianity is viewed as a non-Jewish religion. Marvin R. Wilson, *Our Father Abraham* (William B. Eerdmans Publishing Company, 1989), pp. 65–69. Jewish followers of Jesus prefer to be known as "Messianic Jews" or "Jewish believers."

794   Acts 11:26.

795   Dallas Willard, *Renovation of the heart* (NavPress 2002), p. 267 including note 4. Used by Permission of NavPress, All Rights Reserved. www.navpress. com (1-800-366-7788).

796   Eugene Peterson suggests "company of the baptized" in *The Jesus Way* (Wm. B Eerdmans Publishing Co. 2007), p. 12.

797   1 Cor. 7:14; Eph. 2:19–22; Col. 3:12.

798   Rev. 15:3 (KJV).

799   Deut. 33:5.

800   Isa. 44:2.

801   Isa. 62:2–5.

802   Hos. 1:8–11; 2:1, 23; Rom. 9:24–26; 10:19; 1 Peter 2:10.

803   Eph. 1:6.

Chapter 14

804   The two variations of this name are different transliterations—"Emmanuel" of the Greek, "Immanuel" of the Hebrew.

805   Throughout the Old Testament, *bethulah* is always the word translated "virgin," except for Isa. 7:14 where the Hebrew word is *'almah*. However, *'almah* is used seven times for "maid, maiden, or girl." Apart from Prov. 30:19 (where it could still mean a virgin), *'almah* indicates a young woman, one of whose characteristics is virginity. There is no evidence of its use for one who was not a virgin, or for a married woman. Also, *bethulah* is not a technical term for virgins but speaks of women of marriageable age, including those who are not virgins. Therefore, Isaiah would never have considered using *bethulah* to indicate a true virgin. In fact, something of the opposite argument prevails. Both Gen. 24:16 and Judg. 21:12 have to clarify that *bethulah* means a virgin. In Joel 1:8 it refers to a widow. The word *'almah* requires no such clarification (Gen. 24:43; Ex. 2:8; Ps. 68:25; Prov. 30:18–19; Song 1:3; 6:8).

806   Isa. 9:1–2, 6; 11:1–12:6.

807   Matt. 1:18–19.

808   *Berakoth* 55a. (3rd century AD), probably based on oral traditions.

809   Gen. 2:19–20.

810   Matt. 1:21 (my paraphrase); see also Luke 1:76–77; 2:11, 21; 19:10.

811   The word "incarnation" literally means "in flesh."

812   Heb. 1:1–14.

813   Some examples are captain (KJV), founder (ESV), leader (*Darby*), source (*Holman*), and pioneer (MSG, AB, NIV, RSV).

814   Ex. 33:20.

815   Gen. 3:8.

816   This story is based on an untraceable news broadcast around 2000.

817   KJV has "Son."

818   From p. 29, *The Knowledge of the Holy* by A. W. Tozer, © 1961 Aiden Wilson Tozer. Reprinted by permission of HarperCollins Publishers.

819   *Hark the Herald Angels Sing*, Charles Wesley (1739).

820   *Epeskepsato* from *episkeptomai*, which is used of a visit to check on someone's well-being, for comfort and relief. (Matt. 25:36, 43; Luke 1:68; 78; James 1:27. See also, in the Septuagint, Gen. 50:24–25; Ex. 3:16; 4:31).

821   Jacob (Gen. 28:15), Moses and Israel (Ex. 3:12; 23:20; 33:14), Joshua (Josh. 1:5).

822   Acts 2:38; 10:45.

823   Neh. 9:20; Ps. 143:10.

824   2 Cor. 1:3 (NIV) has "**Father of compassion** and the **God of all comfort**."

825   Heb. 13:14.

Chapter 15

826   Pss. 78:52–53; 79:13; 95:7; 100:3.

827   Ps. 23:4, where the Hebrew word for staff is *mish'enet*.

828   Gen. 22:8, 13–14; Phil. 4:6, 19.

829   Gen. 16:13; Matt. 6:8.

830   Isa. 12:3; John 4:13–14; 7:37–38.

831   Luke 12:22–34.

832   Matt. 10:16–20.

833   Ps. 28:9; Isa. 40:10–11.

834   John 14:26; 15:26; 16:13.

835   Ps. 23:3.

836   His eldest son, John Brookes Keizur, made the very first claim.

837   I am indebted to Dr Jerry McGee for his historical research on the Keizur family as described in his book, *It's a Long Way to Oregon* (Esjay Press, 2007).

838   The root of "perfecter" is *telos*, meaning "end" or "purpose." www.NamesForGod.net/variations shows how different English versions handle these verses.

839   Rev. 3:14. Other versions have "First" (MSG), "Ruler" (NIV), "Origin and Beginning and Author" (AB).

840   Col. 1:15; see also Rom. 8:29; Heb. 1:6.

841   Ex. 4:22; Jer. 31:9.

842   1 Sam. 17:34–36.

843   Job 7:20. *Notser* is also translated "preserver" (KJV) and "keeper" (AB).

844   Pss. 18:1–2; 28:7; 30:10.

845   Ps. 144:2. He promises the same kind of protection to those who walk in integrity (Prov. 2:7) and those who take refuge in Him (Prov. 30:5). See also Gen. 15:1; Deut. 33:29; 2 Sam. 22:3; Pss. 3:3; 7:10; 18:2, 30; 59:11; 84:9, 11; 119:114.

846   Ps. 23:4.

847   Gen. 49:10; Num. 24:17; Ps. 45:6; Mic. 7:14.

848   Matt. 8:16–17.

849   Isa. 53:4–5; 1 Peter 2:24.

850   Acts 3:6, 16; 4:10, 30. In Old English, Jesus was called "*Hælend*," meaning "Healer" or "Savior."

851   Mal. 4:2.

852   Rev. 22:1–2, 17.

853   Ps. 107:20.

854   Ezek. 34:11–16.

855   Matt. 9:36.

856   Deut. 7:9; 32:4; Isa. 49:7; Lam. 3:23; Hos. 11:12; Rev. 19:11.

857   Ps. 23:6.

858   1 Peter 2:25.

859   Matt. 18:13; Luke 15:4–7.

860   2 Sam. 5:2; 7:8; Ps. 78:70–72.

861   Matt. 2:6; Mic. 5:2–4.

862   In Gen. 49:10 *shevet* is a scepter, in Ps. 23:4 it is the rod. In Gen. 49:10 "ruler's staff" is *mekhoqeq* from a root verb "to cut in or inscribe." The same word is translated "lawgiver" in Isa. 33:22.

863   Matt. 18:11; Luke 19:10.

864   Mark 6:32–44.

865   Zech. 13:7 (quoted in Matt. 26:31) seems to connect Jesus with both the shepherd and God's associate ("The man who is close to me" NIV). W. Kaiser, *The Messiah in the Old Testament* (Zondervan Publishing House 1995), pp. 226–7.

866   Matt. 26:55–56; Mark 14:27.

867   John 10:1–4.

868   Luke 2:8.

869   Ps. 78:23–24.

870   Matt. 3:16.

871   John 1:51.

872   Rev. 4:1–2.

873   Matt. 27:51.

874   The thought in Heb. 13:20 may come from Isa. 63:11, which tells of the Exodus from Egypt under shepherd leaders.

875   Acts 20:28; Eph. 4:11.

876   3 John 9–11.

877   1 Peter 5:1–3.

878   Ps. 7:9–11.

879   Ezek. 34:8–24, 31; Matt. 25:31–46.

Chapter 16

880   J. R. R. Tolkien, *The Lord of the Rings* (Book Club Associates, 1979). Aragorn's various names appear on pages: 172, 182,186–7, 237, 249, 265, 395, 533, 617, 811, 821, 881, 900, 905, 913, 919, 922, 1002–4, and the Appendix.

881   John 1:12; 3:18.

882   Phil. 2:6–7.

883   Heb. 4:15–16.

884   Rev. 22:16.

885   Luke 3:38. The English "son of" is *ben* in Hebrew, *bar* in Aramaic, and *bin* in Arabic (e.g. Osama bin Laden).

886   Matt. 1:20.

887   Israel (Ex. 4:22; Jer. 31:9; Hos. 11:1; Mal. 1:6), the king (2 Sam. 7:14; 1 Chron. 17:13; Pss. 2:7; 89:26–27).

888   The New Testament speaks of a "son of peace" (Luke 10:6 KJV), a "son of the devil" (Acts 13:10), a "son of hell" (Matt. 23:15), and "sons of disobedience" (Eph. 5:6). Believers are "sons of light and sons of day" (1 Thess. 5:5) and "children of light" (Eph. 5:8).

889   Matt. 5:44–45; Luke 6:35.

890   Compare Matt. 27:54 and Mark 15:39 with Luke 23:47. KJV and NIV have "righteous" instead of "innocent."

891   Jews began using *Yehoshua'* again to avoid associations with the name *Yeshua'*, and Christians avoided it because it was too sacred. The contemporary historian Flavius Josephus mentions twenty-one men called *Yeshua'* (*JVG* p. 250). Many Talmudic Jews shorten *Yeshua'* to *Yeshu*—an

insulting acronym, "may his name be blotted out." Others suggest it was a way to avoid pronouncing the name of the Christian "god" or perhaps, how Galileans would have pronounced it. Neither *Yeshu* nor *Jesu* are used of Jesus in the Bible. David H. Stern, *Jewish New Testament Commentary* (Jewish New Testament Publications Inc. 1992), pp. 4–5, 14–15.

892 The Galilean towns he lived in.

893 Mark 6:3. Perhaps the latter name came after Joseph's death, or even as a less-than-subtle accusation of illegitimacy.

894 Matt. 13:54–55; Mark 6:3. Other rabbis worked as carpenters and builders, including R. Shammai.

895 J. I. Packer, "Carpenter," in *Dictionary of New Testament Theology*, Ed. Colin Brown (Zondervan, 1986), 1:279.

896 Acts 2:22; 3:6; 10:38.

897 E.g. Ps. 8:4; Isa. 56:2; Jer. 49:18, and 93 times to address Ezekiel.

898 Heb. 2:6–18 quotes Ps. 8:4–6; see also 1 Cor. 15:25–28; Phil. 2:5–8.

899 The parallels with "I" are clearest in Matt. 16:13 (cf. Mark 8:27–30; Luke 9:18–21); 20:28 (cf. Luke 22:27); Luke 6:22 (cf. Matt. 5:11); 12:8 (cf. Matt. 10:22).

900 Judas (Matt. 26:25, 49; Mark 14:45), Peter (Mark 9:5; 11:21), other disciples (John 1:38, 49; 4:31; 9:2; 11:8), Nicodemus (John 3:2), and the multitudes (John 6:25).

901 We met the syllable in Rabshakeh, Sennacherib's commander, in Chapter 8.

902 John 3:26.

903 The Message Bible reflects the fact that *hammoreh litsedaqah* is literally "the teacher of/for righteousness." Other versions speak of rain because another form of *moreh* means rain later in the same verse. See W. Kaiser, *The Messiah in the Old Testament* (Zondervan Publishing House 1995), pp. 139–42, 172–3.

904 N. B. Stonehouse, *The Witness of Matthew and Mark to Christ* (Eerdmans, 1958), p. 254.

905 Matt. 8:2, 6, 8, 25; Mark 7:28; John 4:11, 15, 19, 49; 5:7; 20:15.

906 Compare the parallel verses Matt. 8:25 (*kyrios*), Mark 4:38 (*didaskalos*), and Luke 8:24 (*epistata*). Note the explanation in John 1:38 and 20:16.

907 In John 13:13–14 the underlying Aramaic is likely to be *Rabbi umari* (H. L. Ellison, "Rabbi," in *Dictionary of New Testament Theology*, Ed. Colin Brown (Zondervan, 1986) 3:115–6).

908 Gen. 18:12; 1 Peter 3:6.

909 Three of seven occurences of *despotēs* refer to Jesus (2 Tim. 2:21; 2 Peter 2:1; Jude 1:4). *Epistatēs* occurs in Luke 5:5; 8:24, 45; 9:33, 49; 17:13. In parallels in the other Gospels, it replaces *didaskalos* and *rhabbi*.

910 Luke 2:29; Acts 4:24; Rev. 6:10 (NIV has "Sovereign Lord" in all three).

911 Matt. 23:6–12.

912 John 13:3–5, 12–15.

913 Matt. 1:21, 25; Luke 1:31; 2:7.

914 Matt. 1:23; 2:15; Luke 1:32, 35.

915 Luke 2:25–38; see also Isa. 42:6; 49:6.

916   Being named before birth was so unusual that Rabbis later commented,
       "Six were named before they were created, namely, Isaac, Ishmael, Moses,
       Solomon, Josiah, and King Messiah" (*Pirqe Rabbi Eliezer* 32, dated AD
       80–118). Three other Jewish commentaries say Messiah's name existed
       before creation: *Pesachim* 5a; 54a; *Nedarim* 39b (both on Ps. 72:17); *Targum
       Neviim* (on Zech. 4:7). See also Enoch 48:2–6.

917   Gen. 3:15.

918   Rom. 5:12–21; 1 Cor. 15:22.

919   Taken from *The Normal Christian Life* by W. Nee. Copyright © (2008)
       by Angus I. Kinnear, pp. 39–40. Used by permission of Tyndale House
       Publishers, Inc. All rights reserved. See also N. T. Wright, *The Climax of the
       Covenant* (T & T Clark, 1991), pp. 25–26.

920   Gen. 12:1–3, 7 (*zera'*, meaning "seed," is often translated "descendants");
       13:15; 17:8; 22:18; 24:7; 2 Sam. 7:12–16; Gal. 3:16.

921   Num. 24:7. A 2nd century AD comment on this verse uses the title, "seed of
       Abraham," in a messianic way (*T. Levi* 8:11–15).

922   Acts 13:23 (KJV preserves the meaning of *spermatos*, "seed"); see also 2 Tim.
       2:8.

923   The word translated "wonderful" (*pele*) is only used of God and His
       amazing and inexplicable works (Gen. 18:14; Isa. 28:29; Jer. 32:17). *Targum
       Neviim* says that Isaiah 9:6 is about the Messiah.

924   Matt. 2:23. David H. Stern, *Jewish New Testament Commentary* (Jewish
       New Testament Publications Inc. 1992), pp. 14–15 has *natzrati* as the
       Hebrew equivalent of the Greek, *nazoraios*.

925   *Netser* is interpreted messianically in two Dead Sea Scrolls commenting on
       Isa. 11:1–5, namely 4Q161, col. 3:11–24 and 4Q285, frags. 4:1–10; 7:1–6
       (where the Branch is called "Leader of the congregation") in DSS, Wise *et
       al.* pp. 237–38, 369–70.

926   Isa. 53:3; John 1:46.

927   Mark 14:67.

928   John 19:19.

Chapter 17

929   The contemporary historian Flavius Josephus provides most of the record
       for this period. *Ant.* 17:278–284.

930   Athronges, Judas the Galilean, Menahem ben Judah, Theudas, John of
       Gischala, Simon bar Giora, and Simon bar Kokhba all made some kind of
       claim to messiahship.

931   The abbreviations BC (before Christ) and AD (anno Domini, which
       means "in the year of our Lord") are used to help orient modern readers.
       Of course, it was years before someone devised the system. Historians now
       know that Jesus was born sometime from 6–4 BC, before King Herod the
       Great died.

932   Notes for the following newsclippings.
       172 BC: Antiochus IV ruled 175–164 BC. His epithet "Epiphanes" means,
       "Manifest god." 1 Macc. 1:10–16; 2 Macc. 4:7–15.

167 BC: Events linked to the Maccabean war are retold in 1 and 2 Maccabees, and *Ant.* 12:242–419. See especially 1 Macc. 1:41–54; 2:39–42; 3:27–4:35; 6:1–9 and *JW* 1:1:1–2, 34.

164 BC: Jews still celebrate these events at Chanukah, the Feast of the Dedication mentioned in John 10:22.

933   Notes for the following newsclippings.

139 BC: Simon's confirmation by Jewish leaders, 1 Macc. 14:41.

134 BC: *JW* 1; 2:5; *Ant.* 13:254–300.

934   There were at least six thousand Pharisees. Josephus said that this many refused an oath to Caesar during the reign of Herod I, *Ant.* 17:41–45.

935   *Ant.* 17:149–63; Gal. 1:13–14.

936   *Ant.* 13:298.

937   The Pharisees were subject to them. Paul had to obtain permission to persecute the church (Acts 9:1–2).

938   *War* 2:119, 158, 160; *Ant.* 18:1–25.

939   1QS 9:11 mentions three figures: the Prophet and the Messiahs of Aaron and Israel (the latter a military leader). See DSS, Wise *et al.* p. 131. See also 1 QSa 2:11–22; CD, col. 7:10–15 (manuscript B) and col. 12:22; 4Q174 3:10–18. The idea of dual messiahs may have been a reaction to the combined offices of the Hasmoneans (Matthew Novenson, *Christ Among the Messiahs* (Oxford University Press, 2012), p. 61).

940   CD 1:11; 6:11 in DSS, Wise *et al.* pp. 52, 57.

941   1 QpHab 2:1–5:12; 8:3–10:5; 11:3–12:10 in DSS, Wise *et al.* pp. 81–83, 85–88.

942   References for the following newsclippings.

63 BC: *War* 1:141–159. **36 BC**: *War* 1:248–287. **20 BC**: John 2:20; *Ant.* 15:380–7. **6–4 BC**: Matt. 2:16–18.

943   Jesus warned that false messiahs would arise after Him too (Mark 13:21–23).

944   Notes for the following newsclippings.

March 14, 4 BC: *Ant.* 17:149–63. *War* 1:648–50 says they promised a glorious resurrection to the protesters.

AD 6: One of several governors, Pontius Pilate governed Judea from AD 26–36.

AD 6 census: *Ant.* 18:3–10; *War* 2:118. "While the Jews reluctantly agreed to register their property, a certain Judas of Gamala claimed that this was tantamount to slavery, so he and a Pharisee named Saddok called for revolution." Taken from *Josephus: The Essential Writings* p. 260 © Copyright 1988 by Paul L. Maier. Published by Kregel Publications, Grand Rapids, MI. Used by permission of the publisher. All rights reserved.

Acts 5:37 says that Judas perished. Josephus called the new movement a "fourth philosophy" (after the Pharisees, Sadducees, and Essenes). The total tax burden (including tithes and Roman tribute) may have exceeded 40 percent during this period.

AD 30: *Ant.* 18:106–142.

AD 33: April 3rd, AD 33 is a likely crucifixion date but records are too limited to be certain. Barabbas and the men crucified alongside Jesus were called *lēstai* (brigands or bandits) and Jesus was arrested like a *lēstēs* (Matt. 26:55; 27:16, 38; Luke 23:19, 25; John 18:40).

AD 54: Acts 21:27–39 calls the Egyptian's followers *sikarioi* (assassins). The name derives from their favorite weapon, the *sicae*. The Egyptian caused trouble in Jerusalem in about AD 54. *Ant.* 20:169–72, 185–187; *War* 2:261–63. On Theudas, see Acts 5:36. On Jacob and Simon, see *Ant.* 20:97–102.

AD 66 fortress capture: *War* 2:427–429.

AD 66 murder: *War* 2:422–456.

AD 69: John had 6000 men; Eleazar had 2400. R. A. Horsley & J. S. Hanson, *Bandits, Prophets and Messiahs* (Trinity Press International, 1999).

AD 70: On Simon's execution, see *War* 7: 25–36; 153–8. Josephus' comment about the prediction is in *War* 6:312–15, probably a reference to Daniel 2; 7; 9. Josephus treats the passage as a prophecy, but applies it to Vespasian (as does Tacitus in *History* V, 11 and Suetonius in *Vespasianus* IV). See also *JW* 7:139–162.

AD 74: *War* 7:320–407.

945   Notes for the following newsclipping.

AD 132: On bar Kokhba correspondence, see Matthew Novenson, *Christ among the Messiahs* (Oxford University Press, 2012), p. 92. On rabbinic titles for bar Kokhba, see *Ta'anit* 4:68.

Scepter (*shevet*) and star (*kokhav*) are messianic titles in Targums *Yerushalmi* and *Onqelos*. The passage in question is Num. 24:17. 1QSb 5:20–28 links the scepter with the messianic Prince of the congregation (DSS, Wise *et al.* p. 143). Ecclus. 50:1–11 praises Simon ben Onias, High Priest from 219–196 BC, using the title, Morning Star.

946   M. J. Borg, *Conflict, Holiness, and Politics in the Teachings of Jesus* (Continuum Publishers, an imprint of Bloomsbury Publishing Plc., 1984, 1998), 3f.

947   *JVG* p. 564. I am indebted to Professor N. T. Wright for many insights into the historical and theological context of the events described in these chapters about Jesus as Messiah.

948   Zech. 13:8–9.

949   "The word 'Messiah,' within Jesus' world, does not refer, in itself, to a divine or quasi-divine figure." *JVG* p. 477.

950   J. Klausner, *The Messianic Idea in Israel.* (The Macmillan Company, 1955) p. 525. For a good summary of Jewish beliefs of the time, see E. P. Sanders, *Judaism: Practice and Belief. 63 BCE–66 CE.* (London: SCM; Philadelphia: Trinity Press International, 1992) pp. 298, 303.

951   *Ha'olam hazzeh* and *ha'olam habba'* respectively.

952   The post-maccabean *Testaments of the Twelve Patriarchs* mention royal and priestly messiahs (*T. Levi* 18:1–12 and a messiah with combined roles (*T. Dan* 5:10; *T. Gad* 8:1).

953   Isa. 25:6; Mic. 4:1–3; 1 Enoch 10:17–19; 25:3–5 (2nd century BC); 2 Baruch 29:5–8 (early 2nd century AD); *Ketubbot* 111b; *Sibylline Oracles* 3:356–80, 619–623, 741–761 (2nd century BC); *Baba Bathra* 122a; *Sheqalim* 6:2.

954   1 Kings 4:25; 2 Kings 18:31; Mic. 4:4; Zech. 3:10; 1 Macc. 14:12.

955   Joel 3:18; Amos 9:13.

956   Isa. 2:2–4; Mic. 4:1–3; Zech. 8:20–23.

957   Hos. 13:13; Matt. 24:8; Mark 13:8; see also 1QM 1:9–12; 1 QH 3:6–18; 1 QpHab; 1 QM.

958   Isa. 13:6–10; 42:13–16; Amos 5:18–20; Joel 2:1–2, 30–31; 3:14–15; Zeph. 1:14–15.

Chapter 18

959   Luke 2:11. Like all Jews of the time, they probably spoke Aramaic, which is similar to Hebrew.

960   John notes this in John 1:41 and 4:25 using a Greek transliteration *messias*.

961   Passages like 1 Cor. 15:1–5 suggest that *Christos* was quickly employed as a stand-alone proper name.

962   *Christos kyrios*, exactly as in Pss. Sol. 17:32 "their king shall be the Lord Messiah" (see also Pss. Sol. 18:5, 7). The psalm contains terminology similar to that found in Luke's nativity narrative.

963   Dan. 9:25–26 has two possible exceptions, though verse 25 might tell of an "anointed ruler" and verse 26 might refer to High Priest Onias III who was assassinated around 172/1BC. The Targum interprets 1 Sam. 2:10 as "Messiah." W. Kaiser, *The Messiah in the Old Testament* (Zondervan Publishing House 1995), p. 71.

964   Ps. 133:1–3.

965   Priests (Ex. 28:41; 29:4–7; Lev. 4:3), Prophets (1 Kings 19:16), and metaphorically (Isa. 61:1).

966   1 Sam. 12:1–3; 16:12–13; 1Kings 19:15–16; 2 Kings 9:1–13; Isa. 45:1.

967   Ps. 18:50 is just one example.

968   4Q175 (which was originally called "testimonia" because it gathers texts the writer believed pointed to the coming of Messiah) includes references to all three groups who received anointing: Deut. 18:18–19 (prophet); Num. 24:15–17 (royal Messiah); Deut. 33:8–11 (high priest). DSS, Wise *et al.* p. 258–60.

969   *JVG* p. 11.

970   4Q174 3:10–13 connects the son of 2 Sam. 7:11–14 to the branch of David. 4Q174 3:18–19 applies Ps. 2 to the chosen one of Israel. DSS, Wise *et al.* p. 256–57.

971   Acts 4:25–28.

972   Pss. 89:3–4, 35–37; 132:11–12.

973   The latter title is used in John's Gospel; Son of David is not.

974   Dan. 7:7–8, 24.

975   This prophecy concerns God's king. See also W. Kaiser, *The Messiah in the Old Testament* (Zondervan Publishing House 1995), p. 71.

976   In the Dead Sea Scrolls, *tsemakh Dawid* is a messianic term. 4Q174, col. 3:10–13 says that 2 Sam. 7:14 "refers to the shoot of David, who is to arise with the Interpreter of the law" (DSS, Wise *et al.* p. 257). Targums on Isa. 4:2; Jer. 23:5; 33:15; Zech. 3:8 apply the word "anointed" to the branch. G.

F. Moore, *Judaism in the First Centuries of the Christian Era, The Age of the Tannaim* Part VII (Hendrickson Publishers, Inc., 1960) p. 325 and note 7.

977   Isa. 11:1–5. In the Dead Sea Scrolls, *netser* is understood as the messianic ruler who comes at the end of days (4QpIsa 161, col. 3:11–24). In 4Q285, frag. 7:1–6, *netser Dawid* is called "Leader of the congregation" (DSS, Wise *et al.* pp. 237–38, 370). The Targum on Isa. 11:1 speaks of the King Messiah.

978   Amos 9:11–12.

979   Ps. 89:38–45; Isa. 9:8–10, 14; 10:15.

980   Isa. 53:2 and Ecclus. 47:25 also mention the "root of David."

981   1 Kings 22:17; Jer. 23:4–5; Ezek. 34:23–24; 37:24; Mic. 5:4; 7:14; Pss. Sol. 17:39–42.

982   Isa. 9:6–7; Jer. 33:15, 17, 22. In Jer. 23:5–8 He is said to act wisely, something said of the servant in Isa. 52:13 (RSV).

983   The text is difficult. It might read "until Shiloh comes" or "until the prince/ruler comes" or (with some simple changes) "*shelo*," which translates as "he to whom it (the scepter or rulership) belongs" (W. Kaiser, *The Messiah in the Old Testament* (Zondervan Publishing House 1995), pp. 50–53, 193). 4Q252, col. 5:1–6 says Gen. 49:10 refers to "the Righteous Messiah, the Branch of David." Targums *Yerushalim* (2nd century AD) and *Onqelos* (1st century AD) interpret it as a reference to the Messiah. Rabbi Shila in *Sanhedrin* 98b said it was a name of the Messiah (3rd – 4th century AD). The scepter and staff (*khoqeq*) were symbols of rulership.

984   Zech. 3:8; see also 6:12–13.

985   There are no signs of royal messianic expectations during Maccabean times, but Pss. Sol. 17:21–46 (1st century BC) features a shepherd king purging and judging Gentile rulers. The Eighteen Benedictions (in use by AD 70) include prayers for the royal Davidic messiah, the shoot, and horn.

986   Cf. Pss. Sol. 17:21–25 with Ps. 2:9, which is also quoted in Rev. 2:27; 12:5; 19:15.

987   *JVG* p. 482.

988   *JVG* p. 483.

989   Matt. 2:2, 4, 16.

990   Mic. 5:2.

991   Matt. 9:27; 15:22; 20:30–31; Mark 10:47–48; Luke 18:38–39.

992   Isa. 35:5–6.

993   Rom. 15:12 quotes Isa. 11:10–12 where *nes* is translated "signal." A form of the same word is used in "the LORD is my banner" in Ex. 17:15.

994   Matt. 12:1–8; Mark 2:23–28; Luke 6:1–5.

995   Isa. 62:11; Zech. 9:9; Matt. 21:5; Mark 11:1–10; Luke 19:38. Donkeys were acceptable mounts for rulers (Judg. 5:10; 10:4; 12:14; 2 Sam. 16:1–2; 1 Kings 1:33). Moses entered Egypt on one (Ex. 4:20). Various passages from Zechariah 9–14 are relevant from Jesus' entry through the crucifixion.

996   Matt. 21:9 quotes Ps. 118:25–26; see also Matt. 23:39.

997   2 Kings 9:13.

998   Ezek. 44:1–3 uses the word *nasi'* for prince. It implies elevation over others and in Modern Hebrew means "president."

999	Oral teachings said Zech. 9:9 (*Berachot* 56b) and Gen. 49:11 (*Berachot* 57a) referred to the King-Messiah.
1000	Matt. 21:9, 15.
1001	Ex. 4:22–23; Jer. 3:19; 31:9; Hos. 11:1; Mal. 1:6.
1002	2 Sam. 7:14; see also 1 Chron. 17:13; Pss. 2:7; 89:26–27. A later example of God as Father is *T. Jud.* 24:2 (likely Maccabean).
1003	In Enoch 105:2 (possibly pre-Maccabean) God says He and His Son will reunite with His people. Messiah is called "My Son" in 4 Ezra 7:28–29; 13:32, 37, 52; 14:9 (c. AD 100).
1004	Acts 13:33 and Heb. 1:5; 5:5 quote Ps. 2:7.
1005	Ps. 89:27. W. Kaiser, *The Messiah in the Old Testament* (Zondervan Publishing House 1995), p. 82.
1006	See also Isa. 9:6–7; Dan. 2:44; 4:3, 34; 6:26; 7:14.
1007	4Q174, col. 3:10–13, 18–19 includes 2 Sam. 7:11–14 and Ps. 2:1 about God's Son. 4Q246 2:1 applies the title to a false Messiah (DSS, Wise *et al.* pp. 257, 347).
1008	John 19:7.
1009	R. T. France in *The Illustrated Bible Dictionary* (Inter-Varsity Press, 1980), p. 994.
1010	In Matt. 11:19; Luke 11:29–32 (not in Matthew's account); John 6:27 Jesus spoke to crowds.
1011	A crowd in John 12:34. An angel repeated Jesus' words in Luke 24:7.
1012	For instance in 1 Enoch 37–71, especially 46:1–5; 48:1–10 (c. 105–64 BC).
1013	Matt. 5:11 cf. Luke 6:22. Matt. 16:13 cf. Mark 8:27–30; Luke 9:18–21. Matt. 20:28 cf. Luke 22:27. Matt. 10:32 cf. Luke 12:8.
1014	Several passages link the title to "Son of God": Matt. 10:23, 32–33; 13:37–41; 16:13, 27–28; 17:5, 9; 24:27–44; 26:63–64 (also to "Messiah"); Luke 9:26; John 1:49–51 (also to "King of Israel"); 3:14, 16–18; 5:25–27; 6:53, 57; 8:28; 12:23. Mark 2:3–12 equates Him with God.
1015	Only in visions (Acts 7:56; Rev. 1:13; 14:14) and a quotation of Ps. 8:4–6 in Heb. 2:6–8.
1016	Matt. 9:1–8; 18:11; Mark 2:1–12.
1017	Matt. 12:40; 17:9, 22–23; 20:18–19.
1018	E.g. Mark 8:38; Luke 12:8.
1019	Matt. 25:31–35, 40.
1020	Isa. 60:1. Later rabbis took this verse to mean the Messiah's name was "Light."
1021	Ps. 104:3; Isa. 19:1; Nah. 1:3. 4 Ezra 13:1–4, 21–34, 52–53 (early 2nd century AD) mentions a man from the sea coming in clouds with a voice that melts people. Part of the Talmud from the 3rd – 4th century AD calls the Messiah *bar naphle* "Son of the clouds" (*Sanhedrin* 96b). Also, Rabbi Alexandri said the Son of Man refers to a messianic king (*Sanhedrin* 98a).
1022	Dan. 7:13, 18, 22, 27. See *NTPG* pp. 291–7 on interpreting Daniel 7.
1023	Matt. 16:28.
1024	Acts 1:9 is similar to Dan. 7:13.
1025	*JVG* p. 360–5, 510–19 explains how Mark 13 predicted the Jewish War, and was rooted in Daniel.

1026   Luke 22:69; John 3:14–15; 8:28; 12:23, 32–34.

1027   Matt. 16:16, 19–28.

1028   See Matt. 12:14–21 for another use of Isa. 42:1. 1 Enoch 45: 3–5; 49:1–4
        mention "My Elect One" (pre 64 BC).

1029   Mark 10:45; see also Matt. 16:21–26; 17:9–13.

1030   Luke 18:31–34; see also Matt. 26:24.

1031   There is no reference to a suffering servant in the Dead Sea Scrolls (4Q491,
        Manuscript C, frag. 11, col. 1:15–16 is a possible exception). *Targum
        Neviim*, says Isaiah 52:13 is about the messiah (1ˢᵗ century AD).

1032   See also Ezek. 37:24–25; Mic. 2:12–13; 5:2–4. The latter is quoted in Matt.
        2:6, where *hēgoumenos* is translated "ruler." Luke, using the same word, says
        the leader should be a servant (Luke 22:26).

1033   Isa. 42:1–4; 49:1–6; 50:4–9; 52:13–53:12. Commentators debate exactly
        which verses form part of the songs.

1034   Moses (Deut. 34:5; Josh. 1:1–15; see also Ex. 14:31; Num. 12:7–8), Joshua
        (Josh. 24:29), and Israel (Isa. 42:19; 49:3). Other people are referred to as
        God's servants: Abraham (Gen. 26:24), Caleb (Num. 14:24), David (2 Sam.
        7:5–8), Elijah (2 Kings 9:36), Job (Job 2:3), Isaiah (Isa. 20:3), and other
        prophets (2 Kings 21:10; Amos 3:7).

1035   Isa. 53:4–5; Matt. 8:14–17.

1036   Isa. 42:1–4; Matt. 12:10–21.

1037   Isa. 53:4–12; Matt. 26:63; 1 Pet. 1:19; 2:22–25.

1038   Isa. 53:12; Luke 22:37.

1039   Mark 15:28 (KJV); Luke 22:37.

1040   Isa. 53:12; Luke 23:34.

1041   Isa. 52:14; 53:5; Matt. 27:26. The shepherd in Zechariah was also struck
        (Zech. 13:7) and there are discernable links between Zech. 12:10, the
        pierced firstborn son, and CD 19:7–11.

1042   Isa. 53:9; Matt. 27:57–60.

1043   Acts 8:26–35.

1044   Isa. 53:4–5; Rom. 4:25; see also Isa. 53:12; Heb. 9:28.

1045   Isa. 49:6; see also Luke 2:32; John 3:19; 8:12.

1046   Luke 1:76–79; Isa. 9:1–2; 60:1–2.

1047   Mal. 4:2, where the word for rising in the Greek is *anatelei*. Perhaps Num.
        24:17 is in mind too.

1048   Jer. 23:5; Zech. 3:8; 6:12. *T. Jud.* 24:1–6 (c. 150 BC) connects the sun of
        righteousness with the shoot.

1049   Isa. 9:1–2, 6–7; 42:6; 49:6; 51:4.

1050   Acts 4:27, 30. The word *pais* can mean either child or servant, but here it
        is most likely to mean servant. David is called *pais* in relation to the Lord,
        who is his *despota* in a nearby passage (Acts 4:24–25). *Despota* is a common
        title for rulers, so *pais* can only mean servant there. Also, the Hebrew for
        servant (*'eved*) is translated in the Septuagint using *pais* (340 times) about
        as often as it is translated *doulos* (327 times) (and other words meaning
        "servant" less often). *Ben*, meaning son, is translated *pais* only once, while
        hyios is used 4000 times.

1051   2 Macc. 6:12–17; 7:18–19, 32–33, 36–38; 4 Macc. 6:27–29; 17:20–22; 1QpHab 8:1–3; 1 QS 8:1–4; 9:4–5. *T. Benj.* 3:8 has a lamb of God dying for sinners. 1 QpHab 5:10–11; 11:4–7 tell of the suffering of the Teacher of Righteousness under the Liar/wicked priest. Daniel 11:31–12:10 may be based on Isa. 53 (Dan. 12:3 cf. Isa. 53:11).

1052   Isa. 53:10. The context of the songs is the proclamation and celebration of good news that the penalty of sin had already been paid. See especially the first and last chapters of Isa. 40–55 and Isa. 52:7–12, which precedes the song.

1053   Matt. 20:25–28; Mark 10:42–45; Luke 22:25–27.

1054   The words are part of a song by Angela Oliver, 2012.

Chapter 19

1055   2 Peter 3:8.
1056   John 6: 1–15, 41–42, 51–66.
1057   Matt. 17:24–27.
1058   My interpretation of the meaning behind the question asked in Mark 12:13–17.
1059   *JVG* p. 502–7.
1060   John 7:25–27, 41–44, 52.
1061   Matt. 5:17–48; 23:23–26.
1062   *JVG* p. 646.
1063   *JVG* p. 381.
1064   John 5:17–18; 10:22–39.
1065   Deut. 13:1–18.
1066   Matt. 12:23–24; Mark 3:22; Luke 11:14–15.
1067   Matt. 11:19; Luke 7:34; see also Deut. 21:18–21, which describes a rebellious son as a glutton and drunkard.
1068   Matt. 12:39–42.
1069   John the Baptist pointed this out in Matt. 3:7–12.
1070   N. T. Wright gives a helpful list of statements about the impending judgment on Israel in *JVG* pp. 183–4.
1071   *JVG* p. 274.
1072   Matt. 3:9. *NTPG* p. 369–70 summarizes the perspective of the church in light of what Jesus has done.
1073   Isa. 53:2.
1074   Matt. 25:31–46; John 5:27.
1075   Matt. 9:6; John 3:17.
1076   Mark 8:29–31; 14:21; Luke 9:20–22.
1077   Matt. 26:51–54; John 18:10–11.
1078   John 11:45–53.
1079   Luke 19:39; John 12:19.
1080   Matt. 21:13; Mark 11:17; Luke 19:46 "robbers" translates *lēstai*.
1081   Isa. 56:6–8; Matt. 21:12–14; Mark 11:17.
1082   Acts 17:6.

1083   Matt. 26:63–68; see also Mark 14:61–65; Luke 22:66–71. Mark opts for the phrase "**Son of the Blessed One**" as a polite and oblique version of "Son of God" ("Power" in Matt. 26:64 is an oblique reference to God). In Mark 14:61, the Greek of Caiaphas' question, "Are you the Christ?" is the same as Peter's confession in Mark 8:29 except for the question mark.

1084   See also Matt. 22:41–46; Mark 12:35–37; Luke 20:41–44.

1085   Rabbi Akiva (c. AD 40–137) believed that Dan. 7:9 implied there was a second throne for the Messiah.

1086   Matt. 27:40, 43; John 19:7. Stephen also faced the Sanhedrin and made similar comments about Jesus that provoked his own martyrdom (Acts 7:55–56). John saw the Son of Man standing poised to judge (Rev. 1:13; 14:14).

1087   Luke 23:1–5; see also Matt. 27:1–2, 11–14; Mark 15:1–5; John 18:33. One of the same accusations carried force in Thessalonica against Christians in Acts 17:5–9.

1088   Matt. 27:27–31, 42; Mark 15:16–20; John 19:3, 12–15.

1089   Matt. 27:37; Mark 15:32; Luke 23:36–39.

1090   John 19:19–22.

1091   Acts 5:36–37.

1092   *Ta'anith* 4 and *Midrash Rabbah Lamentations* 2:4.

1093   Mark 15:29–30.

1094   Matt. 27:63. Paul and his team were also called deceivers in 2 Cor. 6:8.

1095   *RSG* p. 558.

1096   *NTPG* p. 472.

1097   Luke 16:31.

1098   Rabbi Gameliel II gave the *Shemoneh 'Esreh* (Eighteen Benedictions or *Amidah*) their present form around AD 70.

1099   Matt. 25:31, 34, 40; Rev. 11:15.

1100   Isa. 11:4; Ps. 2:8–9; Rev. 2:26–27; 12:5; 19:15, 21; see also Pss. Sol. 17:23–24; 1 QSb 5:24–25.

1101   Acts 3:20–21; Heb. 10:37.

1102   Acts 1:6–7.

1103   Luke 24:18–27; Acts 1:9 cf. Dan. 7:13–14.

1104   Acts 2:36; 10:38.

1105   Acts 3:18; 17:3; Phil. 2:5–11.

Chapter 20

1106   Isa. 40:3; John 1:23.

1107   Jewish expectations of a forerunner included different figures: sometimes Jeremiah, usually Elijah (Mal. 4:5) plus either Moses or Enoch. Some authors take Mal. 3:1 as a reference to John the Baptist.

1108   Matt. 11:10, 14; John 1:21.

1109   Luke 1:17.

1110   John 3:29. In *Sanhedrin* 99a the Messiah is the bridegroom.

1111   Matt. 9:14–15; Mark 2:18–20; Luke 5:33–35.

1112   Matt. 25:1–13; Rev. 19:7–9; 21:2, 9.

1113   Mal. 3:1–2; Matt. 3:1–12.

1114   Isa. 29:18–19; 35:5–6; 61:1; 4Q521, frag. 2:1, 7–8, 11–13 tells of the works of an "anointed one." It reads very like Isa. 61:1–2 even mentioning resurrection, which the Isaiah passages do not (DSS, Wise *et al.* p. 531 and *JVG* p. 531 note 188).

1115   John 7:31 is an exception.

1116   Isa. 35:6 in the Septuagint; Mark 7:32–35.

1117   Isa. 8:13–15; Matt. 11:6.

1118   The Greek structure of the phrase strongly suggests underlying Aramaic including the word *talya*, which can mean son, servant, or lamb. J. Jeremias, "Amnos," *Theological Dictionary of the New Testament* p. 339.

1119   Heb. 10:10–14, 18; 1 Peter 1:19.

1120   Isa. 53:7; Acts 8:30–35.

1121   Gen. 22:7–8, 13–14.

1122   The same word (*arnion*) that Jeremiah used of the "gentle lamb led to the slaughter" (Jer. 11:19 in the Septuagint) occurs here. God is pictured as a roaring lion in a few Old Testament verses (Jer. 25:30; Hos. 5:14; 11:10; Joel 3:16; Amos 1:2; 3:4, 8). Gen. 49:9; 4 Ezra 11:36–39; 12:31–32, and 1QSb 5:29 link the lion with Judah, David, and Daniel's son of man. 1 Macc. 3:4 applies Gen. 49:9 to Judah Maccabee.

1123   Rev. 5:12; 6:15–16.

1124   William Barclay, *Jesus as They Saw Him* (William B. Eerdmans Publishing Company, 1978), p. 311.

1125   Matt. 8:29; Mark 5:7; Luke 8:28.

1126   Mark 3:11; Luke 4:41.

1127   James 2:19.

1128   Isa. 11:1–5; see also 1QSb 5:20–26; 4Q161 3:11–24; 4Q285, frag. 7; 11Q14; *T. Jud.* 24:4–6; and 4Q252, col. 5, which interprets Gen. 49:10 as a reference to "the Righteous Messiah, the Branch of David."

1129   Acts 10:38.

1130   Ps. 2:2, 7. A few verses before Isaiah's great description of the suffering servant, Isa. 52:7 tells of the preaching of good news. 11Q13 2:17–19 says the messenger of Isa. 52:7 is the anointed one that Daniel spoke about (likely to be Dan. 9:25–26. DSS, Wise *et al.* p. 592; see *JVG* p. 530 note 186) and the one whose action is described in Isa. 61:2–3.

1131   Matt. 9:9–13; Mark 2:14–17; Luke 5:29–32.

1132   Luke 13:33–34.

1133   Matt. 21:11, 46.

1134   See a similar response from the disciples in Matt. 16:14 (adding Jeremiah); Mark 8:28; Luke 9:19.

1135   Mal. 4:5–6; see also Ecclus. 48:1–10 and (perhaps) the damaged fragment 31 of 4Q382.

1136   Matt. 16:13–14 (John the Baptist, Elijah, Jeremiah, or another); Mark 8:27–28; Luke 9:18–19 (John the Baptist, Elijah, or another); see also Mark 6:15; John 7:40.

1137   G. Vermes, *Jesus the Jew* (William Collins Sons & Co. Ltd, London, 1973), pp. 89–90. Moses and Elijah did similar things—40 days is reminiscent of both (Ex. 24:18, 1 Kings 19:8), judgment of fire (Num. 16:35; 2 Kings 1:9–14). Moses and Elisha healed lepers (Num. 12:9–15; 2 Kings 5:1–19). They both opposed wicked rulers like Pharaoh and King Ahab. See also James 5:16–18.

1138   1QS 9:11 mentions the prophet and the messiahs of Aaron and Israel. 4Q175:5–8 quotes Deut. 18:15–18, showing that the passage was important to the writers and preservers of that scroll. One post-Maccabean work mentions a "unique prophet" (*T. Benj.* 9:2). Rabbis spoke of Moses as a type of messianic redeemer, see J. Klausner, *The Messianic Ideal in Israel* (The Macmillan Company, 1955) pp. 15–17.

1139   John 1:21, 25 actually mentions three characters: Elijah, the prophet, and the Messiah.

1140   John 5:46–47 suggests this, and the crowds seemed to view Him that way (John 6:14; 7:40).

1141   Heb. 3:2–6.

1142   Acts 3:17–26; 7:37, 52.

1143   The Samaritan version of the Torah (*Memar Markah*) says *Taheb* (their name for the messiah) would come and restore worship to Mount Gerazim. Some scholars say that *Taheb* is only mentioned in later manuscripts and that John 4 reflects the Jewish messianic expectation.

1144   They interpreted Deut. 34:10 strictly: that no other prophet would arise after Moses.

1145   John 4:25–26, 29, 42.

1146   Ex. 16:1–36; Num. 11:31–32; 2 Kings 4:42–44.

1147   John 6:14.

1148   Luke 7:11–16; 1 Kings 17:17–24; 2 Kings 4:18–37. Shunem lay over the hill from Nain.

1149   4Q521 2:1–13 mentions it.

1150   Ex. 15:23–25; 2 Kings 2:19–22; John 7:37–44.

1151   2 Kings 5:10 Jesus' miracle is recorded in John 9:1–38. In both miracles, the recipients had to undergo some unusual actions.

1152   Luke 9:51–56.

1153   Num. 16:35; 2 Kings 1:10–12.

1154   Matt. 11:14–18.

1155   Matt. 17:12.

1156   Luke 7:39.

1157   John 1:35–51; see also Gen. 28:12.

1158   John 6:69.

1159   Matt. 14:33.

1160   Matt. 16:17–18, 21–23.

1161   Isa. 4:2–5.

1162   Ps. 78:24–25.

1163   Gen. 49:24.

1164   Ps. 80:8–19; Isa. 5:1–7; 27:2–6; Jer. 2:21; Ezek. 19:10–14; Hos. 10:1–2. Ecclus. 24:17 likens wisdom to a vine. The vine was a prominent decoration on Herod's temple.

1165   Eph. 2:18; Heb. 10:19–20.

1166   1 Cor. 15:20–22.

1167   Isa. 41:4; 43:10–13; 44:6; 45:5–6, 18, 21–22; 52:6. E. Stauffer, *Jesus and His Story*, Translated by R. & C. Winston (Alfred A. Knopf, New York, 1967), p. 183 says God's use of '*ani* and '*ani hu* was a topic of interest in Jesus' day.

1168   Gen. 15:7; 17:1; 28:13; 35:11; Ex. 20:2.

1169   The Septuagint uses the same verb when God "passed by" Moses hidden in the cleft of the rock (Ex. 33:18–23; 34:6) and Elijah on Horeb (1 Kings 19:11).

1170   Luke 24:39.

1171   Isa. 41:10, 13.

1172   Mark 13:6; Matt. 24:5; Luke 21:8.

1173   John 8:24, 28; 13:19.

1174   John 18:5, 6, 8, at Jesus' mock trial. Perhaps the words were interpreted as blasphemy (Mark 14:61–64).

1175   Mark 14:62; Luke 22:70.

1176   Rev. 21:6.

1177   Rom. 3:29–30; 15:9.

1178   Acts 10:36. In Rom. 10:12, Paul might have been speaking of God the Father. The New Testament draws from several Old Testament passages to emphasize His Lordship over the nations: Pss. 2:7–12; 72:1–17; 89:20–27; Isa. 11:1–10; 42:1–6; 49:1–6; Dan. 7:13–14.

Chapter 21

1179   John 11:20–21. Mary used the same words in verse 32.

1180   Daniel 12:2 was quoted by Jesus in John 5:29. See also Isa. 25:8; 26:19; Hos. 6:2; Wisd 3:1–8; 2 Macc. 7:9–23, 29, 36–38; 12:43–45; 14:45–46; *War* 2:163–5; 3:374; *Ant.* 18:14–16; Pss. Sol. 3:11–12; and the second of the Eighteen Benedictions. 4Q385; 4Q386; 4Q391 interpret Ezek. 37 as a resurrection passage. 4Q521 mentions resurrection.

1181   1 Kings 17:17–24; 2 Kings 4:18–37.

1182   Luke 7:11–17.

1183   Matt. 9:18–26; Mark 5:22–43; Luke 8:41–56.

1184   John 6:22–59.

1185   Ps. 77:14.

1186   Jer. 32:27; Rom. 14:9; Deut. 33:27.

1187   1 Tim. 1:17 (*aphthartō*). Ps. 16:10 (quoted in Acts 2:27, 31; 13:35–37) says that Jesus would not undergo decay.

1188   Luke 16:30–31.

1189   My paraphrase of John 17:3 and 1 John 5:20.

1190   Rom. 4:25; 1 Cor. 6:14; 2 Cor. 4:14.

1191   Rom. 6:13–14; 1 Cor. 15:17; Eph. 1:19–20.

1192   Luke 7:36–39 has different details from John 12:1–8, which tells of Mary anointing Jesus.

Chapter 22

1193   *Mere Christianity* by C. S. Lewis, copyright © C. S. Lewis Pte. Ltd. 1942, 1943, 1944, 1952. Extract reprinted by permission.

1194   A record set in the Netherlands in 2009.

1195   1 Cor. 15:3–8.

1196   1 Cor. 15:20–23; Col. 1:18; Rev. 1:5.

1197   Jesus is referred to as the "Christ" thirty times, and Messiah twice (John 1:41; 4:25). Some Bibles substitute the title Messiah for *christos* in a few places.

1198   Acts 5:42; 8:5, 12; 9:22; 10:36, 38; 17:3; 18:5; 28:31; Gal. 1:7. Apollos had the same message in Acts 18:28.

1199   The Septuagint used the word *kyrios*, meaning "**Lord**," to translate "*Yahweh*" and "*'Adonai*" (which even today substitutes for "*Yahweh*" in Hebrew). The adoring cry, *"Kyrie!"* (Greek for "O Lord!"), is found in some worship songs.

1200   Mark 16:19; Luke 24:3.

1201   It occurs sixty-three times, forty of which are at the beginning or end of letters and in other formal settings.

1202   See also Rom. 1:7; 15:6; 2 Cor. 1:2–3; Gal. 1:1, 3; Eph. 1:2–3, 17; 5:20; 6:23; Phil. 1:2; Col. 1:3; 1 Thess. 1:1, 3; 2 Thess. 1:2; 2:16; Philem. 1:3; 1 Peter 1:3.

1203   1 Tim. 1:2; 2 Tim. 1:2. For other exceptions see 2 Cor. 11:31; 1 Thess. 3:11, 13; Jude 1:1.

1204   Titus 1:4. "Savior" is a favorite designation used by Peter too.

1205   Even the single occurrence in Acts 24:24 reports on Paul's message.

1206   See also Titus 2:13; 2 Peter 1:1.

1207   John 1:1, Titus 2:13, and 1 John 5:20 seem clear, though Rom. 9:5 and 2 Thess. 1:12 are ambiguous.

1208   1 Cor. 15:28; Phil. 2:6–7, 11; 1 Tim. 2:5–6.

1209   1 Cor. 8:6.

1210   Gal. 2:20; 4:4–7; Rom. 8:3, 32; 1 John 4:10.

1211   Joel 2:32; Rom. 10:8–13.

1212   Titus 1:3–4.

1213   Eph. 6:23; 2 Thess. 1:2.

1214   Amos 5:18–20; 1 Cor. 1:8; 2 Cor. 1:14; Phil. 1:6, 10; 2:16.

1215   Ps. 29:3. The Greek titles in 1 Cor. 2:8 and James 2:1 are essentially the same.

1216   Rom. 10:9; 12:3; 2 Cor. 4:5; Eph. 4:5; 2 Tim. 2:8. 1 Cor. 8:6 expands the *Shema* of Deut. 6:4 to include Jesus. See also Phil. 2:6–11; Col. 1:15–20; Heb. 1:8–9; 2 Peter 3:18; Rev. 5:13; 7:10.

1217   Matt. 22:41–46; Mark 12:35–37; Luke 20:41–44.

1218   1 Cor. 16:22. This phrase suggests that Jewish believers (who spoke Aramaic) were first to recognize Jesus as Lord.

1219   Rev. 1:8; 21:6 cf. Rev. 22:12–13.

1220   J. A. Motyer, *Introducing the Old Testament* (Church Pastoral-Aid Society, 1960) p.11. Other words that Yahweh said of Himself were also used of Jesus. 1 Peter 2:3–4 applies Ps. 34:8; 1 Peter 3:14–15 adapts Isa. 8:12–13;

Rev. 17:14 and 19:16 are similar to Deut. 10:17. See also Wayne Grudem, *Systematic Theology* (Inter-Varsity Press and Zondervan Publishing House, 1994), pp. 543–49.

1221 Acts 4:24–27.

1222 Acts 16:6–10.

1223 Rom. 8:9.

1224 Spirit of our God (1 Cor. 6:11), Spirit of the living God (2 Cor. 3:3), Spirit of Jesus Christ (Phil. 1:19), Spirit of the Lord (Luke 4:18), Spirit of your Father (Matt. 10:20), Spirit of His Son (Gal. 4:6).

1225 Mark 1:1.

1226 Luke 1:32, 35.

1227 Pss. 65:7; 89:9; 107:29.

1228 Matt. 14:33.

1229 John 11:4, 41–45.

1230 John 5:25.

1231 *RSG* p. 673.

1232 Acts 9:20, 27–28; 2 Cor. 1:19.

1233 Acts 13:33; Heb. 5:5. Heb. 1:5 also applies 2 Sam. 7:14 to Him.

1234 Rom. 1:4. Perhaps an allusion to the decree of Ps. 2:7.

1235 Eph. 5:5; 2 Tim. 4:1; Heb. 1:8–9 (which quotes Ps. 45:6–7 and Isa. 61:3); Rev. 11:15; 12:10.

1236 John 3:18; 20:31.

1237 Acts 8:37; 1 John 4:15; 5:5, 10–13.

1238 Augustus declared his father, Julius, divine at his death. Tiberius did the same in AD 14 to Augustus. Their coins bore the inscriptions "son of the divine Caesar." The eastern empire regarded Tiberius as divine even during his father's lifetime. Gaius Caligula and Nero were more blatant with their claims.

1239 Acts 25:26.

1240 Dan. 2:34–35. There are similarities between Daniel chapters 2 and 7. Chapter 7 includes the Son of Man.

1241 Matt. 21:42–44; Mark 12:10; Luke 20:17–18; see also Isa. 8:14–15. Jesus might have used word association in the original language between the Son (*ben*), and the Stone (*'even*). Zech. 10:3–4 says the cornerstone comes from Judah.

1242 Acts 4:10–11 quotes Ps. 118:22.

1243 Isa. 8:14; 28:16; 1 Peter 2:4–8.

1244 Rom. 9:30–33; Eph. 2:19–22.

Chapter 23

1245 Compound names like this one occur throughout the Old Testament in various forms: "our salvation," "his salvation," "my salvation," etc. For instance, Pss. 24:5; 25:5; 27:1, 9; 65:5; 85:4; Isa. 17:10; 62:11; Mic. 7:7; Hab. 3:18.

1246 Pss. 68:19–20; 79:9.

1247 Ps. 70:5; see also Ps. 40:17.

1248   Isa. 43:11; 45:15–17; Luke 1:47; 1 Tim. 1:1; 2:3; 4:10; Titus 1 :3; 2:10; 3:4; Jude 25.

1249   Darkness (Col. 1:13), uncleanness (Ezek. 36:29), danger (Jer. 30:7), the perverse (Acts 2:40), and illness (Isa. 38:20–21 and many psalms).

1250   Storm (Matt. 8:25), illness (Matt. 9:21–22), persecutions (2 Tim. 3:11), tribulation (Matt. 24:22), and death (2 Cor. 1:10).

1251   Ps. 3:3.

1252   Ps. 81:1; Isa. 49:5.

1253   Jer. 16:19.

1254   Pss. 31:4–5; 43:2; 46:1.

1255   Ps. 27:1; Isa. 25:4.

1256   "Strong tower" is *migdal-'oz.* "Safe" is *nisgav,* related to *misgav* with the idea that a high place is safe and secure.

1257   Pss. 31:3; 71:3; 144:2.

1258   Ps. 148:13. "Exalted" is *nisgav.*

1259   2 Samuel 22 is a copy with a few variations. Ps. 144 is similar.

1260   Ps. 144:1–8 tells of a similar pattern.

1261   In Ps. 71:5, the related word *tiqwati,* parallels *mivtakhi,* "confidence."

1262   Isa. 42:4; Matt. 12:21; Rom. 15:12.

1263   Isa. 63:11–16; see also Ex. 9:13–17; Neh. 9:9–11.

1264   Judg. 2:17–19.

1265   Judg. 2:16; 3:9, 15; Neh. 9:27. In the Greek Old Testament, they are called *sōtēras,* saviors.

1266   Ps. 24:3–6; Mic. 7:18–19.

1267   John 3:17; 5:34; 10:9; 12:47; Acts 2:21.

1268   Heb. 2:10. Other versions have captain (KJV), founder (ESV), leader (*Darby*), source (*Holman*), pioneer (AB, NIV, MSG).

1269   Luke 2:11; John 4:42.

1270   Acts 5:31; 13:23; Eph. 5:23; Phil. 3:20; 2 Tim. 1:10; Titus 1:4; 2:13; 3:6; 2 Peter 1:1, 11; 2:20; 3:2, 18; 1 John 4:14.

1271   In these examples, salvation equaled restored wholeness, so some translators emphasized the practical: "Your faith has made you well," even though the Greek says they were "saved." Hemorrhaging woman (Matt. 9:22; Mark 5:34; Luke 8:48), blind man (Mark 10:52; Luke18:42), demons (Luke 8:36), dead raised (Luke 8:50), lepers healed (Luke 17:19), and sin forgiven (Luke 7:47–50).

1272   Lev. 25:25, 47–48.

1273   Ruth 4:10.

1274   Isa. 59:2.

1275   Ex. 30:12–16.

1276   The word only occurs in the plural (*kippurim*), "atonements."

1277   Ps. 49:7–9, 15; Heb. 10:1–4, 11.

1278   Isa. 53:10 (where "guilt offering" is *'asham*).

1279   John 1:29; Rom. 8:3; 1 Peter 1:18–19. The Old Testament word for a sin offering is *khatta't.*

1280   Rom. 3:23–26 (NIV). NASB says "propitiation." W. Grudem defines the related word, *hilasmos* (which 1 John 2:2; 4:10 also translate as "propitiation") as "a sacrifice that turns away the wrath of God—and thereby makes God propitious (or favorable) toward us." (Taken from *Systematic Theology* p. 575 by Wayne Grudem. Copyright © 1994 by W. Grudem. Used by permission of Zondervan. www.zondervan.com and Inter-Varsity Press.). The atoning sacrifice served two related ends; it cleansed the sinner and thereby turned away the wrath of God. The first aspect is called expiation, the second, propitiation.

1281   Heb. 9–10.

1282   Acts 20:28; 1 Cor. 6:20; 7:23; Eph. 1:7; 2 Peter 2:1.

1283   Both verses use *lytron anti* . . . . In 1 Tim. 2:6 *antilytron* speaks of deliverance from slavery and lawlessness by the payment of an equivalent price (see also Titus 2:14).

1284   In Luke 9:31, Jesus spoke of His *exodus*. English Bibles use the word "departure."

1285   Four verses refer to the exodus as redemption: Ex. 6:6; 15:13; Ps. 106:10; Isa. 51:10.

1286   "Redeemed" (*exagorazo*) means to buy out of the marketplace. See also Deut. 21:23; 1 Cor. 6:20; 7:23.

1287   Jesus' *death* on the tree (at the hand of Roman occupiers and Jewish collaborators) due to our sin was the ultimate curse, the dissolution of relationship with God. He "achieved a specific task, that of taking on Himself the curse which hung over Israel and which on the one hand prevented her from enjoying full membership in Abraham's family and thereby on the other hand prevented the blessing of Abraham from flowing out to the Gentiles." Jesus came out the other side in resurrection "to new covenant life beyond." N.T. Wright, *Climax of the Covenant* (Fortress Press, 1992), pp. 151–2. Used with permission.

1288   Num. 35:1–34; Deut. 19:6, 12; Josh. 20:3–9.

1289   See also Ps. 18:46–49.

1290   Rev. 12:10–11.

1291   1 John 5:19; Heb. 2:15; Col. 1:13.

1292   *Kohen ne'eman* could read "enduring priest." Later in the verse, "enduring house" is *bayith ne'eman*.

1293   John 8:29; Heb. 3:5–6.

1294   Heb 5:5; 9:11 speak of Christ (the anointed) as High Priest just like the anointed priests of Lev. 4:3, 5, 16; 6:22.

1295   Heb. 2:17; 9:24–26.

1296   Heb. 4:14; 9:24–25.

1297   Heb. 7:25; 9:24.

1298   Heb. 1:4–5; 5:5; see also John 10:30, 38.

1299   Heb. 5:5–6, 10; 7:11–17, 21.

1300   Heb. 7:23–27; 9:26; 10:5–10.

1301   Rom. 5:6–11; 2 Cor. 5:18–19.

1302   1 John 2:1–2 gives a fuller sense of the meaning of "Advocate" (*parakletos*).

1303   Heb. 8:6; 9:15–20; 12:24.

1304   Rom. 3:25–26.

1305   1 John 1:7–9.

1306   1 Tim. 2:5–6.
1307   Heb. 2:17; 1 John 2:2; 4:10.
1308   A quotation of Ex. 15:2 appears in Ps. 118:14 and Isa. 12:2.
1309   Deut. 33:29.
1310   Isa. 62:11; Zech. 9:9–10; see also 1 Tim. 6:14–15; Rev. 17:14; 19:11, 16.
1311   Zech. 12:10–11.
1312   Rom. 11:25; see also Isa. 44:21–24.
1313   *Rhyomai* is literally "to draw to oneself." Luke 1:74; 2 Cor. 1:10; Col. 1:13; 2 Thess. 3:2; 2 Tim. 3:11 speak of God's rescue.
1314   Paul quotes the Greek version of Isa. 59:20–21, but God is the *go'el* (Redeemer) in Hebrew. Notice the connection. God delivers the whole world from the deepest, darkest enemy by an act of redemption. The fuller context shows this is His solution to sin's separation (Isa. 59:2) and that the Holy Spirit is evidence that the covenant relationship has been restored.
1315   Rev. 15:1–4. It is unclear whether the reference is to one song or two.

Epilogue

1316   Dan. 7:9–28.
1317   Ex. 32:32; Ps. 69:28; Dan. 12:1; Luke 10:20; Phil. 4:3.
1318   Rev. 14:1; 22:4.
1319   Isa. 62:2–5; Hos. 1:10; 2:23; Rom. 9:25–26; 1 Peter 2:10.
1320   Rev. 2:17; see also Rev. 15:2. Revelation contains other promises: Faithful overcomers escape punishment and enter the New Jerusalem (Rev. 3:5; 20:12–15; 21:2, 27). Those who succumb and worship the beast share his fate (Rev. 13:8; 20:15).
1321   Rev. 19:12.
1322   Rev. 7:3.
1323   Rev. 13:16–18; 14:9–11. *Charagma* comes from the word for engraving. Phylacteries are tiny boxes containing four Scriptures (Ex. 13:1–10; 13:11–16; Deut. 6:4–9; 11:13–21) worn in obedience to God and in memory of His deliverance from Egypt.
1324   Rev. 13:12–16; 14:9–11.
1325   Rev. 13:1; 16:9; 17:3.
1326   Rev. 13:8; 20:4.
1327   Rev. 7:2–3; 14:1.
1328   Rev. 14:9–11; 16:2.
1329   Rev. 17–18.
1330   Rev. 17:1–5; 19:2–3.
1331   Zech. 14:9.
1332   Isa. 45:23; Phil. 2:9.
1333   Rev. 21:2–3, 9–10.
1334   Rev. 21:11, 23; 22:5.
1335   Rev. 21:4; 22:2.
1336   Rev. 21:24–26.
1337   Matt. 25:1–13; John 14:2–4.
1338   Rev. 1:17; 4:1.

Index of

THE NAMES OF GOD

(For information on every name of God visit www.NamesForGod.net)

369

RESOURCES

If you enjoyed reading *The Name Quest* please visit
www.NamesForGod.net

For:
- A newsletter.
- More detailed information about all the biblical names of God.
- Background articles and recommended reading.
- Small Group Bible Study materials and other resources.
- Scheduling a seminar or teaching for your church or group.
- Discounts for missionaries and bulk discounts for events and church book tables.
- Donating a copy of *The Name Quest* to a third world pastor or missionary.
- Donations toward your Christian ministry fundraiser.
- Contacting John Avery.

For Bible Devotions by John Avery please visit
www.BibleMaturity.com

CPSIA information can be obtained at www.ICGtesting.com
Printed in the USA
BVOW04s2046160614

356333BV00001B/1/P